Life in North-Eastern India
IN
Pre-Mauryan Times

(*With special reference to C.* 600 *B.C.*—325 *B.C.*)

Madan Mohan Singh, M.A., Ph. D.
Reader
Department of Ancient Indian History and Archaeology,
Patna University.

MOTILAL BANARSIDASS
DELHI :: VARANASI :: PATNA

MOTILAL BANARSIDASS
BUNGALOW ROAD, JAWAHARNAGAR, DELHI-7
NEPALI KHAPRA, VARANASI (U.P.)
ASHOK RAJPATH, PATNA (BIHAR)

First Edition 1967
Price

Printed in India by Shantilal Jain, at Shri Jainendra Press, Bungalow Road, Jawaharnagar, Delhi-7, and published by Sundarlal Jain, Motilal Banarsidass, Bungalow Road, Jawaharnagar, Delhi-7.

CONTENTS

		Pages
Preface		vii
Abbreviations and Transliteration		ix-xi
Introduction		xiii-xxv

PART I

CHAPTR I.	Caste Organisation	1
	Earlier Period; General features; the Brāhamaṇas; the Kshatriyas; the Vaiśyas; the Śūdras; the Artisans; the Unsettled and Unorganised Castes; the Despised Castes—the Chaṇḍālas, Veṇas, Nesādas, Pukkusas, Rathakāras, etc.	
CHAPTER II.	Slavery	22
	Evidence of Slavery ; Categories of Slaves ; Treatment of Slaves ; Nature of Their Work.	
CHAPTER III.	Marriage	37
	Importance of Marriage ; Polyandry, Polygamy and Monogamy ; Settlement of Marriage ; Qualifications of the Parties : Caste and Family Considerations, Gotra, Brother-Sister Marriage avoided, Cousin-marriage, Marriage Age, Selection of the Bride and Bridegroom ; Forms of Marriages; Remarriage and Divorce; Conjugal Life.	
CHAPTER IV.	Courtesans	64
	An Important Aspect of the City Life ; Their Status in the Society ; Financial Position ; Their Character.	

CHAPTER V. Food and Drink 68

Articles of Food. Meat-Eating ; Drinking Liquor;

CHAPTER VI. Popular Festivals 80

An Important Aspect of Social Life ; General Features ; The Chāturmāsyas—The Kattikā (Kaumudī-Mahotsava) ; The Elephant Festival (Hatthimaṅgala) The Drinking-Festival (Surā-Nakkhata) The Śālabhañjikā-Festival, The Ploughing-Festival.

CHAPTER VII. Religions of the Period 89

Earlier Period and the 7th and 6th Cen. B. C. ; Buddhism ; Jainism ; Ājīvikism ; Doctrines of Pūraṇa Kassapa, Pakudha Kachchāyana, Sañjaya Belaṭṭhiputta, Ajita Kesa-kambalī; Brahmanism and Popular Religion ; Higher Brahmanism ; Popular Brahmanism ; Yakkha-Worship ; Nāga-worship ; Tree-worship ; Bull-worship.

CHAPTER VIII. Monastic Life 123

Gradual Development of the Homeless Stage of Life ; Condition during the days of Buddha ; The Number of Ascetic Orders ; Brahmaṇa Ascetics or the Parivrājakas and the Tāpasas ; Normal Life of the Ascetics ; Jaṭilas ; Order of the Ājīvikas ; Order of the Jainas.

CHPTER IX. The Buddhist Monasteries 149

Coming into Existence of the Monasteries; Admission—Qualifications of the candidate, Qualifications of the

Teacher, Ordinations (Pabbajjâ and Upasampadā) ; The Upajjhāya and the Saddhivihārika ; Seniority and Etiquette : Mutual Relations and Community Life; Common Ownership; Dress and Decoration of the Person—Head-dress, Foot-coverings, Robes, Ornaments, Ointments, etc. ; Food ; The Bhikshuṇīs ; Back-sliding, Reverting to the Worldly Life and Degeneration in the Monasteries; Officers of the Saṅgha.

CHAPTER X. Rural Economy 193

Villages and their Types; Agriculture —Process of Cultivation, Crops Cultivated, Irrigation, State's Interest; Land Holdings; Cattle Farming.

CHAPTER XI. Arts, Crafts, Professions, and Industries 208

Earlier Period; Textile Industry and Luxury Goods; Carpentry; House-Building; Mining and Metallurgy; Smithy; Industry of Precious Metals; Pearls, Gems, and Precious Stones; Ivory-work; Garland-making and Perfumery; Pottery; Dyes, Gums, Drugs and Chemicals; Fish and Meat Production; Liquor Distilling; The Food-Vendor; Sugar Making; Cane and Leaf Work; Leather Work.

CHAPTER XII. Trade and Trade Routes 235

General Condition; Land Trade Routes; River Transport; Oversea Trade.

CHAPTER XIII Organisation of Industry and Trade 247

Guilds—Their Number and Nature;

Localisation of Industries; Partnership.

CHAPTER XIV. Currency, Prices, Fees, Salaries, and Wages 254

Gold Coins; The Silver Standard; Kārshāpaṇa as the Standard Silver Currency; Pre-Mauryan Punch-marked Coins; Viṅśatika and Triṅśatka as Magadhan Standards; Division of Kārshapaṇa; Classification of Pre-Mauryan Silver Punch-marked Coins; Copper Currency; Prices—Fabulous and Actual Prices; Price-Controlling Agencies; Fees and Salaries; Wages.

CHAPTER XV. The Caravans 272

An important Feature of the Trading Community; Problems of the Satthavāhas and their Solution; How the Caravan Proceeded; Problems in course of the journey.

Conclusion 279
Bibliography 281
Index 289
Corrigenda 307

PREFACE

This work is an attempt to represent the social, religious and economic aspects of life in Northern India, with special reference to the region corresponding to modern Bihar and eastern Uttar Pradesh in pre-Mauryan times in general, and particularly between *c*. 600 B.C. to 325 B.C. For this work, we have accepted the two broad cultural divisions of the country, viz., Northern and Southern, divided by the Vindhya ranges. The ranges of the Vindhya system in ancient times formed a great dividing line between Northern and Southern India, and the two great regions developed the most distinctly marked cultural features.

The book substantially represents my thesis approved for the degree of Ph.D. by the Patna University in 1957. As the work is being published after a decade of its completion, I owe an apology to the readers. I am grateful to my *guru*, late Professor A. S. Altekar, under whose inspiring guidance I was able to complete this work. I am thankful to Professor R.S. Sharma who took keen interest in the publication of this book. I wish to thank all those from whom I received encouragement in connection with the writing of this work. Lastly, I express my apology to the readers for my inability to avoid printing mistakes which could not be achieved in spite of my best efforts.

M· M. Singh

Patna,
May, 1967.

PREFACE

ABBREVIATIONS

Ait. Ār.	*Aitareya Āraṇyaka.*
Ait. Br.	*Aitareya Brāhmaṇa.*
A. N.	*Aṅguttara-Nikāya.*
Āp. Dh. S.	*Āpastamba-Dharma-Sūtra.*
Āp. G. S.	*Āpastamba-Gṛihya-Sūtra.*
A. I. N.	*Ancient Indian Numismatics.*
A. S. I.	*Archaeological Survey of India*
A. S. R.	*Archaeological Survey Report.*
Ā. Sū.	*Āvaśyaka-Sūtra.*
Āśva. G. S.	*Āśvalāyana-Gṛihya-Sūtra.*
Aup. Sū.	*Aupapātika-Sūtra.*
A. V.	*Atharvaveda.*
Bau. Dh.S.	*Baudhāyana-Dharma-Sūtra.*
Bhāshya	Patañjali's *Mahābhāshya.*
Bh. Sū.	*Bhagavatī-Sūtra.*
B. I.	*Buddhist India.*
Bṛi. Up.	*Bṛihadāraṇyaka-Upanishad.*
C. H. I.	*Cambridge History of India.*
Chhān. Up.	*Chhāndogya-Upanishad.*
C. L.	*Carmichael Lectures.*
Comy.	Commentary.
C. V.	*Chullavagga.*
Dhp.	*Dhammapada.*
Dia.	*Dialogues of the Buddha.*
Dīp.	*Dīpavaṁsa.*
D. N.	*Dīgha-Nikāya.*
D. P. P. N.	*Dictionary of Pāli Proper Names.*
Early Texts	*India as Described in the Early Texts of Buddhism & Jainism.*
Ed.	Edited by
Fn.	Foot-note
Frg.	*Fragment*
Gau. Dh. S.	*Gautama-Dharma-Sūtra.*
G. S.	*The Book of Gradual Sayings.*
Hi. G. S.	*Hiraṇyakeśin-Gṛihya-Sūtra.*

I. H. Q.	*Indian Historical Quarterly.*
Ins.	*Inscription.*
Jā.	*Jātaka.*
Jā. Up.	*Jābāla-Upanishad.*
J. A. S. B.	*Journal of the Asiatic Society of Bengal.*
J. B. O. R. S.	*Journal of the Bihar & Orissa Research Society.*
J. N. S. I.	*Journal of the Numismatic Society of India.*
J. R. A. S.	*Journal of the Royal Asiatic Society.*
J. U. P. H. S.	*Journal of the Uttar Pradesh Historical Society.*
Kau.	Kauṭilya's *Arthaśāstra.*
Kau. Br.	*Kaushitaki Brāhmaṇa.*
Kau. Up.	*Kaushītaki Upanishad.*
K. S.	*The Book of Kindred Sayings.*
Kā. Saṁ.	*Kāṭhaka-Saṁhitā.*
Kenop.	*Kenopanishad.*
Mahā.	*Mahāvaṁsa.*
Manu.	*Manu-Smṛiti.*
Mai. Saṁ.	*Maitrāyaṇī-Saṁhitā.*
Mānava G. S.	*Mānava-Gṛihya-Sūtra.*
Mbh.	*Mahābhārata.*
Meg.	Megasthenes.
M. N.	*Majjhima-Nikāya.*
Mu. Up.	*Muṇḍakopanishad.*
M. V.	*Mahāvagga.*
Nāradā.	*Nārada-Smṛiti.*
N. S.	*Numismatic Supplement.*
Pā., Pāṇini	*Pāṇini's Ashṭādhyāyī.*
P. E.	*Pillar Edict.*
Pā. G. S.	*Pāraskara-Gṛihya-Sūtra.*
Pari. P.	*Pariśishṭaparvan.*
Parāśara.	*Parāśara-Smṛiti.*
Peta.	*Petavatthu.*
P. T. S.	*Pāli Text Society.*
Ṛig.	*Ṛigveda.*
R. E.	*Rock Edict.*
R. S., *Vinaya.*	Rahula Sanskrityayana, *Vinaya-Piṭaka.*
Sāṅ. G. S.	*Sāṅkhyāyāna-Gṛihya-Sūtra.*
Sabhā.	*Sabhāparva.*
Śata. Br.	*Śatapatha-Brāhmaṇa.*
S. B. B.	*Sacred Books of the Buddhists.*

Ś. B. E.	*Sacred Books of the East.*
S. N.	*Saṁyutta-Nikāya.*
Su. Ni.	*Sutta-Nipāta.*
Social Organisation	*Social Organisation in North-East India in Buddha's Time.*
Vai. Dh. P.	*Vaikhānasa-Dharma-Praśna.*
Vana	*Vanaparva.*
V. Dh. S.	*Vaśishṭha-Dharma-Sūtra.*
Vimāna.	*Vimānavatthu.*
Vinaya	*Vinaya-Piṭaka.*
Vishṇu. Dh. S.	*Vishṇu-Dharma-Sūtra.*
Vāj. Saṁ.	*Vājasaneyī-Saṁhitā.*
Yajñavalkya	*Yājñavalkya-Smṛiti.*

The following are the main points in the scheme of translite-ration followed in this work :—

अ	a	ङ	ṅa
आ	ā	च	cha
इ	i	छ	chha
ई	ī	ञ	ñ
उ	u	ट	ṭa
ऊ	ū	ठ	ha
ए	e	ड	ḍa
ऐ	ai	ढ	ḍha
ओ	o	ण	ṇa
औ	au	श	śa
ऋ	ṛ or ṛi	ष	sha
अनुस्वार	ṅ or ṁ	स	sa
विसर्ग	h		

Modern words and names are generally not attached diacritical marks.

INTRODUCTION

India is a vast country with a fairly uniform culture, which has been made possible due to a fusion of several diverse elements, and to which different regions of India have contributed their own quota. The region corresponding to modern Bihar and eastern Uttar Pradesh made remarkable contribution to Indian culture in different periods of history of the country. But it was in about the 6th century B.C. that the glorious chapter in the history of this region was opened with the rise of Magadha as a great political force. The political horizon of Northern India was marked by the rise of mighty states such as Kośala, Vajji Republic, Vatsa, Imperial Magadha and others. These states dominated the politics of Northern India for sometime, struggled for supremacy, and ultimately Magadha was able to emerge victorious, defeating and annexing her rival kidgdoms. The Vajji Republic was absorbed in the kingdom of Magadha during the reign of Ajātaśatru. This made the boundaries of Magadha correspond approximately to modern Bihar, excluding the major portion of the Chotanagpur plateau to the south, but including the Kāśī state in the west. From this time onwards Magadha became the most important centre of political activities in North-Eastern India, and with the absorption of Kośala and Vatsa by the time of king Śiśunāga, she became a great power in the whole of Northern India. The Nandas, who succeeded the Śaiśunāgas, made Magadha the master of the whole of the Gangetic valley, and probably conquered some portion of the Deccan too. Ultimately, under the Mauryas the Magadha Empire expanded to include almost the whole of India. Thus, politically the period under review records the remarkable expansion of Magdha and its domination in the politics of Northern India.

The rise of the political power of Magadha and the subsequent political unification of almost the entire Northern India resulted in the prosperity of the land. When a country enjoys peace and stable administration under the rule of able and efficient rulers, it makes remarkable progress in the social and economic spheres of life. Economic resources of the land are exploited for the betterment of the people, and arts and crafts, trade and commerce, etc., develop. Mind is diverted towards philosophical speculation, religious thinking, and literary persuits.

The period under consideration makes a great epoch not only in the history of Northern India but also in that of the whole country on account of the rise of Magadhan Imperialism and the advent of the Buddha and Mahāvīra. The rise of Buddhism was to a great extent responsible for the creation of a new social and religious consciousness, which challenged the old notions of social organisation and the authority of the Brāhmaṇas. From the point of view of religious history, this period is specially interesting and important, for Eastern India, specially Bihar was the scene of the rise of several sects, viz., Buddhism, Jainism, Ājīvikism, etc. Bihar, in fact, proved to be the most fertile land for the growth and spread of these sects, and hence the contribution of Bihar to the consolidation and growth of the new religions has received particular attention in this study.

It cannot be claimed that everything is new in the present work, but we have tried to make the treatment comprehensive. There are works which deal with the social and religious aspects of Indian history of this period, but scholars have generally relied upon the Buddhist sources only. Richard Fick was a pioneer in presenting an account of the social conditions of North-East India of the Buddha's time, but he did not sufficiently utilise the Brahmanical sources. Similarly Law's *India as Described in the Early Texts of Buddhism and Jainism* does not make much use of the Brahmanical sources. There are other works on the different aspects of the history of this period, but none has attempted to give a complete picture as revealed from the Buddhist and the contemporary Brahmanical sources, viz., the *Gṛihya-Sūtraṣ* and the *Dharma-Sūtraṣ*. The present work incorporates both the Buddhist and Brahmanical sources, and tries to give a fairly complete picture of the social, religious and economic life of the period. The Buddhist works in several cases give a more faithful account than the Brahmanical, but where they refer to certain aspects of the social and religious life of the Brahmanical society with a view to criticising them, they generally give an exaggerated account. On the other hand, the Brahmanical sources give an account of the higher sections of society ; sometimes the picture is ideal. The Buddhist and the Brahmanical accounts are to a great extent, supplementary to each other, and no picture represented by one source only can be regarded as a faithful account of the society of the period under consideration.

But there is also another side of the picture. The reader will find that the Buddhist account is very considerably supported by the Brahmanical sources, and there is a good deal of agreement between them. The present work shows where these sources agree and where they disagree. Points of differences have been critically analysed and explained, and on the whole it seems that the two sources do not give contradictory accounts, but supplement the information of each other.

The principal source of the present work is the Buddhist Canonical Pāli literature, the *Tripiṭaka* which consists of collections of speeches and conversations of the Buddha, songs of monks and nuns and the rules of the Buddhist Order. We have accepted the date assigned to the Buddhist Pāli Canon by Winternitz[1]. The Pāli *Piṭakas* reveal that it was the Majjhimadesa which remained the scene of the Buddha's activities. The major portion of his life was spent in the region corresponding to modern Bihar and eastern Uttar Pradesh where he delivered the important *Suttas*. It was also by the Bhikshus of this region that the Pāli *Piṭakas* were preserved orally till they were finally compiled in the Third Council at Pāṭaliputra.

1. Winternitz, *A History of Indian Literature*, Vol. II. According to Winternitz the *Vinaya* and *Sutta Piṭakas* on the whole correspond to the Canon compiled in the third century B.C. The Ceylonese tradition says that the Canon, which was compiled in the Third Buddhist Council convened by Aśoka under Moggaliputta Tissa, was taken to Ceylon by Mahinda and was later recorded in writing in its present form in the reign of Vaṭṭagāmani (in the first or fifth century A.D.) According to tradition recorded in the *Chullavagga* (xi), *Dīpavaṁsa* (iv), and Mahāvaṁsa (iii), rules of Dhamma and Vinaya, which were laid down by the Buddha, were chanted by the Theras in the First Council held under Mahākassapa at Rājagṛiha soon after the Nirvāṇa of the Lord. The important *Suttas* delivered by the Buddha and the rules laid down by him for the Bhikshus seem to have been committed to memory and faithfully handed down till they were committed to writing. The reference to certain Buddhist Canonical texts in

The *Jātakas* which form a part of the *Khuddaka-Nikāya* of the *Sutta-Piṭaka* are of great value from the point of view of the cultural history. As stories they refer to the day-to-day life of the people and supply valuable material for reconsrtucting the social, religious and economic aspects of history of our period. We cannot deny that the theme of some stories is very ancient, and a few of them may have been current among the people even before the birth of the Buddha. Rhys Davids accepts the view that the *Jātakas* refer to conditions of the pre-Buddhist period. But this can be true only of some stories, the theme of which is legendary. The stories were framed by the Buddhist monks to explain Buddhism to the masses. They may have adapted some earlier stories for the purpose ; the original form of such stories must have been changed by introducing in them facts of the contemporary society. The story-teller, though referring to ancient times, would have reflected the social conditions of the time when they were told. He must have taken care to see that stories told were in tune with the prevalent conditions. The fact that many things mentioned in the *Brāhmaṇas* and the *Upanishads* are not referred to in the *Jātakas* would suggest that the *Jātaka* literature developed after the age of the *Brāhmaṇas* and the *Upanishads*.

Many of the *Jātakas* are represented in the sculptures of Sānchī and Bhārhut reliefs, often with descriptive titles attached to them. This shows that some of the stories were current in society, before these sculptural representations were attempted. According to the authorities on Indian art the Stūpas of Sānchī and Bhārhut belong to the second century B.C.

Fick has accepted that the *Jātakas* refer to conditions in the time of the Buddha. Rhys Davids holds the view that the stories were current before the third century B.C. According to Būhler the descriptions of the political, religious, and social conditions of the people in the *Jātakas* clearly

the edicts of Aśoka leads to the conclusion that a good deal of the *Sūtra-Piṭaka* and the *Vinaya-Piṭaka* was already compiled before the time of Aśoka. Later sources such as *Milinda-Pañho*, *Dīpavaṁsa*, *Mahāvaṁsa* and commentaries on the *Sūtras* indicate that the *Tripiṭaka* had come into existence by the early centuries of the Christian era.

refer to the time before the rise of the Nandas and the Mauryas, because Rājagṛiha occupies a very prominent position. Takshaśilā also figures prominetly in several stories, and it was so during our period. But Pāṭaliputra, which rose to prominence during the latter half of our period, does not figure much. Kings referred to are generally legendary, which speaks of an earlier period. Under such circumstances we are quite justified in accepting that most of the *Jātakas* depict the state of affairs from *c.* 600 to 325 B.C.

To turn to Brahmanical evidence, we have utilised the Vedic sources to some extent in order to trace the origin and development of certain institutions, customs, and practices.

The *Gṛihya-Sūtras* and the *Dharma-Sūtras* have been utilised as corroborative evidence, because according to competent authorities they were written down between *c.* 800 and 200 B.C. The *Ashṭādhyāyī* of Pāṇini has been used, because so far as Pāṇini is concerned, his relation with Pāṭaliputra during the days of a Nanda king is accepted by scholars. Patañjali's *Mahābhāshya* and *Kātyāyana's Vārttika*, as they are treatises to explain Pāṇini's *Sūtras*, have been sometimes referred to. The *Manusmṛiti* has been also referred to as supporting evidence, because it refers both to an ealier period and the period when compiled. The *Arthaśāstra* of Kauṭilya has been also utilised, because it represents the Maurya period, and the society during the days of the Mauryas was not altogether different from what it was in the pre-Maurya age. Certain conditions would have remained as they were during the earlier period. The *Arthaśāstrā* shows what further progress was made over the preceding period and what conditions were retained. It also enlightens us where the Buddhist evidence is lacking. The *Vaikhānasa-Dharma-Praśna* though of a later period is utilised, because it deals with the rules of Hindu Sanyāsins, which were mostly the same throughout. The account of Megasthenes has been also made use of in a few places. Lastly, there are later sources such as the *Smṛitis* of Yājña-valkya, Nārada and so on referred to with a view to showing later developments.

Like the Brahmanical sources the Jaina sources such as the *Āchārañga-Sūtra*, the *Kalpa-Sūtra*, the *Uvāsagadasāo* and the

Aupapātika-Sūtra have been utilised to provide supporting evidence. Jainism rose in Bihar, and Mahāvīra's activities were mostly confined to this state, hence the early Jaina sources largely refer to conditions in Bihar. The *Bhagavatī-Sūtra*, which belongs to a later period, has also been utilised for an account of the Ājīvikas and their relation to the Jainas. It deals with the life of the Ājīvika leader Makkhali Gosāla and his relations with Mahāvīra, his rival. It is just possible that this treatise may have preserved the ancient tradition faithfully, and we may rely on it where it supplies additional information on a topic which is known from Buddhist sources definitely belonging to our period.

The present work is divided into fifteen chapters dealing with the various aspects of social, religious, and economic life. The first chapter shows that during this period the social life was marked by rigidity of caste laws and the intense feeling based on birth superiority. The Buddha as a reformer exerted himself for liberalising the current notions of the caste system. But he was successful in removing the feeling of caste consciousness only within the monastic fold; outside the Order, his teachings against the feeling of caste distinction proved to be ineffective. He was probably helpless in his efforts to alter the existing caste system, and though theoretically against it, for the interest of his own Order he became a spokesman of the Kshatriya superiority. Sometimes he figures as accepting the ascendancy of the Brāhmaṇas and the Kshatriyas over other castes, and at places as arguing for superiority of the Kskatriyas over the Brāhmaṇas. The situation was that acceptance of Buddhism did not imply the loss of one's caste identity, and in spite of the advent of new social consciousness, the established order remained unshaken. Restriction in interdining was also gradually developing.

The reader will further find an account of the conditions of different castes of this period. As regards the Brāhmaṇas, one finds that though the Buddhist sources give stress on their degenerate condition and the Brahmanical ones refer to their exalted status, yet both the sources show substantial agreement in giving a full account of the position of the members of this caste in the contemporary society. They were divided into two distinct categories, ideal and worldly. A section of the Brāhmaṇās adhered faithfully to the traditional occupations of teaching the *Vedas*, officiating at sacrifices, etc., but on account of economic pressure some of them were taking resort to objectionable professions, such as hunting, carpentry, chariot-driving and so on.

Unlike the Brahmanical sources the Buddhist ones place the Kshatriyas above all. We have discussed the probable reasons of the Kshatriya ascendancy and their actual position in the society.

The Vaiśyas were known by such terms as Seṭṭhi, Gahapati, and Kuṭumbika. The Seṭṭhis were the best representatives of this caste ; they lived in cities, owned considerable property and enjoyed honour in society.

The Śūdras included the followers of several arts and crafts. The main feature of this period was that the artisans were developing into different castes with the characteristics of hereditary professions and separate settlements. There were also certain unsettled, unorganised and wandering castes such as dancers, snake-charmers, and others, who were included among the Śūdras. The reader will further find an account of the despised castes like Chaṇḍālas, Veṇas, Nesādas, Rathakāras, Pukkusas, etc., whose condition was most deplorable.

As regards slavery, dealt with in the second chapter, chief source of information is the Buddhist *Tripiṭaka*. It reveals that the practice of employing Dāsas and Dāsīs was well known in the society of the period. An attempt has been made to make a critical analysis of the categories of slaves, known from different sources, and it is shown that the Buddhist sources give the same number of them as the Brahmanical. The discussion on the treatment of slaves shows that though harsh slave-owners were not unknown, generally they were treated with care and kindness, and some of them could rise to responsible posts, but such cases were few, and most of them were employed for doing the household works. In some cases young masters fell in love with handsome slave girls, resulting in a lifelong union. Sometimes young girls of the master's family fell in love with their slaves, but such unions were not encouraged.

The reader will also find a brief account of the emancipation of slaves, a feature peculiar to our land.

The chapter on marriage deals with such topics as polyandry, polygamy, settlement of marriage, forms of marriages, etc. The Buddhist and the Brahmanical sources no doubt disclose that polygamy was permitted in the society of our period, but they reveal that monogamy prevailed. It was generally the noble and the aristocratic class which used to practice polygamy, and the vast majority of the population was monogamons. The reader will further find that marriage customs and practices were to a great extent similar to those of the present-day Hindu society. The conception of Gotra had developed and it was most probably considered at the time of marriage settlement. The problem of inter-caste marriage has been also discussed and shown that caste restrictions were relaxed only in the higher circles.

The reader will also find a brief discussion on the problem of cousin marriage. The Dharmaśāstras tell us that marrying the daughter of the maternal uncle was a custom of the South, but our sources show that it was in vogue also in Bihar and Uttar Pradesh.

As regards the forms of marriages, we find that the Buddhist sources refer only to Brāhma, Prājāpatya, Āsura, Gāndharva, and Rākshasa marriages. Daiva, Ārsha and Paiśācha are not mentioned, probably because the former two were not differentiated from the Brāhma and Prājāpatya, and the latter may not have been considered as a marriage at all.

Lastly, the subject of remarriage and divorce has been discussed. During our period widow marriage as well as marrying during the lifetime of the husband after seeking a divorce were in vogue, though the latter practice was not encouraged. But whereas the Brahmanical sources favour remarriage only of child-widows, the Buddhist evidence represents those of all ages as marrying again.

The next chapter shows that the gaity and dignity of the cities like Rājagṛiha, Vaiśālī, and Pāṭaliputra were heightened by the courtesans. They were not looked down upon, but enjoyed proper social prestige ; their financial condition also was sound. Bu such was the position of the high class courtesans, who were the custodians of fine arts, and it could be enjoyed by a few. The general conscience of the time did not appreciate the profession of a prostitute.

The chapter on food and drink shows that the people of Eastern India, even during the days of the Buddha, were eating almost the same type of food as today. Some special preparations of that period have survived till modern times. Non-vegetarian food was quite common, and the Buddha, though he preached non-voilence, did not prohibit his followers from accepting meat in alms, nor did he himself refuse eating, if it was offered. Drinking was resorted to by almost all, except ascetics, priests, and students, but on occasions like the Drinking Festival restriction seems to have been relaxed.

Social life in Northern India, specially in the eastern region, was marked by occasional festive celebrations. The reader will find a chapter dealing with the special features of the festivities popular in the society. Details of festive celebrations are available in the Buddhist sources, and we come across many of their interesting features, such as proclamation of the festivals by beating of drums, people flocking in the cities and towns for merry-making, celebrations lasting for days, the king going in a procession round the city and so on. Celebrations of the Kattikā (Kaumudī-Mahotsava), Surā-Nakkhata, Hatthi-Maṅgala, and the Ploughing Festival are quite interesting.

The seventh chapter gives a general outline of the religious conditions. North-East India was then the centre of a very important religious movement, and new schools of religion and philosophy were coming into prominence. Brahmanism, the earlier religion, Buddhism, Jainism, and Ājīvikism were the main religious Orders which were flourishing side by side. Popular Religion, followed by the masses, was nothing but popular Brahmanism, for by this period the latter had absorbed the practices of the lower strata of society.

The chapter deals mainly with those features of Brahmanism which are revealed by the Buddhist sources. Brahmanism of this period can be divided into two aspects—the higher and the lower or popular. A section of the Brāhmaṇas faithfully followed the Vedic religious practices. Sacrifices played a dominant part in higher Brahmanism, and certain aspects of it such as killing elephants, digging the sacrificial pit, etc. are innovations of the period under review. In this period certain Vedic gods like Prajāpati, Agni, Indra and others had retained their popularity, but a few minor deities of the *Vedas* had become prominent. No doubt some Vedic gods were widely worshipped, but the masses also believed in popular cults such as the worship of Yakkha, Nāga, Tree, Bull, etc. which occupied a significant position in the sphere of religious beliefs and practices of the multitude. Shrines of Yakkhas and Nāgas were made for the purpose of worship, but there is no definite reference to image installed in them. The term Yakkhabhavana occurs for the shrine of a Yakkha, but it denotes a raised platform for his worship, and we are not in a position to ascertain what was actually worshipped. Probably terracotta figures of the Yakkhas and Nāgas were worshipped.

The next chapter describes the various aspects of ascetic life for which the term Monastic Life has been used. The homeless stage of life had come into existence long before the period under consideration, but it got momentum from the Upanishadic philosophy, and was further encouraged during the age of the Buddha. During this period there appeared several Orders of the ascetics like those of the Barhmaṇas (Tāpasas, Vānaprasthins, Sanyāsins, etc.), Buddhists, Jainas, Ājīvikas and others. The philosophical theories of the different religions no doubt differed, but there was substantial agreement as regards the discipline of the ascetic life.

The account of the Jaina monastic life is based on the *Āchārañga-Sūtra* which deals with the monastic discipline of the Jaina monks and is regarded by the authorities on the subject as referring to the early days of Jainism. The account brings out the main points of resemblance among the three Orders of the Jainas, the Buddhists and the Brahmanical Sanyāsins.

The following chapter describes life in the Buddhist Monasteries. Scholars such as S.K. Dutta, N. Dutta and others have done considerable work on the subject. But the present work deals mainly with the social aspect of the Bhikshu-life, based mainly on the *Vinaya-Piṭaka* and the *Jātakas*. It is shown that there was a gradual development of the Buddhist monastic life from the wandering stage to the emergence of well-built Vihāras. From the very beginning the Buddha pursued a policy of adaptability, and while laying down rules of monastic discipline, he avoided such practices as would have caused resentment of the people towards his Order. He laid down that antisocial elements like robbers and thieves were not eligible for entering the Buddhist monastic fold. Conscious of the future prosperity of his Order, he carefully framed such rules as would give no place to group rivalry and disunity among the Bhikshus.

The reader will find in this chapter a critical discussion on ordinations and the relations of the Upajjhāya and the Saddhivihārika which was similar to that of a Guru and the Brahmachārin.

In the Buddhist monastery due emphasis was given on the observance of the rules of seniority and etiquette, which was in tune with the age-old tradition of India. One of the reasons for this was that the Buddhist Order was also an educational institution. The senior and the junior members were bound by the sacred tie of mutual duty and assistance. It was no doubt the duty of the junior to obey his elder, but the latter was expected to treat the former like his own son. It was the effort of the Buddha that there should be complete concord, and the feeling of assistance and co-operation among the fellow members should prevail, yet in some cases relations among the Bhikshus could not be ideal as conceived by him.

The ideal before the Buddhist monks was to lead a life of simplicity and moderation, but we find that the Buddha allowed several concessions. According to the rules of the Vinaya, dress was to be simple and unattractive—monks were to use no shoes ; they put on Paṅsukūla robes. But as time marched on changes were introduced by the Buddha himself. He permitted the Bhikshus to put on shoes without linings or cast off ones having linings. Similarly, new robes supplied by the laity were also allowed. Thus, we find that the rules of the Buddhist Order were considerably flexible and that the principle of moderation in laying down them was adhered to by the Buddha. However, there was also a section which found even these concessions insufficient and transgressed the discipline, e.g. the Chhabhaggiyas put on decorated shoes and ornaments, and used several luxury goods.

The Buddha did not favour the entry of women in his Order. The probable causes of his opposition andt he reasoins for women's desire for renunciation have been discussed in full detail. However, by the intervention of Ānanda, they were permitted to enter the Order. Their entry created certain problems for the Saṅgha, e.g., some of them unaware of their conception joined the Order and after sometimes developed signs of pregnancy and so on.

Cases of backsliding and reverting to the worldly life and their reasons have also been discussed. It is further showe that in certain quarters the Bhikshus failed to lead an ideal life and there developed a few monasteries with degenerate line. At the end of the chapter there is a brief account of the officers of the Saṅgha who were looking after the material needs of the Bhikshus.

The tenth chapter deals with rural society which has remained the backbone of Indian economic life. Rural life, during this period, was marked by the rise of several types of villages, out of which those inhabited by people of the same caste or profession and those of the craftsmen draw our attention. The reader will further find a detailed account of agricultural operations and the crops cultivated.

Next chapter dealing with arts, crafts, and industries shows that the industrial genius of the people of this period expressed itself in the advancement of various arts and crafts such as spinning, smithy, carpentry, house-building and so on. The accounts of the manufacture of textile and luxury goods and the works of the carpenter, the blacksmith, the goldsmith, etc. are given in considerable detail in the Buddhist sources. There are certain industries like mining the account of which is available in detail in Kauṭilya's *Arthśāstra*, and it has been presumed that similar may have been the case in pre-Mauryan times. The chapter on trade and trade routes shows that internal as well as foreign trade was in a fairly flourishing condition and that both land and water routes were utilised for the purpose. There was a network of trade routes, connecting almost all the cities and towns, and some of them extended even to famous trade centres outside India.

The succeeding chapter gives an account of the organisation of industry and trade. The organisational genius of the people had attained considerable maturity, and several crafts and also the traders had formed guilds under their respective Jeṭṭhakas. The traditional number of the guilds is eighteen, but by the time of the Buddha, almost all the crafts had formed their organisations. The chapter further discusses the functions and jurisdiction of the guilds.

The fourteenth chapter gives an account of the medium of exchange, prices, fees, salaries, and wages during the period of our study. Though originality cannot be claimed for the account of currency of this period, yet for the completeness of the picture of the economic life, it was thought necessary to give a summary of the work done on the coinage of the period under consideration. This chapter shows that Magadha had an indigenous coinage, and during the reign of the Nandas her coinage was standardised to agree with the currency of other regions. In fact, several states had their own standards, but with the political unification of northern India and also a portion of the Deccan under the Nandas, uniformity in coinage was introduced in the country. It has been shown that silver currency was the standard of the age of which several hoards have been found. As regards prices, fees, salaries, and wages, our findings lead us to the conclusion that generally the popular stories give exaggerated figures, and it is only in a few cases that we come across the reality.

The closing chapter gives a brief account of the caravan life, which was an important aspect of life of the trading community during the period of our study.

importance of the city-based towns, and some of them extended even to small and [illegible] towns of North India.

The succeeding chapter gives an account of the organisation of industry and trade. The organisational set-up of the people had attained considerable maturity and several crafts and also the traders had formed guilds under their respective leaders. The exact total number of the guilds is not known, but by the time of the Guptas, almost all trades had formed their organisations. The chapter further discusses the functions and jurisdiction of the guilds.

The fourteenth chapter gives an account of the medium of exchange, prices, fees, salaries and wages during the period of our study. Though not [illegible] part of [illegible] currency of the period, yet for the completeness of the picture of the economic life, it was thought necessary to give a summary of the work done on the currency of the period under consideration. This chapter shows that Magadha had an indigenous coinage. And while the [illegible] to the Nandas [illegible] stand [illegible] to agree with [illegible] of other [illegible]. In fact, [illegible] with the political unification of the northern India and [illegible], a portion of the Deccan under the Mauryas, [illegible] was introduced [illegible]. It has been shown that silver currency was the [illegible] had been found. A [illegible] salaries and wages, our findings lead us to the conclusion that [illegible] the popular [illegible] and it [illegible] that [illegible] when the [illegible].

The closing chapter gives a brief account of the everyday life, which was an important aspect of the life of the trading community during the period of our study.

CHAPTER I

CASTE ORGANISATION

There is no clear reference in the *Ṛgveda* which can prove the existence of the rigid caste system in contemporary times, as we find during the later period. We only know that during the Ṛgvedic period the four Varṇas, the Brāhmaṇa, the Rājanya, the Vaiśya, and the Śūdra existed as class divisions, and it depended upon the choice of an individual as to which Varṇa he should belong to. There was no sharp difference among the three higher Varṇas; the marked distinction existed only between the Ārya and the Dāsa or the Dasyu. But society gradually developed new ideas. Flexibility of the social organisation slowly gave place to rigidity; professions became hereditary, and caste consciousness became deep-rooted. By the time the *Brāhmaṇas* were composed, the conception of the four Varṇas had taken so deep a root in the social mind that even gods were considered as being divided into these four castes.[1] Thus caste rigidity was slowly and gradually getting accentuated.

Buddhist sources reveal that the Buddha as a reformist exerted himself to liberalise the current notions on the subject, but he was successful in eradicating caste feeling only within the monastic Order. Society as a whole continued to cling to the notions of the caste system as they were being developed.

The Buddhist literature represents the Buddha both as advocating for the worthlessness of the caste system[2] and pleading for the superiority of the Kshatriyas over the Brāhmaṇas. Probably his opposition to the caste feeling refers to the spiritual world; whereas his acceptance of the caste system speaks of the temporal life.

So far as the Holy Order was concerned, the Buddha succeeded in removing the feeling of caste distinction; for he said

1. *Mai. Saṁ.* I. 10. 13; *Śat.* Br. XV. 4. 2. 23-25; *Bṛi. Up.* I. 4. 11-13; *Kau. Br.* IX. 5 *Ait. Br.* XXXIV. 5 referred to by Kane in *History of Dharmaśāstra*, Vol. II, pt. I, p. 42: Agni and Bṛhaspati are Brāhmaṇas; Indra, Varuṇa, Soma and Yama are the Kshatriyas; Vasus, Rudras, Viśvedevas and Maruts are the Viśa, and Pūshan is the Śūdra.

2. *M.N.* II. 147-57; 177-84.

that as rivers after pouring their waters into the great ocean lose their identity, similarly all castes having entered the monastic fold renounced their lineage.[1] It is well known that Upāli, the barber, rose to the position of the chief of the Vinaya. The Bhikshus lived a community life and observed no restriction in inter-dining. Still the influence of the notions of caste was so far-reaching that some of the Bhikshus were known as Brāhmaṇa Bhikshus,[2] high born Bhikshus[3] and so on.

The Buddha's plea for the abolition of the caste distinction was ineffective outside the Order. Caste organisation remained unshaken in society. Acceptance of Buddhism as a lay disciple did not mean losing one's caste identity. The Buddha was even powerless to resist the prevalent notions. Sometimes he is seen arguing for the superiority of the Kshatriyas over the Brāhmaṇas.[4] Sometimes he is found defending the superiority of the Kshatriyas and the Brāhmaṇas over the rest by describing them as worthy of standing in the front rank so far as salutation, offering of seats, and claims of services from lower castes were concerned.[5] In the Buddhist literature the Buddha himself is described as of pure lineage up to seven generations both on the side of the father and the mother.[6] A similar claim is made on behalf of kings, like Ajātaśatru[7] and celebrated Brāhmaṇas, such as Soṇadaṇḍa,[8] Kūṭadanta,[9] Chaṅki[10] and

1. *C.V.* IX. 1. 4.

2. *Udāna*. I. 5, एवं वुत्ते अञ्ञतरो ब्राह्मण जातिको भिक्खु भगवन्तं एतद् अवोच ।

3. *A.N.* I.19. (*K.S.* I.16). उच्चाकुलकानं यदिदं भद्दियो कालिंगोधायपुत्तो ।

4. *D.N.* I. 97-99.

5. *M.N.* II. 128, चत्तारो' मे, महाराजा वण्णा––खत्तिया ब्राह्मणा वेस्सा सुद्दा । इमेसं खो, महाराज, चतुन्नं वण्णानं द्वे वण्णा अग्गं अक्खायन्ति,––खत्तिया च ब्राह्मणा च, यदिदं अभिवादनपच्चुट्ठानञ्चलिकम्मसामीचिकम्मं ति ।

6. *D.N.* I. 131, यं पि भो समणो गोतमो उभतो सुजातो मातितो च पिततो च संसुद्धगहणिको याव सत्तमा पितामहायुगा अक्खित्तो अनुपक्कुट्ठो जातिवादेन ।

M.N. II. 166; *Nidānakathā*, I. 2.

7. *A.N.* IV. 188; *A.N.* II 151 describes an anointed king as of pure origin up to seven generations on the sides of the father and the mother.

8. *D.N.* I. 113.

9. *D.N.* I. 130.

10. *M.N.* II. 165.

others.[1] In some cases feeling of caste consciousness was so high that some Brāhmaṇas did not like to be cremated in a cemetery where out-castes were burnt.[2]

The Buddhist evidence discloses that the society of our period regarded caste system as God ordained. The notion that the Creator Himself made the four castes and assigned to them their well-known duties occurs in some of the *Jātakas*.[3] The Kshatriyas, the Brāhmaṇas, and the Gahapatis (Vaiśyas) were regarded as the higher castes.[4] The Brahmanical literature gives the place of the highest honour to the Brāhmaṇas; but the Buddhist sources, to the Kshatriyas. The next in the rung of ladder were the Gahapatis, the Seṭṭhis, and ordinary Vaiśyas including higher artisans, who did not enjoy the same honour as the first two.[5] After them were the landless labourers occupying a lower position. Lastly, came the despised castes, the Chaṇḍālas, the Nesādas, the Veṇas, the Rathakāras, the Pukkusas and probably others who are described as poor and ill-fed.[6]

The feeling of caste superiority was also intense. The Brāhmaṇas on the one hand considered themselves as superior to all,[7] while on the other the Kshatriyas made the same claim.[3] This was not all. Certain groups within the same caste considered themselves higher than others. The Udichcha Brāh-

1. e.g. Bhadda Assājāniya in *A. N.* IV. 188; the *Brāhmaṇavagga-sutta* (No. 192) of the *Aṅguttara-Nikāya* mentions purity of birth up to seven generations as an essential quality of a Brāhmaṇa. See also *G. S.* I. 146.

2. The *Upasālhaka Jā* (No. 166)

3. *Jā.* VI. 207-8.

4. *M. N.* III. 177, यानि तानि उच्चाकुलानि——खत्तियमहासालकुलं वा ब्राह्मणमहासालकुलं वा गहपतिमहासालकुलं वा।

A. N. IV. 129-34; V. 290-91; *Uddālaka Jā.* (No. 487).

5. *M. N.* II. 128.

6. *M. N.* III. 169, यानि तानि नीचकुलानि——चण्डालकुलं वा नेसादकुलं वा वेणकुलं वा रथकारकुलं वा पुक्कुसकुलं वा——तथ रूपे कुले पञ्चाजायति दलिद्दे अपन्नपाणभोजने कसिरवुत्तके.... ।

K. S. I. 118, *A. N.* II. 85; III. 385.

7. *M. N.* II. 84; 148, ब्राह्मणा, व सेट्ठो वण्णो, हीनो अञ्ञो वण्णो; ब्राह्मणा व सुक्को वण्णो, कण्ह अञ्ञो वण्णो; ब्राह्मणा व सुज्झन्ति न अब्राह्मणा; ब्राह्मणा व ब्रह्मणो पुत्ता ओरसा मुखतो जाता ब्रह्मजा ब्रह्मनिम्मिता ब्रह्मदायादाति ।

8. *D. N.* I. 99; *A. N.* V. 327-28.

maṇas were proud of their origin,[1] thinking themselves higher than other Brāhmaṇas. The Śākya Kshatriyas regarded themselves higher than other Kshatriya clans, and hence they did not give in marriage a princess of their blood to Prasenajit, king of Kośala.[2] The rest of the castes as a general rule regarded the Brāhmaṇas and the Kshatriyas as superior to themselves. A *Jātaka* describes a Lichchhavi girl as a forbidden fruit for a barber boy; and the former is compared with a lioness, while the latter, with a jackal.[3]

Emphasis on the purity of lineage shows that endogamy was normal. But there are also references to inter-caste marriages. This problem is discussed in the chapter dealing with marriage.

As regards inter-dining opinion seems to be divided. The Śākya Mahānāma did not dine with his daughter Vāsabha-Khattiyā, born from a slave girl. He deceived the messengers of the Kośalan king by falsely stating that he had dined with her, and thus convinced them of her pure origin. Āpastamba prescribes that a Brāhmaṇa Snātaka should not dine at the house of any caste other than that of a Brāhmaṇa.[4] From his list of those whose food should not be accepted, it appears that the impure nature of certain professions was responsible for the restriction. People living by arms[5] (except Kshatriyas) and crafts,[6] physicians,[7] messengers,[8] and spies[9] were probably regarded as such. In some cases restriction on inter-dining was imposed as a punishment. Accordingly, userers,[10] drunkards,[11] prisoners,[12] and Brāhmaṇas neglecting[13] their duties were put

1. *Jā.* III. 232, तस्स जांति निस्साय महन्तो मानो अहोसि; *Jā.* I. 3731. We are told that Devadatta used to tell people that Kokālika was born in an chcha Brāhmaṇa family in order to win respect for him from the people of Rājagriha (*Jā.* II. 438).
2. *Kaṭṭhahāri Jā.* (No. 7) and *Bhaddasāla Jā.* (No. 465).
3. *Jā.* II. 5 (No. 152.).
4. *Āp. Dh. S.* I. 6. 18. 9-10.
5. *Āp. Dh. S.* I. 6. 18. 19.
6. *Ibid.* I. 6. 18. 18.
7. *Ibid.* I. 6. 18. 21.
8. *Ibid.* I. 6. 18. 28.
9. *Ibid.* I. 6. 18. 30.
10. *Ibid.* I. 6. 18. 22.
11. *Ibid.* I. 6. 19. 1.
12. *Ibid.*
13. *Ibid.* I. 6. 18. 29. 33.

under the category whose food was not to be eaten. But Āpastamba allows Śūdra cooks in Brāhmaṇa households, provided they were supervised by a member of the three higher castes and observed certain hygienic rules,[1] and in distress food from any caste could be accepted. The Bhikshus accepted food from all sections of society. It appears that one section of society was in favour of observing restrictions on inter-caste dining to a certain extent; while the other was opposed to it.

The Brāhmaṇas :

The Buddhist writers give much emphasis on the degenerate condition of the Brāhmaṇas. They describe them as not adhering to the ideals of their life[2] and engrossed in the pursuit of all worldly pleasures such as highly decorating their persons, eating delicious dishes and drinking liquor, moving in chariots, being attended by women, accumulating wealth, and so on.[3] On the other hand, the Brahmanical sources generally refer to the exalted position of the Brāhmaṇas and describe them as ideal. One may feel that the two sources are self-contradictory. But it should not be overlooked that in the Brahmanical sources there are references to those Brāhmaṇas who were illiterate and could be of no use to literary pursuits. The Buddhist writers refer to the ideal Brāhmaṇas in glowing words. When compared, the two sources do not show contradiction, because there lived in society ideal as well as ordinary Brāhmaṇas, pursuing various professions. Both sources taken together give a clear account of the condition of the Brāhmaṇas, as they existed in the society of the period under discussion.

The Buddhist literature discloses that the Brāhmaṇas were divided into two distinct categories, true and worldly. The first category included ascetics, Vedic teachers, and priests. The *Jātakas* very often refer to the Brāhmaṇas as renouncing

1. P. V. Kane, *History of Dharmaśāstra*, Vol. II, pt. I. p. 161.
2. *Su. Ni.* II. 7, न खो ब्राह्मणा सन्दिस्सन्ति, एतरहि ब्राह्मणा पोराणानं ब्राह्मणंधम्मेति ।
3. *C. V.* XII. 1. 3 ; *D. N. I.* 104-5.
   Dia. III. 276; A. N. II. 53, 54 ; *Jā.* I. 425.

the world and going to the forest, either at an early stage[1] or after passing through the successive stages of Brahmacharya and Gārhasthya.[2] Brāhmaṇas are described as well grounded in the three *Vedas* and versed in the various branches of learning, such as *Nighaṇṭu*, *Vyākaraṇa*, *Lokāyata*, etc.[3] Brāhmaṇas like Sunetta,[4] Sela,[5] and others[6] are referred to as possessed of vast learning, gathering hundreds of students around them, imparting them education and enjoying the respect of the multitude. Some were known as the teachers of world renowned fame (Disāpāmokkha-Āchariyo).[7] However, the Buddhist writers note failings of some of them, who would not always impart everything they knew to their pupils.[8] This criticism is perhaps exaggerated; for when one refers to the dialogue between the Buddha and his teacher Ālāra Kālāma, the Brāhmaṇa teacher is found to be inspired by the highest sense of sincerity towards his pupil.

Sacrifices played a great part in Brahmanism, and as the masses practised popular Brahmanism, it was but natural that the priests should occupy a high position in society and enjoy special honour. As sacrificial priests they made offerings and received rewards which included various objects such as cows, beds, garments, and the like.[9] Land-grants by kings were known as the Brahmadeyya, which in the case of certain Brāhmaṇas like Soṇadaṇḍa, Kūṭadanta and others was one whole village for

1. *Jā.* I. 333, 361, 373, 450; II. 131, 232, 262, 145, etc.
2. *Jā.* II. 85, 394, 411; III. 147, 352.
3. *D. N.* I. 88, 120; *A. N.* III. 223; *G. S.* I 146; *Su. Ni.* III. 7; *M. N.* II. 133—तेन खो पन समयेन ब्रह्मायु ब्राह्मणो मिथिलायं पटिवसति... तिण्णं वेदानं पारगू सनिघण्डुकेटुभानं साखरप्पभेदानं इतिहास पञ्चमानं पदको वेय्याकरणो लोकायत महापुरिसलक्खणेसु अनवयो। The *antevāsī* of this Brāhmaṇa is similarly described (*M. N.* II. 134).
4. *A. N.* III. 371.
5. *Su. Ni.* III. 7.
6. *Jā.* VI. 32, describes an Udichcha Brāhmaṇa at Champā as teaching five hundred pupils; *S. N.* IV. 117 refers to Lohicha as the teacher of several disciples.
7. *Jā.* I. 166, 239, 299; II. 137; III. 215; VI. 32.
8. e.g., *Jā.* II. 221, बोधिसत्ता नाम सिप्पं वाचेन्ता आचरिय मुट्ठिं न करोन्ति।
9. *Su. Ni.* II. 7. 20-22.

each.[1] People organised certain festive occasions called the Brāhmaṇa-Vāchanikāni, and invited Brāhmaṇas for uttering benediction on the occasion; feasts followed the formal function. The Kathāvāchanas of the present Hindu Society are probably a later development of this practice. The royal priest was one of the secular officers of the king.[2] Generally he was the king's Guru in his youthful days and often even in later life.[3] He also participated in the administration of justice.[4] As the fellow companion of the king, he sometimes played dice with him,[5] or accompanied him on the back of the elephant on festive occasions[6], and did not usually abandon him on occasions of misfortune.[7]

The second category consisted of those Brāhmaṇas who took to professions other than those prescribed for them from the orthodox point of view. Due to the changing circumstances and under the pressure of social and economic necessities many of the Brāhmaṇas could not stick to their hereditary professions of teaching and priesthood. The Brāhmaṇa law-givers were quite aware of the changing needs of society, and hence they permitted a Brāhmaṇa to follow other professions for the sake of livelihood. According to Āpastamba[8] and Gautama[9] trade and agriculture were to be taken up by him in times of distress. Manu prescribes that he should follow the profession of a Kshatriya or a Vaiśya.[10] From the Buddhist sources it is gathered that the Brāhmaṇas in the ordinary walk of life appeared as farmers, craftsmen, businessmen, soldiers, administrators, and so on.[11]

1. Soṇadaṇḍa enjoyed Champā as his Brahmadeyya (*D. N.* I. 111); Kūṭadanta was enjoying the village Khānumata in Magadha as the Brahmadeyya by Bimbisāra (*D. N.* I. 127). Similar gift by Pasenadi (Prasenajit) is referred to in *M. N.* II. 164. Honouring the Brāhmaṇas with Brahmadeyya is also referred to in *Jā.* VI. 480.

2. *Jā.* I. 439.

3. *Jā.* III. 28.

4. *Jā.* II. 186-7; V. 1.

5. *Jā.* I. 289.

6. *Kuṇāla Jā.* (No. 536).

7. *Jā.* III. 417.

8. *Āp. Dh. S.* I. 7. 20. 11; II. 5. 10. 4.

9. *Gau. Dh. S.* X. 5.

10. *Manu.* X. 81-82; IV. 6.

11. *M. N. Sutta,* 98; *Su. Ni.* III. 9; *Jā.* II. 165; IV. 207; V. 22.

There were wealthy Brāhmaṇas called the Mahāsālas, like Soṇadaṇḍa, Kūṭadanta, Kasibhārdvāja, Chaṅki, Tārukkha, Jānussoṇi, Todeyya, Pokkharasāti and others[1], who enjoyed all respect of the people of Kośala and Magadha. Some Brāhmaṇas, such as Keṇiya Jaṭila, were so wealthy and resourceful that they could even invite and entertain kings on certain occasions.[2] Some of the Mahāsāla Brāhmaṇas owned considerably big plots of cultivable lands, described as being ploughed by 500 ploughs.[3]

The *Brahmajālā-Sutta* of the *Digha-Nikāya* blames the Brāhmaṇas for following unlawful livelihood and gives a long list of such Brāhmaṇas. The *Dasa-Brāhmaṇa Jātaka* (No. 495) mentions ten categories of the worldly type of Brāhmaṇas. According to this *Jātaka* they were physicians, servants (like chariot-drivers), taxmen (who did not leave, unless they got a reward), wood-cutters, traders, Ambaṭṭha and Vessa (engaged in trade and agriculture), slaughters, cowherds and Nesādas, hunters, and those helping the kings in bathing.[4] This may appear as over-exaggerated, but in other *Jātakas* we get reference to Brāhmaṇas practising the medical profession,[5] ploughing the land,[6] trading[7] and hawking goods,[8] working as a carpenter,[9] as a shepherd (Ajapāla-Brāhmaṇa),[10] as an

1. *Soṇadaṇḍa-Sutta* and *Kūṭadanta-Sutta* of *D. N*; *M. N.* (*Sutta*, 98), II. 203; *Kasibhārdvāja-Sutta* of *Su. Ni.* and *Su. Ni.* III. 9.

2. Keniya Jaṭila of Aṅguttarāpa is described as inviting king Bimbisāra on the occasion of his marriage and *mahā-yajña*, which took place on the same occasion (*Su. Ni.* III. 7).

3. *Su. Ni.* I. 4; *K. S.* I. 216; *Ja.* IV. 276.

4. *Jā.* IV. 363, दस खलु महाराज या ता ब्राह्मण जातियो, तेसं विभङ्ग विचयं वित्थारेन सुनोहि मे... तिकिच्छकसमा, परिचारकसमा, निग्गाहकसमा खानुघातकसमा, वणिजकसमा, समा अम्वट्ठवेस्सेहि, गोघातकसमा, समागोपनिसादेहि, लुद्दका, मलमज्जनसमा ।

5. *Jā.* II. 213; VI. 181.

6. *Jā.* II. 165; III. 162-63; *Jā.* V. 68 describes a Brāhmaṇa as खेत्तं कसित्वा गोणे विस्सजेत्वा कुदालकम्मं कातुं आरभि । Wealthy Brāhmaṇa agriculturists are described as owning 1000 Karisas of land. This shows that among the Brāhmaṇas there were ordinary farmers as well as wealthy agriculturists (*Jā.* III. 293; IV. 276).

7. *Jā.* IV. 15-21; V. 22, 471;

8. *Jā.* II. 15.

9. *K. S.* I. 227; *Jā.* IV. 207, तत्थ एको ब्राह्मण वड्ढकि अरञ्ञा दारुनि आहरित्वा रथं कत्वा जीविकं कप्पेसि ।

10. *Jā.* III. 401.

archer[1] and as a hunter (Nesāda-Brāhmaṇa).[2] There were others who followed the professions of dream[3] and fortune telling (Lakkhaṇa-Pāṭhaka),[4] reading the past, future and the character of an individual from the signs of his body (Aṅga-vijjā-Pāṭhaka)[5] and reading the luck of swords (Asiakkhaṇa-Pāṭhaka).[6] Some of them worshipped demons and practised magic. They possessed Mantras like the Vedabbhamanta,[7] the Paṭhavijayamanta,[8] and the Chintāmaṇivijjā.[9] The art of exorcism was also practised by a few.[10] It appears from these references and from the account of the *Brahmajāla-Sutta* that the Brāhmaṇas could be found in all walks of life, and that some of them took up objectionable practices, such as hunting, carpentary, chariot-driving, etc.

The Kshatriyas :

The place of highest honour, which is given to the Brāhmaṇas in the Brahmanical literature, is occupied by the Kshatriyas in the Buddhist sources where they are generally mentioned as the first caste.[11] The Buddha himself is represented as telling the Brāhmaṇa Ambaṭṭha that whether one compared women with women or men with men, the Kshatriyas were higher and the Brāhmaṇas inferior.[12] No other caste would equal them in the purity of lineage.[13] They were so much

1. *Jā.* III. 219; V. 127.
2. *Jā.* II. 200; VI. 182, 170, ब्राह्मणो... अरञ्ञं गन्त्वा सूलयन्तपासवागुरा ओड्डेत्वा मिगे वधित्वा मंसं काचेन हरित्वा विक्किणन्तो जीविकं कप्पेति ।
3. *Jā.* I. 343; IV. 334-35; VI. 330.
4. *Jā.* I. 272; IV. 79, 335, V. 211.
5. *Jā.* II. 21, 250; V. 458.
6. *Jā.* I. 455.
7. *Jā.* I. 253.
8. *Jā.* II. 243.
9. *Jā.* III. 504.
10. *Jā.* III. 511.
11. *C. V.* IX. 1. 4; *M. N.* II. 128; III. 177, *A. N.* II. 194; III. 214; IV. 129-34; V. 290-91; *Vimāna.* V. 13. 15; *Peta.* II. 6. 12; *Jā.* I. 326; III. 194; IV. 205.
12. *D. N.* I. 98, इति खो अम्बट्ठ इत्थिया वा इत्थिं करित्वा पुरिसेन वा पुरिसं करित्वा खत्तिया व सेट्ठा हीना ब्राह्मणा ।
13. *D. N.* I. 99; *A. N.* V. 327-8.

    खत्तियो सेट्ठो जनेतस्मिं ये गोत्तपटिसारिनो ।
    विज्जाचरणसम्पन्नो सो सेट्ठो देवमानुसेति ॥

proud and conscious of their superiority that in the interview between the Brāhmaṇa Pokkharasāti and king, Prasenajit, the latter never allowed the former, his dependent to see his face; he spoke to him through a curtain.[1] The proud and haughty Śākyas never honoured a Brāhmaṇa; they did not even offer a seat to Ambaṭṭha, when he visited their Council Hall.[2] In the *Jātaka Nidānakathā* the Buddha is represented as reflecting within himself that because the Kshatriyas constituted the highest caste, he would prefer to be born one of them.[3] The Jaina Canon, *Kalpa-Sūtra* gives the story of how the embryo of Mahāvīra was transferred to the womb of Kshatriyāṇī Triśalā from the womb of Brāhmaṇī Devanandā.[4] King Arindama comparing his high birth with that of the Brāhmaṇa Soṇa, the son of the priest, called him a low-born.[5]

What were the factors that led to the rise of such superiority feeling amongst the Kshatriyas? They enjoyed the highest privilege of the right of ruling which could not be claimed by others. It is natural that the ruling class should enjoy power, prestige, and dignity. The Buddhist writers[6] and even Hindu works like the *Gītā* describe the head of the state as the best among men. It was in the Kshatriya caste that during the period under review leaders of the new schools of thought of Buddhism and Jainism were born. It was but natural that the members of the caste from which emerged the Buddha and Mahāvīra should have developed a sense of superiority. It is no wonder to find the Buddhist writers assigning the place of highest honour to the caste of the Lord. In addition to these,

1. *D.N.* I. 103, तस्स राजा पसेनदि कोसलो सम्मुखीभावं पि न ददाति। यदापि मन्तेति तिरो दुस्सन्तेन मन्तेति।

2. *D.N.* I. 90-91, चण्डा भो गोतम सक्य-जाति,... न ब्राह्मणे सक्करोन्ति न ब्राह्मणे गरुकरोन्ति न ब्राह्मणे मानेन्ति न ब्राह्मणे पूजेन्ति न ब्राह्मणे अपचायन्ति न मं कोचि आसनेन पि निमन्तेसि।

3. *Jā.* I. 49, ततो कुलं विलोकेन्तो बुद्धा नाम वेस्सकुले वा सुद्दकुले वा न निब्बतन्ति, लोकसम्मते पन खत्तियकुले वा ब्राह्मणकुले वा ति द्वीसु एव कुलेसु निब्बतन्ति, इदानि च खत्तियकुलं लोकसम्मतं, तत्थ निब्बत्तिस्सामि।

4. *S.B.E.* XXII. 218-229.

5. *Jā.* V. 257, अयं ब्राह्मणो हीनजच्चो समानो असम्भिन्न-खत्तियवंसे जातस्स मम... ।

6. e.g. *Su.Ni.* III. 7. 21.

the general condition in society also favoured the Kshatriya's equality with that of the Brāhmaṇa. Members of both the higher castes received similar education under the same teacher,[1] which enabled the Kshatriyas to have no inferior feeling in relation to the Brāhmaṇas.

The ministers of the kings, the commanders of army, the high administrative officers and feudal lords were mostly Kshatriyas. However, the ministers were often Brāhmaṇas. The Kshatriyas were a warrior class considered as born to lead the army and rule the people. But economic factors had led many of them to adopt other professions also, as was the case with the Brāhmaṇas. The *Jātakas* describe Kshatriya princes as taking to trade,[2] earning livelihood by manual labour[3] and living as potters, basket-makers, florists, and cooks.[4]

The Vaiśyas :

In the Buddhist Pāli literature members of the third caste are represented by words like Vessa, Gahapati, Seṭṭhi, and Kuṭumbika. The term Gahapati means literally a householder, and hence one may doubt whether it actually denotes the third caste. But this term is very often used just after the Kshatriya and the Brāhmaṇa,[5] at the place where we expect the third caste, and at places it is clearly stated that the Gahapati was the third higher Varṇa.[6] Again in the *Jātaka* narratives the hereditary characteristics of the Gahapati are maintained. If he is ruined through the loss of his family fortune and forced to take up lower occupations, he is still known as a Gahapati.[7]

1. *Jā*. I. 259; III. 122, 158.
2. *Jā*. IV. 84.
3. *Jā*. IV. 169.
4. *Jā*. V. 290-93. The story says that a love-lorn prince apprenticed himself successively to a potter, a basket-maker, a florist and a cook and that there was no reproach for his pursuing such jobs when the matter was disclosed.
5. e.g. *M.V.* VI. 28. 4; *D.N.* I. 67, II. 145-46; *M.N.* I. 176, 395, 502, खत्तिय पंडितापि ब्राह्मणपंडितापि गहपतिपंडितापि ।
6. *M.N.* III. 177.
7. A Gahapati of this category is described as dealing in vegetables (*Jā*. III. 21); Another one is seen maintaining his mother and himself by working as a hired labourer— बोधिसत्तो दुग्गत-गहपतिकुले निब्बति... सो वयपत्तो भतिं कत्वा मातापितरो पोसेत्वा... (*Jā*. III. 325.)

We also find the Gahapatis practising endogamy, which is another characteristic of a caste.[1]

Fick admits that the Gahapatis constituted the gentry of the land, the lower land-owning nobility, and the high and rich middle class families of the big cities.[2] But he does not consider the Gahapati to be identical with the Vaiśya caste. It is true that there were Brāhmaṇa as well as Kshatriya Gahapatis.[3] The Vaiśya caste constituted of those who were between the Brāhmaṇas and the Kshatriyas on the one hand and the Śūdra or the serving class on the other. According to Manu their professions were the rearing of cattle, trading, and cultivating the land.[4] We have already seen that the Brāhmaṇas and the Kshatriyas were permitted to take up trade and agriculture for livelihood. These, therefore, may have been known as Brāhmaṇa and Kshatriya Gahapatis. As Gahapati literally means a householder, it may have been used in the same sense in some cases. It should not be a serious objection that because there were Brāhmaṇa and Kshatriya Gahapatis, therefore by the term Gahapati one should not understand a member of the Vaiśya caste.

Like the Kshatriyas and the Brāhmaṇas, the Gahapatis were quite conscious of their position, and are described as high born. In the *Mahāvagga* Yasa, the son of a Seṭṭhi Gahapati is known as a *kulaputta*.[5] Even in the royal court they occupied a high position next to the Kshatriyas and the Brāhmaṇas.[6]

The expression Kuṭumbika is used, like Gahapati, to denote a wealthy citizen at the head of a family[7] (*kuṭumba*), generally belonging to the Vaiśya community. We find them both in cities and villages; in the former mostly as business

1. *Jā*. II. 121, बोधिसत्तो वाराणसितो अविदूरे गामके गहपतिकुले निब्बति। अथ' अस्स वयपत्तस्स वाराणसितो कुलधीतरं आनेसुं।
2. *Social Organisation*, p. 253.
3. *Udāna*, VII 9. *Itivuttaka* 107
4. *Manu I*. 90.
5. *M.V.* I. 7.
6. *Jā*. II. 241. अमच्चा च ब्राह्मण गहपतिरट्ठिकदोवारिकादयो च राजानं परिवारेत्वा अट्ठंसु।
7. *Jā*. II. 267.

men, dealing in corn,[1] practising trade[2] and money-lending,[3] etc. and in the latter as well-to-do cultivators.[4] Some of the Kuṭumbikas figure as very rich citizens (*asītikoṭivibhavo kuṭumbiko*).[5]

The Seṭṭhis living both in cities and villages were the aristocratic and the richest section of the Vaiśya caste. They are represented as respectable tradesmen, enjoying high position of honour among the members of their caste. A Seṭṭhi of Rājagṛha rendered various services to the king as well as to the tradesmen.[6] Anāthapiṇḍika, who was the brother-in-law of the above Seṭṭhi, had spent considerable amount of wealth for providing residences for the Buddhist Bhikshus. It appears from the *Jātakas* that some of them occupied an official position in the royal court. We find the Seṭṭhi going to the king's public Audience Hall (Rājupaṭṭhāna),[7] which he usually visited every day.[8] The *Mahājanaka Jātaka* represents the Seṭṭhis as occupying their seats in the court of the king together with the Amātyamaṇḍala and the Brāhmaṇas.[9] He is also found taking the king's permission, even when he renounces the world.[10] Most probably there used to be a representative of the commercial community at the king's court, who advised the king in matters connected with trade and commerce.

1. *Jā.* II. 267, कुटुम्बिककुले निब्बतित्वा वयपत्तो धञ्ञविक्कयेन जीविकं कप्पेसि ।
2. *Jā.* IV. 370.
3. *Jā.* II. 388, एको कुटुम्बिको एकस्स जानपदस्स सहस्सं कहापणे दत्वा पुन अगहेत्वा व कालं अकासि ।
4. *Jā.* I. 196.
5. *Yā.* IV. 370.
6. *M.V.* VIII. 1. 16, अयं खो सेट्ठिगहपति बहूपकारो देवस्स च एव नेगमस्स च ।

A Magadhan Seṭṭhi is described as donating to the Saṅgha wealth amounting to 80 crores (*Jā.* I. 349).

7. *Jā.* I. 345; III. 299; V. 384.
8. *Jā.* III. 475, सो दिवस्स तयो वारे राजुपट्ठानं गच्छति ।
9. *Jā.* VI. 43.
10. *Jā.* II. 64.

The Seṭṭhis were rich traders and merchants; they carried on trade with distant lands and led big caravans.[1] The wealth of some of them is estimated to have been eighty crores of the current coins.[2] They were usually charitable[3] and a good portion of their wealth seems to have been diverted to the benefit of the poor in the form of charity. Their sons received education along with the Kshatriya and the Brāhmaṇa youths, and offered the teacher high amount as honorarium.[4] They did not marry outside their class.[5]

The Śūdras :

Among the category of the Śūdras there seem to be a number of castes. In the Buddhist Pāli literature we do not find specific mention of castes which were styled as Śūdras. But the status of the low castes makes it quite clear that they were none but the Śūdras. Thus we find the day labourers (Bhatakas), who by the hereditary nature of their profession formed a caste.[6] These people were not much looked down upon, as the *Jātakas* mention even members of higher castes engaged in the day labour for the sake of livelihood in times of distress,[7] which was quite in conformity with the law-books.

Artisans :

The manufacturers and the handicraftsmen were developing into different castes with the characteristics of hereditary professions and a head of their group as observed by Fick.[8] The

1. Jā. I. 270, बोधिसत्तो सेट्ठिकुले निव्वत्तित्वा वयपत्तो पञ्चहि सकटसतेहि वणिज्जं करोन्तो...

In cities of the period like Rājagṛiha, Vaiśālī, Pāṭaliputra, Champā, Śrāvasti, Kauśambī, Vārānasi, and others there must have been several leading Seṭṭhis. Caravans of the Seṭṭhi Anāthapiṇḍika of Śrāvasti were visiting Rājagṛiha and Rājagṛiha Seṭṭhis were visiting Vaśālī, Śrāvasti and other cities for trade.

2. *Jā.* I. 345. III. 128, 300, 444; V. 382.

3. *Jā.* III. 129.

4. *Jā.* IV. 38.

5. *Jāl* IV. 37.

6. *Jā.* III. 406, 444.

7. A poor Gahapati (*Jā.* III. 325) and a Brāhmanī with her three daughters (*Jā.* I. 475) are discribed as engaged in such profession.

8. *Social Organisation*, Chap. X.

potters (Kumbhakāra),[1] smiths (Kammāra),[2] ivory workers (Dantakāra),[3] carpenters (Vaḍḍhaki),[4] etc. belonged to hereditary families and had their own settlements. Their heads were known as the Jeṭṭhakas; e.g., Mālākāra-Jeṭṭhaka,[5] Vaḍḍhaki-Jeṭṭhaka,[6] Kammāra-Jeṭṭhaka,[7] etc.

There were a number of unorganised, unsettled and wandering castes, who earned their livelihood by such arts as amused the people. Thus are mentioned the dancers and singers (Naṭa),[8] acrobats (Laṅghanaṭaka),[9] tumblers,[10] jugglers (Māyākāra),[11] snake-charmer (Ahiguṇḍika),[12] mongoose-tamers (Koṇḍadamaka),[13] musicians (Gandhabba),[14] drummers (Bherivādaka),[15] conch-blowers (Saṅkhadhamaka),[16] and so on. Expressions such as Bherivādakakula,[17] Saṅkhavādakakula,[18] Naṭakakula,[19] Gandhabbakula[20] and the like suggest that they formed separate castes of their own.

Similar in status to these people but leading a more settled life were the cowherds (Gopālaka), cattlemen (Pasupālaka), grass-cutters (Tiṇṇahārka), stick-gatherers (Kaṭṭhahāraka), and foresters (Vanakammika) as they are described in the *Majjhima-Nikāya*[21] and the *Kuṇāla Jātaka*.[22] They probably lived an exclusive life, forming sometimes villages of their

1. *M.N.* II. 18 46; III. 118; *Jā.* II. 79; III. 376.
2. *Su.Ni.* I. 5; *D.N. Sutta*, 33.
3. *D.N.* I. 78; *M.N.* II. 18; *Jā.* I 320..
4. *Jā.* II. 18, 405, IV. 344.
5. *Jā.* III. 405.
6. *Jā.* IV. 161.
7. *Jā.* III. 281.
8. *Jā.* II. 167; III. 61. 507.
9. *Jā.* I. 430.
10. *Jā.* II. 142.
11. *Jā.* IV. 495.
12. *Jā.* I. 370, II. 267, 429; III. 198, 348.
13. *Jā.* IV. 389.
14. *Jā.* II. 249.
15. *Jā.* I. 283.
16. *Jā.* I. 284.
17. *Jā.* I. 283.
18. *Jā.* I. 284.
19. *Jā.* II. 167.
20. *Jā.* II. 248.
21. *M.N.* I. 79,
22. *Jā.* V. 417.

own, away from the towns and the cities which they visited for selling their produce to earn livelihood.

The Despised Castes :

There existed a few castes, which were despised by the higher sections of society, either due to their ethnic origin or on account of the despised nature of their professions. The Buddhist literature makes a difference between the low castes and the low crafts. But gradually those castes that were not looked down upon as untouchables due to their persuing low professions were also being regarded so, e.g. Rathakāra, Nāpita, etc. The Chaṇḍālas, the Veṇas, the Nesādas, the Rathakāras, and the Pukkusas appear as low castes.[1] That members of these castes were considered as contemptible is shown by the use of the words Veṇī and Chaṇḍālī in abusive sense for a lady in the *Takkāriya-Jātaka*.[2] The *Jātaka* descriptions of their position in society show that they were despised and avoided by the higher castes. To understand their real condition, let us look into the social status of the Chaṇḍālas, who occupyied the lowest position in society.

The Chaṇḍālas :

Undoubtedly the Chaṇḍālas constituted the most unfortunate caste, the members of which were despised and forced to live outside the cities and towns, having their own settlements.[3] Their dialect was different, showing their ethnic difference.[4] Being untouchables and unseeables, they did not dare enter the city gates, and we find two Chaṇḍālas showing their art at the gate of a city in the *Chitta-Sambhuta-Jātaka*.[5] Contemptuous terms are used for them, and they are described as the lowest and the meanest on the earth.[6] The *Sigāla-*

1. *M.N.* II. 152, III. 169; *A.N.* II. 85; III. 385 *G.S.* I. 92.
2. *Jā.* IV. 246.
3. *Jā.* IV. 200, 376, 390, तदा उज्जेनिया वहि चण्डाल गामको होति ।
4. *Jā.* IV. 391, सो कम्पमानो सतिं अनुपट्ठापेत्वा चित्तपंडितं ओलोकेत्वा चण्डालभासाय एवं खलु'ति आह । सो पि तथा' एव सतिं अनुपट्ठापेत्वा चण्डालभासाय निग्गल निग्गलाति आह ।
5. *Jā.* IV. 390.
6. *Jā.* IV. 397.

Jātaka compares a jackal with a Chaṇḍāla, the former being low and wretched among animals, and the latter among men.[1] A Brāhmaṇa calls his adulterous wife a Pāpa-Chaṇḍalī.[2] The Chaṇḍālas were regarded untouchables whose touch caused even the wind to be impure. A Brāhmaṇa finding that he had been walking on the same road with a chaṇḍāla cried, "Curse you, ill-omened Chaṇḍāla, get to the leeward," and he quickly went to the windward.[3] Their sight was looked upon as bringing ill-omen. The *Mātaṅga Jātaka* tells us that one day *Mātaṅga*, a Chaṇḍāla, had gone to the town on some business from his settlement. At the entrance of the city gate Dīghamāṅgalikā, the daughter of a merchant, espied him from behind the curtain of palanquin and asked, "who is that ?" The answer was, "Chaṇḍāla my lady." She uttered, "Oh, I have seen something that brings bad luck," and she washed her eyes with scented water and returned back. The people with her cried out, "O vile outcaste, you have lost us free food and liquor today !" In rage they pommelled Mātaṅga with hands and feet, and making him senseless, went away.[4] Similarly in the *Chittasambhūta Jātaka*, when the Chaplain's daughter and a merchant's daughter saw two Chaṇḍāla boys at the city gates, they washed their eyes with perfumed water.[5] The multitude cried, "O vile outcaste, you have made us lose food and strong drink, free of cost !", and belaboured them to the extent of making senseless.[6] When they recovered their sense, they thought that all the misery had come upon them because of their birth, and decided to give up the Chaṇḍāla-work.[7]

1. *Jā*. II. 6.
2. *Jā*. IV. 246.
3. *Jā*. No. 377-III. 233. चण्डालो'हं अस्मीति वुत्ते तस्स सरीरं पहरित्वा आगतवातस्स अत्तनो सरीरे फुसनभयेन नस्स चण्डाल कालकण्णि, अधोवातं याहीति वत्वा वेगेन तस्स उपरिवातं अगमासि ।
4. *Jā*. IV. 376.
5. *Jā*.zV.390-91. चण्डालपुत्ता'ति सुत्वा अपस्सितब्बयुत्तकं वत पस्सिम्हा'ति गन्धोदकेन अक्खीना धोवित्वा निवत्तिसु ।
6. *Jā*. IV. 391. महाजनो अरे दुट्ठचण्डाल तुम्हे निस्साय मयं अमूलकानि सुराभत्तादीनि न लभिम्हा'ति ते उभोपि भातिके पोथेत्वा अनपव्यसनं पापेसि ।
7. *Ibid*. इमं अम्हाकं जातिं निस्साय दुक्खं उप्पन्नं चण्डालकम्मं कातुं न सक्खिस्साम् ।

They pronounced themselves to be Brāhmaṇas and became students under a teacher at Takshaśilā. But one day when it was detected that they were Chāṇḍālas, students cried, O vile outcastes ! You have been tricking us all this while and pretending to be Brāhmaṇa !", and they beat them out.[1] One said to them that it was the fault of their birth.[2]

It becomes quite clear from the above references that the Chāṇḍālas were looked down upon as very low, and to be born as a Chāṇḍāla was the worst curse of one's fate. That they occupied a very low position in society is confirmed by the Dharmaśāstras. According to Āpastamba and Gautama the study of the *Veda* should not be continued in a village, if a Chāṇḍāla is present there, and even in a forest at the sight of him.[3] According to Manu a Brāhmaṇa, while eating, was not to be seen by a Chāṇḍāla.[4] The Chāṇḍālas were to make their residences outside the village, to keep only clay pots, to possess only dogs and donkeys as their wealth, to put on garments of the dead, to eat their food out of the broken pots, to use ornaments of black iron and to be always wandering from one place to other.[5]

Though the details of their professional works are not known from the *Jātakas*, yet from the meagre information available it can be well presumed that they were employed for low works. Some of them were jugglers,[6] some menders of old rubbish (Jiṇṇapaṭi-Saṅkhāraka),[7] and some burners of corpses (Chavadāhaka).[8] Manu says that they should carry the corpse of one who has no relation;[9] they should kill the criminals condemned to death by the king, and they should keep their clothes, beds, and ornaments for themselves.[10]

1. *Jā.* IV. 392, अरे दुट्ठचण्डाला, एत्तकं कातुं ब्राह्मणा व' अम्हाति वत्वा वञ्चयित्थाति उभोपि ते पोथयिंसु ।
2. *Ibid.*
3. *Āp. Dh. S.* I. 3. 9. 15-17; *Gau. Dh. S.* XVI. 19.
4. *Manu.* III. 239.
5. *Manu.* X. 51-52.
6. *Jā.* IV. 388.
7. *Jā.* V. 429.
8. *Jā.* V. 449.
9. *Manu.* X. 55.
10. *Manu.* X. 56.

It has already been seen that the Chāṇḍālas put on rugged clothes, mostly from the dead bodies. They used either reddish or yellowish dress (Kāsāvaṁ, Halidda-pilotikāya).[1] Their under garment used to be ragged (Paṅsu kūla-saṅghāṭiṁ) and the upper one red (Ratta-dupaṭṭaṁ); they had a belt around their body (Kāyabandhana) above which they put on a dirty upper garment;[2] on the head, they wore a yellow cloth.[3]

Though the Chāṇḍālas were so much despised, we come across a few cases in the popular stories where their low origin was ignored and their character taken into account. Mātaṅga, the Chāṇḍāla who had reached the highest fame, was served by the Kshatriyas and the Brāhmaṇas.[4] A young Brāhmaṇa who could not give any answer to the questions of a Chāṇḍāla touched his feet with his head.[5] Another Brāhmaṇa became the pupil of a Chāṇḍāla and rendered him all sorts of service.[6] Such cases in fact do not reflect the actual condition of the Chāṇḍālas in society, but the attitude of the wise one who held the view that one possessed of the right knowledge should be given the highest honour, even if he may have been a Chāṇḍāla or a Pukkusa.[7] But how far such an attitude was translated into practice? The Chāṇḍālas remained in their deplorable condition, and the future law-givers always assigned them a low position. According to Atri, even the shadow of a Chāṇḍāla should not be passed.[8]

The Nesādas (Nishādas) were generally hunters and foresters.[9] According to Manu their profession was to kill fish.[10] Like the Chāṇḍālas they lived outside the towns and the cities.[11] They had probably fallen into a contemptible posi-

1. *Jā.* VI. 156.
2. *Jā.* IV. 379.
3. *Jā.* VI. 156.
4. *Su. Ni.* II. 7. 22-23.
5. *Jā.* III. 233-35 (No. 377).
6. *Jā.* IV. 201 (No. 474) तस्स गेहे कत्तब्बकिच्चानि करोतिः दारुनि आहरति वीहिं कोट्टेति पचति मुखधोवनादीनि देति पादे धोवति ।
7. *Jā.* IV. 205.
8. *Atri Smṛiti.* II. 89.
9. *Jā.* IV. 413; V. 110, 337.
10. *Manu.* X. 48.
11. *Jā.* II. 36; V. 337; तदा नगरतो अविदूरे एकस्मिं नेसाद-गामके ।

tion due to the nature of their work which was of killing fish and animals, as was the case with hunters in Greece.[1]

The Pukkusas are generally mentioned after the Chaṇḍālas when enumerating castes,[2] which shows that they were also despised like the Chaṇḍālas. They were employed for low works; probably one of their occupation was to remove faded flowers from the temples. This suggests that they did cleansing work. Manu puts them under the category of mixed castes, resulting from the union of a female Śūdra and Nesāda.[3]

The Veṇas and the Rathakāras were considered to be low on account of the nature of their profession. They worked on bamboos and wood, both considered as low. The same was the case with the basket-maker, the potter, the weaver, the cobbler and the barber who are described as pursuing low Sippas.[4] The *Jātakas* describe the basket-maker (Nalakāra),[5] the flute-maker (Velūkara).[6] the weaver (Pesakāra),[7] and the barber (Nahāpita)[8] as low professionals. The butcher (Orabbhika), the fowler (Sakuntika), the hunter (Luddaka), the fisherman (Machchhaghātaka) etc.[9] who are described as following bloody profession fall in the same category.

Some of the members of these castes were employed in royal courts. There were court potters (Rāja-Kumbhakāra),[10] court basket-makers (Rājupaṭṭhāka-Nalakāra),[11] and court garland-makers (Rāja-Mālākāra),[12] etc. Their designations suggest that they occupied a rank which raised them above the low position to which the other unfortunate members of their class belonged. Usually, though the barber was held low, in the royal household he rendered many personal services to the

1. *Fick : Social Organisation*, p. 322; *Zimmer : Greek commonwealth.*, p. 236.
2. *Jā.* III. 194-5; IV. 205. 303.
3. *Manu.* X. 18.
4. *Sutta Vibhaṅga Pāchittiya* quoted in *Social and Rural Economy of Northern India*, p. 459.
5. *Jā.* IV. 251.
6. *Ibid.*
7. *Jā.* I. 356. Weaving is described as *lāmaka-kamma.*
8. *Jā.* II. 5; III. 452.
9. *K. S.* II. 171; *A. N.* II. 207.
10. *Jā.* I. 121; V. 290.
11. *Jā.* V. 291.
12. *Jā.* V. 292.

king as shaving his beard, curling the hair, placing the dice on the board in position, etc.[1] and was sometimes raised to the position of the king's friend.[2] He is also described as holding a lucrative post, receiving on certain occasions liberal grants from the king.[3]

1. *Jā*. II. 5.
2. A Videhan King is described as addressing his barbar as a friend (*Jā*. I. 137).
3. A barber was granted a village yielding 1,00,000 current coins by his king when the latter renounced the world (*Jā*. I. 138).

CHAPTER II

SLAVERY

Evidence of Slavery :

The institution of slavery existed in India since very early times and is frequently referred to both in the Brahmanical and the Buddhist sources. The Vedic literature contains many references which prove the existence of the institution of slavery in the contemporary society, though they do not give a sufficiently clear picture. The *Ṛgveda* refers to the gifts of slaves at a number of places. A sage is described as praising his patron, Chaidya Kāsu, who had honoured him by giving him ten noble men, who were like gold in appearance.[1] Another sage speaks of receiving a gift of one hundred donkeys, one hundred fleece-bearing cows, and one hundred Dāsas.[2] Tarasadasyu, son of Purukutsa, gave a sage fifty young women as gift.[3]

The *Saṁhitās*, the *Brāhmaṇas*, and the *Upanishads* all refer to the existence of slaves. The *Taittiriya Saṁhitā* says that the female slaves (Dāsīs) placed on their heads jars full of water, and singing *madhu* and beating their feet against the ground danced round.[4] It also refers to the gift of a horse or a male slave.[5] The *Aitareya Brāhmaṇa* (39.8) mentions that a king gave his Purohita in gift a large number of girls (Dāsīs) and elephants on the occasion of his coronation. The *Bṛhadāraṇyaka Upanishad* states that the king Janaka, having received instruction in the Brahmavidyā from the Sage Yājñavalkya, said to him, "I make a gift to your honour of the Videhas together with myself for being your slave.[6]"

1. *Ṛg*. VIII. 5. 38.
2. *Ṛg*. VIII. 56. 3,
3. *Ṛg*. VIII. 19, 36.
4. *Tai. Saṁ.* VII, 5. 10, उदकुम्भानधिनिधाय दास्यो परिनृत्यन्ति पदो निघ्नतीरिदं मधु गायन्त्यो मधु वै परमन्नाद्यम् ।
5. *Tai. Saṁ.* III 2. 6. 3.
6. *Bṛ. Up.* IV, 4, 23, सोहं भगवते विदेहान् ददामि मां चापि सह दास्याय ।

These references in the Vedic and later literature show that slavery existed during the early and the later Vedic period. The kings owned a large number of slaves, both male and female, and at the times of sacrifices made a gift of them along with other requisites to the priests who were pleased to receive them.

During the period represented by the *Dharmasūtras* slavery continued to exist. The *Āpastamba-Dharmasūtra*, while laying down rules for the attendance on guests, states that if a guest comes, one may stint himself, his wife, or his son (as to food), but by no means a slave who does his menial works.[1] This shows that slavery was common during this period, and the slaves were mainly employed for doing the menial works of the household.

Our main sources on this subject, the *Piṭakas*, reveal that slavery was quite common; slaves could be bought or sold, and they also could be given as gifts. The *Vinaya* texts,[2] the *Nikāyas*,[3] and the *Jātakas* frequently refer to both male and female slaves, revealing thereby that the institution of slavery was well-known in the contemporary society. Slaves could be found in the royal harem,[4] or in the households of rich persons in capital cities, like Rājagṛha,[5] or in the houses of village householders.[6] The references disclose that slavery was not confined to the princely circle and to the royal cities as may be expected, but it existed also in the villages and even ordinary families could keep slaves.

That slaves were bought and sold is mentioned both in the Buddhist and the Dharmaśāstra literature. The *Jātakas* give definite statements on this point and they also mention the price of a slave. In *Jātaka* No. 39, a Saddhivihārika (novice or disciple) is compared to a slave bought for one

1. *Āp. Dh. S.* II. 4. 9. 11.
2. *S. B. E.* XIII. 315; *C. V.* IV. 4. 6-7.
3. *D. N.* I. 64, दासदासी पटिग्गहणो पटिविरतो होति।
   M. N. I. 452, चयो नेकानं दासगणानं चयो नेकानं दासीगणानं चयो।
   II. 187; *G. S.* I. 128; *A. N.* II. 209.
4. *Jā.* No. 92.
5. *C. V.* VI. 4.2.
6. *Jā.* No. 330.

hundred Kahāpaṇas.[1] This suggests that a slave could be ordinarily bought for a hundred pieces of contemporary silver punch-marked coins. *Jātaka* No. 402 states that a Brāhmaṇa after collecting seven hundred Kahāpaṇas thought that the amount was sufficient for buying some male and female slaves.[2] But here unfortunately the number of slaves is not given. Most probably the price of a slave was generally one hundred Kārshāpaṇas, but it might have varied in a few cases. The physical fitness of a male slave and the beauty of a female one might have been responsible for a higher price. In some cases the needy purchaser might have offered a higher price for a slave; while in the other the needy seller might have sold him for a lower price. The Brahmanical sources confirm the Buddhist account of the slaves being bought and sold, but they do not mention the price. Kauṭilya says that the Mlechchhas are not punishable, if they sell or pledge their children, but an Ārya cannot be reduced to slavery.[3] Manu also mentions that Śūdras were often bought and sold.[4]

The practice of giving slaves in gifts was also in vogue, and it existed since Vedic times. Gifts in slaves during the Vedic period have already been referred to. The *Mahābhārata* records that Yudhishṭhira gave each of the 88000 *snātakas* engaged in the sacrifice, thirty female slaves.[5] The *Dīgha* and *Aṅguttara Nikāyas* say that the Buddha had prohibitted the Bhikshus from accepting the gifts of slaves, either male or female.[6] According to a *Jātaka* a Brāhmaṇa demanded a hundred slave girls from a king along with other requisites as his gift, and his demands were fulfilled.[7] These examples show that in most

1. *Jā.* I. 224, मह्यं एको सद्धिविहारिको एकस्मिं ठाने सतेन कीतदासो विय होति ।

2. *Jā.* III. 343, ब्राह्मणो गामनिगमराजधानीसु चरन्तो सत्तकहापण सतानि लभित्वा अलं मे एत्तकं धनं दासीदासमूलाय'ति निवत्तित्वा. . . ।

3. *Kau.* III. 13, म्लेच्छानामदोषः प्रजां विक्रेतुमाधातुं वा न त्वेवार्यस्य दासभावः ।

4. *Manu.* VIII. 413, शूद्रं तु कारयेद्दास्यं क्रीतमक्रीतमेव वा ।

5. *Mbh. Sabhā*, 52. 45-46.

6. *D. N. I.* 64; *A. N.* II. 209.

7. *Jā.* IV. 99, ददामि ते गामवरानि पच्च दासीसतं सत्त गवं सतानि, परोसहस्सञ्च सुवण्ण निक्खे भरिया च ते सादिसी द्वे ददामि ।

cases female slaves were given in gift. This practice survived till modern times, though the institution of slavery died long ago. Females were kept as slaves in the royal harems, a practice adopted by the big Zamindars also. The kings, the chieftains, and big landlords kept in their houses a number of females who were under their full control, and generally at the time of marriage they used to send a number of these along with the bride to the house of the bridegroom. They were sent as maid servants and companions of the bride, but their status was no better than that of slaves, as they were under the complete control of their master. If they were married, it was done through his consent, and usually their husbands would be among the servants of that family. Most of them used to be hereditary servants of their masters. But now, on account of the changed conditions of society this practice has disappeared.

Categories of Slaves :

The number of the categories of slaves is different with different writers. The *Vinaya-Piṭaka* mentions three categories;[1] the *Vidhurapaṇḍita Jātaka*, four,[2] other *Jātakas* refer to three additional categories;[3] the *Arthaśāstra* gives five,[4] and Manu mentions seven.[5] This divergence in number is partly due to a more scientific classification and partly due to recognition of new categories. Taking together the Buddhist and the early Brahmanical sources one would find that they refer to nine categories of slaves.

The first category is of the war-captives, who were reduced to complete subjection under the conqueror. This

1. *Bhikkhuṇī Vibhaṅga Saṅghādisesa*, I. 2. 1, दासो नाम अन्तोजातो धनक्कीतो करमरानितो—quoted by Fick in *Social Organisation*, p. 307.

2. *Jā*. VI. 285, आमायदासापि भवन्ति ह' एके, धनेन कीतापि भवन्ति दासा, सयमपिह' एके उपयन्ति दासा भया पणुन्नापि भविन्त दासा ।

3. *Jā*. I. 200; IV. 22. 99; VI. 545-48; *J.B.O.R.S.* 1923, '*Slavery in the Jātakas*'.

4. *Kau*. III. 13.

5. *Manu* VIII. 415,

ध्वजाहृतो भक्तदासो गृहजः क्रीतदत्त्रिमौ ।
पैत्रिको दण्डदासश्च सप्तैते दासयोनयः ॥

appears to be the earliest category. Later out of the unfortunate enslaved war-captives some may have been either sold or given in gifts to others by their masters. Our authorities accept the categories of those who were either sold or given in gifts. The fourth category is of those who sold themselves as slaves. Manu makes a difference between this category and that of those who were bought, probably because in one case it was the slave who sold himself out of his own accord; while in the other, he may have been sold by his former master. The fifth category is of those who became slaves during the days of scarcity for want of food. This class is very similar to that of those who sold themselves of their own will. But though in both the cases the helpless condition of the family or the individual compelled people to become slaves, in one case there was no question of selling and they could become slaves only for filling their hungry stomachs. The sixth category is of those who became slaves for paying off their debts. This category also is similar to the above two; because indebtedness is generally caused by family poverty, and the debtors finding themselves unable to pay off their debts, either accepted the slavery of the creditor in order to pay off their debts in the form of labour, or they pledged themselves to others for the amount which they owed to their creditors. The seventh and the eighth categories are of those who were born from female slaves and of those who were inherited as ancestral property. Both of these seem to be similar; but while the former consisted exclusively of those who were born of their slave mothers, the latter could have been either bought, or received in gifts, or acquired by any other means by the predecessor of one who inherited them. The ninth category was of those who were condemned to slavery as a punishment for their crimes.[1]

The Buddhist sources do not mention the categories of those who sold themselves as slaves and those who were inherited as ancestral property, as mentioned by Kauṭilya and Manu. It seems that the former was not differentiated from the category of those who accepted slavery of their own will; while the latter was not differentiated from the category of the slaves born in the house of the master. Thus we find that all the cate-

1. *Jā*. I. 200.

gories referred to in the Buddhist sources are mentioned in the Brahmanical texts. There is one category of the *Jātakas* which is not mentioned either by Kauṭilya or Manu. This category is called slaves driven by fear by the *Vidhura-paṇḍita-Jātaka.* But this one can be put under the category of the war-captives. Now, if we put together the categories mentioned by the *Vinaya-Piṭaka* and the *Jātakas* on one side and the categories of Kauṭilya and Manu on the other, we find the following picture :—

Vinaya-Piṭaka and *Jātaka* Stories	Kauṭilya and Manu
1. Slaves born of slave mothers.	1. Slaves born of Slave mothers.
2. Slaves bought by money.	2. Slaves bought by money.
3. Slaves captured in war.	3. Slaves captured in war.
4. Slaves driven by fear.	4. Slaves of their own accord for want of food.
5. Slaves as a punishment for their crimes.	5. Slaves as a result of judicial decrees.
6. Slaves received as gifts.	6. Slaves given as gifts.
7. Slaves for paying off debts.	7. Slaves for paying off debts.
8. Slaves of their own will.	8. Slaves who sold themslaves.
	9. Slaves inherited as the ancestral property.

The number of the categories still increased in later times, and we find Nārada mentioning fifteen kinds of slaves.[1]

Treatment of Slaves :

As regards the treatment of slaves, we get conflicting statements. It depended on the temperament of the master that a slave received good or bad treatment. As in other countries, in India also harsh slave-owners were not unknown. There are cases on record of such slave-owners as harassed their slaves. Sometimes they were punished for their faults and mistakes. A slave, who was elevated to the position of the store-keeper of his master, reflected within himself, "Not always, will one care to let me have the office of a store-keeper; one good day some

1. *Nārada.* V. 25-28.

defect will be noticed in me and the people will thrash me, lock me up, brand me, and give me the food of a slave to eat."[1] A slave girl, who had not brought home her wages of the day, was thrown down at the door of the house and beaten by her master and mistress with rope ends.[2] Beating with a rope as a consequence of the slave's fault is also enjoined by Manu.[3] But sometimes slaves were ill treated merely out of the whimsical nature of their owners. Thus, for instance, the *Aṅguttara-Nikāya* states that the slaves worked with tearful faces for fear of the rod.[4] *Jātaka* No. 63 says that the fierce daughter of a high treasurer used to revile and beat her slaves and servants.[5] The *Vessantara Jātaka* tells us that a Brāhmaṇa, who had received the son and the daughter of a king, bound them with creepers and drove them away beating them with the creeper-ends. He dragged them on with a staff in his hand, holding the creeper tight.[6] As he had to go a long distance, at night he used to tie up the children with osiers and leave them lying upon the ground, but himself in fear of wild beasts would climb up a tree and would sit in the fork of the bough.[7] This account of the treatment of the children is exaggerated and is aimed at depicting the Brāhmaṇa as cruel and selfish to show the contrast between him and the king (Bodhisattva), who gave his children in gift.

It is true that a few slaves received ill treatment from their master; but it can bear no comparison to the treatment of helots of Sparta, colonii of Rome, and the slaves of the planters of the eighteenth and nineteenth century in America. In the western countries, slaves used to work in chains under cruel overseers who took a fiendish delight in exacting a pound of flesh; they used to be made over to the beasts of prey for the delectation and amusement of the rich orders of society, as in Italy; a master

1. *Jā*. I. 451.
2. *Jā*. I. 402, अथ'एकं दासीं भतिं अददमानं सामिका द्वारे निसिदापेत्वा रज्जुया पहारन्ति ।
3. *Manu*. VIII. 299.
4. *K. S.* I. 102; *A. N.* II. 207-8, दण्डतज्जिता भयतज्जिता अस्सुमुखा रुदमाना परिकम्मानि करोन्ति ।
5. *Jā*. I. 295.
6. *Jā*. VI. 548.
7. *Jā*. VI. 573.

could kill not more than two slaves daily to refresh his tired nerves in the warm blood and bowels of the victim.[1]

It was most probably the absence of such atrocities and beastly cruelties of the masters practised on the slaves, that the foreign observers who visited India during the 4th century B. C., missed to notice the prevalence of this system. Megasthenes, who lived for years at Pāṭaliputra, makes no mention of the employment of slaves in Magadha and states that there are no slaves in India. Our sources reveal that very often slaves received good treatment from their masters. In pious households they were supplied with rice, meat, and milk-rice for their food.[2] Some of them were treated as members of the family to which they belonged and were elevated to responsible posts, as was the case of Kaṭāhaka; who grew up in the company of his master's son, got his education along with him, learnt two or three handicrafts and was appointed as the store-keeper of his master.[3] A Brāhmaṇa, the Purohita of a king, when favoured with a boon by his lord, went home and asked the desires of his family members, including the female slave Puṇṇā who expressed her desire for a mortar, a pestle, and a sieve.[4] When the son of a Brāhmaṇa died and was burnt without tear, the female slave of the family was asked, "No doubt you must have been abused, beaten, and oppressed by him, therefore you are glad at his death and weep not"; she replied, 'My lord, speak not so; this does not suit his case. My young master was full of long sufferings, love, and pity for me and was to me as a foster child, reared on the breast.'[5] Such instances of good treatment of slaves show that their relations to the members of the

1. Carlyle : *History of French Revolution*, p. 19.
2. *G. S.* I. 128.
3. *Jā.* I. 451, ते एकतो वड्ढिसु । सेट्ठिपुत्ते लेखं सिक्खन्ते व दासोपि'स्स फलकं वहमानो गन्त्वा तेन' एव सद्धिं लेखं सिक्खि । द्वे तयो वोहारे अकासि ।... सो सेट्ठिघरे भण्डागारिकम्मं करोन्तो चिन्तेसि: ... ।
4. *Jā.* II. 428, सो गन्त्वा ब्राह्मणिञ्च पुत्तञ्च सुणिसञ्च दासिञ्च पक्कोसित्वा "राजा मे वरं देति, किं गण्हामीति" पुच्छि ।...पुण्णा नाम दासी मह्यं उदुक्खल-मुसलञ्च' एव सुपञ्चा' ति ।
5. *Jā.* III. 167, सामि मा एवं अवच, न एतं एतस्स अनुच्छविकं, खन्तिमेत्तानुद्दयसम्पन्नो मे अय्यपुत्तो' उरे सम्बड्ढितपुत्तो विय अहोसीति ।

master's family were often of amity and harmony and that in a good number of cases they enjoyed good treatment.

From the *Arthaśāstra* of Kauṭilya, we know that in case a few masters treated their slaves badly, the state was not to be a silent spectator. On the other hand, the state interfered and such masters were punished for their unfair dealings. If a master beat a slave, or employed him in mean work, he forfeited the purchase value of the slave.[1] If a master raped a slave girl, pledged to him, he not only forfeited the purchase value, but also had to pay a certain amount of money (*śulka*) to her and a fine of twice the amount to the government.[2] Such rules prescribed by Kauṭilya indicate that during the days of the Mauryas the position of the slaves was not very unsatisfactory. Such conditions would have existed even before this period.

In a few cases, slaves enjoyed fullest confidence of their masters. The *Nanda Jātaka* tells as that there was an old squire who had a young wife, a young son and a slave, Nanda. He thought that after his death, his wife being so young, would marry somebody and spend all the money he had, leaving nothing for his son. So one day he went to the forest and buried the money safely under the ground. This matter was known only to the slave Nanda, who had accompanied his master at the time of burying the hoard and who was told by him to show the treasure to the young master, when he would grow up.[3] This shows how a slave could enjoy the confidence of his master more than the latter's wife in some cases.

There was every possibility of young masters falling in love with their young slave girls. What would have been the ultimate result of such unions ? Kauṭilya says that if a son was born as a consequence of a master's union with a slave girl, she was no longer a slave.[4] This suggests the probability of such a slave girl being elevated to the position of a legitimate wife. It is said in the *Vātamiga-Jātaka* that Tissa Kumāra, the

1. Kau. III. 13.
2. *Ibid.*
3. *Jā.* I. 225, घरे नन्दं नाम दासं गहेत्वा अरञ्ञं गन्त्वा एकस्मि ठाने तं धनं निदहित्वा तस्स आचिक्खित्वा, "तात नन्द इमं धनं मम अच्चयेन मह्यं पुत्तस्स आचिक्खेय्यासि ।"
4. *Kau.* III, 13.

scion of a wealthy Seṭṭhi family of Rājagṛha, gained his parents' consent to enter the monastery by resorting to go on hunger-strike. His parents were very much grieved at their son's entry to the monastery. A slave girl, who saw them weeping for their son, consoled them and took up the task of bringing him back to his house again. She was beautiful and by her feminine charm won the heart of her young master, who left the monastery and reverted to the worldly life.[1] The young master abandoned the Order for the sake of a slave girl; what happened to the two in the future is not known. The incident suggests that the ultimate end of their love might have been a lifelong union in the form of marriage. In the *Uddālaka Jātaka* it is stated that the chaplain of a king fell in love with a slave girl. A son was born from their union. He was named Uddālaka and having grown up became a great ascetic, well versed in the sacred books. When he met his father, the latter recognising him as his own son said, "Without doubt you are a Brāhmaṇa." This shows that some recognised sons from slave mothers as belonging to the caste of the father. It may be argued here that Viḍudābha, who was the son of Prasenajit and was born of Vāsabhakhattiyā, daughter of a slave girl from Mahānāmakhattiya of the Śākya clan was reduced from his princely status to the position of a slave by his father due to the servile origin of his mother on her mother's side.[2] But in this case the Kośala king's action was a result of his wrath on the Śākyas for deceiving him by not giving the hand of a girl of their own blood, which fell on his son and wife. Later the king excused them, and Viḍudābha succeeded his father as the heir-apparent. It may be further argued that Viḍudābha was not respected highly by the Śākyas, when he had been at his maternal grand-fathers' house, and some contemptuous terms were used for him. But this was due to the Śākyan pride of lineage, for which they were well known. Customs and practices were different from place to place, and the opinion which was held by the Śākyas cannot be taken as a universal one.

There may have been also a few cases of higher caste ladies falling in love with slaves. It is said in the *Chulla-Seṭṭhi Jātaka* (No. 4) that a rich merchant's daughter in Rājagṛha

1. *Jā.* I. 156-57.
2. *Kaṭṭhahāri Jā.* (No. 7); *Bhaddasāla Jā.* (No. 465)

stooped to intimacy with a slave. Getting alarmed at the idea of her misconduct being revealed to her parents, she eloped with her lover, the slave. She gave birth to two sons. When the elder son reached the age of understanding, he enquired from his mother about his relatives. His mother told him that he was the grandson of a wealthy merchant. At the insistence of the boy to see his grandfather's place, his mother and father started for Rājagṛiha and reached there. But she did not dare to face her father; nor the father liked to see her. However, the father did not disappoint her daughter. She was sent back with wealth and her sons were accepted by their grandfather.[1]

This shows that unions of high born ladies with low born slaves were not encouraged. It was the attitude of society to discourage all unions of low caste males and high caste females. But if a high born lady cultivated intimacy with a slave, such a union was tolerated, though reluctantly. If the mother's father accepted a son born of it, he belonged to his family and caste. It seems that the slave girls enjoyed a better and more favourable position than the male ones in this respect. Very often they came into close contact with their masters and were elavated to the position of wives, losing their servile status as we have observed earlier.

Nature of their Work :

There were only a few slaves like Kaṭāhaka, who were employed on high and responsible posts of store-keepers, treasures, and private secretaries to their masters. Most of them were employed to perform ordinary duties of the household; and their work differed with the social and financial status of the master and the ability of the slaves. Slaves living in the royal palaces and in the household of the rich Seṭṭhis had not to do the same type of work, as the slaves in ordinary families of the villages had to perform. Generally they seem to have been performing two types of works; viz., the household duties, and attendance on the master and mistress. The Buddhist literature represents them as performing household

1. *Jā.* I. 114-15.

duties such as cooking and serving food,[1] fetching water,[2] handling plates and dishes,[3] taking charge of the grannary, spreading rice in the sun and watching it,[4] and the like. Slaves of the farmer's families brought food for their masters at the field,[5] and those of ordinary families had to go out for earning wages.[6] Among the duties of attendance on the master and the mistress, we find them helping them during their bath, such as accompanying them to the bathing tank and looking after their clothes and ornaments, when they entered into the tank,[7] attending on them at the time of their taking meals,[8] and so on. The nature of all these works is by no means low, and there is no indication which may lead to the conclusion that the slaves were generally employed in mean works. On the other hand, as already referred to, we know from the *Arthaśāstra* of Kauṭilya that if the masters employed their slaves for the work of low grade, they forfeited the purchase value of their slaves.[9] The works on which the slaves could not be employed, according to Kauṭilya, were carrying the dead, sweeping ordure, urine, or the leaving of food and attendance by the female slaves, while the masters bathed naked.[10] This reflects the general social attitude that the slaves were not to be employed for such works

1. *C. V.* IV. IV. 7. A slave-girl is represented as serving food to the Bhikshus.'
   C. V. VI. 4. 1. A Seṭṭhi of Rājagṛiha is described as telling his slaves and workmen "Get up early in the morning and prepare congey, rice and delicacies."
   Jā. V. 293 (*Kusa Jā.*).
2. *Jā.* V. 284. Eight slave girls are represented as going to bring water, each carrying a water-pot.
   Jā. V. 413. साकिया-कोलियानं दासीसु उदकत्थाय नदिं गन्त्वा... ।
3. *Jā.* I. 453.
4. *Jā.* I. 484, तस्मिं काले एका भतिया वीहिकोट्टिकदासी वीहिं गेहद्वारे आतपे पत्थरित्वा रक्खन्ति ।
5. *Jā.* III. 163.
6. *Jā*l I. 402. A *dāsī* was beaten for not bringing the days wages.
7. *Jā.* I. 383, इत्थियो अत्तनो सीसूपगगीवूपगादीनि आभरणानि ओमुञ्चित्वा उत्तरासङ्गे पक्खिपित्वा समुग्गपिट्ठेसु ठपेत्वा दासियो परिच्छापेत्वा पोक्खरणिं ओतरिंसु ।
8. *Jā.* I. 453.
9. *Kau.* III. 13.
10. *Ibid.*

which were looked upon as low and impure. To go against this rule was to be a victim of the social censor, which was the forfeiture of the purchase value of a slave.

But later the position of the slaves deteriorated. The conditions of the slaves changed in Gupta times. The *Nārada-Smṛiti* informs us that the slaves could be employed for doing impure works, such as cleansing the entrance to the house, filthy pits, the roads, dung hills; and for scratching the private parts, taking up and throwing away ordure and urine, and doing bodily service to the master, if he so desired.[1] What a contradiction between Kauṭilya and Nārada ! The same works for which a master forfeited his purchase value according to Kauṭilya were prescribed by Nārada. Here is the clear indication that the attitude of society towards the slaves had vastly changed by the time the *Nārada-Smṛiti* was written.

Liberation of the Slaves :

The earliest category of the slaves seems to be of the war-captives. It can be well presumed that slaves of this category could get emancipation, if their defeated side regained its strength and conquered the enemy, who had enslaved them. But such liberation did not happen in the normal course. The Buddhist sources inform us that slaves could be liberated either by accepting Sanyāsa, or by the will of the masters, or by paying them a ransom for their emancipation. The *Dīgha-Nikāya* states that if a slave embraced the life of an ascetic, he was to be greeted with reverence and all the requisites of a recluse were to be provided for him.[2] This shows that acceptance of Sanyāsa led to the termination of one's servile status. According to the *Raṭṭhapālasutta* bringing happy tiding for the master would result

1. *Nārada* : *Abhyupetyāsuśrushā* 6-7. गृहद्वारशुचिस्थानरथ्यावस्करशोधनम् । गुह्यांगस्पर्शनोच्छिष्ट विण्मूत्रग्रहणोज्झनम् । इच्छतः स्वामिनश्चाङ्गै’रूपस्थान मथान्ततः । अशुभं कर्म विज्ञेयं शुभमन्यदतपरम् ।

The *Jātakas* represent them doing such wroks as bodily service to the master and sweeping; but not those prescribed by Nārada.

2. *D. N.* I. 60-61. The Buddhist Order did not accept slaves in order to avoid interference with the right of a third party, but in the beginning they were entitled to enter the monastic fold, and the above statement refers to an earlier period.

in the emancipation of the slave.[1] In the *Sonananda Jātaka* we find a Brāhmaṇa disposing off his wealth and liberating his slaves. The *Vessantara Jātaka* represents a king as uttering after giving his son and daughter as slaves to a Brāhmaṇa, "Son Jāli, if you wish to become free, you must pay the Brāhmaṇa a hundred gold pieces; if your sister would be free, let her pay the Brāhmaṇa a hundred male and a hundred female slaves with elephants, horses, bulls, gold pieces all a hundred each."[2] Definite information on the liberation of slaves is given by Kauṭilya. According to Kauṭilya the slaves, either bought, enslaved for court decrees, or captured in war could get their emancipation by paying a certain amount as ransom to their masters. In the case of one who was bought, the amount would be his purchase value. One enslaved for fines would pay the amount of fine for which he was enslaved. If the master did not liberate his slave, after receiving the required amount of ransom, he was liable to a fine of 12 Paṇas.[3] In case a child was begotten on a female slave by her master, both the child and the mother were free.[4] That practice of liberating the slaves survived in later times is known from the *Nārada-Smṛiti*. We are told there that when a slave saved a master from imminent danger or the latter's life, he became free.[5] One who was pledged, or saved in the famine, or captured in a battle, could be a free man by paying a ransom to the master.[6] One who was forced to be a slave, or carried away and sold by a raider, could be freed by the king.[7] The rule of liberation did not apply to all the slaves indiscriminately; those who were

1. *M.N.* II. 62. The mistress of the house promises to liberate her female slave, if the news conveyed to her by the latter regarding the arrival of the former's son, who had become a Bhikshus, were true.

सच्चे जे सच्चं वदसि, अदासी भक्सीति।

2. *Jā.* VI. 546-47.
3. *Kau.* III. 13.
4. *Ibid.* III. 13.

स्वामिनस्तस्यां दास्यां जातं समातृकमदासं विद्यात्।

5. *Nārada.* V. 30.
Yājñavalkya, III. 32 (p. 190).
6. *Nārada.* V. 31-34. One saved in famine gave a pair of oxen, that captured in a battle gave a substitute for him, and the debter paid off his debts with interest.
7. *Nārada.* V. 38.

either bought, or acquired (by gift or other means), or inherited, or were born in the house, or those who sold themselves could not be freed; except by the favour of the masters.[1] These statements suggest that in a few cases, though the liberation of the slaves was not easy and did not depend on the slaves themselves, yet there was scope for their freedom; because it was prescribed that if the life of the master was saved, all categories of them could be liberated instantaneously. Nārda describes the ceremony of the emancipation of the slaves. He says, "When a master being pleased with a slave desires to make him a free man, he should take from the slave's shoulder a jar full of water and break it; he should sprinkle water mixed with whole grain of rice and flowers on the slave's head, and thrice utter the words, 'you are no longer a slave; he should dismiss him with the (slave's) face to the east."[2] This shows that, though by the time of the *Nārada-Smṛiti*, the Dāsas were being employed in low works, yet the spirit of liberating them existed, and they were in a position to cast off their servility and to breathe once again the fresh air of freedom.

1. *Nārada*. V. 29.
2. *Nārada*. V. 42-43.

CHAPTER III

MARRIAGE

Importance of Marriage :

It is difficult to say when the institution of marriage came into existence. The Vedic literature does not show any indication of a promiscuous society. It represents marriage in the form of a fully developed social institution. The *Ṛigveda* tells us that the tie of marriage was necessary for becoming a householder, performing sacrifices to gods and begetting children.[1] In the later Vedic literature the wife is described as the half of a man's self, and one is said to be incomplete so long as he did not marry and did not beget a son.[2] It was only after marriage that he considered himself to be more complete.[3] Much importance was attached to the procreation of children, and hence a wife was so much glorified and given the epithet *Jāyā*; because the husband was born in the wife as a son, says the *Aitareya Brāhmaṇa*.[4] According to the *Taittirīya Brāhmaṇa* no religious performance could be complete without the participation of the wife.[5] All these references show that society and religion had made marriage an indispensable necessity for an individual. By the days of the Buddha, except those who had renounced the world under the influence of the philosophical and religious ideals of renunciation, nobody whether male or female thought of leading an unmarried life. In the *Sutta-Nipāta* a herdsman

1. *Ṛig.* X. 85. 36, Husband took a woman for *gārhapatya*.

Ṛig. V. 3. 2, Speaks of co-operation of the wife and the husband for worshipping gods.

Ṛig. III 53. 4, The wife herself is the home (*History of Dharmaśāstra*, Vol. II, p. 428).

2. *Śat. Bṛ.* V. 6. 10; अर्धो ह वा एष आत्मनो यज्जाया तस्माद्यावज्जायां न विन्दते नैव तावत्प्रजायतेऽसर्वोहि तावद्भवति अथ यदैव जायां विन्दते ऽथ प्रजायते तर्हि हि सर्वो भवति ।

3. *Ait. Ār.* I. 3. 5, तस्मादपि पुरुषो जायां वित्त्वा कृत्स्नतरमिनात्मानं मन्यते ।

4. *Ait. Br.* 33. 1.

5. *Tai. Br.* II. 2. 2. 6; III. 7. 1.

Dhaniya is described as proud of his obedient wife and the family prosperity.[1] Marriage was more essential for women. The *Aṅguttara-Nikāya* says that the husband is the covering, the shelter and the ornament of a woman (*purisachchhadam purisassaram purisālaṅkāram*).[2] In a *Jātaka* the attitude of the woman-folk to the wedded life is frightfully expressed by a lady in these words, "For a husband is a woman's real covering, and she that lacks a husband—even though she be clad in garments costing a thousand pieces—goes bare and naked."[3] These statements indicate that an unmarried lady was not looked upon with respect and admiration, and it was the married who enjoyed real respect in society, and felt elevated and dignified.

Polyandry :

Polyandry did not exist in society, neither during the earlier period nor during our age. In the *Jātaka* stories there is the single instance of princess Kaṇhā's polyandrous marriage, which is a distorted version of Draupadī's marriage with the Pāṇḍavas. But we know that the decision of Yudhishṭhira to make Draupadī the wife of all the five brothers had shocked all. The *Mahābhārata* offers several explanations for this polyandrous marriage. This incident led some scholars to think that the Pāṇḍavas were non-Aryans. A passage in one of the *Brāhmaṇas* tells us that a man has many wives, but not a woman many husbands. Except in a few uncivilised tribes, polyandry did not exist in any of the cultured sections of the Indian society.

Polygamy and Monogamy :

Polygamy was in vogue since very early times. During the Vedic period it was permitted. It was a patriarchal society and to add to the number of wives may have been looked upon as a means to ensure the numerical strength of the family.

That polygamy was in practice during the period under review is revealed by the Buddhist sources, which frequently

1. *Sū. Ni.* I. 2. 5.

2. *A.N.* IV. 57.

3. *Jā.* I. 307, इत्थिया हि सामिको अच्छादनं नाम, सामिकम्हि असति सहस्समूलं पि साटकं निवत्था इणग्गा एव नाम ।

refer to polygamous marriages. The *Raṭṭhapāla-Sutta* describes Raṭṭhapāla, the son of a Brāhmaṇa Gṛihapati, as having several wives.[1] In the *Aṅguttara-Nikāya* a wealthy and happy householder is described as being waited upon by four wives with all their charms.[2] The *Therīgāthā* tells us that Isidāsī in her former birth was married to a merchant's son, who had already another wife.[3] In one of the *Jātakas* a Brāhmaṇa is represented as giving his four daughters in marriage to a virtuous man, though there were four suitors.[4] It is a story, but the possibility of such incidents taking place in society cannot be completely ruled out. The *Pāraskara-Gṛihyasūtra* states that a Brāhmaṇa should have three wives, a Kshatriya two, and a Vaiśya one, besides one Śūdra wife to all.[5] Thus he allows four wives for a Brāhmaṇa. Vaśishṭha says that a Śūdra wife was only for pleasure and not for performing religious rites.[6] This shows that the higher three castes could easily procure two wives—one for performing religious rites, and the other for pleasure. It seems that during the early days of the Aryan occupation, Śūdra women were being kept as concubines for the sake of pleasure, and this practice continued in a few cases during the period represented by the Dharmasūtras.

From the above references to polygamous marriages both in the Buddhist as well as in the Brahmanical sources it becomes obvious that a second wife was allowed. But what percentage followed the practice of having more than one wife is difficult to say. The *Āpastamba-Gṛihyasūtra* prescribes a charm to be repeated by a wife for suppressing her co-wives.[7] This prescription presupposes unfriendly relations and jealousy amongst the co-wives. The *Āpastamba Dharmasūtra* does not allow a second wife during the life time of the former, if she shares all

1. *M. N.* II. 63, रट्ठपालकस्य पुराणदूतियिके आमन्तेसिः—एष तुम्हे वधुके येन अलंकारेन अलंकता पुब्बे रट्ठपालकस्य कुलपुत्तस्य पिया' होथ मनापा, तेन अलंकारेन अलंकरोथाति ।
2. *G. S.* I. 120.
3. *Therīgāthā*, 446, तस्सापि अञ्ञा भरिया सीलवती गुणवती यसवती च।
अनुरत्ता भत्तारं तस्सा'हं विद्देसनं' अकासि ॥
4. *Jā.* II. 138, ब्राह्मणो तस्स वचनं सुत्वा सीलवन्तस्स'एव धीतरो अदासि ।
5. *Pā. G. S.* I. 4. 8-11.
6. *V. Dh. S.* XVIII. 18, कृष्णवर्णा या रामा रमयामैव न धर्माय ।
7. *Āp. G. S.* III. 9. 8.

religious duties and bears sons. It is only in the absence of either of these two that one should take another wife.[1] Manu allows a second wife, in case the first wife was barren.[2] Kauṭilya also encourages polygamy for the sake of progeny.[3] It appears that as the importance of the son for attaining *svarga* increased, polygamy must have become common for having a son. But the word *dampati* is suggestive of only one wife. The statements of the religious books would indicate that generally monogamy was followed by the vast majority of the people. It was only in special circumstances that a second marriage was resorted to. No doubt the Dharmaśāstras allowed remarriages, but they put the condition that if the wife was unable to discharge her religious duties on account of constant illness, or if she was barren, only then a second one should be brought. Most of the wives would have been neither barren nor diseased. The factor of mutual affection which would have induced many husbands to deviate from the idea of taking resort to a second marriage cannot be overlooked. Economic factor was also there. Even when polygamy was legally permitted in India, generally those would have brought a second wife who could support her also. Similar may have been the condition during our period.

But polygamy was more common among the kings and the nobles. Kings' harems were always overcrowded with many glamorous girls. It is only now and then that a few cases of princes, devoted to the ideal of one wife, like Rāma, are available. In the *Jātakas* most of the princes have been described as polygamous,[4] with the rare exception of prince Suruchi of Mithilā.[5] The *Mahābhārata* says that in kings having a

1. *Āp. Dh. S.* II. 5. 11. 12-13, धर्मप्रजासंपन्ने दारे नान्यां कुर्वीत ।
अन्यतराभावे कार्या प्रागग्न्याधेयात् ॥

2. *Manu.* IX. 81, वन्ध्याष्टमेऽधिवेद्याब्दे दशमे तु मृतप्रजा ।
एकादशे स्त्री जननी सद्यस्त्वप्रियवादिनी ॥

3. *Kau.* III. 2.

4. e. g., The *Chullasutasoma Jātaka* tells us that a king, when he was renouncing the world, was reminded the fate of his seven hundred wives (*Jā.* V.178). In the *Suruchi Jātaka* a queen is represented as telling her husband that the worst misery for a woman was to quarrel with her co-wives (*Jā.* IV, 316).

5. *Jā.* IV. 317, The story says that Suruchi married only one princess, Sumedhā, but as he had no issue, the citizens approached him and requested for bringing other princess for the purpose. He refused to do so. But the queen herself brought to the harem several girls for procuring an issue.

number of wives there is no Adharma.[1] Kings like Bimbisāra, Prasenajit, Udayana, and Ajātaśatru were all polygamous. It was due to the existence of a crowded harem of the kings that even during the later period in the *Abhijñāna Śākuntalam*, Śakuntalā is instructed to have friendly relations with her fellow co-wives.[2] All these show that the passion of the kings to add to the number of their wives was unabated.

Settlement of Marriage :

Buddhist sources reveal that generally marriages were negotiated and settled by the elders of the parties of the bride and the bridegroom. Initiative came from the latter's parents, who sent men for finding out a suitable girl for their son.[3] There are references to fully grown-up girls, whose parents were anxious, for no body selected them for marriage.[4] In some cases grown-up girls were wooed by their suitors and married to those whom their fathers selected. The *Therīgāthā* refers to Anopama as being wooed by several suitors, who approached her with costly gifts and sent messengers to her father for her hand;[5] and a *Jātaka* refers to the four daughters of a Brāhmaṇa, who had four suitors.[6] As a rule marriages were initiated by parents, yet boys and girls both were consulted by them, and it appears that in the case of well grown-up boys and girls their wishes may not have been ignored.

QUALIFICATIONS OF THE PARTIES :—

Caste Consideration :

By this period caste consideration had become the most important factor in determining marriages, and the tendency to preserve the purity of blood through marriages is distinctly marked. Obviously, endogamy was in practice and restrictions were imposed on the intermixture of castes. Incidents of mar-

1. न चाप्यधर्मः कल्याण बहुपत्नीकता नृणाम् । Quoted in *History of Dharmaśāstra*, VI. II, p. 552.
2. *Abhijñāna Śākuntalam*, IV. 18, कुरु प्रियसखीवृत्तिं सम्पत्नी जने
3. *Jā*. III. 93.
4. *Jā*. IV. 219.
5. *Therīgāthā*. 152, पत्थिता राजपुत्तेहि सेट्ठिपुत्ते हि गिज्झिता
   पितु ये पेसयि दूतं, देथ मय्हं अनोपमं ।
6. *Jā*. II. 138.

riages referred to in the Buddhist literature as taking place in the ordinary course of life disclose that the equalities of caste and family status were almost always taken into account.[1] Brāhmaṇas,[2] Seṭṭhis,[3] clansmen,[4] treasurers,[5] and others are mentioned as solemnising marriages with the members of their respective castes of similar family status. When sending men for finding a bride, people advised them to choose one of the equal family and caste.[6] This Buddhist account is supported by the Dharmaśāstras which prescribe that the bride should be a virgin of equal caste.[7]

The equality of caste alone was not taken to be the guarantee of the purity of a family's blood, hence the popular stories almost always mention Kula and Jāti together; and the fact of the parties belonging to pure families of a matching status is emphasised. That the term Kula (family) is used to ascertain the purity of blood is clear from the content and also from the law-books. The *Āśvalāyana-Gṛihyasūtra* says that before settling a marriage, the purity of the family both on the side of the mother and the father should be ascertained.[8] According to Manu one who desires to raise his family to eminence should always endeavour to have marriage relations with the best family and never with the low.[9] But Manu further tells us that if the girl is endowed with beauty and is like a jewel among the womenfolk, she should be accepted, even though she belonged to a low family.[10] And most probably it was due to this social outlook that now and then we come across in the *Jātakas* with

1. *Jā.* I. 199, अथ'अस्स मातापितरो समानजातियं कुलतो दारिकं आनयिंसु ।
Jā. I. 477; II. 229; III. 422.
2. *Jā* III. 162; IV. 22.
3. *Jā.* II. 225.
4. *Psalms of Sisters*, p. 42.
5. *Ibid.* p. 84.
6. *Jā.* III. 93.
7. *Gau. Dh. S.* IV. 1, गृहस्थः सदृशीं भार्यां विन्देतानन्यपूर्वां यवीयसीम् ।
V. Dh. S. VIII. 1, अस्पृष्टमैथुनामरयवीयसीं सदृशीं भार्यां विन्देत ।
8. *Āva. G. S. I.* 5. 1. कुलमग्रे परीक्षेत ये मातृतः पितृतश्चेति यथोक्तं पुरस्तात् ।
9. *Manu.* IV. 244. उत्तमैरुत्तमैर्नित्यं संबन्धानाचरेत्सह ।
निनीषुः कुलमुत्कर्षमधमानधमांस्त्यजेत् ॥
10. *Manu.* II. 238.

such incidents when only the beauty of the girl was counted and family considerations were put aside.

But such cases were exceptional. It was only in the higher circle of society that caste and family restrictions could be relaxed, and the Buddhist evidence[1] like the Brahmanical shows that as a rule it was the bridegroom of a higher family who could accept the bride of a lower family in exceptional cases. It was the love affair which was generally responsible for inter-caste marriage. Thus we find in a *Jātaka* that a king saw a beautiful girl named Sujātā, daughter of a greengrocer selling jujubis, fell in love and made her his queen consort.[2] That marriage of a higher caste girl with a low caste boy known as the Pratiloma form of inter-caste marriage in the Dharmaśāstras was not common is made clear by the *Jātakas*.[3] The other form, known as the Anuloma and permitted by the Dharmaśāstras, took place occasionally. According to the Dharmaśāstras a Brāhmaṇa may marry a lady of any caste; a Kshatriya can marry a woman of any caste, except a Brāhmaṇa lady; a Vaiśya may take as a wife a Vaiśya or a Śūdra girl, and a Śūdra only a Śūdra one.[4] It seems that during the earlier period this type of marriage was fairly frequent, but by this time, it had ceased to be a common practice; and only the higher classes practised it, though not often.

Gotra and Marriage :

During the Vedic period Gotra denoted a cow-pen, and had nothing to do with marriage. But gradually the term assumed quite a different meaning. The Buddhist as well as the

1. A *Jātaka* describes Senāpati Ahipāraka as marrying Ummadantī, a merchant's daughter (*Jā*. V. 211).

2. *Jā*. III 81.

3. It is said that a barber's son fell in love with a Lichchhavi girl at the first sight and conveyed to his father his desire of getting her. The father told him that he was no match for a Lichchhavi girl, a high-born Kshatriya lady, and that he would secure a bride for him of his own caste—
हीनजच्चो त्वं नहापितपुत्तो, लिच्छविकुमारिका खत्तियधीता जातिसम्पन्ना,
न सा तुय्हं अनुच्छविका, अञ्ञं ते जातिगोत्तेहि सदिसकुमारिकं आनेसामीति आह,
(*Jā*. II. 5).

4. *Pā. G. S.* I. 4.8-11; *Bau. Dh. S.* I. 8. 2-5; *Vishṇu, Dh. S.* 24. 1-4
V. Dh. S. I. 24-25, तिस्रो ब्राह्मणस्य भार्या वर्णानुपूर्व्वेण द्वे राजन्यस्य
एकैका वैश्य शूद्रयो । शूद्रामप्येके मन्त्रवर्जं तद्वत् ।

Brahmanical sources reveal that by the period under discussion Gotra came to be used in the sense of lineage or ancestry. When king Prasenajit asked the Gotra of Aṅgulimāla's parents, the latter replied that his father was of the Gārgya Gotra, and the mother of the Maitrāyaṇī.[1] In the Buddhist literature sometimes Gotra is differentiated from the name,[2] and sometimes from the caste,[3] which suggests that it denoted the lineage of the family. It appears from certain references that Gotra consideration was taken into account in marriages. The *Majjhima-Nikāya* informs us that if anybody loved a lady, he was required to know her caste and Gotra.[4] A verse in the *Kachchhapa Jātaka* suggests that generally parties united in wedlock belonged to different Gotras.[5] Pāṇini and Patañjali by referring to compound words of two Gotras suggest that marriages were not performed within the same Gotra.[6] But Gotra did not play the same part in marriage as during the later period. Some of the law-givers (e.g. Gautama, Baudhāyana) are silent on the point. Some of them prohibit Sagotra marriage. This shows that opinion was divided; some disfavoured Sagotra marriages, while others did not.

Brother-sister marriage which now appears to be repulsive was once in practice. It was customary among the Egyptians. The *Avestā* shows that it was prevalent among the Iranians. The Vedic literature refers to the incident of Yama and Yamī.[7]

1. *M. N.* II. 102, गग्गो खो, महाराज, पिता मन्ताणी माताति ।

2. *D. N.* I. 92; M. N. III. 118; II. 40, एवं-नामा एवं-गोत्ता इति वा ति. . . . ?

Buddhaghosha, *Sumaṅgalavilāsinī* I. 257, पञ्ञत्तिवसेन नाम, पवेणि-वसेन गोत्तं ।

3. *Sū. Ni.* III. 1-19, आदिच्चा नाम गोत्तेन, साकिया नाम जातिया ।
Sometimes we get reference to *Jāti*, *gotta* & *kula* (*Jā.* II. 3).

4. *M. N.* II. 40, अम्भो पुरिस, यं त्वं जनपदकल्याणिं इच्छसि कामेसि, जानासि तं जनपदकल्याणिं:—खत्तिया वा ब्राह्मणी वा वेस्सी वा सुद्दी वा ति ?. . . एवं नाम एवं गोत्ता इति वा ति. . . ?

5. *Jā.* II. 360.

6. *Pā.* IV. 3. 125.

Patañjali II. 4. 62; I. 492.

7. Instances of brother-sister marriage in Vedic texts have been collected by S. C. Sircar in his book *Some Aspects of Earliest Social History of India*.

The Buddhist literature speaks of the Śākyas marrying their sisters for the sake of continuing their line.[1] Gradually marital relation between a full brother and a full sister was given up. Some of the *Jātakas* refer to the marriages of half brothers and sisters, either their fathers or mothers being different.[2] Generally it was among kings and nobles that such marital relations could be established during the early period, but later this also was stopped totally in India.

Our sources disclose that cousin-marriage was in vogue. Generally one would marry his maternal uncle's daughter, though in some of the *Jātakas* marriage with one's father's brother's daughter is also recorded.[3] The Brahmanical sources also refer to the custom of marrying one's maternal uncle's daughter; but whereas they show that this practice was confined to the south,[4] the Buddhist sources reveal that even in the north it was customary. The *Jātaka* stories refer to the marriages of Kāśī and Śivi princes with their maternal uncle's daughters.[5] The sister of the Kośala king Prasenajit was married to Bimbisāra and his daughter Vājirā was wedded to Ajātaśatru, the son of Bimbisāra.[6] The marriage of Jyeshṭhā to Nandivardhana, the elder brother of Mahāvīra also falls under this category. These instances would suggest that princes often resorted to such marriages. But the popular stories refer to several cases of cousin marriages taking place among the common folk. One story tells us that a wicked woman having hurled her husband down a precipice in a forest fled away with a robber, whose limbs had been mutilated. When people enquired from her in what relation she stood to the robber whom she was carrying on her shoulder, she replied in a tone mixed with pride that he was the son of her father's sister and to him she was given by her parents.[7]

1. *Dia*. II. 115; *Jā*. V. 413 (No. 536).
2. *Jā*. Nos. 458; 461.
3. *Jā*. VI. 486; *Mahā-Janaka Jā*. (No. 539).
4. *Bau. Dh. S*. I. 1. 19-26.
5. *Jā*. I. 457, अपरभागे भागिनेय्यस्स रज्जं दत्वा धीतरं महादेविं अकासि ।
Jā. II. 327.
Jā. VI. 486.
6. *Jā*. II. 237, 403-4; IV. 342-43.
7. *Jā*. II. 119, अहं एतस्स मातुलधीता, पितुच्छापुत्तो मे एस, एतस्स'एव मे अदंसु ।

Marriage Age :

There is no clear statement in the *Vedas* on the strength of which the exact marriageable age of the boys and the girls in the contemporary society can be finally determined. But whatever stray references are available, they indicate that both the sexes were fully matured at the time of their wedding. The description of the bride as possessed of blossoming youth and yearning for a husband,[1] and as able to rule over the family members,[2] clearly indicate that a bride was not a child at the time of her wedding. The consummation took place soon after the marriage.[3] Love affair was not unknown and youthful maidens approaching their cherished youth can be seen.[4]

Our sources indicate that the marriage age of the girls and the boys was more or less the same as in the earlier period. There are frequent references to prove beyond doubt that the usual age of the bride at the time of her wedding was sixteen. The bridegroom used to be older than his partner, and it can be well presumed that his age for marriage was at least eighteen or twenty.

The *Therīgāthā* states that Isidāsī in her former birth was married at the age of sixteen.[5] From the same work it can be presumed that Bhikshuṇīs like Dhammadinnā and Kuṇḍalakesā, who had renounced the world before their marriages, were either of the age of sixteen or of the age of discretion.[6] The commentary on the *Dhammapada* describes the girls of sixteen years as eagerly pining for being united with husbands.[7] The *Jātakas* clearly state that girls of this age were regarded as ripe

1. *Ṛig.* X. 85. 22;x.85.9.
2. *Ṛig.* X. 85. 46.
3. *Ṛig.* X. 85.
4. *A. V.* II 30. 5.
5. *Therīgāthā.* 445, अथ सोलसमे वस्से दिस्वान मं पत्तयोब्बन ।
कञ्ञं ओरुद्ध तस्स पुत्तो गिरिदासो नाम नामेन ॥
6. *Therīgāthā*, 12 and 46 and commentary.
7. Commentary on the *Dhammapada*, 120, quoted in the *Position of Women in Hindu Civilisation*, 102. राजगहे तु एका सेट्ठिधीता सोलस्सवस्सुदेसिका अभिरूपा अहोसि दस्सनाय । तस्मिं च वये थिता नारिणे । पुरुसज्ञासाय होंति पुरुसलोला ।

for marriage, and possessed of beauty and all signs of youth.[1] Cases of elopment[2] and love marriages mentioned in the Buddhist sources support the view that the age of sixteen was the proper age of marriage for girls throughout Northern India.

The Sūtra literature by using the adjective Nagnikā for a bride[3] has given rise to the view that girls were married at an age when they did not care to cover their body. But this interpretation of the term Nagnikā has not been accepted by scholars. The commentators are not themselves unanimous. While the *Gṛihyasaṅgraha*, the commentary on Gobhila interprets Nagnikā as denoting a girl who has not attained her puberty,[4] Māṭridatta commenting on the *Hiraṇya-Gṛihyasūtra* states that Nagnikā means one whose menstrual period is near, i. e. one who is fit for intercourse.[5] The *Mānava Gṛihyasūtra* says that Nagnikā is a girl who has not yet experienced the impulses of youth,[6] which may simply mean the pre-puberty age or a virgin. The *Hiraṇya Gṛihyasūtra* on the other hand states that Nagnikā at the time of her marriage should also be a virgin.[7] Such a statement could be applicable only to a grown-up girl. Mostly the references in the Sūtra literature concerning marriage refute the assumption that a bride was a mere child as the time of her marriage. At one place in the *Mahābhārata* the term Nagnikā

1. *Jā.* III. 93, सा सोलस्सवस्सकाले अभिरूपा अहोसि पासादिका देवच्छरपटिभागा सब्बलक्खणसम्पन्ना ।

It was at this age that princess Phusati of Madra was married to prince Sañjaya (*Jā.* No. 547) and a King of Vārāṇasī became anxious for his daughter's marriage (*Jā.* I. 456).

2. *Therigāthā*, 47, Gātha of Paṭāchārā; she had eloped with a servant.

3. *Bau. Dh. S.* IV. 1. 12, दधाद्गुणवते कन्यां नग्निकां ब्रह्मचारिणे ।

4. *Gṛihyasaṅgraha on Gobhila Gṛihya.* III. 4. 6, नग्निकान्तु वदेत्कन्यां यावन्नर्तुमती भवेत् । .... अव्यञ्जिता भवेत्कन्या कुचहीना च नग्निका ।
(Quoted by Kane in *History of Dharmaśāstra*, VI. II, pt. I, p. 440).

5. *Māṭridatta on Hi. G. S.* I. 6. 19. 2, नग्निकामासन्नार्तवाम् । .... तस्माद्वस्त्रविक्षेपणा ह्या नग्निका मैथुनार्हेत्यर्थः ।
(Vienna edition, 1889 edited by J. Kirtse, p. 127).

6. *Mānava. G. S.* 1. 7. 8. Quoted in the *History of Dharmaśāstra*, VI. II, p. 440, बन्धुमतीं कन्यामस्पृष्टमैथुनामुपयच्छेत... यवीयसीं नग्निकां श्रेष्ठाम् ।

7. *Hi. G. S.* I. 6. 19.2, ताभ्यामनुज्ञातो भार्यामुपयच्छेत् सजातां नग्निकां ब्रह्मचारिणीमसगोत्राम् ।

is used for a girl of 16.[1] Pāṇini describes a maiden of the marriageable age as *varyā,* i. e. one to be wooed freely without any restriction.[2] This also supports that she was fully developed at the time of her marriage. The Dharmaśāstras permit marriage of girls three years after menses. In such cases girls would have been of the age of 14 or 15. In some cases where the boys are described as being married at the age of 16, girls would have been of the above age, because both could not have been of the same age.

There was a general tendency to lower the marriageable age; 14 or 15 was preferred to 16 or 17. Three years constituted the period of grace. The popular practice prevalent was to settle the marriages of girls soon after their attaining puberty. According to the *Dharmasūtras* of Vaśishtha and Baudhāyana a girl should not remain at her father's house for more than a period of three years after her menses.[3] Gautama goes so far as to declare that a girl is to be married within three months of her menses; and if her parents fail to settle her marriage within this period, she should herself find out a suitable match for her.[4] The *Pāraskara-Gṛihyasūtra* prescribes that the married couple should not have intercourse for a period of a year, or six months. or twelve nights, or three nights in the last resort.[5] This prescription was to test the self-control of the couple. The idea was to abstain from intercourse for a longer period, but if that was not possible, celibacy was to be observed at least for three nights. Other *Gṛihyasūtras* also prescribe the fourth night as suitable for the consummation of marriage,[6] which was technically known as the Chaturthikarma, equivalent to the Garbhā-

1. A. S. Altekar: *The Position of Women in Hindu Civilisation,* p.61.
2. *Pā.* III. 1. 110 (*India as known to Pāṇini*, p. 88).
3. *V. Dh. S.* XVII. 67-68, कुमारी ऋतुमती त्रीणि वर्षाण्युदीक्षेत् ।
उर्ध्वं त्रिभ्यो वर्षेभ्यः पतिं विन्देत्तुल्यम् ॥
Bau. Dh. S. IV. 1. 15, त्रीणि वर्षाण्यृतुमती कांक्षेत पितृशासनम् ।
Also Manu. IX. 90.
4. *Gau. Dh. S.* XVIII. 21, त्रीन्कुमार्यृतूनतीत्य स्वयं युज्येतानिन्दितेनोत्सृज्य पित्र्यालङ्कारान् ।
5. *Pā. G. S.* I. 8. 21, त्रिरात्रमक्षारालवणाशिनौ स्यातामधः शयीयातां संवत्सरं न मिथुनमुपेयातां द्वादशरात्रं. . . . त्रिरात्रमन्ततः ।
6. *Āśva. G. S.* I. 8. 10; *Āp. G. S.* III. 8. 10.

dhāna Saṅskāra of the later writers. These references show that a girl at the time of her marriage used to be fully developed from the physical point of view.

Post-Sūtra literature does not indicate the prevalence of pre-puberty marriage. Kauṭilya says that there is no offence if a man of equal caste and rank has connection with a maiden, who has been unmarried three years after her first menses.[1] This suggests that a girl was to be married within three years of her first menses, after which she was free to choose her mate. This rule is similar to that of Vaśishṭha, who also allows a girl to wait for three years after her menses at her father's house. Manu also prescribes the same rule. He says that a girl at the expiry of three years after her first menses, should herself choose a husband for her.[2]

The *Jātakas* mention 16 as the usual marriage age for the boys.[3] But as 16 was the marriage age for the girls, boys' age should have been a few years' more than this. But in case a girl was of 14 years, there is no wonder that the husband would have been of the age of 16. We may not take this to be the popular practice, but the possibility of boys in a few cases being married at the age of 16 cannot be overruled, in the light of the definite statements in the *Jātaka* stories. The *Jātakas* state that by the age of 16, the three *Vedas* and the eighteen branches of knowledge were taught.[4] This statement seems to be a conventional way of describing the expiry of the student life, and it should not be taken for granted that by this age all the branches of knowledge were really taught. According to the *Sūtra* literature the initiation took place at the age of eight, eleven, and twelve for the Brāhmaṇas, the Kshatriyas, and the Vaiśyas respectively;[5] the study period being 12 or 24 or 36 or 48 years, taking a period of 12 years for each *Veda*.[6] This arrangement does not seem to be in practice, except in the priestly class. The public seems to have been following the practice of retaining the studentship until one learnt the *Vedas*.[7] It seems

1. *Kau.* IV. 12.
2. *Manu.* IX. 90.
3. *Jā.* I. 456; VI. 72 (No. 540); VI. 486.
4. *Jā.* I. 259; IV. 33.
5. *Āśv. G. S.* I. 19. 1-4; *Pā. G. S.* II. 2. 1-3. *Āp. Dh. S.* I. 1.1.19.
6. *Pā. G. S.* II. 5. 13-14; *Āp. Dh. S.* I. 1. 2. 12-16.
7. *Pā. G. S.* II. 5. 15.

that the studentship started at the age of 7 or 8. The *Milindapañho* informs us that Brāhmaṇas started their education at the age of seven.[1] If we assume that one started his education at the age of 8, by the age of 16 or 18 he would have been well trained for entering the life. Higher studies were not for all, and the general public may not have been in favour of a prolonged studentship. It seems very probable that by the age of 16 to 20 parents thought it proper for their boys to start their household. As the marriageable age of the bride was usually 16, we may take that grooms were older than their partners by 2 or 4 years. Then their age would be at about 18 or 20 years. This assumption is supported by the *Kāmasūtra*, which says that the bridegroom should be three years older than the bride.[2] Child marriage was not popular. Girls were married at the post-puberty age, which was generally 16. Boys were married at about the age of 18 to 20. But cases of unequal marriages were not unknown in society. The *Sutta-Nipāta* discourages bringing wife in advanced age.[3] Even old persons were suitors for young girls.[4] Though old persons were not always successful in having young wives, in a few cases they secured young girls as their brides. The *Nanda Jātaka* tells us that an old squire was apprehensive of his young wife remarrying after his death.[5] We are told in the *Vessantara Jātaka* (No. 547) that a Brāhmaṇa, Jujaka, had married quite a young girl named Amittatāpanā. When she went to the well for bringing water, other women observed :

'A "foe" indeed your mother was, a "foe" your father too,
To let an old decrepit man wed a young wife like you.'

Such a description in a popular story would suggest that marriages of young girls with old persons were ridiculed. In the *Mahābhārata* also we find a simile of girls not liking husbands of

1. *Milindapañho*. I. 22, सो अनुक्कमेन वड्ढन्तो सत्तवस्सिको जातो । अथ खो नागसेनस्स दारकस्स पिता नागसेनं दारकं एतदवोच—इमस्मिं खो तात नागसेन ब्राह्मणकुले सिक्खानि सिक्खेय्यासी' ति ।

2. *Kāma-Sūtra* III. 1. 2.

3. *Su. Ni.* I. 6. 20.

4. *Jā.* II. 138, एकस्स वद्धव्यं वद्धभावो महल्लकता अत्थि ।

5. *Jā.* I. 225.

sixty years.[1] These references no doubt disfavour marriage in the old age, but at the same time they point out that such marriages took place, though their percentage would not have been high.

Selection of the Bride and the Bridegroom :

Marriage has been looked upon as the most important event in the life of an individual, whether male or female. It is an inevitable accident of life, and its effects are far-reaching and lifelong. Our sources reveal that marriage, being such an important event in life, could not be settled without proper selection of the bride and the bridegroom. The parents of our period were quite conscious of the future happiness of their sons and daughters, and it was their endeavour to have proper selection of boys and girls, so that their conjugal life would result in perfect mutual harmony and bliss. The Buddhist sources of this period do not inform us much of the qualities sought for in a bride or bridegroom and of the mode of selection. They only inform us that the brides were selected, either by the suitors or by the parents, and that beauty and intelligence were taken into consideration.

The Sūtra literature informs us that the party of the bridegroom looked for a girl who possessed intelligence, beauty, good character, auspicious characteristics, and freedom from disease.[1] Any girl who was physically deformed like a haunch back one was not selected for a bride.[2] Sound health of body and mind was an essential quality, and a girl who suffered from some mental disorder or physical disease was not selected for marriage.[3] Even the earlier texts recommend for marriage a girl possessed of beauty. The *Śatapatha Brāhmaṇa* considers slender waist and broad hips as signs of beauty.[4] But there can be no norm of beauty, as it is to a great extent subjective in nature; and a

1. *Mbh. Sabhā.* 64. 14; *Vana.* V. 15, ध्रुवं न रोचेद्भरतर्षभयस्य पतिः कुमार्या इव षष्टिवर्षः।

1. *Āp. G. S.* I. 3. 18-19; *Āva. G.S. S.* I. 5. 3, बुद्धिरूपशीललक्षण-सम्पन्नांमरोगामुपयच्छेत् ।

2. *Āp. G. S.* I. 3. 11.

3. *Āp. G. S.* I. 3. 10. One should not choose a girl who is asleep or weeps or has left the house when persons come to her for selection.

4. *Śat. Br.* I. 2. 5. 16.

girl who is lovely and soothing to the eyes of one may not arouse soft feelings in the heart of another. It is due to this factor that the *Āpastamba-Gṛihyasūtra* points out that if a girl on whom the eyes of the bridegroom are fixed is taken as a wife, the marriage would really bring happiness to the couple.[1] A girl who was not favoured by nature had to wait till she was selected as a bride. We find in a *Jātaka* a mother observing that though her daughter had come to age, no body selected her as a wife.[2]

Similar qualities were sought for in a bridegroom, but virtue and wisdom counted much in his case; probably because the father liked to give the hand of her daughter to a person, who was known for his good conduct and thereby would enjoy respect in his after life. The priest of the family advised the father of a girl to give his daughter in marriage to a man possessed of virtue.[3] The *Baudhāyana-Dharmasūtra* expresses the same view.[4] Āśvalāyana says that the girl should be given in marriage to a man endowed with intelligence.[5] According to Āpastamba he should be endowed with good character, auspicious characteristics, learning and good health.

Forms of Marriage :

Marriages referred to in the Brahmanical sources are o eight forms, viz., Brāhma, Daiva, Ārsha, Prājāpatya, Āsura, Gāndharva, Rākshasa, and Paiśācha. From the Buddhist sources it appears that Brāhma, Prājāpatya, Āsura, Gāndharva, and Rākshasa marriages were common. Daiva and Paiśācha forms of marriages are not mentioned, probably because th former was not differentiated from the Brāhma and the Prājāpatya, and the latter was not regarded as marriage at all. It may be that there may have been no occasion of mentioning them. As Ārsha was a disguised form of Āsura, it does not

1. *Āp. G. S.* I. 3. 20, यस्यां मनश्चक्षुषोर्निबन्धस्तस्यामृद्धिर्नेतरदाद्रियेतेत्येके ।
2. *Jā.* IV. 219 (No. 477), मम धीता वयप्पता नं च नं कोचि वारेति ।
3. *Jā.* II. 138, अत्थो अत्थि सरीरस्मिं, वद्धव्यस्स नमो करे ।
अत्थो अत्थि सुजातस्मिं, सीलं अस्माक रुच्चतीति ॥
4. *Bau. Dh. S.* IV. 1. 12, दद्याद्गुणवते कन्याम् ।
5. *Āva. G. S.* I. 5. 2, बुद्धिमते कन्यां प्रयच्छेत् ।

figure. According to the Dharmaśāstras Brāhma and Prājāpatya marriages were the most popular , and similar may have been the case during the period under discussion. Marriages which took place on account of love, or where force was applied could easily get place in the popular stories; but the Brāhma and the Prājāpatya marriages which took place in the ordinary course of life would not figure prominently in the stories. When the Buddhist sources tell us that marriages were settled by parents, auspicious days were fixed for the marriage ceremony,[1] the bridegroom's party reached the house of the bride on the fixed day,[2] the bride was carried in a car to the bridegroom's place escorted by a number of people[3] and so on; they suggest that generally marriages were performed in line with the custom of the present-day Hindu society, which follows the rules of the Brāhma and Prājāpatya forms of marriages. The Buddhist sources do not refer to the details of these marriages. Their full details are available in the Brahmanical sources.[4] Pāṇini refers simply to the marriage rituals,[5] (he does not mention the various forms of marriage) which would also suggest that the Brāhma and the Prājāpatya forms, performed according to the prescribed rituals, were common.

The Āsura form of marriage in which a wife was procured by paying a substantial amount to her father also seems to be fairly common. One of the *Jātakas* tells us that an old Brāhmaṇa begging for alms received a thousand pieces of the current coin, deposited them in a Brāhmaṇa family and went for alms again. By the time he returned back, the Brāhmaṇa family had spent all his money, and unable to repay the deposit, gave him a daughter instead.[6] Expressions like *kito dhanena bahunā*,[7] *bhariyā yā pi dhanena hoti kītā*,[8] *yā cha bhariyā dhanakkītā*[9] are

1. *D. N.* I. 11; *Jā.* I. 258.
2. *Jā.* I. 258.
3. *Kuṇāla Jā.* (No. 536).
4. *Āśva. G. S.* I. 6. 1-8; *Gau. Dh. S.* IV. 6-13.
5. He refers to marriage by the term *Upayamana* (I. 2. 16), and explains it as *sva-karṇa*, i.e. the bridegroom making the bride his own (I. 3. 56). *Pāṇigrahaṇa* was the most important ritual (*Vārttika* on IV. 1. 52; *Bhāshya*, II. 221—*India as known to Pāṇini*, p. 85).
6. *Jā.* III. 342, ब्राह्मणो कहापणे दातुं असक्कोन्तो अत्तनो धीतरं तस्सा पादपरिचारिकं कत्वा अदासि।
7. *Jā.* II. 185.
8. *Jā.* IV. 122.
9. *Jā.* V. 269.

sufficient proofs to justify the remark that a wife could be procured for money. Sometimesse rvice at the bride's house by the bridegroom may have served the purpose of the bride-price, as we find in the *Mahā-Ummaga Jātaka*.[1]

The Dharmaśāstras do not allow the sale of a bride; but this practice assumed a disguised form under the name of Ārsha marriage, in which the bride's father received a bull and a cow at the time of her daughter's marriage.[2] Manu first discourages giving the bride-price for a matured girl,[3] then he says that if one who had deposited the bride price is dead before marriage, the girl should be married to the younger brother of the deceased.[4] This shows that the practice existed in spite of denunciation, and, as practical law-givers, Smṛitikāras had to take notice of it. Manu's vehement opposition to this practice even in the case of a Sūdra probably reflects his personal views.[5] But he approved of the Ārsha marriage, which amounts to the acceptance of the practice in a different form.[6] It appears that the practice of buying a wife was encouraged by old persons who contracted a second marriage, and also by poor parents of the girls, who would lose their services after they were given to other families.

The Gāndharva or love marriage was also not an uncommon affair. Among nobles it was fairly common. The *Mahā-Ummaga Jātaka* says that prince Mahosadha of Mithilā did not cherish the idea that his sister Udumbarā should choose a wife for him, and he went on search for a bride of his own choice. He met a village girl Amarā, had a prolonged courtship with her and finally carried her away[7]. The *Kaṭṭahāri Jātaka* states that a king who saw a girl merrily singing in his pleasaunce fell in love with her. Later he had her as his queen consort[8]. Another *Jātaka* speaks of a Brāhmaṇa pupil of a teacher of

1. It is said that Golakāla of the kingdom of Mithilā obtained a wife named Dīghatālā after working for seven year's in her father's house—गोलकालो नाम पुरिसो सत्त संवच्छरानि घरे कुम्भं कत्वा भरियं लभि (*Jā* VI. 337 No. 546).

2. *Āśva. G. S.* I. 6. 4; *Gau. Dh. S.* IV. 8; *Manu.* III. 29.

3. *Manu.* IX. 93.

4. *Manu.* IX. 97.

5. *Manu.* IX. 98.

6. *Manu.* III. 24.

7. *Jā.* VI. 364 f.

8. *Jā.* I. 134-36.

world-wide fame of Vārāṇasī who fell in love with a girl and made her his wife.[1] Stories of Udayana's love are well known. These references lead us to conclude that now and then love marriages were taking place in society.

Rākshasa marriage in which the bride was procured by force figures frequently in the *Jātakas*. Thus, at one place a king is described as killing his enemy king and making the widowed queen his own wife.[2] Another story says that a robber-chief kidnapped a village maiden and made her his wife.[3] This form of marriage was quite popular among the warrior class from very early times. Among the Oraons of Chotanagpur the bridegroom observes the custom of snatching away his wife from the party of the bride. This practice of the aboroginals speaks of its hoary antiquity.

Remarriage and Divorce :

Remarriage was permitted to man in ancient times. But as a woman's place was subordinate to that of man in society, the question whether she had any right to choose a new husband, if the earlier one had predeceased, presented a knotty problem. During the Vedic period Niyoga was in practice, which was prevalent also in the contemporary societies of other countries. But we find a clear reference to remarriage in a hymn of the *Atharvaveda*, which speaking of a woman who married a second time, prescribes an offering to be made to gods by the new couple for not being separated in future life.[4] The term Punarbhu is used for her which is applied in later literature to a widow who remarried. The *Taittirīya Saṁhitā* uses the word *Dvaidhishavya*,[5] most probably for a widow's son. These references

1. *Jā*. I. 300, एकाय इत्थिया पटिवद्धचित्तो हुत्वा तं भरियं कत्वा तस्मिं एव वाराणसीनगरे वसन्तो द्वे तिस्सो वेलाय आचरियस्स उपट्ठानं न गच्छति ।
2. *Jā*. V. 425-6.
3. *Jā*. I. 297.
4. *A. V.* IX. 5. 27-28, या पूर्वं पतिं वित्त्वाथान्यं विन्दतेऽपरम् ।
पञ्चौदनं च तावजं ददातो न वि योषतः ॥
समानलोको भवति पुनर्भुवापरः पतिः ।
यो ऽजं पञ्चौदजं दक्षिणाज्योतिषं ददाति ॥
5. *Tai. Saṁ*. III. 2. 4. 4.

show that widow could marry during the Vedic and the later period.

Evidence of widow-marriage during the period under review is conflicting. There are cases of permission as well as prohibition. Probably they refer to different sections of society. The Brahmanical sources generally take an idealistic view, and hence, what they disapprove should not be regarded as non-existent in society. They are more sympathetic to child widows, but the popular stories show that widows of tender age or those having children both could remarry. The Dharmaśāstra rules were followed by the priestly class and the higher section of society, but the ordinary folk mostly followed local customs. It appears that while only a few among the higher section took recourse to widow-marriage, a high percentage of the lower stratum practised it as is the case even to-day. Widows of some sections may have taken to adultery. In the higher circles, widows having no issue may have found it easier to remarry than those who had the burden of looking after their sons and daughters. According to the *Nanda Jātaka* a squire who had a young wife was apprehensive of her marrying after his death and transferring the movable family property to her new husband.[1] The *Susīma Jātaka* describes the priest of a king marrying the widowed queen. In the *Aṅguttara-Nikāya* on the other hand, we find a lady assuring her husband on his death-bed that she would never remarry, but would look after the household and the children.[2] The *Uchchhaṅga Jātaka* states that when a lady had to make a choice among her husband, brother, and son, who had been condemned to death, she said, "If I live, I can get another husband and another son; but as my parents are dead, I can never get another brother.[3]" This incident refers to that section where widow-marriage was common.

The Dharmaśāstra literature shows that both Niyoga and widow-marriage were practised in some sections. The *Sūtra* writers place the son from Niyoga next to the Aurasa. The

1. *Nanda Jā.* (No. 39), अयं इत्थिया तरुणता मम्' अच्चयेन किंचिद् एव पुरिसं गहेत्वा दयं धनं विनासेय्य, पुत्तस्स मे न ददेय्य ।

2. *A. N.* III. 295.

3. *Jā.* I. 307, अहं देव जीवमाना एकं सामिकं लभिस्सामि पुत्तं लभिस्सामि' एव मामापितुन्नं पन मे मतत्ता भाता व दुलभो, भातरं मे देहि देवा'ति ।

term Punarbhu is used to denote a widow who remarried.[1] The widow predeceased by her husband before the cosummation of marriage is regarded as a maiden by Vaśishṭha, who pleads for her remarriage.[2] In the opinion of Kauṭilya, an issueless widow should remarry after seven menses and having son, after a year.[3] Manu's statements are conflicting and hence they may be taken as referring to the different sections of the society.

The Dharmaśāstra writers are of the opinion that generally the remarriage of the widow should be confined to a member of the family of her deceased husband. The reason of this was the popularity of Niyoga from the earlier period. According to Kauṭilya if a widow married a man other than the one selected by her father-in-law, she forfeited whatever had been given to her at the time of her former marriage by him and her deceased husband. This shows that marriage outside the deceased husband's family could be contracted at the cost of the property acquired by the widow at the time of her former marriage. It would appear from the Buddhis sources that there was no such restriction. Probably liberal rules were followed by people of the eastern part of the country where widows had more freedom in the selection of their new husbands, than those of the Madhyadeśa.

In ancient India apart from her widowhood a lady had to face the problem of remarriage, when her husband either became a recluse or went abroad and did not come back. The problem of remarriage after the husband had become a Sanyāsin had come to the forefront during the Upanishadic period, but it had not become acute. The sixth century B.C. had created a peculiar situation in the region now covered by eastern Uttar Pradesh and Bihar on account of the rise of new ascetic orders; and especially Buddhism, with its organised monastic life, attracted a large number of the young men, who renounced the world in their youthful age abandoning the young wives. In the beginning the people of Magadha did not welcome the Buddha's Order of renunciation, and they described him as

1. *V. Dh. S.* XVII. 20.
2. *V. Dh. S.* XVII. 74, पाणिग्राहे मृते बाला केवलं मंत्रसंस्कृता ।
सा चेदक्षतयोनिः स्यात्पुनः संस्कारमर्हति ॥
3. *Kau.* III. 4.
4. *Kau.* III. 2.

the harbinger of widowhood.[1] But this opposition did not last for a long time; the monastic order flourished day by day, and the number of deserted wives also increased. We learn from the *Jātakas* that such wives, whose desires and cravings for their youthful pleasures were still unsatisfied, remarried and restarted their conjugal lives, though some of them followed their husbands. In some of the *Jātakas* husbands are represented as expressing their views that their wives would take new husbands, after they had renounced the world.[2] The Brahmanical sources tell us that in case a husband became an ascetic, or went abroad and did not return, the wife was to marry within a limited time. According to Vaśishṭha even a Brāhmaṇa lady having children was to wait only for five years; then she should marry a near relative, but should not wed outside the family, if an eligible person is available within it.[3] Kauṭilya says that she should wait for seven menses (*saptatīrthānyākāṅksheta*) only, if without any issue, and for a year, if with child.[4] He is also of the opinion that she should wait from two to eight years, if provided with maintenance, or maintained by her *jñātis*, after which she is free to marry.[5] According to Manu the wife should wait for a period of three to eight years according to the nature of the work for which the husband had gone abroad.[6]

Our sources further tell us that a few cases of marriages after divorcing the wife or the husband on certain grounds were also not unknown. The Buddhist sources refer to such incidents; the Dharmaśāstras permit divorce in exceptional cases. As the Dharmaśāstra literature represents an ideal picture of society, it does not refer to these customs of the lower sections which it disapproved. But the Buddhist literature refers to the customs

1. *S. B. E.* XIII. 150.
"The samaṇa Gotama causes fathers to beget no sons;
the Samaṇa Gotama causes wives to become widows;
the Samaṇa Gotama causes families to become extinct".

2. *Chullasutasoma Jā.* (No. 525).
"Their sorrows soon another will console,
For they are young in years and fair to see,
But I am bent upon a heavenly goal
And so right fain am I monk to be."

Vessantara Jā. (No. 547 original in *Jā.* VI. 495), "And if no man should wish to be thy husband, when I am gone,
Go, seek a husband for thyself, but do not pine alone."

3. *V. Dh. S.* XVII. 78-80.

4. *Kau.* III. 4.

5. *Ibid.*

6. *Manu.* IX. 76.

of all the sections of society, high and low. It shows that divorce and remarriage were to a great extent liberally practised in some sections of society. Even today, people belonging to the lower strata of society are liberal in this direction, and similar may have been the case even during the period under consideration. The *Piyajātika-Sutta* of the *Majjhima-Nikāya* states that the relatives of a lady, who did not like her husband, intended to separate her from him and to unite her with another person.[1] A *Jātaka* relates the story of princess Phusati of Madra, who wanted to get rid of her ugly husband, Kusa (the Bodhisattva) of Kusāvatī and to marry another prince who would be handsome, according to her wishes. It is stated in the story that many princes demanded her hand, but none succeeded on account of the valour of prince Kusa.[2] According to Vaśishṭha one can seek a new husband, if the former proves to be either impotent, mean, or insane.[3] Kauṭilya makes provision for dissolving a marriage by the consent of both parties concerned on account of continued enmity.[4] This rule was a check on the unfaithful wife or husband, who would have divorced one's partner to serve his or her own selfish ends. Hence, mutual consent was needed. But this rule was laid down during the days of the Mauryas, when the administration had become well organised; and in earlier period no such condition was probably necessary.

But what percentage of people availed the practice is difficult to say. As already observed, people of the lower sections may have been practising it liberally. Family tradition and local customs always play an important part in controlling social practices. Females are more devoted to the family customs and they hardly like to transgress it. A *Jātaka* story tells us that a wife, who disclosed her indifference towards her husband, when asked by him the reason of her not abandoning him and having a new husband said, that the custom of the family was not to take a newer mate for a wedded wife, and she followed

1. *M. N.* II, 109, तस्सा ते ञातका सामिकं अच्छिन्दित्वा अञ्ञास्स दातुकामा, सा च तं न इच्छति ।
2. *Jā.* No. 531 (*Kusa Jā.*)
3. *V. Dh.* S. XVII. 20.
4. *Kau.* III. 3.

that custom.[1] This shows that in spite of the lack of deep-rooted love for the husband, generally the wife did not exercise her right of divorcing him, but preferred to remain in her uncomfor table condition. Similar may have been the case with some husbands also. It is said that a Brāhmaṇa who was asked, whether he would keep or abandon his wife found guilty of adultery, expressed his view against deserting her and remarrying.[2] It appears that it was only in very few cases that divorce may have been resorted to. Stories generally refer to extreme cases, whether good or bad. Hence, it can be concluded that divorce was resorted to only in extreme cases; among the lower castes, for whom in most cases marriage tie has never been very exacting like that of the higher castes, it was fregment. The situation remained the same even during the later period. Later Smṛiti writers like Nārada[3] and Parāśara[4] permit divorce only in extreme cases. But society changed gradually and by the 12th century A.D. the law-givers declared that neither widow-marriage, nor divorce, nor remarriage could be practised in the Kali-Yuga.[5] Yet these customs went out of vogue only among the higher caste Hindus.

Conjugal Life :

The Buddhist as well as the Brahmanical sources reveal that the conjugal life of the wife and the husband was generally ideal and happy, marked by mutual respect and deep-rooted affection. But we come across stories referring to several cases of unhappy conjugal life as a result of the wives's wickedness and infidelity, and in some cases due to the husband's unfaithfulness. As the stories take delight in exaggerating certain incidents, their evidence should be used with caution. The *Jātaka* narratives, which speak of the unfaithful nature of women,

1. *Jā.* IV. 35, आरा दूरे न इध अत्थि परम्परा नाम कुले इमस्मिं, तं कुलवत्तं अनुवत्तमाना नाहं कुले अन्तिमगन्धिनी अहुं एतस्स वादस्स जिगुच्छमाना अकामिका वद्ध चरामि तुह्यं ति ।

2. *Jā.* III. 351, ब्रह्मण, किं सा येव भरिया होतु उदाहु अञ्ञा गण्हिस्ससीति । सायेव मे होतु पंडिता' ति ।

3. *Nārada*. XII. 97.

4. *Parāśara* IV. 28, quoted in *The Position of Women in Hindu Civilisation* p. 180.

5. Devaṇabhaṭṭa, *SCS*, p. 221; Laghu-Āśvalāyana, XXI, 14; The *Position of Women in Hindu Civilisation*, p. 182.

are primarily intended to warn Bhikshus against the danger of falling from their ideal of celibacy. They were to keep themselves aloof from feminine charm, which overcomes man's reason. It is with this aim that every attempt is made to depict womanfolk as wicked and unfaithful. A *Jātaka* story says, 'The ways of women are difficult to understand;[1] their mind is fickle like that of a monkey.'[2] Another story says that a husband who quenched the thirst of his wife by his own blood was got rid by her; because she fell in leave with a robber, though the latter's limbs were mutilated.[3] There are stories describing how wives used to enjoy with their paramours in their husbands' absence.[4] There are some stories of wives exposing the husband to the ridicule of the multitude, like that of the *Ruhaka Jātaka*.[5] We also come across stories which describe the wife fleeing with another and the husband chasing her.[6] The *Chullavagga* refers to woman conceiving from her paramour and bringing about an abortion.[7]

The stories do not mention only the infidelity of the women, but they also refer to men, who did not remain faithful to their wives. They are shown intriguing with others' wives.[8] Some wives being disappointed with their conjugal life entered monastery.[9] Some husbands gave sound drubbing, threw outside the door and discarded their wives due to the latter's misconduct, as we find it in the *Takkala Jātaka*.[10] Sometimes the wife seems to have been discarded on ordinary grounds. Thus it is said in a *Jātaka* that a girl named Kānā, who had gone to her mother's house, did not turn up in spite of her husband's sending messenger thrice, and her husband brought another wife.[11] There may have been a few unfaithful husbands who would be ready to part away from their wives for serving their

1. *Jā.* V. 446.
2. *Jā.* V. 445.
3. *Jā.* II. 116-18.
4. *Jā.* Nos. 62, 130, 199, 212, 257 and others.
5. *Jā.* II. 113-15.
6. *Jā.* VI. 338.
7. *C. V.* X. 13. 1.
8. *Jā.* V. 61.
9. A *Jātaka* story says that a lady whose husband used to enjoy elsewhere neglecting his wife joined the Order (*Jā.* II. 229).
10. *Jā.* IV. 45-49.
11. *Jā.* I. 477.

selfish motives, as we find in the *Ummadantī Jātaka.*[1]

But in spite of such references to unfaithful wives and husbands, the Buddhist sources reveal that the conjugal life was happy. Faithful wives and husbands were not lacking in society. The ideal before the married couple was of a happy married life. At the time of the betrothal, the best benediction that an aged and respected member would bestow upon the couple was to express the hope for their indissoluble friendship[2]. This very ideal is expressed by Brahmanical sources, which states that there should be absolute identity in the aesthetic, material, and moral interests of the couple.[3] The Buddhist as well as the Brahmanical sources reveal that the wife was regarded as the best friend.[4] There were wives whose love for their husbands was so intense that they pined for reunion with them even in the after-life.[5] The Brāhmaṇa, Dhaniya was proud of his faithful wife, says the *Sutta Nipāta.*[6] In the *Jatākas* are cited illustrations of faithful, virtuous, and dutiful wives, such as Sujātā,[7] Sambulā[8] and others, whose conjugal life was marked by joy, unity, and oneness of mind.

Instances of faithful husbands are also not lacking. It is said at one place that people never love others as they do a beloved wife.[9] A husband, though his wife was found to be guilty of adultery, did not discard her as already observed. It is well known that the Dharmaśāstras do not favour discarding faithful wives. A few cases of discarded wives, who were found

1. *Jā.* No. 527. The story says that the commander-in-chief of a king, finding the latter infatuated by his wife's beauty, said to him that he was ready to abandon his wife for his master's pleasure. Probably the general was in fear of his being an innocent victim of the king's wrath as a result of his wife's glamour and beauty, and hence with a viwe to saving his life and to gain the king's favour he showed such indifference to her honour.

2. *Jā.* VI. 323, अजेय्यमेसा तव होतु मेत्ती भरियाय कच्चान पियाय सद्धि ।

3. *Āp. Dh. S.* II. 6. 14. 16-20; *Manu.* IX. 101.

4. *K. S.* I. 52. 'The wife is here below comrade supreme; *Ait. Br.* VII. 13.

5. *A. M.* II. 61.

6. *Su. Ni.* I. 2. 5.

7. *Jā.* II. 121-5.

8. *Jā.* V. 88-98, She is described as serving her leprosy-stricken husband in the forest.

9. *Jā.* VI. 458, सत्ता हि पियभरियासु विय सेसेसु आलयं न करोन्ति ।

to be unfaithful, are in accordance with the Dharmaśāstra rules. But such cases would have been only a few. The law-givers regard the violation of the vow of conjugal fidelity as the greatest sin. That is why they neither favour the wife disregarding her husband, nor the husband discarding his faithful wife. Āpastamba prescribes that a husband who discarded his wife was to beg in seven houses, clad in ass's skin with the hair turned outside.[1] Manu prescribes the imposition of a fine by the state on such a husband.[2] A wife forsaking her husband was to go through the *kṛichchhra* penance.[3]

1. *Āp. Dh. S.* I. 10. 28. 19.
2. *Manu.* VIII. 389.
3. *Āp. Dh. S.* I. 10. 28. 20.

CHAPTER IV

THE COURTESANS

There is no doubt that our period was one of prosperity in the history of Northern India. The region corresponding to Eastern Uttar Pradesh and Bihar was studded with a number of flourishing cities and towns, and had developed a busy urban civilisation. Rājagṛiha, Vaiśālī, Śrāvastī, Kauśāmbī, etc.[1] were among the foremost cities; later Pāṭaliputra also rose to eminence and surpassed others. The courtesans were the special feature of the city life, and they added to its gaity and dignity. The presence of a courtesan in a royal city was a matter of pride for its citizens. This is shown by the way in which Sālavatī was installed as a courtesan of Rājagṛiha. It is said that a merchant of Rājagṛiha went to Vaiśālī and saw the flourishing condition of that city, beautified by the grace of Ambapālī. After returning from Vaiśālī, he approached the Magadhan king Seṇiya Bimbisāra and said: 'Vaiśālī, Your Majesty, is an opulent, prosperous town. ....And there is the courtesan Ambapālī, who is graceful, beautiful, pleasant, gifted with the highest beauty of complexion, well versed in singing, dancing, and lute-playing, much visited by desirous people. Through her Vaiśālī becomes more and more flourishing. May it please Your Majesty, let us also install a courtesan.'[2] The king said, "Well, my good Sir, look for such a girl whom you can install as a courtesan."[3]

Now at that time there was at Rājagṛiha a girl Sālavatī by name, who was beautiful, graceful, pleasant, gifted with the highest beauty of complexion. The girl Sālavatī was installed as a courtesan.[4] It seems that selection of a courtesan was made in recognition of the beauty and art possessed by her; and hence Śālavatī took it as a pride.

1. In the 7th and 6th centuries B.C. there existed a number of cities and towns in the country among which Rājagṛiha, Champā, Vaiśālī, Mithilā, Sāketa, Śrāvastī, Kauśāmbī, Vārāṇasī, Mathurā, Kāmpilya, Ujjaini, Pratishṭhāna and Roruka were the important ones—(Rys Davids, *Buddhist India*).
2. *M.V.* VIII. 1. 2.
3. *M.V.* VIII. 1. 2.
4. *M.V.* VIII. 1. 3.

The *Vinaya-Piṭaka* bears an eloquent testimony to the fact that courtesans enjoyed a respectable status in society. They were not only a means through which the nobles satisfied their thirst for beauty, but they were also the real custodians of such fine arts as singing, dancing, and music, through which the aesthetic emotions of the people were aroused and satisfied. As the place of dancing and singing was very high in ancient India, it seems that the courtesans appeared in the royal palaces on festive occasions to give the finest exhibitions of dancing and singing. The fact that the Buddha accepted the invitation extended to him by Ambapālī and went to her residence with the Bhikshu Saṅgha for the meals,[1] and that she dedicated the Ambapālī grove for the Saṅgha,[2] shows that a courtesan occupied no mean position. The way in which Ambapālī proceeded to see the Buddha at the Koṭigāma with a number of magnificent vehicles[3] shows that her paraphernalia was almost royal. That the great physician Jīvaka was born of a courtesan of Rājagṛiha, named Sālavatī[4], shows that some of the sons of the courtesans could rise to a high position in society.

The *Jātakas* inform us that generally the courtesans enjoyed sound financial status. They tell us that Sāmā,[5] Sulasā,[6] Kālī[7] and others[8] earned one thousand Kahāpaṇas every night. Sulasā lived with a train of five hundred girls.[9] Kālī used to spend daily five hundred pieces of money for clothes, perfumes, garlands, and one who visited her had to put on clothes supplied by her.[10] Such accounts in the popular stories are no doubt undue exaggerations. But the information of the *Vinaya Piṭaka* appears to be quite correct, and we may accept fifty to one hundred silver punch-marked coins as their daily income, which

1. *M. V.* VI. 30. 2.
2. *M. V.* VI. 30. 5.
3. *M. V.* VI. 30. 1.
4. *M. V.* VIII. 1. 4; Prince Abhaya was conceived by Ambapālī.
5. *Kaṇavera Jā.* (No. 318).
6. *Sulasā Jā.* (No. 419).
7. *Jā.* IV. 248. (No. 481, *Takkāriya Jā*).
8. e.g. *Aṭṭhāna Jā.* (No. 425).
9. *Jā.* III. 435.
10. *Jā.* IV. 249.

would have enabled them to live a luxurious life.[1] In the *Jātaka* stories we come across courtesans of both high as well as low character, which is but natural. It is not known whether the percentage of those possessed of fine qualities was high. The courtesan Kālī is described in the *Takkāriya Jātaka* as one possessed of the qualities of social decency and self-respect. She had a brother, Tuṇḍila, who was a debauch, a drunkard, and a gambler, and he wasted her wealth. She tried to restrain him, but in vain. One day he was beaten and deprived of his clothes he was clad in. When he went to his sister wrapped in a rag of loin-cloth, she drove him out with the help of the maid-servants.[2] Another *Jātaka* speaks of a courtesan who had became poor, because of her waiting for a youth for three years, from whom she had received one thousand pieces of coins, accepting not even a piece of betel from another man.[3] The *Sulasā Jātaka* represents Sulasā as a woman of rare wisdom and courage. She had saved the life of a robber, and as she was in love with him, she did not welcome any visitor. But the robber one day took her at the top of a hill with the mean mentality of killing her and possessing the ornaments. She prayed him for sparing her life, but no mercy was aroused within his cruel and greedy heart. Seeing no way of escape, she with the pretence of embracing him, threw him down the precipice to be crushed to pieces.[4]

There is also the other side of the character of courtesans. A story describes how a courtesan, who was paid by her lover, a young merchant a thousand pieces of current coins daily, did not welcome him, when one day he went to her without money. She said, "Sir, I am but a courtesan, I do not give my favours without a thousand pieces, you must bring the sum." All his entreaties proved to be futile, and she ordered her maids

1. Ambapālī is described as earning 50 Kahāpaṇas per night (*M. V.* VIII. 1. 1.), whereas Sālavatī is said to have charging 100 Kahāpaṇas (*M.V.* VIII 1. 3). This shows that the income of the Rājagṛiha courtesan was higher than that of Vaiśālī. Probably the standard of living was high in Rājagṛiha, and the nobility could afford to pay more for the courtesan as would have been the case in Vaiśālī or other towns of that period. Similar would have been the case later on at Pāṭaliputra, when it became the capital of the Magadhan Empire. The charges of the courtesans of Vārāṇasī as given in the *Jātakas* are unrealistic.

2. *Jā.* IV. 248-9.

3. *Jā.* II. 380.

4. *Jā.* III. 435-38. (No. 419.)

to drive him away. Being discontented he became an ascetic.[1] The *Kaṇavera Jātaka* speaks of another courtesan of low character, Sāmā who fell in love at the sight of a robber and saved his life by replacing him by her lover, a young merchant.[2]

Courtesans of high order like Ambapālī, Sālavatī and others, who adorned the royal cities, enjoyed respectable position in society. The *Jātakas* mostly refer to them. Ordinary courtesans, who sold their flesh for money, were looked down upon. The profession is described as a vile trade (*nīchakamma*).[3] The expressions like a house of ill fame (*nīchcha-ghara* or *gaṇikā-ghara*)[4] and a low woman (*duratthi kumbhadāsī*)[5] indicate that the profession of the prostitutes was not considered to be respectable.

1. *Jā.* III. 475-76.
2. *Jā.* III. 59-60.
3. *Jā.* III. 60.
4. *Jā.* III. 61; IV. 249.
5. *Jā.* VI. 228.

CHAPTER V

FOOD AND DRINK

Articles of Food

Rice was the staple food of the people of North-Eastern India during our period too. The Buddhist[1] and the Brahmanical[2] sources mention several varieties of rice, such as Sāli (Śāli), Vīhi (Vṛīhi), Taṇḍula, Hāyana, Shashṭikā and Nīvāra which seem to have been cultivated in this region. Śāli of Magadha is highly praised by Patañjali.[3] Mahāśali seems to have been a superior variety of Śāli, and according to Hwui Li it was grown only in Magadha.[4] The rice of superior quality was enjoyed by the rich sections of society, whereas the inferior variety was the food of the people belonging to the lower strata[5]. Generally people preferred to eat three year old rice as is the case today.[6] Such rice also could have been available to the higher sections of society, not to the poor, who earned their livelihood either by day labour or by serving others.

Cooked rice was called Bhatta or Bhakta (modern Bhāta).[7] Pāṇini calls it also Odana.[8] Bhatta was not eaten alone. It was ordinarily eaten with Sūpa (pulses) and vegetables[9] as we do. The *Jātakas* inform us that the dish constituted of rice and meat or fish was the favourable one; even ascetics are seen relishing it[10]. If ghee was added to, it became more delicious. Śāriputta is represented as serving rice, red fish and new ghee

1. *M. N.* I. 57; III. 90., *Jā.* I. 429, 484; II. 110, 135, 378; IV. 276; VI. 367.
2. *Āśva. G. S.* I. 17. 2; *Śāṅ. G. S.* I. 24. 3; I. 28. 6; *Pā.* III 1. 48; III. 3. 48; V. 1. 90; V. 2. 2.
3. Bhāshya, I. 19.
4. Agrawala, *India As Known to Pāṇini*, p. 103, Hwui Li states that Huen Tsang while staying at Nālandā was entertained with this variety of rice.
5. *Jā.* I. 486.
6. *Jā.* Nos. 23 & 26.
7. *Jā.* IV. 43 (*Takkala-Jā.*); *Pā.* IV. 4. 100.
8. *Pā.* IV. 4. 67.
9. *Jā.* VI. 372 (*Mahāummaga-Jā.*).
10. *Kesava-Jā.*

to Bimbādevī. Pāṇini, while giving examples of eatables, tells us that meat, Sūpa, vegetables, Guḍa, ghee, etc. were added to Bhāta[2].

Rice-milk was highly praised by the Buddha, and he recommended it for the Bhikshus as a morning breakfast.[3] Honey was also mixed to it. Yavāgū (rice or barley gruel) was a common liquid food. In modern Bihar and Bengal rice-gruel is the food of the commoners.[4]

Sattu,[5] so common in Bihar of today, was also eaten during our period and is referred to both by the Buddhist and Brahmanical sources. Pāṇinī informs us that it was mixed with water and eaten.[6] Udamantha or Udakamantha was another variety of Sattu which was made of fried rice (Bhujiyā ke Sattu of modern times).[7] Kummāsa or Kulmāsha was a coarse food of the poor.[8]

There were a few special preparations which also in most cases have been retained till today. Sweet cake, modern Puvā, was a favourite sweet. Puvā is prepared either from powdered wheat or rice. According to the *Illīsa Jātaka* it was prepared from rice, milk, sugar, ghee, and honey.

Piṭṭhakhajjaka (modern Khājā) was another sweetmeat liked by all.[9] Sāriputta was fond of it, but took a vow not to eat it, for it tended to make him greedy.[10] A king is seen entertaining an ascetic with Yavāgū and Piṭṭhakhajjaka.[11] Palala was a delicious sweetmeat mentioned by Pāṇini.[12] It was made of powdered Tila and sugar or Guḍa. Modern equivalent of it is Tila-Kuṭa with which Northern India is well acquainted. Gayā is famous in Bihar for its Tilakuṭa, and during

1. *Jā.* No. 292.
2. *Pā.* VI. 1. 128.
3. *M.V.* VI. 24-25.
4. Rice-gruel or the Yavāgū Bhāta is prepared in this way : 'Water is added to the cooked rice at night; in the morning mustard oil, tamarind, chilli and salt are added to it. Then it is eaten.
5. *Sattubhasta Jā.* (No. 402).
6. *Pā.* VI. 3. 59.
7. *Pā.* VI. 3. 60.
8. *Kummāsapiṇḍa Jā.* (No. 415).
9. Khājā is a popular sweetmeat in Bihar. A place named Silāo, near Rājgir, is famous for its Khājā, and it appears that during our period Rājagriha may have been known for it.
10. *Jā.* I. 31. *Visavanta-Jā.* (No. 69).
11. *Brahachhatta-Jā.* (No. 336).
12. *Pā.* VI. 2. 128.

our period this sweet may have been well known in Magadha and the adjoining regions.

Pishṭaka, prepared from the ground paste of rice, seems to have been fairly common. It is well known in the villages of Bihar and is called Piṭhā.

In addition to these, there may have been other preparations also.

Milk and milk-products, like curd, butter and ghee were largely eaten[1].

Vegetables and fruits have always formed a considerable part of the Indian dietary. During our period vegetables like pumpkins, gourds, cucumbers, etc. and fruits like mango and jamboo (Jambū) were included in the diet of people.[2]

Meat-Eating

Meat was eaten during the Vedic period. In the *Ṛigveda*, Indra and Agni are described as eating the meat of oxen and cows.[3] Horses, bulls, oxen, cows, and rams were sacrificed for Agni.[4] In the *Śatapatha Brāhmaṇa*, meat is described as the best kind of food[5], and the Sage Yājñavalkya is represented as eating the meat of cows and oxen[6]. All these show that during the Vedic and the later period meat-eating was quite common.

The Buddhist literature makes it quite clear that during our period non-vegetarian diet was popular. The Jaina and the Buddhist philosophies of non-injury to living beings had in no way affected the practice of meat-eating. Those who preached the doctrine of non-violence accepted meat, if offered. The *Mahāvagga* represents the Bhikshus accepting it in alms.[7] In the *Mahāparinibbāna-suttanta* the Buddha himself is described as eating pig-meat (Sūkara-maddava),[8] and in a *Jātaka* story he is found cherishing cooked meat at the house of a house-

1. *A. N.* II. 95.
   Pā. IV. 3. 160; IV. 2. 18; II. 4. 14.
2. *Jā.* V. 37; *Pā.* IV. 1.42; VIII. 4. 5; IV. 3. 165.
3. *Ṛig.* X. 86. 14. Indra Says, 'They cook for me 15 plus 20 oxen'.
   Ṛig. VIII. 43. 11.
4. *Ṛig.* X. 91. 14.
5. *Śat. Br.* XI. 7. 1. 3.
6. *Śat. Br.* III. 1. 2. 21.
7. *M. V.* VI. 23. 10-15.
8. At Pāvā, the Buddha was served with *Sūkara-maddava* by Chunda Karmāraputra (*D. N.* II. 127; *Udāna*, VIII. 5).

holder.[1] He is also found arguing that there is no sin in eating meat; one who kills an animal and cooks its meat is a sinner.[2] This logic is not quite convincing; because killing takes place for those who eat meat, and people may be compelled to slaughter animals for them. Both are equally culpable. It seems that the custom of meat-eating was so common that the Buddha did not prohibit it, except for the Bhikshus, who could accept it only in alms and could not procure it otherwise.

The Buddhist literature refers to the cattle-butcher,[3] the sheep-butcher,[4] the goat-butcher,[5] the pig-butcher,[6] the deer-hunter[7], the fowler[8] and the slaughter-houses (Sūnā),[9] implying thereby that the wide prevalence of the practice of meat-eating had given rise to professionals who saught their livelihood by killing various animals and supplying their meat to the people. Meat was carried on carts to the towns and cities for being sold in the open market.[10] Meat and fish were important items of diet in the royal kitchen.[11] On the festival days and on occasions like marriages meat was lavishly consumed.

In the *Jātakas* the Brāhmaṇas also are described as relishing meat and fish with great delight. They enjoyed the non-vegetarian diet on the occasions of sacrifices[12] and the Śrāddha ceremony.[13] In the latter case, they generally killed the goat.[14] This *Jātaka* account that the Brāhmaṇas ate meat is confirmed by the Dharmaśāstra literature. Āpastamba says that a Vedic teacher should not eat meat in the months from Upākarma to Utsarga.[15] This shows that a Brāhmaṇa teaching the *Vedas* could take meat in the other months of the year. From this it can be assumed that Brāhmaṇas other than the Vedic

1. *Jā.* II. 262.
2. *Jā.* II. 263.
3. *M. N.* I. 364; II. 193; *K. S.* II. 170-11.
4. *K. S.* II. 171.
5. *G. S.* I. 229.
6. *K. S.* II. 171.
7. *Ibid.*
8. *Ibid.*
9. *M. N.* I. 364.
10. *Maṁsa-Jā.* (No. 315).
11. *Jā.* I. 242.
12. *Jā.* III. 429.
13. *Jā.* I. 166 (No. 18).
14. *Ibid.*
15. *ĀP. Dh. S.* II. 2. 5. 16.

teachers and priests could eat meat without any restriction. Āpastamba further says that if meat was offered to a guest, the merit was equal to the performance of the Dvādasah sacrifice[1]. It is well known that it was eaten on the occasion of Madhuparka. There is no reason to believe that the Brāhmaṇa guests were not served with meat. On the other hand, it seems more probable that a Brāhmaṇa guest would have been served with the best possible delicacies including meat with a view to reaping the fruits of the merit of honouring him. Manu says that the Brāhmaṇa should be served with meat at the time of Śrāddha.[2] For the non-acceptance of the non-vegetarian diet on this occasion, he is cursed for being born as an animal for twenty-one births.[3] This religious sanction leaves no doubt that on occasions like religious sacrifices and Śraddha, etc., and when offered by a host, the Brāhmaṇas ate non-vegetarian diet. This is further supported by the accounts of the Greek writers, who tell us that the Brāhmaṇas ate meat at the expiry of the studentship, when they became householders.[4]

There were a few animals whose flesh was not eaten. Buddha had prohibited the meat of elephant, horse, dog, lion, tiger, panther, bear, and hyena.[5] Āpastamba[6] and Manu[7] do not allow the meat of animals with five nails, except Śvāvidha (bear or hedgehog), porcupine, iguana, rhinoceros, hare and tortoise, and among animals with one hoof, only of the camel. It seems that only a few animals were prohibited; others were eaten.

Deer was a favourite animal whose meat was eaten. Hunters engaged in killing deer were known as Mig-luddakas.[8] Deer-meat was carried on carts to the markets of towns and cities for sale.[9] The First *Rock Edict* of Aśoka tells us that before the king's prohibition of non-vegetarian diet in the royal kitchen, antilope-meat was included in his favourite dish. The

1. *ĀP. Dh. S.* II. 3. 7. 4.
2. *Manu.* III. 227.
3. *Manu.* V. 35.
4. *Meg.*, p. 99. *Strabo*, XVI. 1. 59.
5. *M. V.* VI. 23. 10-15.
6. *ĀP. Dh. S.*, I. 5. 17. 37.
7. *Manu.* V. 18.
8. *Jā.* III. 49.
9. *Ibid.*

Buddhist literature by mentioning the pig-butcher[1] and describing the pig-meat as a good gift[2] shows that it was largely eaten. The pig was generally killed on the wedding-day for the marriage-feast.[3] As a squire is described as killing a pig on the day of his daughter's marriage,[4] it appears that not only the low caste people, but also the aristocrats were fond of it. Sometimes we find pigs being fattened before killing.[5] The Dharmaśāstra writers allow the meat of the wild pig only, and not of the village one,[6] but it is not so in the Buddhist literature.

As regards the killing of cattle, our sources show that in certain sections of society cows and oxen were slaughtered, but there was growing a tendency to revere the cow and to spare the useful bull. There are references made to the cow-butcher (Goghātaka) and his apprentice,[7] the place of slaughtering cows (Goghātaka-sūnaṁ)[8] and the razor for killing them,[9] which would show that cattle-meat was included among eatables; on the other hand, a *Jātaka* story tells us that an old ox was killed during the days of famine,[10] which suggests that some people did not like killing of the useful cattle. But the Dharmaśāstras allow the meat of milch cows and oxen.[11] Cow was killed in Śrāddha[12] and for entertaining guests in the Madhuparka.[13] The bull was killed in the Sūlāgava sacrifice.[14] The Brahmanical literature thus shows that cattle meat was eaten on special occasions by the priests.

The *Jātaka* stories mention among birds, pigeons,[15] geese,[16]

1. *K. S.* II. 171.
2. *A. N.* III. 49.
3. *Jā.* I. 196-97; II. 419.
4. *Jā.* I. 196-97.
5. *Ibid.*
6. *ĀP. Dh. S.* I. 5. 17. 29.
7. *D. N.* II. 294; *M. N.* I. 58; II. 193.
8. *M. N.* I. 364.
9. *M. N.* I. 449; II. 193.
10. *Jā.* II. 135.
11. *Āp. Dh. S.* I. 5. 17. 30-31.
12. *Āp. Dh. S.* II. 7. 16. 26; *Bau. G. S.* II. 11. 51; *Hi. G. S.* II. 5. 15. 1.
13. *Āśva. G. S.* I. 24. 30-33; *V. Dh. S.* IV. 8.
14. *History of Dharmaśāstra*, Vol. II, p. 777.
15. *Romaka Jā.* (No. 277).
16. *Puṇṇandī Jā.* (No. 214).

herons,[1] peacocks,[2] crows,[3] and cocks[4] as eatables. The Dharmaśāstras[5] prohibit the flesh of birds which are carnivorous, subsist on raw flesh, that dwell in the villages, that scratch dunghills and the flesh of Chātakas, parrots, geese, cranes and so on. There was a notion that the qualities of a bird eaten would be transmitted to the eater,[6] and therefore it was responsible for prohibiting the flesh of cruel birds. Domesticated birds were not eaten due to the feeling of compassion for them. Though the flesh of domesticated cock was not permitted, it was eaten. It seems quite probable that the strict rules of the Dharmaśāstras were followed only by the priestly class; others preferred a liberal path.

Both the Buddhist as well as Brahmanical sources disclose that fish was freely eaten. In the houses of nobles and in the royal kitchen several varieties of it were cooked.[7] Brāhmaṇas also ate it.[8] According to the *Pāraskara-Gṛihya-sūtra* it was given to a baby at the time of the Annaprāśana.[9] But the Dharmaśāstra writers do not allow all the species of fish to be eaten. Āpastamba prohibits the Cheṭa, the Makara, those with snake-like heads, those having strange forms and those subsisting on dead flesh.[10] Manu no doubt expresses his opinion against meat-eating, but allows the lion-faced and those having scales to be eaten usually, and the Pāṭhina and the Rohita, if used in rites for gods and manes.[11] We do not know how far these rules were observed. In the Buddhist literature fishery is described as being practised on a large scale, which suggests that a high percentage of the total population cherished fish-diet. People of North Bihar and Bengal are even today very fond of it, and the same may have been the case during the period under review.

1. *Puṇṇandī Jā.*
2. *Ibid.*
3. *Ibid.*
4. *Jā.* II. 412.
5. *Gau. Dh. S.* XVII. 29 and 34-35; *Āp. Dh. S.* I. 5. 17. 32-36; *V. Dh. S.* XIV. 48; *Manu.* V. 11-14; *Vishṇu-Dh.S.*, 51. 29-31.
6. *Pā. G. S.* I. 19.
7. *Jā.* II. 242-43.
8. *Jā.* III. 429.
9. *Pā. G. S.* I. 19. 9.
10. *ĀP. Dh. S.* I. 5. 17. 38-39.
11. *Manu.* V. 14-16.

The *Jātakas* mention that lizards and snakes were also eaten.[1] The religious books do not allow these creatures to be eaten. But even today some backward people eat snakes. Similar might have been the case in the past also. Lizard is not known as being eaten. But the *Jātakas* mention that even ascetics ate lizards. Thus in one place it is said that lizards were caught in a great number, cooked, and served to an ascetic with vinegar and salt, and he was very pleased with the savoury dish;[2] at another place we find that he so much relished lizard-meat at the house of a householder that he planned to kill one and cook it.[3] Representing ascetics in such a manner may be due to the Buddhist bias of describing them greedy, but even persons like the Kuṭumbikas figure as enjoying roasted lizards.[4] Eating of lizards appears rather unusual, but it may have been in practice among people of the lower stratum of society.

Meat-eating was quite common. High and low, both cherished the non-vegetarian diet. But the religious sects of Buddhism and Jainism discouraged killing and meat-eating for the monks. Because Buddhism did not discourage the lay followers from eating meat, the practice prevailed in the land of the Buddha, in spite of his preaching of non-injury to all living beings. The priest class following the commands of the religious books did not eat the flesh of a number of animals and birds; but the common man followed the local customs, and hence he ate the meat of such animals and birds also which were prohibited.

Drinking Liquor

The *Ṛigveda* refers to Soma and Surā as intoxicating drinks, the former probably reserved for being offered to gods and drunk by priests; while the latter as a drink for common man. The *Atharvaveda*[5] by stating that the reward for the performance of sacrifices is heaven, where there are lakes full of

1. *Jā.* V. 163 (Nos. 524, 138),
मयं अज्ज गोधपोतकं पि न लभिम्ह, इमं नागराजं वधित्वा खादिस्साम ।
2. *Jā.* I. 480-81 (No. 138), गामवासिनो निक्खमित्वा गोधा गहेत्वा सिनिद्धसम्भारयुत्तं अविलानम्बिलं गोधमंसं सम्पादेत्वा तापसस्स अदंसु ।
3. *Godha. Jā.* (No. 325).
4. *Jā.* III. 106-7.
5. *A.V.* IV. 34. 6.

ghee and honey, and wherein liquor flows like water, shows that wine was quite popular. The *Brāhmaṇas* tell us how Surā was prepared[1] and that in the Sautrāmaṇī sacrifice a Brāhmaṇa was hired for drinking its dregs offered in it.[2] But the *Kāṭhaka Saṁhitā* states that liquor should not be drunk by a Brāhmaṇa and that a Kshatriya does not incur sin by drinking,[3] and thus shows a tendency towards restraining the religious section of society from indulging in drinking even during the early period. But there is no reference to its restriction so far as other castes were concerned.

The Buddhist, the Jaina, and the Brahmanical sources disclose the wide prevalence of the practice of drinking with the exception of the religious class. There are references to Surā and Meraya (Maireya) as intoxicating drinks.[4] The Brahmanical literature by mentioning that Surā was offered to the female manes at the time of Śrāddha shows that it was not looked upon as an objectionable drink.[5] The *Jātakas* inform us that there were crowded taverns, where liquor was kept filled in jars and sold.[6] The owners of the taverns kept apprentices, who helped them in their business.[7] We do not find people of low grades maintaining taverns; but generally they used to be Seṭṭhis, who were the aristocratic Vaiśyas owning considerable property. References which tell us that people went to the taverns for drinking with their wives,[8] that persons like Illīsa whose wealth is estimated to have been worth eighty crores drank liquor,[9] and so on show that drinking was not looked down upon.

The Buddhist and Jaina sources further inform us that the

1. *Śat. Br.* XII. 7. 3. 5; *S.B.E.* XLIV. 223.

2. *Tai.Br.* I. 8. 6, quoted in *History of Dharmaśāstra*, Vol. II, p. 793. ब्राह्मणं परिक्रीणीयादुच्छेषणस्य पातरम् । ब्राह्मणो हि आहुत्य उच्छेषणस्य पाता ।

3. *Kā. Saṁ.* XXII. 12, quoted in *History of Dharmaśāstra*, Vol. II, p. 793.

4. *C.V.* XII. 1. 3. *A.N.* II. 53, सुरं पिवन्ति मेरयं पिवन्ति । II. 54; IV. 5; 246; *Itivuttaka*, 74; *Pāṇini*, II. 4. 25; VI. 2. 70.

5. *Āśva. G.S.* II. 5. 5; *Pā. G.S.* III. 3. 11, स्त्रीभ्यश्चोपसेचनं च कर्षूषु सुरया तर्पणेन चाञ्जानुलेपनं स्रजश्च ।

6. *Jā.* I. 251-52 (Nos. 47, 78).

7. *Ibid.*

8. *Jā.* IV. 114.

9. *Jā.* No. 78.

festive occasions were marked by feasting, drinking, and merry-making.[1] As described in the following chapter, there used to be a festival known as the Surā-Nakkhata (drinking-festival) dedicated to unrestricted drinking, feasting, and dancing.[2] On such occasions even ascetics are described as resorting to drinking, which appears to be rather unusual.[3] In one of the *Jātakas* an interesting practice of drinking is referred to. It is said that a king sitting on the splendid pavilion in the palace courtyard, on a royal throne, surrounded by his courtiers drank liquor before the gathering of the citizens, who also did the same.[4] This description shows that neither any hesitation in drinking nor any secracy about it was observed. But the story tells us that the king on the interference of Sakka realised that drinking was a sinful act.

What percentage of the total population indulged in drinking is difficult to determine. The Buddhist, the Jaina, and the Brahmanical sources agree that the priests were not to drink liquor. According to the rules of the Vinaya, the novices were not to drink strong drinks and intoxicating liquors,[5] and the same rule applied to the elders. However, in sickness a Bhikshu could take oil decoction mixed with strong drink.[6] But this refers only to an exception for an emergency period. According to a *Jātaka* the Brāhmaṇas regarded it a sin to indulge in drinking.[7] A virtuous man was expected to be immune from this bad habit.[8] The same is the case with the Jaina *Sūtras*, which prohibit the Jaina monks from visiting festive gatherings, where drinking took place.[9]

We learn from the Dharmaśāstras that the Brāhmaṇas were not allowed to indulge in drinking. Āpastamba says that liquor was never to be drunk by a Brāhmaṇa (सर्वं मद्यमपेयम्).[10]

1. *Infra.* p. 82; *S.B.E.* XXII, pp. 94-95.
2. *Jā.* I. 362; 489.
3. *Jā.* I. 362. (No. 81).
4. *Kumbha Jā.* (No. 512).
5. *S.B.E.* XIII. 211, 215.
6. *M.V.* VI. 14. 1.
7. *Jā.* V. 467; तात अयुत्तं ते कतं सोत्थियकुले जातेन सुरं पिवन्तेन, मा पुन एवं अकासीति ।
8. *Jā.* VI. 15. (No. 538).
9. *S.B.E.* XXII, pp. 94-95.
10. *Āp. Dh. S.* I. 5. 17. 21.

According to Gautama all intoxications were prohibited to a Brāhmaṇa, but only Paishṭi to a Kshatriya and a Vaiśya.[1] Vaśishṭha says that if a Brāhmaṇa wife drinks Surā, she is not permitted by the gods to reach the world of her husband.[2] He further tells us that even the husband is guilty, if his wife drinks liquor, because she is his half portion.[3] Gautama and Manu prescribe severe penance for a Brāhmaṇa, if he drank liquor.[4] According to the *Vishṇu-Dharmasūtra* intoxications of ten kinds were forbidden only for the Brāhmaṇas, but not, for the Kshatriyas and Vaiśyas.[5] From these references it becomes quite clear that a Brāhmaṇa was not allowed to drink any intoxicating drink; but people belonging to other castes were not subjected to such restrictions . Intoxication is responsible for undesirable acts, and hence the idea was that a Brāhmaṇa who should always have a clear intellect should not drink liquor. Drunkenness might lead him to such acts as a Brāhmaṇa should not do.[6] The Jaina *Sūtras* express a similar view on the consequences of drinking.[7] One of the *Jātakas* tells us how people broke their heads, feet, and hands on *Surā-Nakkhata* days, after drinking hard which led to quarrelling.[8] The principle of abstinence applied also to the students, and Brahmachārins of all castes had to abstain completely from all kinds of intoxications.[9] This shows that generally the householders of all castes except the Brāhmaṇas indulged in drinking. But Manu prohibits all the twice born from drinking.[10] This shows

1. *Gau. Dh. S.* II. 26.
2. *V. Dh. S.* XXI. 11, या ब्राह्मणी च सुरापी न तां देवाः पतिलोकं नयन्तीहैव ।
3. *V. Dh. S.* XI. 15, पतत्यर्धं शरीरस्य यस्य भार्या सुरां पिवेत् ।
4. *Gau. Dh. S.* XIII. 1; *Manu,* XI. 90-92.
5. *Vi. Dh. S.* XXII. 84, अमेध्यानि दशैतानि मद्यानि ब्राह्मणस्य च ।
राजन्यश्चैव वैश्यश्च स्पृष्ट्वैतानि न दुष्यति ॥
6. *Manu.* XI. 96, अमेध्ये वा पतेन्मत्तो वैदिकं वाप्युदाहरेत् ।
अकार्यमन्यत्कुर्याद्वा ब्राह्मणो मदमोहितः ॥
7. *S. B. E.* XII. pp. 94-95.
8. *Jā.* IV. 115-16.
9. *Āp. Dh. S.* I. 1. 2. 23; *Manu.* II. 177.
10. *Manu.* XI. 93, सुरां वै मलमन्नानां पाप्मा च मलमुच्यते ।
तस्माद्ब्राह्मणराजन्यौ वैश्यश्च न सुरां पिवेत् ॥

Vaśishṭha prescribes the Kṛichchhra penance for a Brāhmaṇa who drank liquor (*V. Dh. S.* XX. 19).

that a tendency was rapidly growing in a section of society that even the Kshatriyas and the Vaiśyas should not drink. How far this new ideology was followed is not known.

Now it can be concluded that during this period drinking was fairly common. The religious class and the Brahmachārins of all castes did not drink. But in view of the *Jātakas* representing them as indulging in drinking on the days of the festivals, it is difficult to assert that all the Brāhmaṇas did not drink. By this period, professions had become manifold; and the Brāhmaṇas also were taking recourse to agriculture, trade, and crafts. It is quite possible that such Brāhmaṇas might have been drinking on festival days. Manu says that a Brāhmaṇa should abandon a wife who drank liquor. This indicates that there were some Brāhmaṇa families which practised drinking, and the prescription of Manu was for the ideal Brāhmaṇas, who had married in such families. What percentage of the Kshatriyas and the Vaiśyas was addicted to drinking is also not certain. The religious class was discouraging them to drink, and it is quite possible that many of them might have given up this habit. The warriors, the nobles, the rich people like the Seṭṭhis and the general public occasionally drank liquor. There were occasions like festivals when drinking was almost universal and social censor was relaxed. Manu's prohibition of drinking for the Kshatriyas and the Vaiśyas seems to refer to a later attitude of society. On days of festivals, the Gṛihasthas are described as freely drinking strong drinks in the *Jātakas* and the Jaina *Sūtras*.

CHAPTER VI

POPULAR FESTIVALS

Our ancient literature reveals that the occasional celebrations of festivals were an important aspect of the social and religious life of the people. The Vedic people organised festive occasions, when they amused themselves by games like chariot races. The later sources inform us that not only the people but also the state took an active part in initiating the celebrations of the festive occasions. The *Rāmāyaṇa* says that festivities and the popular gatherings add to the popularity of the state.[1] Kauṭilya had recommended the organisation of Yātrā, Samāja, Utsava, and Pravahaṇa by the state.[2] From the First *Rock-Edict* of Aśoka we know that there used to be festive gatherings, both religious as well as secular, and he discouraged such gatherings where animals were killed. King Khāravela entertained the citizens of Kaliṅga capital by the organisation of a festive occasion, where took place the display of contests, music, songs and dances before large gatherings.[3] Thus, we find that the festive celebrations were a very important aspect of the social life of the people from the Vedic time downwards.

The Buddhist and the Jaina sources reveal that the people of the period were very keenly interested in merry-making through occasional celebrations of the festivities. The festive celebrations were either religious or secular. Both the occasions were marked by feasting, dancing, singing and so on. The word Samajja, referred to as Samajyā by Pāṇini in the sense of a place where people flock together,[4] occurs often in the Buddhist literature to denote a festive gathering. In the *Vinaya-Piṭaka* a festival on a high place at Rājagriha is described as Girajjasamajja.[5] That it took place at the top of a hill, probably a sacred place,

1. Quoted by B. M. Barua, *Ins. of Aśoka*, Pt. II, p. 224.
2. *Ibid.* According to commentary: यात्रा देवतानां, समाजो लोकसमुदयः, उत्सवः इन्द्रवसन्तोत्सवादिः, प्रवहणमुद्यानभोजनादि ।
3. *Hāthīgumphā Ins.*
4. *Pā.* III. 3.99; *Bhāshya*, II. 152, समजन्ति तस्यां समज्या ।
5. *C.V.* V. 2.6; VI. 2.7.

points to the religious nature of the gathering. It is also said that high officials were invited and provided with special seats. The *Sigālovāda-Sutta* informs us that in a Samajja there used to be dancing, singing, music, recitations, conjuring tricks, and acrobatic shows. The *Jātakas* show that the word Samajja meant either a popular gethering for merry-making or a simple fair. But the occasions on which the Samajjas took place would have been probably religious or at least on auspicious consteilation of stars. In the *Jātakas* Nakkhata (Nakshatra) has been very often used to mark a festive occasion; this shows that it was on special occasions, probably on days auspicious for religious performances, that normally a Samajja took place. However, there used to be occasional gatherings organised by the king, which took place in the courtyard of the royal palace.[1] Wrestling was the usual game which took place on such occasions.[2] There were also amusements such as tournaments of archery,[3] parade of elephants[4] and horse-races,[5] dramatic representations[6] (Nāṭakāni), music competitions,[7] etc. Such festive gatherings seem to have been held on purely secular occasions and may be compared with the festival held annually by Chandragupta Maurya for animal fights of rams, wild bulls, elephants, and rhinoceros and races of chariots drawn by two oxen with a horse between them.[8]

It is difficult to indicate the nature of other festive occasions, because both the religious and secular gatherings had assumed the form of fairs lasting for several days. Means of amusement were similar in both. The *Dīgha-Nikāya* tells us that people used to enjoy in a number of ways. There were dances, singing of songs, instrumental music and shows at fairs.[9] There were band music, chanting of bards, tom-tom playing,

1. *Jā.* II. 253,
सब्बे नागरा सन्निपतिंसु। राजंगणे चक्कातिचक्के मञ्चातिमञ्चे बंधिसु।
2. *Jā.* III, 160; IV. 81-82; VI. 277.
3. *Jā.* VI. 311-312.
4. *Jā.* II. 46-9.
5. *Jā.* VI. 275.
6. *Jā.* V. 282.
7. *Jā.* II. 253.
8. Aelian , quoted by R. K. Mukherjee, *Aśoka,* 2nd ed., 1955, p. 129.
9. *Brahmajāla-Sutta* of *D. N.* (II. 6).

fairy scenes and acrobatic feats by Chaṇḍālas.[1] There used to be animal and bird fights,[2] boxing and wrestling, sham-fights and manoeuvres. The *Jātakas* tell us that on festival days people gathered in a large number to witness the entertainments of the fair,[3] which represented manifold items of great interest. The tumblers and jugglers represented spectacular scenes with their dances and tricks, which made people burst into laughter.[4] Their assemblage in thousands must have been the most attractive scene. Feats like rope-dancing and jumping over javelins (Laṅghanasippaṁ) were very exciting and were performed by the Naṭas.[5] At times the Javelin-dancers met their tragic ends by falling down.[6] The snake-charmers (Ahiguṇḍika)[7] would have equally attracted large gatherings; while the conch-blowers (Saṅkhadhamaka)[8] and the drummers (Bherīvādaka)[9] created an atmosphere of great pleasure by their musical melodies. People profusely consumed garlands, scents, perfumes, unguents, and food;[10] eating meat and fish and drinking liquor were usual features.[11] The Jaina *Sūtras* inform us that the festive entertainments were characterised by feasting, drinking, and amorous acts.[12]

The centres of the festivals were the cities and towns, where gathered people from the neighbouring villages to enjoy them. In the royal cities the festival was usually proclaimed by the king, and at the first sounding of the festive drums outpoured the townsfolk to observe holiday.[13] Ordinary daily pur-

1. *Brahmajāla-Sutta of D. N.* (II. 6).
2. *Ibid*; combats of elephants, horses, buffaloes, bulls, goats, rams, cocks and quails, etc. (*Jā.* III. 82 speaks of cock fight).
3. *Jā.* II. 13, उस्सवे घोसिते महासमज्जं अहोसि, बहु मनुस्सा च देवनागसुपण्णादयो च समज्जदस्सनत्थं सन्निपतिंसु ।
4. *Jā.* No. 489. We are told of how a dancer (*nataka*) at Mithilā made everybody present at the courtyard burst into laughter (*Jā.* IV. 324).
5. *Jā.* I. 430.
6. *Ibid.*
7. *Jā.* II. 267; III. 198.
8. *Jā.* I. 284.
9. *Jā.* II. 283.
10. *Jā.* II. 248, उस्सवे घुट्ठे चंदकं संहरित्वा बहुं मालागन्धविलेपनञ्च खज्जभोजनादिनि आदाय कीलनट्ठाने सन्निपतिता ।
11. *Jā.* III. 435.
12. *S. B. E.*, XXII, pp. 94-95.
13. *Jā.* I. 250, नक्खत्तभेरिसद्दसवनकालतो पट्ठाय सकलनगरवासिनो नक्खत्तनिस्सितका हुत्वा विचरन्ति ।

suits, like the ploughing of the land, were stopped; feasting and drinking were resorted to, and friends were invited.[1] The Brāhmaṇas were feasted with meat and rice, and homages were paid to the deities, whom they worshipped.[2] The Jaina *Sūtras* state that the Brāhmaṇas, Śramaṇas, guests, paupers, and beggars were fed.[3] The *Dummedha-Jātaka* (No. 122) describing a festival at the city of Rājagṛha, the capital of Magadha, says that the city was adorned on the occasion of a festival, like a city of gods, and the king mounted on an elephant in all its trappings, made a solemn procession round the city, attended by a great retinue.[4] The royal cities during the festival days displayed great pomp, and people believed that gods from heaven came to witness the festive occasions.[5] The enthusiasm of the people to celebrate festivals shows that the whole land of Northern India keenly observed and enjoyed such occasions in a befitting manner.

The references to festivals indicate that they normally lasted for seven days.[6] But this was not the limit; we come across festive holidays lasting for one full month, devoted to merry-making and feasting.[7]

The Chāturmāsyā Festivals

The Chāturmāsyas were old seasonal festivals. The *Taittiriya Brāhmaṇa* speaks of the reward obtained by the performance of the Chāturmāsyas, which were simply sacrificial performances. The *Āpastamba-Gṛihya-Sūtra* tells us that there were three Chāturmāsya festivals, each celebrated at an interval of four months, which indicated the advent of three seasons, viz., spring, rains, and winter. They were celebrated on the full-moon days of Phālguṇa, of Āshāḍha and of Kārttika. The end of the rainy season and the commencement of the winter,

1. *Jā.* VI. 328. (No. 545).
2. *Ibid.*
3. *S.B.E.*, XXII. 92.
4. *Jā.* I. 444, अथ' एकस्मिं छणदिवसे सकलनगरं देवनगरं विय अलंकरित्वा सब्बालंकारपतिमण्डितं मंगलहत्थिं अभिरुहित्वा महन्तेन राजानुभावेन नगरं पदक्खिणं अकासि ।
5. *Jā.* III. 87, देवा च आगन्त्वा उस्सवं ओलोकयिंसु ।
6. *Jā.* III. 434 (No. 418; No. 546).
7. *Jā.* VI. 329 (No. 545), छणो मासेन ओसानं अगमासि ।

when the sky became clear of clouds and the fields rich with ensuing harvest, was a very joyful occasion, and so the Chāturmāsya of the Kārttika month was celebrated whole-heartedly.

Kattikā (Kaumudī-Mahotsava)

The Chāturmāsya festival of the month of Kārttika was known as the Kaumudī or the Kattikā. It is referred to several times in the Buddhist literature, but the details of its celebrations are described only in the *Jātakas.* Everywhere the night is described as lovely and pleasant. In the *Sāmaññaphala-Sutta* of the *Dīgha-Nikāya*[1], on the Kaumudī night king Ajātaśatru of Magadha is described as sitting on the upper terrace roof of his palace, surrounded by his Ministers and uttering :

How pleasant, friends, is the moonlight night !
How beautiful, friends, is the moonlight night !
How lovely, friends, is the moonlight night !
How soothing, friends, is the moonlight night !
How grand a sign, friends, is the moonlight night !

The *Jātakas* show that the Kattikā or the Kaumudī was the most popular festival, when all persons high or low, young and old, men and women, participated in the enjoyment with equal zeal and interest. The *Saṅkichcha-Jātaka* (No. 530) tells us that the king on this day mounted on a magnificent chariot, drawn by thorough-bred horses, and escorted by a number of courtiers went round the city with all his pomp, when flowers from the balconies of the palaces were showered upon him. He halted at the houses of certain outstanding members of his court. The beauty of the festival lay in the night decorations of the cities and towns. The *Sañjīva-Jātaka* (No. 150) tells us that when Ajātaśatru was the king of Magadha, on the Kattikā festival day, the city of Rājagṛiha was decorated like a city of gods.[2] All the royal cities of Northern India represented similar grandeur on the occasion of this festival ; and we are informed of similar scenes in the cities of Vārāṇasī[3]

1. *D.N.* I. 47; *S.B.B.* II. 66.
2. *Jā.* I. 508,
अथ' अस्स राजगह नगरे कत्तिकरत्तिवारे सम्पत्ते देवनगरं विय नगरं अलंकते ।
3. *Jā.* I. 499.

and Śrāvastī.[1] People kept holiday with no exception.[2] At night everybody came out of his house to enjoy the decorations and other entertainments.[3] Ladies liked to adorn themselves with fine and colourful clothes, and we find one entreating her husband for having a saffron coloured cloth to put on.[4] People belonging to the lower stratum of society used to go out with their wives, the latters' hands resting round the necks of their husbands, as we generally find among the aboriginals of Chotanagpur. A lady who had no good clothes was sorry that she would not be able to go about at the night festival with her hands round her husband's neck.[5]

The festival lasted for seven days[6] and was proclaimed by the king,[7] as in the case of other festivals. It was just like a fair devoted to merry-making for a week. The Full-Moon night of Kārttika enjoys importance even today, and the whole night is spent in keeping awake (Jāgaraṇa) in some parts of the country.[8]

The Elephant Festival (*Hatthi-Maṅgala*)

The Hatthi-Maṅgala (Elephant Festival) is described as a royal festival,[9] being celebrated in the courtyards of the kings. It seems quite proper that this festival was performed for the enjoymnt of the nobility, which was associated with royal dignity. The festival must have been a costly affair. The *Susīma-Jātaka* (No. 163) describes an Elephant Festival, which was held yearly in the royal courtyard. It is said that the Brāhmaṇas flocked to the king and said, "O Great King ! the season for an Elephant Festival has come, and a festival should

1. *Jā*. I. 433.
2. *Jā*. I. 433, 499.
3. *Jā*. I. 499.
4. *Ibid*., इच्छाम' अहं सामि कुसुम्भरत्तं निवासेत्वा एकं ।
5. *Ibid*., तव कंठे लग्गा कत्तिकरत्तिवारं चरितुं ति ।
6. *Jā*. I. 433, सत्ताहे वातिवत्ते नक्खत्तं ओसितं ।
7. *Ibid*.
8. As observed above, Kaumudī-Mahotsava had assumed the form of a fair, and the modern Sonpur fair most probably is the continuation of the old Kattikā festival. This assumption seems to be correct, for the modern fair also takes place on the occasion of the Full-Moon day of Kārttika. The citizens of Patna still celebrate the Kaumudī-Mahotsava, though in a different way. Today the occasion is enjoyed by organising Kavi-sammelan, musical performances, etc., and the celebration takes place on Āśvin Pūrṇimā.
9. *Jā*. II. 46-49; IV. 91; V. 286.

be celebrated.[1]" It is said further that a hundred elephants were set in array with golden trappings, golden flags, all covered with a net-work of fine gold. The courtyard of the palace was fully decked. The chaplain of the king conducted the festival; and he was expected to know the three *Vedas* and the elephant-lore (Hatthisuttaṁ). In the absence of such an able person the festival could be held up. The festival was in reality an exhibition of the feats of the elephants in a spectacular manner.

The Drinking Festival (*Surā-Nakkhata*)

There are a number of references to the Drinking Festival. A Drinking Festival at Rājagṛiha is mentioned in the *Sigāla-Jātaka*.[2] On that occasion every body drank hard.[3] People put on good clothes just as on the occasions of other festivals, ate meat and danced merrily. On the festival day liquor and meat were sold side by side.[4] There were some other festive occasions or fairs where meat and liquor were consumed accompanied by singing, dancing and music; but the mention of a festival dedicated only to drinking and eating points out that drinking was so much in vogue that people thought it necessary to organise festivals in honour of a popular habit. The festival is described as very wet, when everybody drank to his utmost capacity.[5]

Another *Jātaka* tells us of a Drinking Festival held at Vārāṇasī.[6] A large number of ascetics were staying at the royal pleasure-garden, and on the day of the Drinking Festival they were supplied with the best spirits by the king. They drank, sang, and danced in drunken hilarity.[7] This statement reveals that even the higher class people were given to drinking on such occasions, and that even ascetics, for whom drinking is strictly prohibited, were led astray. But this can be partially true, as we are told from other sources that drinking was prohi-

1. *Jā*. II. 46, महाराज, हत्थिमंगलछणो सम्पत्तो, मंगलं कातुं वत्तति ।
2. *Jā*. I. 489.
3. *Ibid*., ये भुय्येन मनुस्सा सुरं पिबन्ति, सुराछणो येव किर सो ।
4. *Jā*. I. 489.
5. *Ibid*.
6. *Jā*. I. 362.
7. *Ibid*., तापसा सुरं पिवित्वा उय्यानं गन्त्वा सुरामदमत्ता हुत्वा एकच्चे उट्ठाय नच्चिसु एकच्चे गायिसु ।

bited, and the ideal ascetics abstained from drinking. The occasion was characterised by unrestricted enjoyments of drinking and dancing. At times drunkenness led to quarrelling.[1] Women also drank hard, danced, and sang in a large number.[2] All these show that people during this period were so keen about merry-making that they organised festivals even in the name of drinking.

The Śālabhañjikā Festival

Śālabhañjikā means plucking the Śāla flowers. From the descriptions of this festival in the Buddhist literature it appears that multitudes of people assembled on certain days at the Śāla groves, plucked the Śāla flowers, sported, and spent the time in making merry. According to Pāṇini this festival was peculiar to the eastern people.[3] Śālabhañjikā appears in the Indian art; and Vogel remarks, "It is interesting that these games are said to be peculiar to Eastern India, as this tallies with the mention of the Śālabhañjikā Festival in Buddhist literature. It is evidently Magadha, the cradle of Buddhism, and the neighbouring countries, that may be taken to have been its home."[4]

The *Jātaka Nidānakathā* describes the Śālabhañjikā Festival in these words; "Now between the two towns (Kapilavatthu and Devadaha) there is an auspicious grove of Śāla trees belonging to the people of both cities, and is called Lumbinī Grove. At that time from the roots to the topmost branches it was one mass of full-blown flowers; and amidst the branches swarms of five-coloured bees, and flocks of birds of different kinds roamed, warbling sweetly. The whole of Lumbinī-vana was like a wood of variegated creepers, or the well-decorated banqueting hall of some mighty king. The queen beholding it was filled with the desire of disporting herself in the Śāla grove; and the attendants entered the wood with the queen."[5]

The *Avadānaśataka* gives a vivid description of this festival:

1. *Jā.* IV. 116 (No. 459).
2. *Jā.* V. 11 (No. 512).
3. *Kāśikā* on VI. 2. 74; III. 3. 109; II. 2. 17,
उद्दालक-पुष्प-भञ्जिका वीरण-पुष्प-प्रचायिका, शालभञ्जिका, ताल-भञ्जिका ।
4. The Woman and Tree or Śālabhañjikā in Indian Literature and Art, *Act a Orientalia*, Vol. VII, pp. 203-4.
5. *Jā.* I. 52.

"Once the Lord Buddha dwelt at Śrāvastī in the Jatavana, the garden of Anāthapiṇḍika. Now at that very time the festival called Śālabhāñjikā was being celebrated at Śrāvastī. Several hundred thousand beings assembled there and having gathered Śāla blossoms, they played, made merry and roamed about."[1] It appears from the description that the festival was a popular one.

The Ploughing Festival

The *Kāma-Jātaka* (No. 467) describes a festival which was known as the Ploughing Festival. It is said there that on that day the king held the plough. Ploughing is the means through which we get corn from the land. From times immemorial the earth has been worshipped as the mother goddess. Therefore ploughing the earth was a sacred act. Most probably the first ploughing at the beginning of the rains was observed as a sacred day and celebrated as a festival. The king, who enjoyed a divine status, started the ploughing. The *Sāṅkhyāyana-Gṛihyasūtra* lays down that ploughing should be done under the Nakshatra Rohiṇī.[2] Before ploughing started, at the eastern boundary of the field, a *bali* was offered to heaven and earth. When the plough was being put into motion first, a Brāhmaṇa was to touch it reciting a Vedic mantra and to perform worship of the different directions. This religious rite at the beginning of the ploughing seems to have been developed in the form of a festival, when even the king attended to grace the occasion of the first ploughing of land on the eve of the agricultural season. The Earth was known as Sītā and the wife of Indra.[3] Offerings were made to Sītā, and Indra was invoked for rains.[4]

In addition to these important festivals, there were other minor ones held in honour of gods like Indra, Skanda, Rudra, and Mukunda; there were festivals of Demons, Yakshas, and Nāgas; there were festivals to honour shrines and tombs, and there were festivals to worship trees, cows, wells, tanks, ponds, rivers, lakes, seas, and mines.[5] Thus we find that the life of the people was liberally interspersed with festivities.

1. The woman and Tree or Śālabhañjikā in Indian Literature and Art, *Acta Orientalia*, Vol. VII. p. 201, quoted by V. S. Agrawala in *India as known to Pāṇini*, p. 159.
2. *Sāṅ. G. S.* IV. 13.
3. *Pā.* G. S., II. 17. 9.
4. *Ibid.*
5. *S.B.E.* XXII, p. 92.

CHAPTER VII

RELIGIONS OF THE PERIOD

During the Vedic period the religious side of life had been considerably elaborated. Vedic religion in essence was simple, but that it was no longer in a primitive stage, is revealed by the magnitude of its pantheon. The objects of worship were grand phenomena of nature, which were conceived all alive and divine throughout.

During the days of the *Brāhmaṇas*, the Pantheon became still enlarged. A number of spirits, goblins, demons, and allegorical personifications became objects of worship. Certain old mystic representations of the *Ṛigveda*, it seems, were losing their importance, and the language of the old hymns had become unintelligible to the multitude and obscure to the priests.[1]

The Age of the *Upanishads* was an era of philosophical speculation. The Vedic rituals and ceremonies were not regarded as the best means of attaining salvation. The new philosophical activity paved the way for the rise of various novel religious sects.

By the 7th and 6th centuries B.C. the field giving rise to new religious movements seems to have become exceptionally fertile. An old Buddhist text mentions sixty-three schools of philosophy, many of which were probably non-Brahmanical.[2] The Jaina literature mentions a large number of the schools of the heretics. But such statements appear to be exaggerations. The Buddhist texts generally refer to six main heretical sects which flourished during the days of the Buddha in the north-eastern region of India.[3] Among the religious leaders of the period, Gautama, the Buddha, Mahavīra, and Makkhali Gosāla were the most outstanding personalities. It appears that there was a natural rivalry among them for supremacy,

1. Barth, *The Religions of India*, pp. 40-41.
2. *S.B.E.* XII, p. 93; referred to in the *C.H.I.* I. 150.
3. *D.N.* I. 47-49; *M.N.* I. 198, 250, II. 2; *Su. Ni.* III. 6.

and it was the Buddha who surpassed his rivals and gathered more followers around him.

Buddhism

The Buddhist evidence reveals that Buddhism was born in Magadha, from where it spread all over Bihar and the eastern portion of Uttar Pradesh during the lifetime of the Buddha; and henceforth it remained as one of the leading religions of these regions of the country for several centuries. The Buddha attained Sambodhi at Uruvelā, on the banks of the Nerañjarā river. At that time, says the *Mahāvagga*, Brahmā Sahampati uttered, 'The Dhamma hitherto manifested in the country of Magadha has been impure, thought out by contaminated men. But do thou now open the door of the Immortal; let them hear the doctrine discovered by the spotless one.'[1] The Buddha after his attainment of Sambodhi went to Isipattana (Sārnāth), where he delivered his first sermon before the five Bhikshus and thus set the wheel of Dhamma in motion.[2] The citizens of Vārāṇasī gave a good response to his call to follow his teachings. Yasa, a Seṭṭhiputta, renounced the world and entered the Order.[3] Hearing this, Vimala, Subāhu, Puṇṇagi, and Gavampati also belonging to respectable Seṭṭhi families did the same.[4] They were followed by fifty more members.[5] Thus the number of Bhikshus reached sixty.[6] But the work of major conversion started from the place where the Buddha had attained enlightenment. Uruvelā, the place of the Buddha's Sambodhi, was then a great centre of Vedic religion. The three Kassapa brothers, Uruvela Kassapa, Nādi Kassapa, and Gaya Kassapa, who were Jaṭilas, had built their Āśramas on the banks of the Nerañjarā river and gathered 1000 disciples[7]. To convert these Brāhmaṇa ascetics, who were the adherents of Vedic rites and enjoyed respect of the people, was the principal aim of the Buddha, for it would have produced a magical effect on popular mind. According to the *Mahāvagga*, he was suc-

1. *M.V.* I. 5. 7.
2. *M.V.* I. 6. 10-29.
3. *M.V.* I. 7.
4. *M.V.* I. 9.
5. *M.V.* I. 10.
6. *Ibid.*
7. *M.V.* I. 15. 1.

cessful in changing the heart of the 1000 Jaṭilas along with their leaders, who entered the Order.[1] After this great conversion, he went to Gayāsīsa, and then to Rājagṛiha.[2] His popularity was spreading fast, and when the Magadhan king heard of his presence at Rājagṛiha, he went to see him.[3] King Bimbisāra heard a religious discourse from the Buddha, entertained him with food and dedicated the Veluvana to the Saṅgha.[4]

It was at Rājagṛiha that the next major conversion after those of the Jaṭilas took place. Like Uruvelā, Rājagṛiha was another centre of Brāhmaṇa ascetics. Sañjaya Parivrājaka was residing there with two hundred and fifty disciples among whom Sāriputta and Moggallāna were the foremost.[5] Sāriputta was the first to resolve to embrace the faith and was followed by Moggallāna.[6] These two friends tried to persuade their teacher Sañjaya to see the Buddha, but failing to convince him, abandoned him and proceeded to the Buddha, followed by all the disciples of Sañjaya and received the *Upasampadā* from him.[7] It was after this incident that some Magadhan noblemen of Rājagṛiha raised their voice against the Buddha.[8] The opposition was mainly on account of admitting youngmen into the Order, causing thereby separation of sons from their parents, wives from their husbands and extinction of families.[9] But the Buddha instructed his disciples to face this opposition peacefully by telling the people that the great Samaṇa led men by means of true doctrine, by the power of Truth.[10] And, as the *Mahāvagga* says, the opposition lasted only for a week.[11]

Now, it was at this stage, when the number of Bhikshus had gone over 1250, that the Buddha started to enact rules of monastic discipline, and most of them were laid down in Bihar where he spent a considerable portion of his life. Aspects of monastic life have been discussed in a following chapter. The

1. *M.V.* I. 20. 17-24.
2. *M.V.* I. 21-22.
3. *M.V.* I. 22.
4. *Ibid.*
5. *M.V.* I. 23. 1.
6. *M.V.* I. 23. 2-10.
7. *M.V.* I. 24. 1-4.
8. *M.V.* I. 24. 5.
9. *Ibid.*
10. *M.V.* I. 24. 6.
11. *M.V.* I. 24. 7.

Vinaya-Piṭaka shows that the Buddha spent considerable time at Rājagṛiha,[1] receiving honour from Bimbisāra and enjoying the privilege of the services of Jīvaka, the renowned Magadhan physician.[2] It was after establishing firm the foundation of Buddhism in Magadha that the Buddha left Rājagṛiha for Kapilavastu.[3] The Buddha's association with Rājagṛiha continued lifelong, where according to the Buddhist sources he spent after the Sambodhi his 1st, 3rd, 4th, 7th, and the 20th Vassas.[4] He spent the 11th Vassa at Eknāla, a Brāhmaṇa village to the south of Magadha.[5] It was here that he preached the *Kasibhārdvāja-sutta.*[6] Even when he stayed at Śrāvastī, he used to visit Rājagṛiha occasionally. Several important Suttas, like *Āṭānāṭiva*, *Udumbarika*, *Kassapasīhanāda*, *Jīvaka*, *Mahāsakuludāyī* and *Sakkapañha* were delivered at Rājagṛiha.[7] Even his last journey was started from the Gijjhakūṭa[8] on the outskirts of Rājagṛiha. Vaiśālī and Champā, the other two great cities of Bihar during the days of the Buddha, were also several times visited by him. The first visit of the Buddha to Vaiśālī in which he was honoured by the courtesan Ambapālī by the dedication of the Ambapālī grove is well known. Mahāvana was also a favourite halting place of the Buddha. He preached the *Mahāli*, *Mahāsīhanāda*, *Chulasachchaka*, *Mahāsachchaka*, *Tevijja*, *Vachchhagotta*, *Sunakkhata* and *Ratan Suttas* at Vaiśālī.[9] Similarly Champā, which he visited many times and where he stayed at the grove on the banks of the Gaggarāpokkharaṇī,[10] was the scene of the preaching of the *Soṇadaṇḍa*, *Dasuttara*, *Kandaraka*, and *Kāraṇḍava Suttas*[11].

It was by the Buddha's wanderings and preachings that Buddhism spread in Bihar and outside, but it was to a great extent by his disciples of Bihar that his religion was consolidated.

1. *M.V.* I. 25-53.
2. *M.V.* I. 39.
3. *M.V.* I. 54. 1.
4. *D.P.P.N.* II. 722 & I. 799.
5. *S.N.* I. 172; *Su. Ni.* I. 4. It was near Dakshiṇāgiri.
6. *Ibid.*
7. *D.P.P.N.* II. 722.
8. *D.N.* *II.* 81.
9. *D.P.P.N.* II. 943.
10. *M.V.* IX. 1. 1; *S.B.B.* (Dia.) II. 144; *S.N.* I. 195; *A.N.* IV. 59, 168; V. 151, 189,
11. *D.P.P.N.* I. 856.

Bihar's contribution to the consolidation of Buddhism during the period under review and later cannot be underestimated.

The Buddha's chief disciples Sāriputta, Maggallāna, and Mahākassapa belonged to Magadha; others like Ānanda and Upāli hailed from Kapilavastu. Sāriputta was regarded as the *aggasāvaka* (Chief disciple) of the Buddha.[1] In the assembly of monks and nuns he was declared by the Buddha foremost among those who possessed wisdom, being inferior only to the Master.[2] The Buddha had so much faith in his wisdom that sometimes he merely suggested a topic and he preached a sermon, winning his approval.[3] The *Dasuttara* and the *Saṅgīti Suttas* are the most famous discourses of Sāriputta.[4] But in spite of the Buddha's open praise of his wisdom,[5] he never transgressed any rule laid down by the Lord, unless the latter permitted him. His loyalty to the Buddha is revealed from the incident of his declining to take garlic in his illness till the Master gave permission, though Sāriputta knew that he would be cured by doing so.[6] It was at Nālandā that Sāriputta uttered the lion's roar (*Sīhanāda*) affirming his faith in the Buddha, shortly before his death.[7]

Moggallāna was second among the chief disciples of the Buddha. He was born at Kolitagāma, near Rājagṛiha on the same day as Sāriputta.[8] Both were great friends and renounced the world together. When Sāriputta conveyed to him the news of his conversion into Buddhism, he also did the same.[9] His pre-eminence lay in his possession of the *iddhi*-power.[10]

Mahākassapa, who possessed in his body seven out of the thirty-two marks of a great being, was born in the Brāhmaṇa

1. *D.P.P.N.* II. 1108.
2. *A.N.* I. 19; *S.N.A.* II. 45.
3. *M. N.* I. 13-16; III. 46-61; 248-52.
4. *D.P.P.N.* II. 1113.
5. e.g. *M.N.* III. 25-29, पंडितो, भिक्खवे, सारिपुत्तो; महापञ्ञो, भिक्खवे, सारिपुत्तो; पुथुपञ्ञो, भिक्खवे, सारिपुत्तो; हासुपञ्ञो, भिक्खवे, सारिपुत्तो; जवनपञ्ञो, भिक्खवे, सारिपुत्तो; तिक्खपञ्ञो, भिक्खवे, सारिपुत्तो; निब्बेधिकपञ्ञो, भिक्खवे, सारिपुत्तो।
6. *Vin.* II. 140. *D.P.P.N.* II. 1115.
7. *S.N.* V. 159-61.
8. *D.P.P.N.* II. 541.
9. *M.V.I.* 23. 6-10.
10. e.g., *A.N.* I. 19.

village Mahātittha in Magadha.[1] He was regarded as chief among those who upheld minute observances of form.[2] It was under his presidentship that after the Buddha's death five hundred monks assembled at Rājgṛiha and recited the *Dhamma* and the *Vinaya* in a council, which is known as the First Baudha Saṅgīti.[3]

The Buddha had to face internal dissension as well as external opposition in Bihar. The Chhabbaggiya Bhikshus almost always appear in the *Vinaya-Piṭaka* as transgressing the laws of monastic discipline.[4] Devadatta figures as a schismatic, who is said to have taken 500 Bhikshus to Gayāsīsa, with a view to establishing a rival Order to that of the Buddha.[5] But Sāriputta and Moggallāna, who were sent by the Buddha to bring them back, were successful in their mission for the time being.[6] Devadatta, however, soon started to work against the Buddha. He had conceived from the time of his admission into the Order an ambition for securing a supreme position in the Saṅgha.[7] He was unnecessarily envious of the Buddha.[8] In order to fulfil his ambition, he planned several times to deprive the latter of his life. He bribed the royal archers, but they were won by the Lord.[9] Next, a great rock was hurled over him from the Gijjhakūṭa, but only the Blessed One's toe was injured which was dressed by Jīvaka.[10] Lastly, the royal elephant Nālāgiri, intoxicated with toddy, was let loose in a

1. *D.P.P.N.* II. 476-77.
2. *A.N.* I. 19.
3. *Mahāvaṁsa*, III. This recital is called the Therasaṅgīti or Theravāda.
4. Two of the Chhabbagiyas lived near Rājagṛiha, two near Kiṭāgira and two in Kośala. They acted against the rules of monastic discipline, e. g. laid ban upon the novices without the consent of their Upajjhāyas (*M. V.* I. 58), drew the novices of the senior Bhikshus to themselves (*M. V.* I. 59), gave Nissaya to shameless Bhikshus (*M. V.* I. 72) and so on. A number of their transgressions are referred to in the chapter dealing with the Buddhist monasteries.
5. *C. V.* VII. 4. 1.; *Lakkhana Jā.* (No. 11); *Sigāla Jā.* (No. 113); *Virochana Jā.* (No. 143).
6. *C. V.* VII, 4. 3; *Jā.* Nos. 11 & 143.
7. *Vinaya.*, II. 184 (*D. P. P. N.* I. 800). When the Buddha was advanced in age, Devadatta asked him to give up the leadership of the Saṅgha for him (*C. V.* VII. 3. 1).
8. *Kālabāhu Jā.* (No. 329).
9. *C. V.* VII. 3. 6-9; *Kālabāhu Jā.* (No. 329).
10. *D. P. P. N. I.* 800.

narrow lane where the Buddha was going for begging, but the animal was overpowered by his overpowering love.[1] But all these had no effect on the Buddha, and his Order remained firm as long as he lived.

The opposition of the Magadhan noblemen to the Buddha has been already referred to. That many Brāhmaṇas from Magadha, Aṅga, and Vaiśālī were also against him is shown by the fact that Soṇadaṇḍa,[2] Kūṭadanta[3] and others had to face the opposition of their class, when they paid their visits to the Buddha. The Brāhmaṇa Parivrājaka Sañjaya was decidedly against the Buddha, and he did not agree to approach him in spite of the persuasion of Sāriputta and Moggallāna, his disciples, as already referred to. Kāsibhāradvāja in the beginning disputed with the Buddha, and then became a great admirer of him.[4] It has been already seen that there were six heretical sects during the days of the Buddha, and that Gosāla and Mahāvīra were his opponents. Some of the *Jātakas* refer to the opposition of the heretics and the loss they had to sustain due to the growing popularity of Buddhism. According to two of the *Jātakas* the heretics tried in vain to bring disgrace upon the Buddha.[5] But their efforts resulted in the loss of their popularity and the growth of the Buddha's influence. According to *Jātaka* No. 472 the heretics lost all their honours and no

1. *C. V.* VII. 3. 11-12; *Jā.* V. 333-37. The *Chullavagga* (VII. 3. 12) says that the Buddha caused the sense of his love to pervade the elephant Nālāgiri; and the elephant, touched by the sense of his love, put down his trunk, and went up to the place where the Blessed one was, and stood still before him. And the Blessed one, stroking the elephant's forehead with his right hand, addressed him. And Nālāgiri, the elephant, took up with his trunk the dust from off the feet of the Blessed One, and sprinkled it over its head, and retired, bowing backwards while it gazed upon the Blessed one. (Letting loose of Nālāgiri is referred to also in *Jā.* Nos. 329 and 358).

2. *D. N.* I. 111-12.

3. *D. N.* I. 129-31.

4. *Su. Ni.* I. 4.

5. *Maṇisūkara Jā.* (No. 285) tells us that the heretics engaged Sundarī, a beautiful lady, for the purpose. She used to visit the Buddha every evening with flowers, scents, perfumes, camphor, condiments, and fruits. She told the people that she went to the Buddha to spend the night. The heretics hired some ruffians to murder her, and her dead body was thrown before the chamber of the Buddha. But the ruffians were caught by the police. They revealed the secret, which resulted in the disgrace of the heretics, and the Buddha became more popular.

Jātaka No. 472 says that due to their losing influence, the heretics employed Chinchamānavikā for disgracing the Buddha. Such stories are obviously exaggerations and are fabricated for the purpose of standering an opponent sect. But the fact that the heretics were opponents of the Buddha cannot be ruled out.

gifts were given to them. They stood in the streets and used to cry, "What, is the ascetic Gotama, the Buddha ? We are Buddhas also ! Does that gift only bring great fruit, which is given to him ? That is given to us also has great fruit for you ! Give to us also, work for us !" But no honour or gift was given to them. This shows that probably the heretics' opposition was of no avail, and the Buddha spread his religion in spite of all oppositions which finally subsided, as his popularity increased.

Buddhism was patronised by a number of Magadhan rulers during the period under review. Bimbisāra was very favourable to Buddhism, and he was probably also a friend of the Buddha. He dedicated Veluvana to the Order. His son Ajātaśatru, being under the influence of Devadatta[1], was in the beginning not favourably inclined to Buddhism. Later, when his father died in the prison, he turned to the Buddha who restored the lost peace of his mind.[2] He is represented as approaching him and hearing religious discourse.[3] He is said to have built at Rājagṛiha a cairn over the relics of lord Buddha which he had obtained as his share.[4] In addition to Ajātaśatru, the Lichahavis of Vaiśālī, the Śākyas of Kapila vastu, the Bulis of Allakappa, the Brāhmaṇas of Beṭṭhadīpa, the Mallas of Pāvā and the Mallas of Kusinārā were the first sharers of the Buddha's relics, and all of them are said to have built Stūpas for worship.[5] Thus, in the beginning, eight Stūpas were built. According to the *Mahāvaṁsa*, on the suggestion of Mahākassapa, the king Ajātaśatru gathered seven *doṇas* of the Buddha's relics deposited at various places, except that at Rāmagāma, and deposited them over a large Stūpa from where Aśoka obtained relics for his Stūpas.[6]

It was in the reign of Ajātaśatru that the First Buddhist Council was convened at Rājagṛiha. Soon after the death of the Buddha, a large number of Bhikshus assembled at Rājagṛiha under the presidentship of Mahākassapa and compiled

1. *C. V.* VII 3. 4-6. Ajātaśatru even helped Devadatta in depriving the Buddha of his life by giving orders to his men to obey whatever said Devadatta (*C. V.* VII. 3. 6.)
2. *Jā.* V. 262-63.
3. *Sāmaññaphala Sutta* (*D. N.* I. 47-86).
4. *D. N.* II. 166.
5. *Mahāparinibbāna Suttanta* (*D. N.* II. 164-67).
6. *Mahā.* 31. 21-22; *Ṭīkā.* 564.

the rules of Dhamma and Vinaya,[1] known as the doctrine of the Theras, i.e. Theravāda, or the First or Primitive doctrine, according to the *Dīpavaṁsa*.[2] Among the leading Theras participating in this Council in addition to Mahakassapa were Ānanda, Upāli, Anuruddha and others, each learned in a specific branch of Buddhist theology.[3]

During the reign of Kālāśoka Śaiśunāga there took place another Council of the Buddhists at Vaiśālī, after a hundred years from the Nirvāṇa of the Buddha.[4] For these hundred years the religion of the Buddha had remained pure, but at the beginning of the second century there happened a great schism, which was created by the Bhikshus of Vaiśālī.[5] As the *Chullavagga* and the *Dīpavaṁsa* tell us, 12000 Vajjians proclaimed ten indulgences permissible.[6] In order to subdue the rise of such forbidden practices, a large number of Bhikshus assembled in the *Kūṭāgāraśālā* at Vaiśālī and excommunicated

1. According to the *Chullavagga* (XI. 1) the decision to hold the Council was taken only after a week of the Buddha's Nirvāṇa, and it was held during the Vassa. According to the *Dīpavaṁsa* this event took place in the fourth month. (*Dīp*. V. 4-5).

According to Oldenberg the First Council was not at all held. He calls the tradition recorded in the *Chullavagga* as an invention of very early times. His main argument is that both the *Chullavagga* and the *Mahāparinibbāna Suttanta* refer to the conduct of Subhadda, but the latter does not record the holding of a Council at Rājagṛiha. Rhys Davids (*S. B. E.* XI. Introduction to *Mahāparinibbāna-Suttanta*) has pointed out that probably the author of the *Mahāparinibbāna-Suttanta* considered the mention of the Council unnecessary, as it had no bearing on the subject of his work—he was not describing the history of the Canon or the Order. But as pointed out by Rhys Davids the *Suttanta* does not close with the account of the Great Decease, but it also refers to the distribution of the relics and the feast celebrated in their honour. It refers to the arrival of Kasapa, the president of the Council, but there is no reference to it. Probably, when the work was composed, the tradition of the First Council may not have been held commonly. Probably it was composed before the account of the Council was included in the concluding portion of the *Chullavagga*. Most probably the account of the First Council was added to the *Chullavagga* after the incident of the Second one. It appears that the importance of the First Council was much emphasised after the Schism created by the Vajjiputtakas, in order to maintain the true nature of the Buddha's teachings. This importance of the First Council may not have been realised, when the book of the Great Decease was composed. And hence it is not correct to hold that the First Council did not take place.

2. *Dīp*. IV. 13-14; V. 14-15.
3. *Dīp*. 3-9; V. 8-13.
4. *C. V.* XIII; *Dīp*. IV. & V.
5. Ibid.
6. *C. V.* XII. 1. 1; *Dīp*. IV. 47-49; V. 17-18. The ten points promulgated permissible by the Vajjians are these:—

(a) Storing salt in a horn.

the Vajjians.[1] The excommunicated members held a Council and settled a doctrine contrary to the original one.[2] This dissension led to further schisms, resulting in the formation of new schools.[3] Probably it was due to this tendency that in a later period Aśoka took steps to check schisms by threatening to expel the schismatics.

Bihar was no doubt the stronghold of Buddhism, but it does not mean that the gospel of the Buddha did not spread outside the present boundaries of Bihar. The definition of Majjhimadesa[4] and the wanderings of the Buddha[5] in the *Tripiṭaka* give an idea of the region where spread Buddhism. To the East the Buddha did not go beyond the Kajaṅgala Nigama (Kaṅkajola in Santhal Pargana district of Bihar) which was the Eastern boundary of the Middle country. The Salalavatī river (in Hazaribagh district) formed the Southern boundary of the Majjhimadesa, and the Buddha is not known crossing it. But he visited the Suṁsumāragiri. The Buddha visited Kauśāmbī and Avanti to the South-West. Avanti had only a few followers according to the *Mahāvagga*. To the West the Buddha went up to Mathurā according to the *Aṅguttara-Nikāya* and up to Thulakoṭṭhita (in Kuru) according to the

(b) Taking midday meal, when the sun's shadow showed two finger breadth after noon.
(c) Eating food after the regular meal, when going to the villages.
(d) Holding Uposatha separately by Bhikshus in the same boundary.
(e) A saṅgha not at unity within itself could carry out an official act, undertaking to inform Bhikshus of it (obtaining the consent of the fraternity, not before, but after an act.)
(f) It was permissible for a Bhikshus to do anything adopted as a practice by his Upajjhāya (Practice of acting according to example).
(g) Curd might be eaten by one who had finished his midday meal (or practice of drinking milk-whey).
(h) Drinking toddy.
(i) Sitting on seats covered with cloths without fringes.
(j) Possessing gold and silver.

1. *Dīp.* V. 20-29.
2. *Ibid.* V. 30-38.
3. *Ibid.* V. 39-50, 53-54.
4. *M. V.* V. 13. 12—Defines the Majjhimadesa as the region bounded by Thūṇa to the West, Usīradhvaja to the North, Kajaṅgala to the East, Salalavatī to the South-East and Setakaṇṇika to the South.
5. The *Nikāyas* tell us that the Buddha did not go beyond Mathurā and Thullakoṭṭhita to the West, Sāpuga and Usīradhvaja to the North, Kajaṅgala to the East and Suṁsumāragiri to the South. (See Introduction to the *Majjhima-Nikāya* by Rāhula Sānkṛityāyana).

Majjhima-Nikāya. The *Mahāvagga* knows the Brāhmaṇa Nigama Thūṇa (Thāneswara) as the Western limit of the middle-country. Buddhism does not seem to have spread beyond the limits of the modern Uttar Pradesh to the West and the North.

Usīradhvaja, near Haridwār, was the northern boundary of the Majjhimadesa. Śrāvastī, the scene of the utterances of many Sūttas, was the headquarters of the Buddha for about 25 years.[1] The places frequently visited by the Buddha were in the modern eastern Uttar Pradesh and Bihar, and the natural conclusion at which we arrive is that next to Bihar Eastern Uttar Pradesh was the stronghold of Buddhism, and it also spread to Central India as far as Ujjainī.

Jainism

Jainism was one of the important religions during the period under review. Vaiśālī was its stronghold where Mahāvira, the last Tīrthaṅkara of the Jainas was born as a scion of the Jñātṛi clan. He is known as Nigaṇṭha Nātaputta by the Buddhists.[2] After renouncing the world he led a life of hard austerity, the account of which has been well preserved in the Jaina Canon, the *Āchāraṅga-Sūtra*.[3] He wandered about in regions inhabited by wild tribes, enduring painful treatment at their hands. Probably it was the forest region of South Bihar. He occasionally visited Rājagṛiha and other towns, where he received the highest honour from the people. During this period he visited Nālandā where he met Gosāla. It was after the austerities of 13 years that he attained supreme knowledge,[4] and became the head of the Order of the Nigaṇṭhas. After this he wandered about preaching his doctrine for 30 years about which not much is known. According to the *Kalpa-Sūtra* he dwelt at Rājagṛiha, Nālandā, Champā, Vaiśālī, Mithilā, and Śrāvastī.[5] According to the Buddhist sources the activities of Mahāvīra and his followers were concentrated at these places.[6] He died at Pāvā near

1. *D.P.P.N.* I. 799.
2. *D.N.* I. 49, 57-58; *M.N.* I. 198.
3. *S.B.E.* XXII. 79-87.
4. *S.B.E.* XXII. 263.
5. *S.B.E.* XXII. 264.
6. Law, *Mahāvīra, His Life and Teachings*, p. 7.

Rājagṛiha, a place still visited by thousands of Jaina pilgrims.[1] Thus we find that Bihar remained the scene of the most of his activities.

Mahāvīra stood for extremely austere practices; whereas the Buddha favoured to follow the middle course. Naturally, these religious teachers proved to be rivals. The Buddha denounced the Nigaṇṭhas for their practices of false Dhammas,[2] and he is said to have caused considerable loss to the religion of Mahāvīra. He converted the commander-in-chief of the Lichchhavis, a lay disciple of the Nigaṇṭhas.[3] Ajātaśatru approached Mahāvīra for a satisfactory explanation concerning matters of religion, but he was disappointed and hence turned to the Buddha.[4] Upāli of Rājagṛiha was a lay-follower of Mahāvīra; he made an attempt to convince the Buddha of his wrong views, but was easily upset by him. At this he treated Mahāvīra with arrogance, which so much shocked him that he vomited hot blood.[5] Mahāvīra's greatest rival was Makkhali Gosāla. Both recommended the same mode of living, such as nakedness and uttar deprivation of the comforts of life. About the mutual relations of Mahāvīra and Gosāla, we do not know much, but it appears that their followers may have come into occasional conflicts. The *Bhagavatī-Sūtra* records the last meeting between these religious leaders at Śrāvastī, when Mahāvīra caused the death of his opponent by his magical power. When the Jaina Tīrthaṅkara had been to Śrāvastī, Gosāla told a Jaina monk that if Mahāvīra continued to slander him, he would reduce him to ashes.[6] Hearing this Mahāvīra instructed his followers to suspend all associations with the Ājīvikas.[7] At this Gosāla filled with anger visited Mahāvīra and explained his doctrine of Niyati.[8] But Mahāvīra told him that he was like a thief chased by villagers, feverishly trying to hide himself.[9] Full of anger, he cursed Mahavira; he also employed

1. Pāvā, according to the Buddhist sources, was among the centres of Mahāvīra's activities (*Mahāvīra : His Life & Teachings*, p. 7). He died in about 468 B.C. at the age of 72 years (*C. H. I.* Vol. I, p. 163; *I.A.* 1914, p. 177).
2. *A. N.* V. 150.
3. Jacobi, *Jaina Su.*, p. XI.
4. *Sāmaññaphalasutta of D. N.* & *Sabhiya-Sutta of Su. Ni.*
5. *M. N.* I. 371. 387 (*Upālisuttaṁ*).
6. *Bh. Sū.* XV. 547.
7. *Bh. Sū.* XV. 549.
8. *Bh. Sū.* XV. 550.
9. *Bh. Sū.* XV. 551.

magic power against him, but in vain.[1] It is said that he died on the 7th day of this incident by the magic power of Mahāvīra.[2]

Mahāvīra survived the death of his opponent Gosāla for 16 years,[3] and probably Jainism spread with rapidity during these years. The Jainas claim both Bimbisāra and Ajātaśatru as the followers of lord Mahāvīra, which shows that these rulers honoured Jainism in spite of their patronage to Buddhism. Ajātaśatru was probably more liberal to Jainas in spite of his faith in the Buddha. He is described as often approaching Mahāvīra at Vaiśāli and Champā.[4] In the *Aupapātika-Sūtra* (Su. 30) he is represented as declaring his faith in Mahāvīra, who had expounded the true path of religion based on renunciation and non-violence. The Jainas do not brand Ajātaśatru a parricide. Ajātaśatru's son Udāyi proved to be a great patron of Jainism. The *Pariśishṭa-parvan* credits him with the building of a Jaina temple in the centre of Pāṭaliputra.[5] During the reign of this ruler Jainism may have spread rapidly in Bihar. Jaina monks had easy access in his palace, and it was a disguised Jaina monk who murdered this king.[6] The Nanda rulers seem to have been not unfavourably inclined to Jainism. The removing of the image of the Jina from the capital of Kaliṅga to Pāṭaliputra may have been due to the Jaina faith of the Nanda[7] king. That Jainism was an important sect of Magadha is also shown from the association of the first Maurya emperor with the Jainas.

The teachings of the Buddha and Mahāvīra are well known, and it is needless to enter into their details. We should only refer to the main doctrines of Buddhism and Jainism. They show many points of resemblance such as the observance of the five Śīlas, belief in Ahiṅsā, denial of the authority of the *Vedas* and the Brāhmaṇas, and the existence of a Creator and so on. But the two teachers, the Buddha and Mahāvīra, differred in

1. *Bh. Sū.* XV. 552-53.
2. *Bh. Sū.* VX. 554-55. (*History and Doctrine of the Ājīvikas*, pp. 60-61 by Basham gives the full detail of the last meeting of Mahāvīra and Gosāla and their duel resulting in the death of the Ājīvika teacher.
3. *Bh. Sū.* XV. 553.
4. *Aup. Sū.* 12, 27, 30; *Ā. Sū.* pp. 684, 687; *Pari.* P. IV.
5. *Pari. P.* VI. 34.
6. *Ibid.* V. 208.
7. *Hāthīgumphā Ins. of king Khāravela*, line, 12.

their outlook, and their teachings gave rise to two different religions and philosophies.

The aim of the Buddha's teaching was not to solve the complexities of metaphysics by logic, but to find out a simple path based on ethical practices, for securing emancipation from the sufferings of life. He was not concerned with the origin of things, but took them as they appeared to him. He expounded his doctrine in four Noble Truths, viz.,[1]

I. Dukkham (Existence of Pain)

II. Dukkh-Samudāya (Cause of Pain)

III. Dukkh-Nirodha (Cessation of Pain possible)

IV. Dukkh-Nirodha-gāminī-Pratipadā (way leading to the Cessation of Pain).

The first Noble Truth is that life is full of misery. The existence of pain in life is so gross that it cannot be rejected. The second Noble Truth is that there is cause of pain, which is not one, but there is a chain of causes. This is explained by the conception of the twelve Nidānas, which are Jarāmaraṇa (Old age and death), Jāti (Birth), Bhava (Existence), Upādāna (Clinging to Existence), Tṛishṇā (Desire), Vedanā (Sensation), Sparśa (Contact of senses with objects), Shaḍāyatana (Sensibility), Nāmarūpa (Individuality) Vijñāna (Consciousness), Saṅskāra (Pre-dispositions of mind which determine our action) and Avidyā (Ignorance).[2] Each successive Nidāna is the cause of the preceding one, and hence Avidyā, i.e. Ignorance is the root cause of all sufferings. The third Noble Truth is that cessation of pains by removing the root cause is possible. The Buddha disagreed with those who believed that emancipation from pain lay in the full enjoyment of the worldly pleasures like the Chārvākas, and also from those who advocated the necessity of practising severe austerities like the Jainas. He avoided both the extremities, and took a medium course by propounding the doctrine of Madhyama-Pratipadā (middle-course), which is also known as the Ārya-Ashṭāṅgika-Mārga[3] (The Noble Eightfold Path). The Eightfold Path constitutes of Samyak Jñāna (Knowledge of the Noble Truths), Samyak-Saṅkalpa (Determination), Samyak-Vachana

1. *D.N.* I. 83-84; II. 304.

2. *Mahānidāna-Sutta of D.N.* (No. 15) *Mahāsatipaṭṭhāna-Sutta of D.N.* (No. 22); *Mahātaṇhāsaṅkhava-Sutta of M.N.* (No. 38).

3. *Mahāsatipaṭṭhāna-sutta of D.N.* (No. 22); *S.N.* V. 8-10.

(Speaking the Truth), Samyak-Karmānta (Avoiding Killing, Envy, etc.), Samyak Ājīva (lawful living), Samyak-Vyāyāma (Avoiding Evils and endeavouring for the Good), Samyak-Smṛiti (Right Mindfulness) and Samyak-Samādhi (Right Concentration). According to the Buddha the practice of these eight practices leads to salvation.

For the attainment of enlightenment or knowledge, the purity of body is an essential factor. For this purpose he advocated the practice of the Three Ratnas (Tri-Ratna),[1] viz., Śīla, Samādhi and Prajñā. Śīlas are five. Samādhi is of four types and Prajñas are three. The doctrine of the Tri-Ratna may be regarded as the substance of the teachings of the Buddha.

As regards the religious and the philosophical doctrines propounded by Mahāvīra, we do not know much. The Jaina Canons were compiled centuries after the Nirvāṇa of Mahāvīra, and they are far from the direct representatives of the teachings of the last Tīrthaṅkara. The Jaina philosophy began to develop from *c.* first century B.C., after Umāsvāti of Magadha, who wrote the *Tattvārtha-Sūtra* and the *Tattvārtha-Nigama.*[2] The *Dīgha-Nikāya* refers to the doctrine of the Chāturyāma-Saṁvatsara of the Nigaṇṭhas. According to this doctrine the Nigaṇṭha is restrained with a fourfold self-restraint. He lives restrained as regards water and evils, he has washed away all evils and lives suffused with the sense of evil held at bay.[3] Pārśvanātha prescribed the observance of Ahiṁsā, Satya, Asteya and Aparigraha. Mahāvīra added also Brahmacharya. The main doctrine of the Jaina Philosophy is Syādvāda or the Saptabhaṅgī-Naya which was elaborated after Mahāvīra, but he is represented in the *Bhagavatī-Sūtra* as speaking of *Syādasti, Syānnāsti* and *Syādavaktavyaṁ.* Mahāvīra must have derived this idea from the Upanishadic philosophy. Jainism accepts the existence of life in every particle of the universe. It be-

1. *Sāmaññaphalasutta of D. N.* (No. 2)—Refers to various Śīlas and Prajñās, but five Śīlas and three Prajñās are the main.

2. The contemporary of Umāsvāti was Kund Kundāchārya of the South, who is regarded as a great Jaina philosopher. He wrote a number of books, out of which three are regarded by the Jainas equivalent to *Upanishads, Brahma-Sūtra* and *Gītā* of the Hindus (*Bhāratīya Darśana* by B. Upadhyaya, p. 145).

3. *D. N.* I. 57, निगण्ठो चातुयामसम्वरसम्वुतो होति...सब्बवारिवारितो च होति, सब्बवारीयुतो च, सब्बवारीधुतो च, सब्बवारीफुट्ठो च ।
S.B.B. (*Dia.*), II, pp. 74-75.

lieves in the observance of non-voilence in every sphere of life. According to Jainism Man's personality is dual, i.e. material and spiritual and that man is not perfect, but the human soul can attain perfection. It is after the subjugation of matter that the soul attains perfection, freedom and happiness; then one becomes the *Jina* (conqueror). Jainism does not make man an irresponsible agent like Ājīvikism, but it believes that man alone is responsible for all that is good or bad in his life.[1] Mahāvīra is represented in the Buddhist sources as an exponent of the doctrine of action (Kiriyāvāda).[2]

Ājīvikism

Our sources reveal that besides those of the Buddhists and the Jainas, the Order of the Āijīvikas was important in Bihar and Eastern Uttar Pradesh. Probably Ājīvikism already existed before the emergence of the celebrated Ājīvika leader Makkhali Gosāla, the contemporary of the Buddha and Mahāvīra, though its earlier history is shrouded in mystery.[3] Makkhali Gosāla's headquarters lay at Śrāvastī which would suggest that his religion was popular in Kośala, but that Ājīvikism had a strong footing in Magadha is shown by the fact that it was probably the first doctrine preached in Magadhan dialect.[4] The fact that Makkhali Gosāla had associations with Mahāvīra in Magadha,[5] that Upaka, the Magadhan Ājīvika born at Nāla near Nālandā, had met the Buddha on the road to Gayā,[6] that Paṇḍuputta, son of a Rathakāra of Rājagṛiha, was an Ājīvika[7] and that a kinsman of king Bimbisāra had embraced Ājīvikism[8] are sufficient to show that the Order of the Ājīvikas was established in Magadha. When we are told that it was an Ājivika who had informed Mahākassapa of the Buddha's death,[9]

1. *Outlines of Jainism*, Jaini, J. R., pp. 1-6.
2. *A. N.* IV. 180-81.
3. The Jaina *Bhagavatī Sūtra* (XV, 554) describes Makkhali Gosāla as the 24th Tīrthaṅkara; Buddhist sources link his name with Nandā Vachchha and Kisa Saṅkichcha (Basham, *History and Doctrine of the Ājīvikas*, pp. 27-30).
4. Basham, *History and Doctrine of the Ājīvikas*, pp. 24-26.
5. *Ibid*, pp. 39-41; *Bh. Sū.* IV, 541; It is said that Mahāvīra and Gosāla lived in the same house at Nālandā.
6. *M. V.* I. 6. 7-9; *M. N.* I. 170-1; *Jā.* I. 81; *D. P. P. N.* I. 385.
7. *M. N.* I. 31.
8. *Vinaya*, IV. 77.
9. *C. V.* XI. 1. 1.

when a *Jātaka* story refers to the Āśrama of Guṇa kassapa, the Ājīvika at Mithilā,[1] when the *Bhagavatī-Sūtra* suggests that ascetics of the type of the Ājīvikas visited places like Magadha, Videha and Champā,[2] when one finds the mention of the Ājīvika ascetics along with the Śramaṇas and the Brāhmaṇas in the inscriptions of Aśoka, and when cave dedication to them in the Barābar hill are taken into account, one is led to conclude that Ājīvikism was an important Order in the eastern region of the country before the beginning of the Christian era.

The hostility of the Jainas to the Ājīvikas, has already been referred to. That the Buddhists were in no way favourably inclined to them is revealed by the terms used for the Ājīvikas in the Buddhist literature, such as *Michchhājīvo*,[3] *Ājīvikanaṁ michchhātapaṁ*,[4] *Ājīvikanaña' eva anuchchhairika*[5] and so on.

Makkhali Gosāla propounded the doctrine of Niyati 'or the Automatic function through Transmigration'. 'According to him there is no cause, either ultimate or remote, for the depravity of beings; they become depraved without reason and without cause. The attainment of any given condition does not depend on one's acts, or on the acts of others', or on human effort. Creatures have no power of their own, and they are regulated by their fate. They are bent this way or that by their fate, by the necessary conditions of the class to which they belong and by their individual nature.[6]'

According to Makkhali Gosāla's theory of 'purification through transmigration' one will make an end of pain after wandering through various births for the allotted term. There are eighty-four hundred thousand periods during which both fools and wise alike, wandering in transmigration, shall at last make an end of pain. Neither the wise nor the fool can get rid of the Karma—there can be no increase or decrease thereof. Everything is predestined. Just as when a ball of string is cast forth it will spread out just as far, and no farther, than it can unwind, just so both fools and wise alike, wandering in

1. *Jā.* VI. 222-23.
2. Basham, *History and Doctrine of the Ājīvikas*, p. 95.
3. *S. N.* V. 14, 76, (*J. B. O. R. S.* Vol. XII, p. 54.)
4. *Jā.* I. 493.
5. Norman, *Dhammapada Comy.*, 1911, I. 309, II. 55-6; *J. B. O. R. S.* vol. XII, p. 54.
6. *D. N.* I. 53; *S. B. B.* (*Dia.*). II. 71.

transmigration exactly for the allotted term, shall then and only then, make an end of pain.[1]

The above doctrine is referred to also in the *Jātaka* literature. The Ājīvika Guṇa Kassapa, who lived in a deer park near Mithilā with a large number of followers and enjoyed the respect of the people, is described as expounding his doctrine which corresponds to that of Makkhali Gosāla. One day he told king Aṅgati of Videha, "There is no fruit, good or evil, in following the law; there is no other world, O King,—who has ever come back hither from thence ? All beings are equal and alike, there are none who should receive or pay honour; there is no such thing as strength or courage ; —how can there be vigour or heroism ? All beings are predestined (Niyatāni), just as the stern rope must follow the ship. Every mortal gets what he is to get, what then is the use of giving ? There is no use giving—the giver is helpless and weak : gifts are enjoined by fools and accepted by the wise."[2] He is further described as pronouncing the theory of the Automatic function of Transmigration, as we have already seen in the case of Makkhali Gosāla. He says that there is neither the destroyer nor the destroyed ; there are eighty-four great aeons (Mahākappas) through which all beings have to pass and it is then that they become pure. Every thing is guided by destiny.[3]

In the same story the doctrine of Guṇa Kassapa is refuted by Rujā, the daughter of king Aṅgati, who says that if a man is purified by the mere course of existence, then Guṇa's own asceticism is useless; like a moth flying into the lighted candle, the idiot has adopted a naked mendicant's life. Having accepted the idea that all will at last be purified through transmigration, in their great ignorance many corrupt their actions; and being fast caught into the effects of former sins, they find it hard to escape, as the fish from the hook.[4]

Pūraṇa Kassapa and Pakudha Kachchāyana

The doctrines propounded by Pūraṇa Kassapa and Pakudha Kachchāyana are similar to the Niyati-vāda of Makkhali

1. *D.N.* I. 54; *S. B.B.* (*Dia.*), II. 72-73.
2. *Jā.* VI. 225.
3. *Jā.* VI. 226.
4. *Jā.* VI. 234.

Gosāla. Later sources associate them with Ājīvikism.[1] It appears that there were several sects of the Ājīvikas, which were developed by different teachers with slight differentiation in their method of approach.

Pūraṇa Kassapa is described as a well reputed religious teacher in the *Sāmaññaphala-Sutta*. He expounded the theory of Non-Action[2] (no future rewards or punishments, as translated by Gogerly). According to this doctrine man is an irresponsible agent, because his action neither brings any merit nor demerit. Neither mutilation, robbery, adultery, lies, oppression, killing and so on cause any guilt; nor charity, generosity, self-mastery, and truthfulness bring any merit or increase of merit.[3]

According to Pakudha Kachchāyana there is neither creator nor created; there is neither slayer nor causer of slaying. When one with a sharp sword cleaves a head in twain, no one thereby deprives any one of life; a sword has only penetrated into the interval between seven elementary substances.[4] He believed in seven eternal elements—earth, water, fire, air, life (soul), joy and sorrow.[5] He also included a part of Gosāla's doctrine.

Sañjaya Belaṭṭhiputta was a great sceptic. He neither denied the existence of the next world nor accepted it. Whether the beings are produced by chance, or whether there is any fruit of good or bad action, or whether a man who won the truth continues after death—to all these questions he gave the same answer.[6] His doctrine was of neither acceptance nor denial.

According to the doctrine of Ajita Kesakambalī, there is neither fruit nor result of good or evil deeds. There is no such thing as this world or the other. There is neither father nor mother, nor beings springing into life without them. There are in the world no recluses or Brāhmaṇas who have reached the highest point (Arhatattva), who walk perfectly, and who having understood and realised by themselves alone, both this

1. Tamil Sources, such as (a) *Nīlakechi*, (b) *Maṇimekhalai*, (c) *Chivañāna-chettiyār*, and (d) *Tarka-rahasya-dīpikā* of Guṇaratna referred to by Basham in the *History and Doctrine of the Ājīvikas*, Chap. V.
2. *D.N.* I. 53; *S.B.B.* (*Dia.*), II.6 9-70.
3. *D.N.* I. 52.
4. *D.N.* I. 56; *S.B.B.* (*Dia.*), II. 74.
5. *Ibid.*
6. *D.N.* I. 58-59; *S.B.B.* (*Dia.*), II. 75.

world and the next, make their wisdom known to others.'[1] His view is similar to that of the Chārvākas. According to his belief a human being is built up of four elements, and when he dies the earthly in him returns and lapses to the earth, the fluid to the water, the heat to the fire, the windy to the air, and his faculties pass into the space.[2] He believed in the theory of annihilation.

Brahmanism and Popular Religion

Buddhism spread far and wide; Jainism and Ājīvikism also spread in a considerable area and there also existed various minor religious sects; but the beliefs, superstitions, and practices of the vast majority of the commonfolk had nothing to do with the doctrinal side of the various schools. Even the Buddha did not oppose the prevalent customs, except those which caused slaughter of animals. The social order remained unshaken; religious beliefs and superstitions of the masses remained practically as they were before the advent of the Buddha and Mahāvīra. In fact, Buddhism was to a great extent genuine Brahmanism in its texture. It shared with Brahmanism its dominant religious ideas, such as the conception of Sorrow, Deliverance, Desire, *Karman* and Rebirth. It did not, however, accept the belief of Brahmanism in the authority of the *Vedas*, the efficacy of animal sacrifices and so on.

Both in the doctrinal as well as the practical side of religious life the Buddha introduced redical reforms, which were directed in good part against Brahmanism. Buddhism and Jainism adopted in their ascetic practices and in their whole mode of life the rules which had been already fixed by their Brāhmaṇa antagonists. The rules laid down for Jaina monks show closer similarity to those of the Brāhmaṇa mendicants.[3] In various matters of religious practices the Buddhists and Jainas were not innovators.

Though the Buddhists and Jainas revolted against the authority of the Brāhmaṇas and the efficacy of the Vedic Yajñas and rituals, they did not go against the prevalent customs and practices of the people, but they tried to replace a few of them

1. *D.N.* I. 55; *S.B.B.* (*Dia.*), II. 73.
2. *Ibid.*
3. Jacobi, *Jaina Sū.*, Introduction.

by similar disguised practices in order to attract the masses. They tried to get rid of those Brahmanical practices which involved killing of life. In case of Yajña, the Buddha opposed the slaughter of animals, but approved a Yajña performed otherwise.[1] He is silent about the Pākayajñas and the Pañchamahāyajñas. People used to consult the Brāhmaṇas for interpreting their dreams.[2] This belief of the commonfolk was not overlooked by the Buddha, and hence he is described as one who could interpret dreams better than the Brāhmaṇas.[3] People believed in the efficacy of benediction by priests. The Buddhists prescribed chanting of the *Maṅgalasutta*;[4] the Jainas introduced eight Maṅgalas.[5] They further praised the selfless and enlightened Brāhmaṇa. Though they challenged the orthodox view of the high position of the Brāhmaṇas, they placed the Kshatriyas above all, and valued the purity of blood. Thus we find that popular beliefs and customs did not die out with the advent of novel religious outlook. And, it can be said that Brahamanism, which had already assimilated all popular cults, did not receive a set-back due to the rise of Buddhism and Jainism and that the popular Brahmanism was in spirit nothing but popular religion, which consisted of spells, charms, incantations, exorcism, witchcrafts, occultism, interpretation of dreams, signs, and cries of beasts and birds and so on, the roots of which lay in the *Atharva-Veda*. The observation of Hopkins that Vedic religion or Brahmanism was confined to a small section of the people of India and that it was rather an island in the sea, the majority of the people following their own religions, which consisted of beliefs, spells, incantations, charms, and spirits[6] is correct, if by Brahmanism one understands the religion of the law-books, which represent the ideal religion practised by a few. Even today the religious practices of the lower sections of the Hindu society are different in many respects from those of the higher sections. Similar was the case in ancient days. When we speak of the religious practices of the people

1. *D.N.* I. 141-42.
2. *S.N.* I. 76; Jā. III. 43-44.
3. *Jā.* I. 335.
4. *Khuddakapāṭha*, p. 3.
5. *Aup. Su.*, Sec. 49.
6. Hopkins, *Religions of India*, Chap. IX, quoted in *India as described in Early Texts of Buddhism and Jainism*, p. 202.

during the period under review, there are before us the two aspects of Brahmanism, viz., the Higher and the Popular.

The complete picture of higher Brahmanism is represented by the *Āraṇyakas*, *Upanishads*, *Gṛihyasūtras*, *Dharmasūtras* and so on; it held good in the case of the Brāhmaṇas in particular and the Dvijas in general. The Buddhist and the Jaina writers also refer to the religious practices of the Brāhmaṇas, but the orthodox sections refer only to those customs which they intend to criticise, and hence they do not reveal the complete picture of higher Brahmanism. But they add to our knowledge of Brahmanism of the period under review.

The Buddhist sources disclose that the Sotthiyas and the Brāhmaṇa Mahāsālas of the age were custodians of the Vedic religion or higher Brahmanism, which was mostly sacrificial. The Buddhist literature refers only to animal sacrifice which it vehemently criticises.[1] But it does not mention other forms of Yajñas which did not involve loss of life. As already observed, the Buddha was not against it.

Performance of Yajñas was an important aspect of Brahmanism as in the Vedic period. The Brāhmaṇa Mahāsālas sometimes performed sacrifices for themselves, and sometimes officiated as priests in the Yajñas performed for kings. Descriptions of the preparations of the Mahāyajñas of the Brāhmaṇa Kūṭadanta of Magadha,[2] of the Brāhmaṇa Uggatasarīra of Sāvatthī,[3] and of king Pasenadi of Kośala[4] throw a good deal of light on the method of Yajñas. Animals sacrificed included cows, bulls, steers, heifers, goats, sheep, poultry, pigs, horses, elephants and so on,[5] which shows that some animals such as elephants, which were not sacrificed during the Vedic period, were also killed in the Yajñas. The number of animals for

1. e. g., *Su. Ni.* II. 6. 12-32 (*Dhammachariya-sutta*).

2. *D. N.* I. 127, तेन खो पन समयेन कूटदन्तस्स ब्राह्मणस्स महायञ्ञो उपक्खटो होति, सत्त च उसभ-सतानि सत्त च वच्छतर-सतानि सत्त च वच्छतरि-सतानि सत्त च अज-सतानि सत्त च उरभ-सतानि थूनूपनीतानि होन्ति यञ्ञत्थाय।

3. *A. N.* IV. 41.

4. *S. N.* I. 76.

5. *D.N.* I. 127; *S.N.* I. 76; *A.* N. IV. 41; II. 42; 207; *Jā.* III. 44.

sacrificing had also gone high; sometimes each in the number of 500 or 700 were killed. As the Buddhist writers give exaggerated accounts of the Yajñas involing killing of living beings[1] on account of their antagonism towards Brahmanical religion, all that they say may not be true.

The Buddhist sources refer to the performance of the Assamedha, the Purisamedha, the Sammāpāsa and the Vājapeyya sacrifices.[2] The interpretation of the term Purisamedha as human sacrifice is doubtful. It appears that it has been mentioned by way of tradition. It has also been suggested that it meant corn sacrifice.

Yajñas were performed with grandeur. It has already been observed that animals in huge numbers were killed. Trees were cut for constructing sacrificial posts (Yūpas).[3] Sometimes a sacrificial pit was dug and numerous victims were fastened to the stakes. Fastening animals to the stakes is not Vedic. Probably it was a new development. Multitudes of people must have gathered to witness the sacrifices. Brāhmaṇas enjoyed considerable respect of all sections of society, and when a Yajña like that of the Brāhmaṇa Kūṭadaṅta took place, it was quite natural that people may have flocked to see it. The great Yajñas of the Kassapa brothers, at Uruvelā, were eagerly attended by the people of Aṅga and Magadha.[4] Yajñas were attended by big feasts, offerings, gifts, distribution of charities and so on.[5] Brāhmaṇas received liberal gifts such as cows, beds, garments, women, chariots, carpets, and palaces filled with corn.[6] The picture of the Yajñas thus revealed by the Buddhist sources is similar to that disclosed by the Brahmanical sources, leaving aside a few exaggerations. There is mention of the Vedic *ṛishis*, like Aṭṭhaka, Vāmaka, Vāmadeva, Viśvāmitra, Jamadagni, and Bhṛigu.[7] It is said that hymns composed by

1. *Jā*. III. 44.
2. *S.N.* I. 76, अस्समेधं पुरिसमेधं सम्मापासं बाजपेय्यं ।
   निरग्गलं महारम्भा न ते होन्ति महप्फला ।।
   A.N. II. 42; *Su. Ni.* II. 7. 20.
3. *D.N.* I. 142; *A.N.* IV. 42, अगिंग ब्राह्मण आधेन्तो यूपं उस्सापेन्तो
4. *S.B.E.* XIII. 124.
5. Law, *Early Texts*, p. 205.
6. *Su.Ni.* II. 7. 20-22.
7. *D.N.* I. 239; *M.N.* II. 200; *A.N.* IV. 61.

these *ṛishis* were sincerely repeated by the Brāhmaṇas.[1] Here we find that the Buddhists were acquainted with the Vedic *ṛishis* and that they were against the practice of repeating these Mantras composed by them. By this period, Vedic texts had become more important than the gods. The Brāhmaṇas also appear as teachers representing various Vedic schools, such as the Addhariyas (Aitareyas), Tittiriyas (Taittiriyas), Chhandokas (Chhāndogyas), Chhandāvas and so on.[2] It would appear from such references that a section of the Brāhmaṇa community sincerely followed the Vedic religious tradition. The Brāhmaṇas worshiped Indra, Soma, Varuṇa, Isāna, Prajāpati, Brahmā, Mahiddhi, Yama and so on.[3] Among these gods all are Vedic, except Isāna, who is frequently referred to in the *Gṛihya-Sūtras*. The Brāhmaṇas invoked them and offered prayer.[4]

When the Buddhist sources use the terms Devadhammikas and Devavatikas to distinguish the masses from the ascetics as the worshippers of gods,[5] and when Pāṇini refers to the devotees of Vāsudeva-Kṛishṇa as Vāsudevakas[6], we are led to assume that the cult of Bhakti was in existence.

The Vedic god Brahmā retained his popularity during our period. The Buddhist writers are not found criticising his worship as they sometimes do that of Agni,[7] but he is described as the highest god by the Buddhist writers. But it was in the age

1. *D.N.* I. 239, 104' ये ते अहेसुं ब्राह्मणानं पुब्बका इसयो मन्तानं कत्तारो मन्तानं पवत्तारो येसं इमं एतरहि ब्राह्मणा पोरानं मन्तपदं गीतं पवुत्तं समिहितं तद् अनुगायन्ति तद् अनुभासन्ति भासितं अनुभासन्ति वाचितं अनुवाचेन्ति ।

2. *D.N.* I. 237, किञ्चापि भो गोतम ब्राह्मणा नाना-मग्गे पञ्ञापेन्ति—अद्धरिया ब्राह्मणा, तित्तिरिया ब्राह्मणा, छन्दोका ब्राह्मणा छन्दावा ब्राह्मणा ब्रह्मचरिया ब्राह्मणा—।

3. *D.N.* I. 244, इन्दम् अह्वयाम, सोमम् अह्वयाम, वरुणम् अह्वयाम, इसानम् अह्वयाम, पजापतिम् अह्वयाम, ब्रह्मम् अह्वयाम्, महिद्धिम् अह्वयाम, यमम् अह्वयामीति ।

4. *D.N.* I. 245.

5. *Chulla-Niddesa*, p. 173 f.; Law, *Early Texts*, p. 195; Barua in I.H.Q. III, 1927, p. 151.

6. *India as known to Pāṇini*, pp. 358-60.

7. *Theragāthā*. 219, 341.

of the Buddha that various Brahmās such as Sanankumāra, Prajāpati, Sahaṁpati and so on were conceived for worshipping.[1]

The Vedic god Indra described in the Brahmanical as well as Buddhist literature as the lord of gods residing in heaven appears as the most popular deity. He is mentioned by various names such as Sakka.[2] Vāsava[3], Maghavā[4] and so on. The Buddhist literature enables us to know in greater detail than the Brahmanical sources about his activities, residence, etc. It represents him as one whose throne grows hot, when somebody acquires extraordinary merit,[5] or when one is in distress.[6] He is also described as descending to this world for helping the virtuous[7] and punishing the evil-doers.[8] He is all-seeing (*Samantachakkhu*)[9] and hence is called the thousand-eyed (*Sahassanetta* or *Sahassākkha*).[10] But he is not eternal, because one can be born in the heaven as the Sakka on account of his merit of virtue,[11] and so he is almost always under the fear of losing his Sakkahood.[12]

The Buddhist literature gives us more information than the Brahmanical sources about the abode of Sakka, his gardens, and so on. He resides in the palace known as Sudhammā,[13] Vejayanta[14] and Missakasāra[15] in the beautiful Tāvatiṁsa heaven.[16]

1. *M. V.* I. 5. 4; *D. N.* I. 244; *S. N.* I. 219: *K. S.* I. 281, 191-2, 298; *A. N.* II. 21.
2. *Mahāvoginda Suttanta of D. N.* ; *Dia* III. 259 f; *M. N.* I. 251; *K. S.* I. 284, 293-307; *S. N.* IV. 101-2; *G. S.* I. 127; *A. N.* III. 370; IV. 162, etc.
3. *K. S.* I. 285-303; *Jā.* VI. 127, 289.
4. *Dhp.* 30; *Jā.* III. 146.
5. *Jā.* III. 129.
6. *Jā.* III. 146.
7. *Jā.* II. 123-24, No. 186 (*Dadhivāhana Jā.*) ; VI. 72-73.
8. *Jā.* No. 540.
9. *Su. Ni.* II. 12. 3-4.
10. *K. S.* I. 295; *Su. Ni.* II. 12. 4; *Vimāna.* IV. 10. 10;
11. *Jā.* II. 101, 312; IV. 63. V. 383.
12. *Jā.* II. 312, III. 129, 132.
13. *Jā.* I. 204; VI. 127, 278.
14. *K. S.* I. 301-2; *Jā.* VI. 278.
15. *Jā.* VI. 289.
16. *K. S.* I. 284-307; *Jā.* II. 312 (तावतिंसलोको रमणियो). The thirty-three gods occur also in the Vedic mythology.

The Sudhammā palace is also the Assembly Hall of gods.[1] In the heaven there are beautiful gardens like Chitralatā, Nandana, Phārusaka, and Missaka for the enjoyment of Sakka.[2] His two constant companions are Mātali, his charioteer, and Pañchasikha, the musician.[3] His chariot is known as the Vejayanta.[4]

Agni occupied an important place in Brahmanism on account of the importance of Agnihotra. The *Gṛihyasūtras* and the *Dharmasūtras* prescribe a number of domestic sacrifices for which Agni is needed. Again, Agni was given a high position due to his place in the Yajña, which is referred to also by the Buddhist writers.[5] They no doubt ridicule Agni-worship, but their statements reveal its popularity among the Brāhmaṇas. When the Buddhist writers speak of the Brāhmaṇas retiring to the forest with the sacrificial fire,[6] when they describe Brāhmaṇas as making offerings and worshipping fire at the Āśramas, like that of Sundarika Bhāradvāja,[7] or when they speak of the Jaṭilas at Uruvelā performing Agnihotra,[8] they give a true account of the place of Agni-worship in Brahmanism. When they ridicule Agni-worship as in the *Santhava Jātaka*, they show Buddhist antagonism to it, which was probably due to its association with Yajña, involving slaughter of living beings.

In the *Vedas* the Sun occupies an important position, but the Moon is insignificant. From the Buddhist literature it appears that the latter also had become a popular deity, because both are described as being worshiped by the people.[9]

The Vedic deity Parjanya (Pajjuna) did not lose his position during this period. He was worshipped as the custodian

1. *D.N.* II. 220; *K.S.* I. 284; *Jā.* VI. 97, 126.
2. *A.N.* III. 40; *Vimāna.* 1. 13. 6; 14. 6; II. 1. 1 and 14; IV. 2. 2, 10. 10; *Jā.* VI. 278, फारुसकं चित्तलतं मिस्सकं नन्दनं वनं । *Jā.* VI. 132.
3. *K.S.* I. 284-303; *S.N.* IV. 103; *Jā.* III. 222; IV. 63; VI. 126.
4. *Jā.* II. 254. Vejayanta is the name of his palace as well as the Chariot.
5. *Su.Ni.* III. 7. 21.
6. *Nāguṇṭha Jā.* (No. 144); *Santhava Jā.* (No. 162).
7. *Su.Ni.* III. 4.
8. *S.B.E.* XIII. 129, 132.
9. *Therīgāthā*, 87; *Jā.* I. 474; VI. 1. 263.

of rain water, whom people prayed for sending forth rains.[1]

Siri or Sirimā was a popular deity of our period.[2] She is described as the daughter of Dhataraṭṭha and the goddess of Fortune and Luck.[3] She manifested herself with raiment and ointment of golden hue and ornaments of golden brightness.[4] She is represented in Bhārhut sculptures as seated on a full blown lotus,[5] which is the same as the representation of Lakshmī. Maṇimekhalā was regarded as the goddess presiding over the oceans who protected victims of shipwreck.[6] This deity must have been worshipped by the sea-farers for safe journey.

Of the abstract deities that were worshipped,[7] some were Vedic and others, new additions. Saddhā (Śraddhā) is a Vedic deity, but Āsā and Hiri are non-Vedic.

There are four Lokapālas (Chātumahārājika Devas)[8] in the four quarters. Dhataraṭṭha Mahārājā, Virulhaka Mahārājā, Virupakkha Mahārājā, and Vessavaṇa Mahārājā are the lords of the East, the South, the West and the North respectively.[9] These four Lokapālas appear in the Bhārhut *Jātaka* scenes.

There is mention of various minor gods. There are picturesque descriptions of various heavens and hells. The popular belief was that those who perform virtuous acts attain heaven while those who indulge in evil acts go to hell.

1. *Jā.* I. 331.
2. She is referred to also in the Jaina Canon, e.g. *Kalpa-Sūtra,—S. B. E.* XXII. 232.
3. *Jā.* III. 262, महाराजस्स अहं धीता धतरट्ठस्स सिरिमतो,
अहं सिरि च लक्खी च भूरिपञ्ञाति मम विदु ।
4. *Jā.* III. 261.
5. *Barua & Sinha*, 186.
6. *Jā.* VI. 35; IV. 17.
7. *Jā.* V. 392, तदा सक्कस्स आसा सद्धा, सिरि हिरीति चतस्सो धीतरो होन्ति ।
8. *M. V.* I. 6. 30; *M. N.* II. 194.
9. *D. N.* II. 220-21.

पुरत्थिमाय दिसाय धतरट्ठो महाराजा पच्छाभिमुखो निसिन्नो होति देवे पुरक्खत्वा
दक्खिणाय दिसाय विरुल्हको महाराजा उत्तराभिमुखो निसिन्नो होति देवे पुरक्खत्वा
पच्छिमाय दिसाय विरुपक्खो महाराजा पुरत्थाभिमुखो निसिन्नो होति देवे पुरक्खत्वा ।
उत्तराय दिसाय वेस्सवणो महाराजा दक्खिणाभिमुखो निसिन्नो होति देवे पुरक्खत्वा

Yakkha Worship

The term Yaksha occurs several times in the *Ṛigveda* and the *Atharvaveda*.[1] It is also referred to in the *Brāhmaṇas*[2] and the *Upanishads*.[3] In the Vedic literature it means a supernatural being, or a ghost like appearance.[4] Sometimes it means the ghost of an expired person,[5] and sometimes it is used for the attendants of Kubera.[6] Our sources, which very frequently refer to the Yaksha or Yakkha, reveal that the central conception of it is that of a non-human being, a spirit, an ogre, a ghost and so on.[7] Sometimes it is said that a Yakkha is a being to whom a sacrifice is given,[8] sometimes he is called a Devatā[9] or Devaputta.[10] The functions of the Yakkhas are diverse. They are kind and interested in the welfare of those in whose contact they come; they save sinners from doing evil.[11] They are guides in the inferno.[12] Sometimes they are represented dangerous, like one who threatened to kill Ambaṭṭha,[13] or the other who intended to slay Sāriputta.[14] Female ones are more dangerous than the males, who entrap and kill the travellers, whom they eat.[15]

The Buddhist literature refers to the cities and haunts of the Yakkhas. Their cities were known as Yakkhanagaras, usually in islands, deep forests, and deserts. A *Jātaka* story mentions a Yakkhanagara called Sirisavatthu in Tambapaṇ-

1. *Vedic Index*, II. 182.
2. *Tai. Br.* III. 12. 3. 1; *Śat. Br.* XIV. 8. 5. 1.
3. *Kau. Up.* 95; *Kenop.* 15.
4. *St. Petersberg Dictionary*.
5. *Ṛig.* IV. 3. 13.
6. *P. T. S. Pāli Dictionary*.
7. *Ibid.*
8. *Vimāna. Comy.* 224, यजन्ति तत्थ बलिं उपहरन्ति ति यक्खा।
333, पूजनीयो भवतो यक्खो ति वुच्चति।
9. *S. N.* I. 205.
10. *Peta-Comy.* 113, 139.
11. *Chariyā Piṭaka*; *Peta.* IV. 1.
12. *Peta.* IV. 11; *Chariyā.* IV. 3.
13. *D. N.* I. 95.
14. *Udāna*, IV. 4.
15. *Jā.* I. 395-96.

ṇidīpa[1] and the another in a forest.[2] But some had individual haunts.[3]

The Buddhist literature refers to several individual Yakkhas, and more than thirty are mentioned by name.[4] That some of them are described as residing in Magadha, some are represented in the Bhārhut sculptures and that huge Yakkha figures were found at Mathurā suggest that Yakkha-worship was widespread in the country. Yakkha Sūchiloma had his haunt near Gayā.[5] He is represented in the Bhārhut sculptures in the shape of a man with turban, on the straight roof, consisting of a massive slab.[6] The *Saṁysutta-Nikāya* and the *Sutta-Nipāta* describe him as discoursing with the Buddha.[7] Yakkha Khara also, who is represented as discoursing with Sūchiloma, seems to have been worshipped at Gayā.[8] Yakkha Indrakūṭa haunted the Indrakūṭa hill at Rājagṛiha.[9] For Yakkha Maṇimāla there was the Maṇimāla Chetiya.[10] Ajakalāpaka resided at Pāṭaliputra[11] in the Ajakalāpaka Chetiya. The *Udāna* commentary gives a terrible description of this Yakkha.[12]

Yakkhas appear in the Buddhist, the Jaina[13] and the Brahmanical[14] sources as objects of worship. There are references to Yaksha shrines,[15] but what was worshipped therein is not very clear. They were worshipped with offerings of deer, pig, fish, drinks, etc.[16] Buddhist and Jaina sources further

1. *Jā.* II. 127; There are references to other Yakkhanagaras, e. g. *Jā.* I. 240.
2. *Jā.* I. 399.
3. *S. N.* I. 207; *Jā.* II. 16.
4. *P. T. S. Pāli Dictionary*.
5. *S. N.* I. 207; *K. S.* I. 264; *Su. Ni.* II. 5.
6. *Barua & Sinha*, 177.
7. *S. N. I.* 207; *Su. Ni.* II. 5.
8. *S. N. I.* 207; *Su. Ni.* II. 5.
9. *S. N.* I. 206; *K. S.* I. 262.
10. *S. N.* I. 208, *K. S.* I. 266.
11. *Udāna*, I. 7.
12. Barua, *Barhut Jātaka Secenes*. Book II, pp. 60-61. Edition, 1934.
13. *S. B. E.* XXII. 92.
14. *S. B. E.* XXX. 219.
15. *S. N.* I. 206, इन्दकूटे पब्बते इन्दकस्स यक्खस्स भवने ।
S. N. I. 207; *Su. Ni.* II. 5, टङ्कितमञ्चे सूचिलोमस्स यक्खस्स भवने ।
Udāna, I.7.
16. *Jā.* I. 425; IV. 115.

inform us how festivals for making offerings to them were proclaimed.[1]

Nāga Worship

Nāga worship seems to have a non-Aryan origin. The Nāga was not worshipped during the Vedic period, and it seems that the cult was adopted by the Aryans, partly as a consequence of absorption of non-Aryan deities into Hindu fold, and partly as a protection against snake-bites. The Brahmanical literature represents Nāgas as hostile to Aryan gods from the earliest period. The *Ṛigveda* shows the hostility of Vṛitra and Ahi, the Nāgas to Indra, who vanguished them.[2] In the *Mahābhārata* we find Arjuna burning the Khāṇḍava-vana, which was the residence of the Nāgas. Again, Janamejaya performed the Sarpayajña to kill them. These references indicate that the Nāga was definitely a non-Aryan deity. Probably he was originally worshipped by the tribe known after them as Nāga which was not Aryan.

The *Mahābhārata*[3] which refers to the images and temples of Nāgas at Rājagṛiha shows that Magadha which was under a non-Aryan ruler Jarāsandha was a great centre of Nāga worship. That Magadha remained a centre of Nāga-worship from very early times supports the view that it was originally a non-Aryan land.

The Nāgas were also worshipped with the idea of getting protection against snake-bites. The Buddha advised the Bhikshus to honour the royal families of the Nāgas, so that they could be protected from snake-bites,[4] and the regions which were covered with dense forests may have given impetus to snake-worship. Till the present day this idea is unchanged among the countryfolk of Bihar. If somebody is bit by a snake, the family members promise to worship the Nāga-Devatā in future, provided the victim is saved. Even if he is not saved, the deity is worshipped in some cases for the fear of other members of the family falling a prey to the wrath of the

1. *Ibid.*, *S.B.E.* XXII, p. 92.
2. *Ṛig.* I. 32.
3. *Mbh. Sabhā.* XXI. 9.
4. *A.N.* II. 72.

Nāga. It appears that the fear of snake-bite was to a considerable extent responsible for the origin of the cult. Even if we take it to be a non-Aryan cult, it may have originated among the non-Aryans due to this factor and may have been easily absorbed in the Hindu society, when the Aryans penetrated forest regions like Magadha. Nāga-worship has remained in vogue even today among the Hindus, and the fifth day of the bright fortnight of the month of Śrāvaṇa, the Nāgapañchamī is the day dedcicated to the worship of Nāga.

The Jaina[1] and the Buddhist[2] sources frequently refer to Nāga-worship, and it appears that, like those of Yakkhas, terracotta figurines of Nāgas were made for the purpose. Their images and temples are referred to in the *Mahābhārata*;[3] Kauṭilya speaks of the images of Nāgas[4] with hoods. And, it is not unlikely that they may have been installed in shrines for the purpose of worship, as we find the structural remains of the Maṇi Nāga temple at Rājagṛiha belonging to a later period.[5] Nāgas are so prominent in the Buddhist sculptures that this does not seem improbable.

The Buddhist sources tell us that Nāgas were worshipped by the offerings of milk, rice, fish, meat, strong drink and the like.[6] According to the *Gṛihya-Sūtras* they were offered fried grain, flour of fried barley and flour over which ghee had been poured.[7] Water was poured; flowers and thread were also offered.[8] Even today milk and fried corn are offered. Probably the *Gṛihya-sūtras* prescribe this ritual for the higher castes.

Tree Worship

The *Ṛigveda* refers to the worship of Arṇyānī, the forest

1. *Nāyādhammakahā*.
2. *Jā*. I. 498; II. 149.
3. *Mbh*. Sabhā; XIX. 9.
4. *Kau*. V. 2.
5. *A.S.R.* 1936-37, p. 46.
6. *Jā*. I. 498, तस्मि काले मनुस्सा समुद्दतीरे खीरपायासमच्छमंससुरादीहि नागबलिकम्मं कत्वा पक्कमिंसु ।
7. *S.B.E.* XXIX, pp. 128-29; 201-2; 328-30.
8. *Ibid.*

spirit,[1] but there is nothing to suggest the worship of any individual tree. Aśvattha[2] and Pippala[3] are no doubt referred to, but not as objects of worship. It is in the *Atharvaveda*,[4] *Aitareya Brāhmaṇa*[5] and the *Upanishads*[6] that one finds the trace of tree worship. The *Atharvaveda* contains a number of non-Aryan religious practices. It presents that stage when many non-Aryan objects of worship were absorbed in Brahmanism. Probably due to the absorbtion of the non-Aryan tribes in the Aryan-fold and recognition of their deities as objects of worship the *Atharvaveda* attaches sanctity to the tree.

That the tree was a non-Aryan object of worship is confirmed by the Harappan or Indus Valley Civilisation. Some of the seals and sealings show that the Pippal tree was worshipped by the Indus Valley people in two forms, i.e. in its natural form and the other in which the tree-spirit was shown emerging from the tree.[7]

According to Hutton sanctity was attached to the tree by the Negrito substratum of the Indian population, who were the earliest inhabitants of India and South-East Asia from whom it was adopted by the Aryans.[8] The cult appears among the Andamanese, who were a Negrito race, and among those whose kinship among the Negrito is established, such as the people of Malaya, Indian Archipelago, etc. Magadha, which was a non-Aryan land, may have been among the centres of this cult.

Our sources disclose that during the period under consideration tree-worship was well known. The belief that trees were abodes of spirits was responsible for their being regarded as objects of worship. Generally trees were considered as residences of some divine spirits like gods, fairies, Apsaras and so on,[9] who were worshipped by the multitude for fulfilling

1. *Vedic Index*, I. 33.
2. *Ibid.*, I. 43.
3. *Ibid.*, I. 531.
4. *A.V.* V. 4. 3.
5. *Ait. Br.* VII. 30-33 (Haug's pp. 190-91); VIII. 16 (Haug's p. 205)
6. *Chhān. Up.* VIII. 5. 3; *Kau. Up.* I. 3.
7. Marshall, J., *Mohenjodaro & Indus Valley Civilisation*, pp. 63-65.
8. *I. H. Q.* 1943.
9. *Jā.* I. 259, 328, 412, 425; II. 440.

their desires for sons, daughters, honour, wealth and so on.[1] Sometimes trees were regarded as abodes of evil spirits like Pretas and Nāgas,[2] and people worshipped them out of fear to please the spirit, so that he may not harm them. This belief survives even today among the countryfolk, and people regard certain trees as the haunts of Bhūtas.

Bull Worship

India being primarily an agricultural land has always been depending upon the bull for ploughing the fields, and it is quite natural that the agriculturists should express their gratitude to him by honouring and worshipping him. Secondly, the bull is the Vāhana of Śiva, and the cult of Śaivism is among the earliest religious practices in India which can be traced back to the days of the Harappan Civilisation. On the authorities of Pāṇiṇi,[3] Kauṭilya,[4] and Patañjali[5] it can be said that Śiva, whose images were made and probably sold in the market and installed in shrines, was worshipped in Northern India from c. 5th B.C. onwards. Buddhist sources speak of the honour shown to the bull, sometimes in normal course[6] and sometimes on occasions like his death.[7] The association of the bull with Śiva is not referred to; its first pictorial representation is found in the Kushāṇa coins, where Śiva appears along with his bull. Even if we deny the possibility of bull being worshipped during our period as a Vāhana of Śiva, the custom of showing reverence to him on account of his assistance in agriculture cannot

1. *Jā.* I. 259, एकस्मिं महन्ते वटरूक्खे महाजनं सन्निपतितं तस्मिं रूक्खे निब्बतदेवताय सन्तिके पुत्तधीतुयसधनादिसु यं यं इच्छन्ति तं तं पथेन्तं ।
2. *B.I.* pp. 56, 232.
3. *Pā.* V. 3. 96; *India as known to Pāṇini*, p. 361.
4. *Kau.* II. 4; V. 2., *India as known to Pāṇini*, p. 362.
5. *Bhāshya*, II. 429.
6. *Jā.* II. 225.
7. *Jā.* IV. 326—The *Pañchuposatha Jātaka* (No. 490) refers to the worship of a bull when he was dead in a Pachchantagāma of Magadha. The story says that at the sudden death of the bull multitudes of people gathered, decorated the dead body with garland, flowers, etc., and weeping carried it to the place of burial.

be put aside. In the present-day society, the villagers of Bihar respect both the cow and the bull on the occasion of Dīpāvalī, the day of worshipping Lakshmī. The worship of bull and cow on this occasion speaks of the inner idea of accepting their share in agriculture and adding to the wealth of the family. The people of Mahārāshṭra worship the bull on the Full-Moon day of Āshāḍha which is due to his helpfulness in the work of agriculture. It can be concluded that the bull was worshipped partly due to this assistance in agriculture and partly due to his association with Śiva.

—:0:—

CHAPTER VIII

MONASTIC LIFE

Gradula Development of the Homeless Stage of Life and the Main Ascetic Orders

The expression monastic life is not used here in the strict sense of life in the well-built monasteries, but to denote the ascetic or homeless life in general. The earliest trace of the homeless life is found in the *Ṛigveda* where the Munis[1] and the Yatis[2] are referred to. That they put on antelope-skin, grew beard, practised asceticism and discarded the desire for worldly life is suggested by a passage in the *Aitareya Brāhmaṇa* which shows contempt for Sanyāsa.[3] Thus, we find that the order of the ascetics, or the order of the third and fourth stages of life, i.e. the Vānaprastha and the Sanyāsa was started long ago, but was not popular. Till the days of the *Chhāndogya-Upanishad*, there was also no clear line of demarcation between the two stages of Vānaprastha and Sanyāsa and they rather coalesced with each other[4]. People as a rule retired to the forest after the completion of the householder's stage. Yājñavalkya is described as telling his wife that he was going into a life of Pravrajyā from being a householder[5]. The *Muṇḍaka Upanishad* tells us that by penance one acquires the knowledge of the Brahman[6] and that one knowing Him should live on begging.[7] We find the mention of the four Āśramas in the *Jābālopanishad* where it is stated that one could become a Sanyāsin, after passing successively through the three earlier stages of life ; or at any time when the urge for the realisation of the Brahman was

1. *Ṛig.* X. 136. 2,4.
2. *Ṛig.* VIII. 3.9 ; VIII. 6. 18 ; X. 72. 7.
3. *Ait. Br.* (VII. 13) by Martin Haug, Vol. I, p. 178,
   किन्नु मलं किमजिनं किमु श्मश्रूणि किं तपः;
   पुत्रं ब्राह्मण इच्छध्वं स वै लोको वदावदः ।
4. *Kane, Hist. of Dh. Śā.*, VI. II, Pt. I, p. 421.
5. *Br. Up.* VI. 5. 2.
6. *Mu. Up.* III. 2-6.
7. *Mu. Up.* I. 2. 11.

felt, one was to renounce the world.[1] This shows that though the general practice was to become an ascetic after the householder's stage, one could entei the forest even during the early stage of his life.

The reason of the rise of the ascetics' order was the desire for spiritual realisation, through the quest for Ātman. The *Bṛihadāraṇyaka Upanishad* says, "Knowing him, the Ātman, the Brāhmaṇas relinquish the desire for children, the desire for wealth, the pursuit of worldly weal and go forth as mendicants[2]." This most probably refers to those who renounced the world at the early stage, following the principle of *Yadahareva virajet-tadaharevapravrajet.* It was the spiritual urge which gave rise to the homeless life. Hence it appears that the appearance of the doctrine of the Brahman and the origin of the monastic life in India are two aspects of the same issue. It seems that the realisation that real happiness did not lie in the enjoyment of sensual pleasures, but in realising the Brahman, the all-pervading, non-perishable Being, that the urge for renouncing the world in quest of Him became intense, and gradually there came into existense the order of the hermits. It was the realisation of the perishable nature of the external world that gave rise to a number of speculations during the Upanishadic period, and later during the days of the Buddha a number of ascetics' orders came into existence. New philosophical ideas changed the aim of life. What appears important to the natural consciousness of ordinary men were of no value for those whose aim was the realisation of the eternal truth. For them sacrifices and external observances were considered to be incapable of raising the spirit to the Ātman, to disclose

1. *Jā. Up.* IV, quoted in *History of Dharmaśāstra*, Vol. II, p, 421,
ब्रह्मचर्यं परिसमाप्य गृही भवेद् गृही
भूत्वा वनी भवेद् वनी भूत्वा प्रव्रजेत् ।
यदि वेतरथा ब्रह्मचर्यादेव प्रव्रजेत् गृहाद्वावनद्वा ।
यदहरेव विरजेत्तदहरेव प्रव्रजेत् ।

2. *Bṛ. Up.* IV. 4.22.
एतं वै तदात्मानं विदित्वा ब्राह्मणाः पुत्रैषणायाश्च वित्तैषणायाश्च
लोकैषणायाश्च व्युत्थाप्य भिक्षाचर्यं चरन्ति ।

to the individual ego his identity with the universal ego.[1] Thus it was in quest of the universal soul that the forest life was started. Probably the Brāhmaṇas first started seeking deliverance as beggars or forest hermits in retirement from worldly concerns, but there is nothing to show that it was their exclusive right to lead the homeless life[2]. It can be, therefore, assumed that all those who desired to strive after spiritual attainment renounced the world, though the number of the Brāhmaṇas would have been large.

We have already seen that the Order of the Sanyāsins or the Parivrājakas had come into existence much earlier than the days of the Buddha. But we do not know how many schools of ascetics existed during the early period. The existence of a number of ascetic orders during the days of the Buddha would suggest that probably a few centuries before his birth various shools of the homeless life had taken their root in the Indian society, though we do not possess much information about them. But it is quite apparent that the Sanyāsins had made numerous hermitages in the forest lands of the past. The *Rāmāyaṇa* shows that there existed several Āśramas of *ṛishis* such as those of Viśvāmitra, Gautama and others ; and during their journey from Ayodhyā to Mithilā, Rāma and Lakshmaṇa came across many hermitages. The Buddhist *Suttas* like the *Isigili-sutta*, *Khaggavishāṇa-sutta*, and others refer to a number of legendary ascetics of the past, which tell us that ascetic life was quite common before the birth of the Buddha.

The Buddhist and the Jaina sources of our period inform us that during the days of the Buddha, not only the earlier practice of retiring to the forest for the attainment of spiritual insight continued, but there rose to eminence various ascetic orders under their respective teachers. The north-eastern part of India was in a state of religious and philosophical ferment, and it was in the land of Bihar and Eastern Uttar Pradesh that a number of new philosophical doctrines were propounded, and new religious orders were established during the period under review. The new schools of philosophy

1. Oldenberg, *The Buddha*, p. 61.
2. *Ibid.*, p. 62.

and religion exhibit a common tendency of encouraging the homeless life. The Buddhists, the Jainas, the Ājīvikas, the Achelakas and others gave impetus to a life of disinterestedness to the world. But the field for these schools had been created by the Upanishadic philosophy of deliverance of the soul which was a dominant factor in regulating the Brahmanical Ascetic Order. The contemporary literature shows that people, whether they were the adherents of Brahmanism, Buddhism, or Jainism, or of any other sect, all cherished intense yearning and attraction for the forest life. The forests, which were the usual place of residence for hermits, were found to be resounding with the bustle of busy life, led by hundreds of ascetics living together in huts.

The usual and the common terms used in the Buddhist literature to denote one's passing to the homeless state from the household one are *agārasmā anagāriyaṁ pabbajati*[1] and *isipaabbajjāṁ pabbajitvā*.[2] The way in which the glory of the homeless life is sung and the worthlessness of the worldly life is described in the *Suttas* of the *Dīgha*,[3], *Majjhima*[4] and *Saṁyutta Nikāyas*,[5] the *Therīgāthā*,[6] the *Sutta-Nipāta*[7], and in some of the *Gāthās* of the *Jātakas* suggest that there had been a wave of asceticism during the 6th century B.C. Wordly life was regarded as an obstacle for the attainment of spiritual insight, because sensual pleasures, which are various, sweet and charming, agitate the mind under their different shapes.[8] People in large numbers renounced the world. Neither wealth nor affection for family members could stand in the path of one who resolved to enter the homeless life. The Brāhmaṇa Mahāsālas who were considerably wealthy quite gladly renounced the world for the sake of leading the forest life. While leading this life they wandered from place to place, with meagre possession, subsisting on roots

1. *D. N.* I. 60-61 ; *M.N.* I. 163, 179 ; II. 75 ; *A.N.* II. 123 ; *Udāna*, III, 2. *Therī-gāthā*, 46, etc.
2. *Jā.* I. 140, 295, 406, etc.
3. *Sāmaññapala-Sutta of D. N.*
5. *M.N.* I. 240, 267 ; II. 211.
5. *S.N.* V. 250-51.
6. *Therīgāthā*, 301.
7. *Khaggavishāṇa-Sutta* (*Su. Ni.* I. 3).
8. *Ibid.*

and fruits and on alms, during their journeys through the haunts of men.

The desire of the forest life had so much penetrated into the religious mind of the people that sometimes even parents encouraged their young sons to retire to the wood and practice asceticism for the attainment of the higher state of spiritual enlightenment. In a *Jātaka* (No. 61) a mother is seen encouraging her son for entering the homeless life, by pointing out to him the evils of women[1]. It seems that there had grown an antipathy to the family life, and in their zeal for renunciation people had become prejudiced towards women. One who desired to part with all the ties of the family life and the attachments of the world found that woman was a great hindrance in his path, and hence he felt that she was the greatest evil. One who resolved to become a recluse expressed his feelings towards women in these words—

> In lust unbridled, like devouring life
> Are women,—frantic in their rage.
> The sex renouncing, fain would I retire
> To find peace in a hermitage.[2]

What was the reason that asceticism became so popular during this period? Tapas—literally means burning or glowing. It presupposed self-control which was often supplanted by self-torture. Later it acquired the secondary sense of retirement into solitude in the forest for the purpose of practising austerity for higher attainments. People believed that by the practice of asceticism it was possible to attain mystic and marvellous results. It was the belief that extraordinary superhuman faculties could be acquired by Tapas. Common man attached importance to austerities and believed in the infinite possibilities of the Yoga practice, which was considered to be capable of producing superhuman powers such as becoming invisible, flying in the air,

1. *Jā.* I. 285,
अथ नं माता इत्थिनं दोसं दस्सेत्वा अरञ्ञं पेसेतुकामा ।
2. *Jā.* I. 288.

walking on water, or going to the other side of a hill or a wall in spite of the obstructions and similar extraordinary acts[1]. The Yogī was considered to be possessed of tremendous power, and he was compared with a potter who could make pots of any shape he liked out of properly prepared clay.[2] One who could exhibit greater psychic power would attract more people and would be considered as superior to other Yogīs, who would not be able to compete with him. Now and then we get references to the performance of miracles by the Buddha, so that he could establish his superiority over the leaders of the contemporary ascetic orders. It is said that at the Aśrama of Uruvela Kassapa he conquered the fire of the Nāga by his own fire, threw him into his almsbowl and said to the Jaṭila Uruvela Kassapa, "Here you see the Nāga, Kassapa, his fire has been conquered by me.".[3] The Jaṭila teacher thought, "Truly the Samaṇa possesses high magical faculties, since even the four Mahārājās come to hear his preachings.[4]" The incident took place when the annual festival of the Jaṭilas was approaching. The Jaṭila teacher was apprehensive of the fact that if the Buddha would perform a wonder before the great assembly of the people of Aṅga and Magadha, the latter would gain honour, while the esteem of the former would diminish.[5] It is said that the Buddha possessed superiority over all on account of his experience of the highest state of consciousness through the ninth *Samāpatti* called *Saññavedayitanirodha*.[6] His miraculous magic power is described as even greater than that of Su-Brahmā and Suddhavāsa.[7] Similar is the case with other religious personalities, who are described as possessing superhuman power. Mahāmoggallāna is described as endowed with immense psychic power.[8] Mahāvīra is described as all-

1. *S. B. B.* II, p. 88.
2. *S. B. B.* II, p. 89 ; D.N. I. 78.
3. *S. B. E.* XIII, p. 120. The Buddhist literature very often refers to the Buddha exhibiting supernatural power, e. g., *G. S.* I. 170 describes him flying in the air. Similar and other forms of performances are quite common is the *Jātakas*.
4. *S. B. E.* XIII, p. 123.
5. *Ibid.*, p. 124.
6. *M. N.* I. 296.
7. *K. S.* I. 185.
8. *A. N.* I. 19, इद्धि मन्तानं यदिदं महामोग्गल्लानो ।

knowing, all-seeing, and possessed of infinite knowledge.[1] It was through his magic power that he humbled Gosāla. Tīthaṅkara Gosāla was regarded among the three great Avadhūtas in history[2]. Rohitassa is described as possessed of immense psychic power, when he was the son of Bhoja and lived as a hermit. He performed deeds like walking in the air and so on.[3]

It is true that the common man regarded asceticism as a means of securing supernatural powers, but all did not renounce the world with a view to acquiring miraculous psychic faculties ; we have already seen that the main cause of renunciation was spiritual enlightenment. Generally references show that the realisation of the transitory nature of worldly pleasures led to the idea of retirement to the forest. Prince Gautama and Mahāvīra renounced the world for the realisation of the Truth. The *Jātaka* stories show that the evil nature of the worldly desires led to the idea of renunciation. It is a different thing that the common man's respect and devotion for the ascetics were guided by the idea of the latter's possession of superhuman power.

The common people showed proper respect to all the various orders of mendicants. An ordinary man was not concerned with the minute differences of doctrines. For him, those persons whose life was dedicated to spiritual enlightenment, occupied a high position. The Buddhist sources tell us that the Śramaṇas and the Brāhmaṇas were respected and shown hospitality alike by the people[4] and that they were invoked for protection together with the deities.[5] According to the Jaina *Sūtras* it was a meritorious work to honour the mendicants with food. Śakra (Indra) is seen instructing

1. *M. N.* I. 92f.,
निगण्ठो आवुसो नाथपुत्तो सब्बञ्ञू सब्बदस्सावी अपरिसेसं ञाणदस्सनं पटिजानाति……चरतो च मे तिट्ठतो च सुत्तस्य च जागरस्स च सततं समितं ञाणदस्सनं पच्चुपट्ठितन्ति ।
2. *A. N.* III. 384.
3. *A. N.* II. 48.
4. *D. N.* I. 51 (*Sāmaññaphala-Sutta*, 14.)
समण ब्राह्मणानं उद्धग्गिकं दक्खिनं पतिट्ठापेन्ति सोवग्गिकं सुखविपाकं सग्गसम्वत्तनिकं ।
5. Senart, *Mahāvastu*, III. 310.5.

king Nimi, "Offer great sacrifices, feed the Samaṇas and the Brāhmaṇas, give alms, enjoy yourself and offer sacrifices : thus you will be a true Kshatriya."[1] We are told that they were feasted on festive occasions.[2] In the royal court, the Śramaṇas and the Brāhmaṇas appeared as teachers of religious faiths and received proper honour. Inscriptional evidence also shows that they enjoyed high esteem in society. In the inscriptions of Aśoka, Śramaṇas and Brāhmaṇas appear together occupying equal position, and people are instructed always to pay respect to them and also to be liberal to them in charity.[3] That the Ājīvikas, who were looked down upon by the Buddhists were also shown proper respect, is revealed from the inscriptions of Aśoka and Daśaratha, which refer to their dedications of cave dwellings for the Ājīvika ascetics.

There is nothing to show in the Buddhist sources that members of all the castes were not eligible for entering the homeless life. It is true that in the earliest stage the Brāhmaṇas started the practice of renouncing the world, and were imitated by a few Kshatriyas, like Janaka, Aśvapati and others, but members of other castes also may have been entering the homeless order of life. During our period there existed several ascetic orders, to which all the castes were freely admitted. It may be argued here that the reason for this liberal outlook was the advent of Buddhism. But this does not seem to be totally true, because Buddhism was not able to do away with the feeling of caste distinction. Even in the Buddhist Order, at the early stage, feeling of caste superiority was not completely absent. From the stories of Chaṇḍālas receiving proper respect in society in the form of ascetics, like Mātaṅga, and from statements which tell us that even a Śūdra,[4] or a slave[5], or a Chaṇḍāla[6] who became a mendicant could receive proper respect, it appears that there was a section which favoured the entry of all castes in the homeless order. The inner idea was that by becoming a mendicant one lost his caste identity, which is expressed in

1. *Jaina Sū.* II. p. 39.
2. *S.B.E.* XXII. 92-93.
3. *R. E.* IV, IX, XI; *P.E.* VII.
4. *Sāmaññaphala-Sutta. of D. N.*
5. *S. B. B.* (*Dia.*) II. 76-77
6. *Jā.* III. 235 ; IV. 201.

the *Mahāvagga* and the *Sāmaññaphala-Sutta*. The Dharmaśāstras permit only the twiceborn to become Vānaprasthins and Sanyāsins, probably because the Śūdras performed no Vedic rituals. The actual situation seems to be that the percentage of the Śūdras becoming ascetics was very low. As their position in society was low, all sections did not favour their entry into the order of the ascetics.

The Buddhist texts refer to the existence of various ascetic orders. The *Udāna* says that mendicants both Samaṇas and Brāhmaṇas of various denominations of different views, opinions, inclinations, and doctrines were agitating the mind of people[1]. Though this statement belongs to a latter period, yet it is true of the 6th century B.C. when various orders of the ascetics under different teachers had risen to eminence.

Our sources give varying lists of the several ascetic orders. The *Sāmaññaphala-Sutta*[2] and the *Mahāparinibbāna-Suttanta*[3] of the *Dīgha-Nikāya* speak of six main orders of the Samaṇas under their renouned teachers, who were known as the leading thinkers and enjoyed the esteem of the multitude during the days of the Buddha. They were the orders of Pūraṇa Kassapa, Makkhali Gosāla, Pakudha Kachchāyana, Ajitakesakambalī, Sañjaya Belaṭṭhiputta, and Nigaṇṭha Nātaputta. Other texts mention also Muṇḍasāvakas, Paribbājakas, Magaṇḍikas, Tedaṇḍikas, Aviruddhakas, Devadhammikas, Pisāchillikas (Probably worshippers of Piśāchas), Achelakas, and Ekasāṭikas.[4] A Jaina commentator of the 9th century A.D. quotes a very old hemistich which mentions only five orders of the Samaṇas, i. e. the Nigaṇṭhas, the Śākyas, the Tāpasas, the Gairikas, and the Ājīvikas.[5] The inscriptions of Aśoka reveal that the Brāhmaṇa, Buddhsit, Jaina and Ājīvika monks formed the main religious orders of the period.

1. *Udāna*, VI. 4-5.
2. *D. N.* I. 47-49, *S. B.B.* (*Dia.*) II, pp. 66-76.
3. *D. N.* II. 150 ; *S. B. E.* XI. 106.
4. *S. B.B.* (*Dia.*) II. 220-2 ; *S. N.* I. 78.
   Udāna, VI. 2.
   तेन खो पन समयेन सत्त च जटिला सत्त च निगण्ठा सत्त च अचेला सत्त च एकसाटा सत्त च परिब्बाजका परूल्हकच्छनखलोमा खारिविविधमादाय भगवतो अविदूरे अतिक्कमन्ति ।
5. *Jaina Sū.* Pt. I, p. 128, Footnote 1.

The texts belong to different periods and differ in their enumerations of the mendicant sects. The reason of this confusion seems to be partial and defective knowledge, inadequate appreciation of the distinction between genus and species, and confusion between tradition and personal knowledge.[1] Many of the external characteristics are common to the various schools of asceticism, and the task of giving distinct pictures of all the ascetic orders is rendered difficult. The terms generally used in the Pāli Buddhist literature to denote an ascetic in general are Paribbājaka, Bhikkhu, Samaṇa, and Tāpasa. While Paribbājaka is very common in the *Nikāyas*, Tāpasa occurs frequently in the *Jātakas*. The Jaina *Aupapātika-Sūtra* (Sec. 74) probably speaks of Tāpasas living as Vānaprasthins. They are described as family men owning property, or fire-worshippers, or performers of sacrifices and funeral rites.

The Brāhmaṇa ascetics were probably divided into two classes, i. e. the one retiring to the forests as Vānaprasthins and then passing to the stage of Sanyāsa, and the other consisting of the wandering mendicants. According to Rhys Davids the Paribbājakas or the wandering mendicants were teachers or sophists who spent eight or nine months of every year wandering about, and they very often lodged in the Public Halls where conversational discussions were held on philosophical and religious questions.[2] The learned scholar further tells us that they were different from the ascetics.[3] But he seems to have been misled in his assumption. The Paribbājakas lived on alms collected from door to door, and their other characteristics also show that they belonged to the class of ascetics, though formed a distinct and separate group.

The Parivrājakas formed two distinct groups, i.e. the Brāhmaṇa Parivrājakas and the Aññatitthiya Parivrājakas. The former were the members of the Sanyāsa-Āśrama. The *Jātakaș* use the terms Tāpasa and Parivriājaka, and the descriptions show that these words denote the Vānaprasthins and

1. S. K. Dutta, *Early Buddhist Monachism*, p. 45.
2. *B.* I. p. 161.
3. *Ibid.*
4. *A. N.* I. 157.

the Sanyāsins. The main feature of the Brāhmaṇa-ascetics of this period is that they formed large groups under various teachers. The *Nikāyas* inform us that there were about forty-seven leaders, probably of the Brāhmaṇa Parivrājaka contemporaries of the Buddha. Poṭṭhapāda,[1] Bhaggavagotta,[2] Paṭika-putta[3], Nigrodha,[4] Sakula-Udāyi,[5] Pilotaka,[6] Dīghanakha,[7] Māgandiya,[8] Samaṇa-Maṇḍikāputta Uggahamāṇa[9], Vekhaṇasa,[10] Potaliputta,[11] Timbaruka,[12] Susīma,[13] Suchimukhī (Paribbājikā),[14] Vachchhagotta,[15] Jambukhādaka,[16] Sāmaṇḍaka,[17] Nandiya,[18] Kuṇḍaliya,[19] Sarabha,[20] Annabhāra,[21] Varadhara,[22] Potaliya,[23] Moliyasīvaka,[24] Sutavā,[25] Sajjha,[26] Samandakāni,[27] Uttiya,[28] Kokanuda,[29] Ajita[30], Sabhiya[31], and Sañjaya[32] figure as prominent leaders of the orders of Parivrājakas. We are also told of Subhaddha,[33] Pessa[34], Kandaraka,[35]

1. *D. N.* I. 178-203.
2. *D. N.* III. 1-2.
3. *D. N.* III. 12-35.
4. *Ibid*, pp. 36-57.
5. *M. N.* II. 29-39 ; *A.N.* II. 29, 176.
6. *M.N.* I. 175.
7. *M. N.* I. 497-501.
8. *M.N.* I. 502-13.
9. *M.N.* II. 22-29. He lived in Śrāvastī.
10. *M.N.* II. 40-44.
11. *M.N.* III. 207, 209.
12. *S.N.* II. 22.
13. *S.N.* II. 119-28.
14. *S.N.* III. 238-40.
15. *M. N.* I. 481-83 ; *S. N.* III. 257-63 ; IV. 395-403, *G.S.* I. 143.
16. *S. N.* IV. 251, 403.
17. *Ibid.* pp. 261, 403.
18. *S.N.* V. 11.
19. *S.N.* V. 73-75.
20. *G.S.* I. 167.
21. *A.N.* II. 29-39, 176.
22. *A.N.* II. 29, 176.
23. *A.N.* II. 100-1.
24. *S.N.* IV. 230-31 ; *A.N.* III. 356
25. *A.*N. IV. 369-71.
26. *Ibid*, p. 371-72
27. *A.N.* V. 121.
28. *Ibid.* p. 193.
29. *Ibid. p.* 196.
30. *Ibid.* pp. 229-30.
31. *S.N.* IV. 403 ; *Su. Ni.* III. 6.
32. *Dhp. Ṭīkā*, Vol. I. 88-90, *Mahāvastu*, III. 59.
33. *D.N.* II. 148-53.
34. *M.N.* I. 339.
35. *Ibid.*

Agivachchhagotta,[1] Sandaka,[2] Anugāra,[3] Uttiya,[4] Samaññakāni[5], Katriyana,[6] Migasira,[7] Paviṭṭhakolita,[8] Upatissa,[9] Pasura,[10] Laduyāyi,[11] and Palāyi[12]. Almost all of these religious teachers except Māgandiya[13] belonged to Bihar and Eastern Uttar Pradesh, and almost half of them either actually belonged to Bihar or lived in some Āśrama for some time. The famous Parivrājaka Sañjaya lived at Rājagṛiha[14]. Sakula-Udāyi also figures as staying at Rājagṛiha[15]. The *Aṅguttara-Nikāya* refers to Annabhāra, Sarabha, and others as staying in the Parivrājakārāma at the banks of the Sappiniyā river.[16] Potaliputta[17] and Dīghanakha[18] also lived at Rājagṛiha. Anugāra and Varadhara are mentioned as staying at Moranivāpa Parivrājakārāma[19] (in Rājagṛiha), and Vachchhagotta stayed at Vaiśālī in the Puṇḍarika Parivrājakārāma.[20] There is also mention of Moliyasīvaka[21] meeting the Buddha at Rājagṛiha, and Jambukhādaka meeting Sāriputta at Nālakagāma (in Magadha)[22] and Ukkavela (in Vajji).[23] Sabhiya appears as staying at Rājagṛiha and meeting the Buddha.[24]

It is shown by the Buddhist sources that the Brāhmaṇa ascetics (Tāpasas and Parivrājakas) such as Sañjaya, Uggahamāṇa

1. *M. N.* I. 483-89.
2. *M.N.* I. 513-24. He lived near Kauśāmbī.
3. *M.N.* II. 1.
4. *A. N.* V. 193-95.
5. *Psalms of Brethren*, p. 40.
6. *Ibid.*
7. *Ibid.* pp. 138-39.
8. *Dhp. Comy.* Vol. I. 88-90.
9. *Ibid.*
10. *Su. Ni.* IV. 8.
11. *Ibid.*
12. *Jā.* II. 216.
13. He lived at Kammāsadamma Nigama in the Kuru Country (*M.N.* I. 501).
14. *M. V.* I. 23.1.
15. *M. N.* II. 29, *A.N.* II 29, 176
16. *A. N.* II 29, 176.
17. *M. N.* III. 207.
18. *M. N.* I 497.
19. *M. N.* II 1-22.
20. *M. N.* I. 481.
21. *S. N.* IV. 230.
22. *S. N.* IV. 251.
23. *S. N.* IV. 261.
24. *Su. Ni.* III. 6.

and others had gathered large numbers of disciples at the parks and woodlands where they lived. Sañjaya lived with two hundred and fifty disciples[1], and Uggahamāṇa had seven hundred Parivrājakas[2] under him. The *Jātakas* refer to the Tāpasas as gathering five hundred disciples each[3], which is a conventional number. The leaders of the Brāhmaṇa ascetics were known as the *gaṇasatthās*.[4] Satthā was probably used for the heads of all ascetic orders, and we find that the Buddha was also called a Satthā.

The *Jātakas* most probably depict the life of the Vānaprasthins and the Sanyāsins, but there is no demarcation made between the two. It is only in the Dharmaśāstra literature of a later period that a clear distinction is made between the two stages of life. The *Jātakas* show that renunciation of the world was permitted at any stage of life. Some renounced the world very early in life, apparently without fulfilling their duties as scholars (Brahmachārins) and householders (Gṛihasthas)[5]. Some became ascetics after completing their studies, i.e. after the completion of the stage of Brahmacharya,[6] and some passed on to the homeless life from the stage of the householder's life, after fulfilling their duties towards the family members[7]. Generally a householder renounced the world after begetting children, but he would do so at any moment he liked. It is also interesting to note that one could take with him his wife and children, and make them members of the homeless order.[8]

Now, how far does the above account correspond with that of the Dharmaśātras? According to *Baudhāyana-Dharmasūtra* one could renounce the world after the student life, or

1. *M. V.* I. 23. 1.
2. *M. N.* II. 22-29.
3. *Jā.* I. 140 ; 406, 431, etc.
4. *Jā.* II. 72.
5. E. G., *Jā* I. 333, 361, 373, 450 ; II. 131, 145, 232, 262, 269, III. 45,
ब्राह्मणकुले निब्बत्तित्वा वयपत्तो कामे पहाय इसिपब्बज्जं पब्बजित्वा झानाभिञ्ञं उप्पादेत्वा झानकीळं कीळन्तो हिमवन्ते रमणीये वनसण्डे वसन्ति ।
6. *Jā*, II. 57, 72, 85 ; III. 64, 110, 119, 228-9, 249, 308 ; V. 152. 193,
वयपत्तो उग्गहितसिप्पो इसिपब्बज्जं पब्बजित्वा…।
7. *Jā.* II. 269, 437 ; III. 147 ; V. 312-13.
8. *Jā.* II. 269 III. 147 ; V. 312-13.

after being a householder, or from the forest.[1] Āpastamba and Vaśishṭha permit option of becoming an ascetic, after the completion of the Brahmacharya stage, or after becoming a householder.[2] Thus, we find that the Brahmanical sources support the Buddhist account. In view of the fact that there had been a wave of asceticism during the days of the Buddha, the information derived from the Buddhist sources, mainly from the popular stories, seems to be substantially true. The later Dharmaśāstra writers do not encourage renunciation, before the completion of the Gṛihastha Āśrama. Manu is dogmatic in not permitting one to renounce the world before fulfilling his duties as a householder.[3] Living in the forest as a Vānaprasthin and preparing for the final stage is not shown by the Pāli texts; they refer to ascetics as a whole.

Considerable light is thrown upon the normal life of the Parivrājakas by the Buddhist, Jaina and Brahmanical sources; though these religions differed in their philosophical theories, they seem to be substantially in agreement on the discipline of the wandering Bhikshu. Regular monastic orders with their permanent buildings, which were so prominent a feature of the life in the country after *c.* 200 B. C., were yet to come into existence. Monks as a rule lived under trees, in caves, or in groves and orchards[4], usually on the vicinity of important towns, like Rājagṛiha, Vaiśālī, Śrāvastī, Kapilavastu, etc. Rājagṛiha had several delightful spots like Veluvana[5], Ghijjhakūṭa mountain[6], Moranivāpa[7], the Parivrājakārāma on the bank of the Sappiniyā river[8], Tapodārāma[9], Jīvaka's

1. *Bau. Dh. S.* II. 10. 2-6 ; *S. B. E.* XIV. 273.
2. *S. B. E.* II. 153 ; XIV. 40, 46.
3. *Manu.* VI. 1, 34-37, 87-88.
4. *M.N.* I. 56, 269, 274, 346, 440; *A.N.* II. 210; III. 91; *D.N.* I. 71, विवित्तं सेनासनं भजति, अरञ्ञं रूक्खमूलं पब्बत्तं कन्दरं गिरिगुहं सुसानं वनपत्थं अब्भोकासं पलालपुञ्जं ।
5. *D.N.* II. 116-17; *M.N.* III. 13.
6. *D.N.* II. 116; *M.N.* I. 497.
7. *M.N.* II. 1-22, 29-39.
8. *A.N.* II. 29; 176.
9. *D.N.* II. 116-17; *A.N.* V. 196.

Amravana[1], Sītavana,[2] Maddakuchchi[3] and so on which were resorted to by a large number of Parivrājakas. These had made Rājagriha famous as a halting place for the wandering monks. There was another pleasant and delightful Āśrama at Uruvelā with the river Nerañjarā (modern Nīlāñjana or Phalgu)) with her glassy streams, showing the bathing places with gradual descents of steps.[4] Pavārika's mango grove at Nālandā,[5] Gaggarā Pokkharaṇī at Champā,[6] Mahāvana near Vaiśālī,[7] Mallikārāma in Śrāvastī[8] and others were important places during this period utilised by the Parivrājakas. Monks used to visit the towns and villages for alms by the midday;[9] this procedure is expressly enjoined by the Buddhist, Jaina, and Brahmaṇical authorities. The Buddha permitted the concession of accepting occasional invitations from the laity for midday meals. This practice prevails among the Hindu Sanyāsins of the present day and may not have been unknown in the 5th century B.C. During our period a beginning was made to have some kind of permanent structures in some of the orchards like Jetavana, but these were few. Monks usually lived in thatched huts (Paṇṇasālaṁ) in the Āśramas, even in the rainy season.[10] We get an idea of some of them from sculptures in Sānchī and Bhārhut.

A section of the Parivrājakas, however, preferred to stay away from haunts of men in deep forests where they felt they could practice their spiritual exercises better.[11] When the Buddhist sources like the *Kassapasīhanāda-Sutta*[12] and the *Udum-*

1. *D.N.* I. 49, II. 116-17.
2. *D.N.* II; 116. *Dia.* III 123; *S.B.E.*XI. 56.
3. *Ibid.* Other delightful spots mentioned here are Gotamanigrodha, Chora-papāta, Sattapaṇṇiguhā, Kāla-Silā in Isigili.
4. *M.N*· I. 166-7; Mahāvastu, III. 123; *Lalitavistara*, Mitra's edition, p. 311.
5. *D.N.* I. 211; II. 81; III. 99.
6. *M.V.* IX 1.1.
7. *D.N.* 119. Vaiśālī had several pleasant and beautiful spots suitable for being utilised by the wandering monks; they were Gotamaka Chetiya, Udena Chetiya, Chāpāla Chetiya, Sītambavana Chetiya, Sarandada Chetiya, and Bahuputta Chetiya(*D. N.* II 117-18).
8. *M.N.* II 22.
9. *Manu.* VI. 56; Vai. Dh. P. III. 6.9.
10. *Theragāthā*, 127. *Udāna*, III. 3; *Jā.* I. 506.
11. *Theragāthā*, 59. 541.
12. *D.N.* 1.166.

barika-Sīhanāda-Suttanta[1], the *Jātakas*[2], and the *Sutta-Nipāta*[3] refer to monks living upon roots of trees, fruits, etc., or when the Dharmaśāstras lay down that Vānaprasthins and Sanyāsins should subsist upon herbs, roots, fruits, wild cereals and so on,[4] they have this section of the Parivrājakas in view. Begging alms was not possible for these monks, because they were far away from haunts of men. They, however, used to get salt and vinegar either by way of presents or they used to visit towns and villages for that purpose on occasions[5].

The dress and general appearance of the ascetics differred according to their austerity practices. Views about the extent of austerities were divergent. Some wanted to carry austerities to the extreme, like the Nigaṇṭhas and the Achelakas. The Nigaṇṭhas were in favour of hard austerities and did not like to cover the body with clothes. Some of the ascetics put on hides, feathers of owl, horses' tails, human hair and so on.[6] Others preferred to cover the body with barks of trees or grass[7]. The practice of putting on rags picked up from cemetery or a dust heap was also there.[8] In the beginning the Buddhist Bhikshus were putting on *paṅsukūla* robes. But later probably because the Bhikshus were moving a good deal in society, they replaced this early practice of putting on

1. *D.N.* III. 41.,
   सो साक-भक्खो वा होति, सामाक-भक्खो वा होति, नीवार-भक्खो वा होति, दद्दुल-भक्खो वा होति, हट-भक्खो वा होति, कण-भक्खो वा होति, आचाम-भक्खो वा होति, पिञ्ञाक-भक्खो वा होति, तिण-भक्खो वा होति, गोमय-भक्खो वा होति, वन-मूल-फलाहारो यापेति, पवत्त-फल-भोजी । मूल-फलेहि यापेन्तो रमणीये वनसण्डे वसि ।
2. *Jā.* III. 37.
3. *Su. Ni.* II. 2.1.
4. *S.B.E.* II. 155, 157; *Manu.* VI. 13; *Vai. Dh. P.* II. 4.5; 5.5.
5. *Jā.* I. 333; 406; II. 55,
   लोणम्बिल सेवनत्थाय गिज्झकूटे पण्णसालायं विहासि ।
   The stories do not always mention the purpose of the ascetic's visit to the towns and villages (e. g., *Jā.* I. 373), but it is obvious that he visited for begging, procuring salt and vinegar or for the Varshāvāsa.
6. *D.N.* I. 166-67; III. 41,
   अजिनानि पि धारेति, अजिनक्खिपमपि धारेति······केसकम्बलमपि धारेति, वालकम्बल धारेति, उलूकपक्खमपि धारेति ।
7. *Ibid*; *Jā.* I. 304.
8. *D.N.* I. 166-67. III. 41,
   छव-दुस्सानि पि धारेति, पंसुकूलानि पि धारेति ।

rags by yellow (*kāshāya*) robes of rough material. Another reason for this seems to be the Buddha's teaching of moderate austerity practices. The Buddhist as well as the Brahmaṇical sources disclose that a Brāhmaṇa ascetic put on bark of trees and antelope hide[1]. He was also permitted to put on rough and old clothes of yellow colour.[2] All depended on the extent of austerity one preferred. The underlying idea was also of looking unattractive and showing disinterestedness in the world. As regards his general appearance, it is said in the *Jātakas* that in the garment of barks and hides, the ascetic appeared sometimes with a knot of his tangled locks of hairs in a coil on the top of his head, and with a yoke on his back from which hung two baskets.[3] The Brahmanical sources tell us that whereas the Vānaprasthin grew hairs, beard, moustaches and nails[4]; the Sanyāsin or the Bhikshu cut off hairs, beard, moustaches and nails.[5] This practice of the Hindu Sanyāsins was shared by the Buddhist monks. The Ājīvikas followed the extreme practice of plucking the hairs.

Our sources disclose that monks of various orders resorted to several austerity practices. Their practices were divergent; because, while some ascetics went to an extreme, others preferred the medium course. The Achelakas, the Ājīvikas, the Jainas, some of the Brahmaṇa Sanyāsins and others resorted to severe austerities; while the Buddhists preferred moderate asceticism. The *Kassapasīhanāda-Sutta*,[6] the *Mahāsīhanāda-Sutta*[7] and the *Aṅguttara-Nikāya*[8] throw considerable light on the austerity practices of the Achelaka ascetics, who took recourse to about thirty-five methods of Tapas in respect to food and clothing among which one had to make a choice. It is difficult to say how many of these were actually taken recourse to, because many of them appear to be fantastic.

Some of the *Jātakas* refer to the practices of the Ājīvika ascetics, such as enduring the extremity of cold during the

1. *Jā.* I. 304. V. 132; VI. 21, 73; *Manu.* VI. 6; *ĀP. Dh. S.* II. 9.22.1; *Bau. Dh. S.* II. 6.11.15.
2. *Manu.* VI. 44 ; *Vai. Dh. P.* III. 6.
3. *Jā.* I. 304; V. 132.
4. *Manu.* VI. 6; *Vai. Dh. P.* III. 5.7.
5. *Bau. Dh. S.* II. 10. 11; *Vai. Dh. P.* II. 6.
6. *D.N.* I. 167-68.
7. *M.N.* I. 77-8.
8. *A.N.* II. 206-7.

winter by remaining in the open for the whole night and torturing the body by remaining in the sun for the whole day in the summer.[1] The Brahmaincal authorities also prescribe similar austerity practices for the Vānaprasthin.[2] But the Ājīvikas seem to have gone further in taking recourse to painful practices of asceticism, for they are described as squatting on their heels, swinging in the air like bats, reclining on thorns, scorching the body with the five fires, lying on beds of thorns, staying in the water and so on [3]

The Jaṭilas and the Ājīvikas

The *Vinaya-Piṭaka* speaks of three settlements or colonies of the Jaṭilas under three Kassapa brothers in the three divisions of the Gayākhetta at Uruvelā on the banks of river Nerañjara[4]. They were Uruvela Kassapa, Nādi Kassapa, and Gaya Kassapa, each at the head of 500, 300 and 200 *Jaṭilas*.[5] They were brothers born in a Brāhmaṇa family of Magadha and were highly respected by the inhabitants of Aṅga and Magadha.[6]

The Jaṭilas were so called on account of their matted hairs.[7] They were fire-worshippers and offered sacrifice which suggest that they were the followers of Vedic religion. Most probably they were Naishṭhika Brahmachārins. It is said that Uruvela Kassapa held annually a great sacrifice, which was shared by the people of Aṅga and Magadha, who went to the place of sacrifice with abundant food.[8] Again on the occasion of the Ashṭakās, in the snowy cold winter nights, the Jaṭilas are described as plunging and emerging out of water repeatedly into the river Nerañjarā.[9] The *Udāna* also speaks of their plunging into the river in the cold nights of the

1. *Jā.* I. 390
2. *Manu.* VI. 23.
3. *Jā.* Nos. 144, 322, 377, 487.
4. *S.B.E.* XIII. 118; Jaṭila Uruvela Kassapa is mentioned also in *Ja.* VI. 219-20.
5. *Ibid.*
6. *M.V.* I. 15; Law, B. C., *India as Described in Early Texts*, p. 220.
7. *D.P.P.N.* I. 931; *Udāna Aṭṭhakathā*, 74,
   जटिला ति तापसा, तेहि जटाधारिताया इध जटिला ति वुत्ता ।
8. *S.B.E.* XIII, p. 124.
9. *Ibid.*, XIII, p. 130.

winter and of the worship of the fire.[1] The *Therīgāthā* also refers to their belief of purification by bathing in the river[2]. It is said that when the Jaṭila Uruvela Kassapa accepted the supremacy of the Buddha and embraced Buddhism, his 500 followers flung their hairs and braids and their provisions and the things for Agnihotra into the river.[3]

That the three brothers who were leaders of this sect, had gathered large numbers of followers and had made three colonies of them, shows that they had developed a congregational life. In the opinion of Dr. B.M Barua there was no corporate life, and among the Jaṭilas forming three distinct groups the tie in each group was rather domestic than congregational.[4] But during the days of the Buddha it was a common feature of the leading religious orders to have the corporate life, though details of all are not available.

Probably during the days of the Buddha also people from all parts of the country made pilgrimages to Gayā and performed the holy ablution in the Phalgu or Nerañjarā, so that their sins would be washed off. As the Jaṭilas were the upholders of the popular belief of the sanctity of water and fire, they enjoyed the respect of the people of Aṅga and Magadha. The Buddhists, however, looked upon this belief as an outcome of superstition, and passed bitter and scathing remarks at the holy ablution.[5]

The Ājīvikas also like the Buddhists and the Jainas lived in communities. A place inhabited by the Ājīvikas is called Ājīvika-seyya in the *Vīnaya-Piṭaka* which[6] appears to be the same as Ājīvikasabhā (Ājīviyasabhā) of the *Uvāsagadasāo*[7]. When Makkhali Gosāla visited the town Polāsapura, he first

1. *Udāna*, I. 9.
तेन खो पन समयेन सम्बहुला जटिला सीतासु हेमन्तिकासु रत्तीसु अन्तरट्ठके हिमपातासमये गयायं 'उम्मुजन्ति' पि निमुज्जन्ति पि उम्मुज्जनिमुज्जं पि करोन्ति ओसिञ्जन्ति' पि अग्गिं पि जुहन्ति इमिना सुद्धिति ।
2. *Therīgāthā*, 236-37.
3. S. B. E. XIII, p. 132.
4. Barua, *Gayā and Bodha-Gayā*, Vol. I. p. 99.
5. *Therīgāthā*, 237 ; *Udāna*. I. 9.
6. *Vinaya*. IV. p. 223 (*History and Doctrine of the Ājīvikas*, p. 116).
7. Hoernle, *Uvāsagadasāo*, VII. 214.

went to the Ājīvikasabhā and deposited his almsbowl. This shows that some sort of monastic establishment was evolved.

As among the Buddhists and the Jainas, so among the Ājīvikas there were both ascetics and laymen, and we come across some of them in our sources. Thus, for instance, Paṇḍuputta, the son of a Rathakāra of Rājagṛiha, is described as watching the work at the shop of his father.[1] Later we find that an Ājīvika was attached to the court of Bindusāra as an astrologer.[2]

As the Ājīvikas believed in severe austerities, they preferred to discard clothes, like the Digambara Jainas. They are generally described as naked.[3] One of the Ajanṭā fresco figures represents Pūraṇa Kassapa naked.[4] Hoernle and Basham presume that Mahāvīra reformed his dress under the influence of Gosāla,[5] and this should not be doubted, because while the Jainas appear with a loin cloth,[6] the Ājīvikas are represented completely nude, suggesting that they had gone a step further than the Jainas in this direction.

As regards severe asceticism attributed to the Ājīvikas, it can be said that the account is sufficiently exaggerated. The Buddhist writers describe them practising loathsome austeri ties, but it appears from a few references that they did not resort to all the practices referred to as being practised by them. Jambuka, who had developed the habit of remaining naked and eating the ordure and who refused to go for alms, was expelled from the Order on account of his disgusting behaviour.[7] Hence, it appears that, although the Ājīvikas preferred hard austerities, they generally did not prefer resorting to repulsive practices.

1. *M.N.* I. 31.
2. *Mahāvaṁsaṭīkā,* I. p. 190; *Divyāvadāna*, pp. 370-71.
3. *Ja.* VI. 225,

अजानन्तं नग्गभोगं निस्सीरीकं अन्धवालं आजीविकं;

Sumaṅgalavilāsinī, I. pp. 142-4; *Bh. Sū.* XV. 541; *Divyāvadāna,* p. 165.

4. Basham, *History and Dactrine of the Ājīvikas,* p. 107.
5. *Ibid.* p. 109.
6. *Āchārāṅga-Sūtra,* 1. 7,7,1.
7. *Dhp. Comy.* II, pp. 52f.

The Order of the Jainas

The Jaina and the Buddhist monastic orders were inspired by and modelled after that of the Brahmanical Sanyāsins; and hence the Hindu, the Jaina and the Buddhist orders show close affinity[1] Like the Buddhist Bhikshus, the Jaina monks also depended on begging, possessed meagre material belongings, practised non-violence and truth, observed Brahmacharya and Asteya, abstained from music, intoxicants, high beds, garlands and eating at forbidden hours.[2] The main difference between the two orders was that while the Buddhist system stressed on following a middle course (Majjhimapatipadā), the Jaina monks aimed at practising extreme ascetictism.

At the time of entering the monastic fold, the Jaina monk had to take the five great vows of *Abiṅsā*, *Sunṛīta*, *Aiteya*, *Brahmacharya* and *Aparigraha*.[3] These five vows, when compared to the eight precepts of the Buddhists, show a striking resemblance, suggesting that one borrowed from the other. But the reason of close resemblance between the two is due to their being adopted from the five vows of the Brāhmaṇa Sanyāsins.[4] The first vow of non-violence (Ahiṅsā) prohibited killing in any form of all living-beings, including plant life. It aimed at restraining the monks from using even harsh words or speaking such truth which might hurt anyboby; for this also was a form of violence in the Jainistic outlook.[5] According to the second vow the monk was always to speak the truth and to dissociate himself with any word of untruthfulness.[6] He was also expected to use moderate and restrained language.[7] Though the vow of truthfulness was taken, but

1. The points of resemblance among the orders of the Brahmanical Sanyāsins, the Jainas and the Buddhists and the indebtedness of the latter two to the former have been scholarly dealt with in detail by Jacobi in his introduction to the *Jaina Sūtras* (*SBE*, XXII).
2. *SBE*, XXII Introduction.
3. *Ibid.*, XXII, pp. 202-209.
4. *Ibid.*, XXII, Introduction.
5. *Ibid.*, XXII, pp. 146-47; 202.
6. *Ibid.*, XXII, pp. 204-5.
7. *Ibid.*, XXII, p. 149.

truth liable to harm one was to be avoided, as already referred to above.[1] The vow of *Asteya* prohibited the monk from taking possession of anything which did not belong to him.[2] This vow reveals that the material possession of the Jaina monk consisted of what he obtained by begging, i.e. he had to subsist on begging. According to the fourth vow of *Brahmacharya* all sexual pleasures were to be given up both physically and mentally.[3] The fifth vow of *Aparigraha* aimed at renouncing all attachments to the pleasures of the five senses.[4]

The Jaina monks remained all along wandering from place to place, avoiding visit to certain places.[5] Places of musical performances and merrymaking, parks, gardens, playgrounds and the like were prohibited for them, as these might lead them to moral lapses, either physically or mentally. Places disturbed by riots, quarrels and revolutions were to be avoided for the reasons of personal insecurity. Woods and mountains were haunted by robbers and so they also were unsafe. Market towns and halting places of caravans were not to be visited by the monk, as he might be mistaken for a thief or an agent of the robbers.

Generally he stayed at a place for the maximum period of a month.[6] It was during the rainy season that he like the members of other orders stayed in one place.[7] The Jainas adopted this practice for two reasons; firstly, living-beings were trodden and killed by walking, and secondly, it became difficult to trace routes due to the growth of grasses and weeds and accumulation of rain water.[8] A village or town suitable for study and religious practices, where alms could be available easily, and which was not haunted by members of rival orders and beggars, was regarded as a suitable place for the Varshāvāsa.[9] Usually, after staying for four months, one

1. E.G., if a monk was asked, 'O long-lived Śramaṇa, did you see a man, or a cow, or a buffalo, or a snake, he observed silence or denied (*SBE*, XXII, pp. 146-47).
2. *SBE*, XXII, pp. 206-9.
3. *Ibid.*
4. *Ibid.*
5. *Ibid.*, pp. 183-84.
6. *Ibid.*, XXII, p. 126.
7. *Ibid.*, XXII, p.136. It is called *pajjusana* in the *Jaina Sūtras.*
8. *Ibid.*
9. *Ibid.*, XXII, pp. 136-37.

was to leave the place of Varshāvāsa, provided roads were comparatively free from living-beings and a large number of travelling ascetics (Śramaṇas and Brāhmaṇas); otherwise he did not leave it till the end of the month of Mārgaśirsha.[1]

The Jaina monk begged a lodging from the householder where he desired to halt for sometime.[2] The lodging for him was not to be in crowded places like assembly halls, temples, family quarters, garden houses, etc.[3] He generally avoided to meet members of rival orders, and hence did not prefer to halt in temple-like places, haunted by members of religious orders. Family quarters were not commended for him with the apprehension of his indulging in the pleasures of senses, either physically or mentally, or being a party to family quarrels, or contacting contagious diseases, or causing inconvenience to the family members due to his uncleanliness.[4] He stayed in such a lodging which was suitable for the life of the Jaina mendicant and the acceptance of which did not interfere with the vows of his ascetic life.[5] For sleeping, he begged a couch of the prescribed quality.[6] If several monks stayed in the same room, beds were not spread closely, but at such intervals that no monk could touch the limb of the other.[7] This rule was laid down with the apprehension of arousing sex-desire by physical contact.

The Buddhists aimed at moderation in asceticism and allowed the Bhikshus to possess material objects necessary for a life of their ideal. The Jainas stood for extreme austere practices, and hence permitted the monks to possess objects of humble nature like robes, shoes, staff and umbrella essential for the Bhikshu life.[8] The ideal before them was to possess as meagre as possible. In the Buddhist Order all the material objects were allotted to the individual Bhikshu by the Saṅgha which received them from the laity; in the Jaina Order the monks directly begged them from the householders. But both

1. *SBE.*, XXII, p. 137.
2. *Ibid.*, XXII, pp. 120, 130-31.
3. *Ibid.*, XXII, pp 126-27.
4. *Ibid.* XXII, pp. 122-24.
5. *Ibid.*, XXII, pp. 120-21.
6. *Ibid.*, XXII, p. 132-33.
7. *Ibid.*, XXII, p. 135.
8. *Ibid.*, XXII, p. 171.

specified the qualities of such objects and also the number to be possessed by a monk. The Buddhist Bhikshu possessed even trifles like needles etc., but objects of this nature were borrowed by the Jaina monks from the householders when needed and were returned back to them.[1]

Like the Brāhmaṇa Sanyāsin and the Buddhist Bhikshu, the Jaina monk shaved his head.[2] But in respect to dress, unlike the former two, he went to the extreme simplicity of remaining naked. Those who did not go upto this extent, put on white dress,[3] unlike the Brahmaṇical and Buddhist Bhikshus who wore Kāshāya clothes. Both the Jaina and Buddhist monks were in the beginning putting on cast off rags, but this practice was modified and clothes were begged from the householders. In the Buddhist Order robes were donated by the donors to the Saṅgha which distributed them among the needy Bhikshus, but in the Jaina Order every monk begged his set of robes from the householder individually,[4] and this was in line with the practice of the Brahmaṇical Sanyāsins. When begging a garment from the laity, he specified its fabric (one out of wool, silk, hemp, palm-leaves, cotton, Ārkūṭa, or the like)[5] and the type (upper one or the under garment).[6] The Buddha permitted to possess a set of three robes; Mahāvīra allowed to put on either the upper one, or the under-garment, or both, exception being in the case of the weak and the diseased monk.[7] In winter he could possess even four pieces of clothes.[8] However, the nun possessed four pieces (two of 3 cubits each and two of 2 and 4 cubits).[9] Here also he begged for one which was intended for donation.[10] But unlike the Buddhist Bhikshu, he was permitted to borrow a robe from another monk for a limited period

1. *SBE.*, XXII, p. 172.
2. *Ibid.*, XXII, Introduction, p. XXV.
3. *Ibid.*, XXII, p. 163.
4. *Ibid.*, XXII, p. 159.
5. *Ibid.*, XXII, pp. 157-58.
6. *Ibid.*, XXII, pp. 157-159.
7. *Ibid.*, XXII, pp. 68-69. 71, 157.
8. *Ibid.*, XXII, 67-68.
9. *Ibid.*, XXII, p. 157.
10. *Ibid.*, XXII. p. 159.

subject to certain conditions.[1] This provision seems to have been made considering the Jaina monk's possession of only one garment generally.

It has been already referred to above that the Jaina monk did not put on dyed clothes. He was further prohibited from using washed, perfumed, or those of costly fabrics.[2] As a rule he abstained from washing his clothes, but if washing became necessary, scanty water was used for the purpose.[3] With the idea of ensuring personal safety and observing non-viloence, clothes were not spread for drying on a raised place like a pillar, or one which was not stable, or where there was possibility of the existence of living-beings.[4]

Monks acquired their almsbowl by begging from the laity.[5] But bowls made of precious metals of stones or the ornamented ones were not to be accepted by them.[6] The bowl bought for the sake of the monk concerned was also prohibited for him.[7] With the ideal of causing no inconvenience or monetary burden on the part of the laymen, bowls made of ordinary materials like wood or clay or bottlegourd, etc. were permitted for the use of the Jaina monks.[8] A used one or the left of required by no other ascetic could be accepted.[9] At the time of begging a bowl it was the duty of the monk to specify the quality out of the permitted ones,[10] because he could possess only one almsbowl, besides a drinking vessel.[11] Conscious of the observance of non-violence, he was to inspect it thoroughly at the time of receiving to see that it did not contain living-beings, seeds or grass.[12] If any of these were present there (inside the

1. *SBE.*, XXII, pp. 163-64. According to the prescribed rules the monk who borrowed a robe from his fellow mendicant was to return it within five days and not to change its colour. He was also not to give it to some one else for use.
2. *Ibid.*, XXII, pp. 158, 160-61, 163.
3. *Ibid.*, XXII, p. 162.
4. *Ibid.*, XXII, p. 162.
5. *Ibid.*, XXII. pp. 160, 170.
6. *Ibid.*, XXII, pp. 166-67.
7. *Ibid.*, XXII, pp. 166. The same rule applied to robes also (*Ibid.* pp. 157-58).
8. *Ibid.*
9. *Ibid.*, XXII. p. 167
10. *Ibid.*
11. *Ibid.*, XXII, p. 166.
12. *Ibid.*, XXII, pp. 167,169.

bowl), he removed them and wiped off the dust; but if the bowl was wet or moist he did not wipe or rub it, obviously apprehending the presence of life therein.[1] Thus the rules laid down by Mahāvīra for the manks show that they were mainly guided by the ideal of non-violence.

(1) *SBE.*, XXII, pp. 169-70.

CHAPTER IX

THE BUDDHIST MONASTERIES

Coming into Existence of the Monasteries

It has already been seen that North East India of the 6th centuary B. C. was the scene of the rise of several ascetic orders, among which the orders of the Buddhists, the Jainas, and the Ājīvikas were the most prominent ; and the Order of the Buddha came out to be the foremost, surpassing the two. The Buddha, in the beginning, followed a course which was similar to other ascetic organisations and advocated the importance of renunciation. Early Buddhism had no Saṅgha life, lived in the well-built monasteries. The Buddhist monastic life was gradually evolved. During the initial period the Buddhist Order was a wandering one, each Bhikshu living a solitary life. It was only during the rains that suitable residences were utilised. The shelter of the nature was regarded as the ideal dwelling place for a Bhikshu ; and at the time of Upasampadā Ordination he was told, "The religious life has dwellings at the foot of a tree for its resource. Thus you must endeavour to live all your life[1]." Very often the Bhikshu is described as residing in the forest, under the shade of a tree, on a hill, in a cave, at cremation grounds, forest lands, in an open field, or on the heap of straw.[2] The ideal of living at cremation grounds, or in open field, or on the heap of straw may not have been in actual practice. We get definite statements of Bhikshus residing in huts at the forests.[3] The sculptures at Sānchī and Bhārhut give an idea of these small

1. *S.B.E.* XIII. 173.
2. *M.N.* I. 269, 274, 346, 440; III 105-6.
   अरञ्ञं रुक्खमूलं पब्बतं कन्दरं गिरिगुहं सुसानं वनपत्थं अब्भोकासं पलालंच···।
3. *S.N.* III. 116, IV. 117; *Theragāthā*, 59.
   सद्धयाहं पब्बजितो अरञ्ञे मे कुटिका कता ।
   Udāna. IV. 2; *Jā*. I. 106; IV. 130-31. Places like Veluvana, Mahāvana and other forest regions adjoining towns and cities were made suitable for Bhikshus.

huts. The practice of dwelling in caves appears to be equally common.[1]

Though the Buddha advocated a medium path of asceticism, he felt the necessity of sending Bhikshus to the forest for getting themselves trained in the spiritual insight, because it was not possible for a new-comer to practice meditation among the multitude.[2] In the forest, the Bhikshu was required to live a regulated life in a hut, living on doles of food, received in alms from the neighbouring forest dwellers and the adjoining villages.[3] He rose betimes, placed his bowl in the bag, hung it over his shoulders, arranged his upper robe over his back, got on his sandals, put the utensils and the earthenware in order, closed the doorway and lattice, and then left his hut for alms,[4] which was his daily routine. The practice of constructing huts on the riverside was also common[5]. Thus we find that early Buddhism shows close resemblance to the Brahmanical practice of having hermitages at the forests and on the riversides. Sometimes villages were also selected for the purpose of leading a solitary life. Dhammadinnā had retreated to a country abode.[6]. Sāriputta and Moggallāna once spent the Vassa at the house of Kokālika unknown by anybody.[7] Apparently, they lived there for the purpose of meditation. This shows that during the initial period of the Buddhist Order, a Bhikshu could utilise the house of his trusted friend as his residence for sometime.

The solitary and wandering life gradually went through transformation. The devoted lay followers began to dedicate Ārāmas (Parks) to the Bhikshu Saṅgha.[8] In the beginning these were used as the Vassa residence, but soon were turned into permanent residences. "The Ārāmas dedicated to the

1. *Theragāthā*, 887; 925,
अरञ्ञे रुक्खमूले कन्दरासु गुहासु च ।
Preceding references also.
2. *Psalms of Sisters*, pp. 16-17; *Jā*. No. 481.
3. *Jā. No.* 71.
4. *C. V.* VIII. 6.2.
5. *Theragāthā*, 127.
तिण्णं मे तालपत्तान गंगातीरे कुटी कता ।
Udāna, III. 3.
6. *Psalms af Sisters*, pp. 16-17.
7. *Takkāriya Jā*. (No. 481).
8. *C. V.* VI. 4.8-10.

Order were neither too far away from the town, nor too near it. They were easily accessible to all who wished to visit and convenient for the Bhikshus for going out for alms and coming back. They were not too crowded at day time and exposed to too much noise and alarm at night. They were well protected from the wind, hidden from men, and fitted for the retired life.[1] The existence of such parks, under the possession of the Order where Bhikshus could live a retired and solitary life, dispensed with the need of going to the forest.

The lay disciples further built Vihāras. They spent lavishly for erecting new buildings for the Saṅgha. Anāthapiṇḍika spent 54 crores of current coins over monasteries only.[2]

With the existence of Vihāras for the Bhikshus, there arose the need of regulation regarding the lodgings. As the lodgings were the common property of the Saṅgha, they were allotted by it for the use of the individual Bhikshus. There was an apportioner for lodgings, and whosoever was in need of a lodging place was provided with.[3] Even when Vihāras had become common, the Bhikshus did not live at one place for the whole year. It was only during the rains that they lived at one Vihāra or Ārāma, otherwise they remained wandering, and at whichever establishment they arrived at, they were provided with a lodging for the duration of the period they lived there.

As the life in the monasteries became well organised, established, and regulated, it was felt that students of the same branch of thought should have one lodging place, so that they might be helpful to one another, and they were grouped accordingly.[4]

Admission

The *Vinaya* texts reveal that in the beginning admission into the Order was open to all those who were willing to join the religious life, except women. But later a few classess of

1. M. V. I. 22. 16-17, *C.V.* VI. 4.8-10.
2. *C.V.* VI. 5.1, *Jā.* 1. 226, अनाथपिंडिको हि बिहारं' एव आरभ चतु-पण्णासकोटिधनं बुद्धसासने विकिरित्व······।
3. *C.V.* VI. 11. 1-2.
4. *Ibid.*, IV. 4. 4.

people were debarred from entering the Order. It was found that the criminal class, whose whole life was spent on mean and antisocial activities, was not fit for religious life. Robbers and thieves were disqualified from seeking admission in the Saṅgha;[1] the case of Aṅgulimāla was an exception. Hunters and fishermen, who were given to slaughter, were not able to follow the Law. Sāriputta taught them; they obeyed him out of respect, but could not follow his instructions.[2] Religious life required a proper background, and the soil where the seeds of religion were to be shown had to be fertile. Hence, those who were considered to be incapable of grasping the Law, were not admitted in the Order.

As time marched on, the Buddha realised that the admission of the antisocial elements in the Saṅgha was bound to bring disgrace to the Order and hinder the progress, prosperity, and expansion of his gospel. The honour and respect, esteem and devotion, that the Saṅgha received from society, depended on the admission of the right type of persons, as desired by the prevalent public opinion. The policies of Buddhism were very much influenced and determined by the attitude of society. Hence, those whose entry might arouse social agitation or interfere with the rights of the third parties, were excluded from admission into the Saṅgha. Robbers and thieves were a menace to society and a headache to the state. Apart from their personal inability to receive the Law, their presence in the Saṅgha was likely to create social annoyance, legal hindrance, and state interferences. The entrance of debtors[3] and slaves[4] clashed with the rights of the third parties. Taking into view these problems, robbers, thieves, debtors, and slaves were disqualified for admission into the Saṅgha. The astitude of the state was properly and carefully watched, and it was decided that in the best interests of the Order, men belonging to the administrative class should not be ordained. The Buddha said, 'Let no one, O Bhikshus, who is in the royal service, receive the

1. *S.B.E.* XIII. 196.
2. *Jā.* III. 170-71 (*No.* 356).
3. *S.B.E.* XIII. 199, 230.
4. *Ibid.*

Pabbajjā.[1]' Henceforth, they were not admitted in the Saṅgha, and at the time of the Upasampadā Ordination inquiry was made whether the candidate belonged to the royal service.[2] People suffering from contagious diseases like boils, leprosy, dry leprosy and consumption were debarred from entering the monastic life.[3] Buddhism had caused separation of a good number of parents from their sons, who, though not mature in age, embraced the religious Order. There were parents who had only one son, very much loved and the only hope for their old age and the family. What would have been their condition, after losing that son ? When a certain merchant entered the monastery, his parents became so poor that they began to subsist on alms received by begging in their old age.[4] When the Buddha had renounced the world, his parents had only Rāhula to console their withered hearts, but when he was also enunciated to the Pabbjjā Ordination, the last ray of hope vanished from the heart of old Suddhodana. He requested the Buddha that his Order should not admit any son, without the consent of his parents, and the request was accepted.[5] Thenceforth, a son who had not received the permission of parents, was not admitted in the Saṅgha.[6] The *Raṭṭhapāla-Sutta* of the *Majjhima-Nikāya* shows that parents having only one son dissuaded him from embracing the monastic life, thinking that he would not be able to face the hardship of the Bhikshu's life, as he had been brought up very affectionately and knew no misery.[7] There seemed to be another reason why a novice could not get admission in the Saṅgha, without his parents permission. The only son could not be given in adoption (*dharmakārya*). If the only son entered monastery, the family would cease to continue. In the beginning only sons were being admitted.[8] Later it became a custom to ask the

1. *S.B.E.* XIII. p. 196.
2. *Ibid.*, p. 230.
3. *Ibid.*, pp. 193-4, 230.
4. *Jā.* VI. 69 (No. 540).
5. *S. B. E.* XIII. 209-10.
6. *Ibid.*, pp. 210, 230.
7. *M.N.* II. 58.
त्वं खो, तात रट्ठपाल, अम्हाकं एकपुत्तको पियो मनापो सुखे ठितो सुखपरिभतो, न त्वं, तात रट्ठपाल कस्सचि दुक्खस्स जानाति ।
8. E. G., Yasa of Vārāṇasī.

permission of the parents, before entering the monastery as a novice.[1] That a son had to seek his parents' permission for entering the monastery, whether he was the only son or one in many, suggests that it was the misery of parents after his departure which was responsible for making parents' consent obligatory. In case of only sons, it was probably more the fear of the extinction of the family line than any other consideration which stood in the way of their initiation.

Qualifications of the Teacher who Admitted

At the earliest stage, the Buddha himself was conferring the Pabbajjā and the Upsampadā Ordinations.[2] Bhikshus took to him those desirous of embraciug the brotherhood, and they were ordained and admitted by him in the Order. But soon this procedure was found to be inconvenient, because the Bhikshus had to cover long distances, and much time was wasted in reaching the Buddha. So the Lord said to the Bhikshus, "Confer, henceforth, O Bhikhshus, in the different regions, and in the different countries, the Pabbajjā and the Upasampadā Ordinations yourselves."[3] This step widened the scope for the spread of the Buddha's religion, as the Bhikshus could confer the two Ordinations in different regions, resulting in the establishment of Bhikshu Saṅghas in different localities, through which spread the gospel of the Lord.

But the freedom of the Bhikshus to confer the Ordinations had two dangers. Firstly, there was the possibility of unfit persons being admitted to the Order by less qualified Bhikshus. Secondly, this could give rise to a tendency on the part of the elder Bhikhus to gather as large a number of disciples and followers as possible. This ambition was natural, but against the interests of the Order ; because such tendencies ultimately lead to the formation of groups and create rivalries for leadership. Due to the realisation of this fact it was prescribed that only he who had completed ten years or more as a full-

1. *Milindapañho*, I. 26.
अथ खो नागसेनो दारको मातापितरो उपसङ्कमित्वा आह—अम्म तात···अथस्स मातापितरो पब्बजित्वा'पि नो पुत्तो मन्तं गण्हातु। गहेत्वा पुन आगच्छिस्सती' ति मञ्ञमाना—गाह पुत्ताति अनुजानिसु।
2. *S. B. E.* XIII. 114.
3. *Ibid.*

fledged Bhikshu was competent to confer the Upasampadā Ordination.[1] But this also involved another difficulty, because there were a number of ignorant Bhikshus who had completed their ten years. There were cases where the pupil possessed better intellect than the teacher. Therefore, it was decided finally that only those who had completed ten years as full-fledged Bhikshus and were really possessed of spiritual insight, could confer the Upasampadā Ordination.[2]

Thus, we find that the Order of the Buddha was quite conscious of the interests of the Brotherhood and intended to avoid disunity, strifes, and group rivalry, which are the main factors responsible for the disruption of any organisation. The task of showing path to the new-comers was entrusted to those who were really noble and could be relied upon to safeguard the interests of the Order.

Ordinations

It was through the Pabbajjā and the Upasampadā Ordinations that one was properly admitted into the monastic fold. In the beginning these Ordinations were conferred simultaneously, and there was no rule as regards the age of those admitted. Later the Pabbajjā Ordination was conferred at the age of fifteen,[3] followed by the Upasampadā at the age of twenty.[4] While the former marked the preliminary stage of Brotherhood, the latter marked admission to its full privileges. The five years' gap between the two Ordinations was a period of probation[5], during which the newly admitted Bhikshu went through proper training under his teacher for entering the higher order. Pravraja means going forth, which is equivalent to going forth from the household life to the homeless state. Pāli Pabbajjā (Pravrajyā), i.e. going out, was used as a mark of the change of a layman into an ascetic. In the Brahmanical system the

1. *S.B.E.* XIII. 177.
2. *Ibid.*, p. 178.
3. *M.V.* I. 50.
4. *S. B. E.* XIII, pp. 46, 203, 230 ; *Milindapañho*, I. 28.
   अथ खो कोटिसता अरहन्तो आयसमन्तं न।गसेनं परिपुण्णवीसतिवस्सं रक्खततले उपसम्पादेसुं ।
5. *Jā.* I. 106.
   पब्बजित्वा उपसम्पदाय पञ्चवस्सिको हुत्वा...।

homeless state had two stages; the first, being the Vānaprastha or Vaikhānasa and the second, the Sanyāsa or Bhikshu-Āśrama[1]. The Vānaprasthin endeavoured for spiritual attainment, lived at the root of trees and begged alms from the householders.[2] Later when he entered the Sanyāsa-Āśrama, he shaved his hair, put on yellow robe, and took an almsbowl.[3] He cut off all attachment to the worldly life and lived solely with the aim of spiritual enlightenment. In the Buddhist monachism the five years of Pabbajjā bore some resemblance to the Vānaprastha stage, and the Upasampadā marked the attainment of Sanyāsa. Again, in the Brahmanical system, there was option to one's entering the forest just after the completion of the first stage or after becoming a householder[4]. The stage of studentship was regarded as a necessary preliminary for becoming a Sanyāsin.[5] The Buddhist system combined the Brahmacharya and the Vānaprastha stages into one period of Pabbajjā, when the Pabbajita one was called the Sāmaṇera. The Sāmaṇera combined in him the duties of the Brahmachārin and the Vānaprasthin. The Bhikshu life was modelled in line with the Brahmacharya, Vānaprastha, and Sanyāsa stages of life, according to the Brahmanical system. The correspondence of the duties of the novice with that of the Brahmacharin is pointed out, while discussing his relation to his teacher. There is close similarity between the duties of a Bhikshu during the Pabbajjā stage and those of the Vānaprasthin whose stage was a stepping to full-fledged Sanyāsa. Both were required to abstain from destroying any life, speaking false, drinking intoxications, eating at untimely hours, using garlands, flowers, scents, high seat or bed, and so on.[6]

Prior to the existence of the five years' probation there was a period of four month's duration, before the Pabbajjā and the Upasampadā known as the Parivāsa.[7] Evidently,

1. *Āp. Dh. S.* II. 9. 21; *Gau. Dh. S.* III. 2; *V.Dh.S.* VII. 1-2; *Vai. Dh. P.* I. 1. 13,
तदाश्रमिणश्चत्वारो ब्रह्मचारी गृहस्थो वानप्रस्थो भिक्षुरिति।
2. *Vai. Dh. P.* III. 5. 13.
3. *Ibid.* II. 6. 2.
4. *S. B. E.* II. 153; XIV. 273 ; Manu. II. 247-48; VI. 2.
5. *S. B. E.* II. 153.
6. *S. B. E.* XIII. 211; *Vai. Dh. P.* I. 26.
7. *S.* B. *E.* XIII. 187-88.

this probation was intended for the Aññatitthiya Paribbājakas, who entered the Buddhist Order.[1] When Seṇiya, Vachchhagotta, and Sabhiya, who all embraced the Buddhist Order, expressed their intention of entering the Saṅgha, they were told that they would have to go through the Parivāsa of four months[2]. However, the Jaṭilas, the fire-worshippers, and the Śākyas were admitted to the Order, without any probation.[3] Probably this represents the stage when the idea of Parivāsa was not conceived. Later the members of other schools had to go through the Parivāsa, before becoming a Bhikshu. After sometime it may have been found that the new-comers, who were the followers of a sect much opposed to Buddhism, should develop a new mental and psychological background, favourable for the growth of the new faith. Accordingly, Parivāsa was prescribed. During Parivāsa one had to attain such a stage of mental state where he could feel joy, even when somebody spoke against his old faith; and be intolerant, when one spoke against the Buddha.[4]

In the beginning, Pabbajjā and Upasampadā had not become so technical, and both were conferred simultaneously. In the case of the earliest disciples of the Budda and as regards Achela Kassapa,[5] Pukkusāti[6], Kasibhārdvāja[7] and Nand-Gopālaka[8], we are told of the conferring of both the Ordinations simultaneusly. One who desired to enter the Order had simply to provide himself with adequate robes and alms-bowl which constituted the equipment of a Bhikshu.[9]

1. *M.V.* I. 38. 1 ; *S.B.B.* (Dia.) II. 239-40
2. *M.N.* I. 391, 494.
   सचे भन्ते अञ्जतित्थियपूब्बो इमस्मिं धम्मविनये आकंखंति पब्बज्जं आकंखंति उपसम्पदं सो चत्तारो मासे परिवसति चतुन्नं मासानं अच्चयेन आरद्धचित्ता भिक्ख पब्बजेन्ति उपसम्पादेन्ति भिक्खुभावाय।
   Su. Ni. III. 6.
3. *S.B.E.* XIII. 190-91.
4. *Ibid.*, pp. 189-90.
5. *M. N.* III. 127.
6. *M. N.* III. 247.
7. *Su. Ni.* I. 4.
8. *S. N.* IV. 181.
   अलत्थ खो नन्दो गोपालको भगवतो सन्तिके पब्बज्जं अलत्थ उपसम्पदं।
9. *M. N.* III. 247.

During the earliest period of the Order, the methods of conferring the Pabbajjā and the Upasampadā Ordinations were very simple, and both were conferred simultaneously. When the first five disciples of the Buddha were ordained at Sārnāth, they received their Ordinations simply by listening to the sermon of the Buddha.[1] By this method Ordinations were conferred on Yasa, his four friends, and fifty more Bhikshus.[2] When Bhikshus were entitled to confer the Ordinations, they were directed to do so by the declaration of the holy triad.[3] The method was this : 'One desirous of receiving the Pabbajjā and the Upasampadā Ordinations first shaved his head and beard and put on yellow robes. He adjusted his upper robe so as to cover one shoulder, saluted the feet of the Bhikshus with the head, then sat down squatting and raising his joined hands uttered, "I take my refuge in the Buddha, I take my refuge in the Dhamma, I take my refuge in the Saṅgha." This was uttered thrice and the Bhikshu received the Upasampadā.[4] This simple method was subsequently replaced by a formal act of the Saṅgha.[5] The duration of time between the Pabbajjā and the Upasampadā, of which no trace in the beginning is available, widened and a gap of five years came into existence. It was through the approval of the Bhikshu Saṅgha consisting of at least ten fully qualified elders that a novice was raised to the status of a full-fledged Bhikshu[6]. The novice had to speak before the assembled Bhikshus, lowering reverently on the ground and raising his joined hands to his forehead, "I entreat the Order, reverend Sirs, for initiation. May the Order, reverend Sirs, raise me up to itself; may it have pity on me. And for the second—and for the third time I entreat the Order, reverened Sirs, for initiation. May the Order, reverend Sirs, raise me up to itself; may it have pity on me." Then the novice was asked whether he was a freeman, whether he was not indebted, whether he was not in the royal service, whether he had

1. R. S., *Vinaya*. pp. 82-83.
2. *Ibid.*
3. *S.B.E.* XIII. 115.
4. *Ibid.*
5. *S.B.E.* XIII, 169-70.
6. *M. V.* I. 31. 2; IX. 4. 1.

obtained his parents' consent, whether he was of full twenty years of age, and so on.[1] He had to answer these questions in the affirmative. Then a motion was moved before the Saṅgha : "Reverend Sirs, let the Order hear me. N.N. here present desires as pupil of the venerable N. N. to receive Ordination. He is free from the obstacles to Ordination. He possesses alms-bowl and robes. N. N. entreats the Order for Ordination with the said N.N. as his teacher. Whosoever of the venerable is for granting the said N. N. Ordination with the said N.N. as his teacher, let him be silent. Whosoever is against it, let him speak." This motion was repeated thrice and if no dissenting voice was heard, it was declared passed; and the novice was raised to the status of a Bhikshu.

Even this rule was not rigid, because Buddhism was very much adapting itself to the situations. The border[2] countries enjoyed special rules for the Upasampadā Ordination. In those regions the Upasampadā could be held in the meeting of only four Bhikshus, besides the chairman who was to be the Vinayadhara.[3] This concession was allowed, because the border countries had very few followers.

The Buddhist Order further permitted another exception as regards the rules of Upasampadā Ordination. If a Bhikshu or a Bhikshuṇī could not be present in person before the Saṅgha due to unavoidable reasons and begged admission through some body else, he or she was conferred the Ordination by a Bhikshu duly empowered and sent for the purpose by the Saṅgha. What mattered was that the Bhikshu sent to confer the Upasampadā was not to be a novice or a dull one.[4]

1. *S. B. E.* XIII. 230.
2. *M.V.* V. 13. 12. The border countries were the regions adjoining the boundaries of the Majjhimadesa. The *Mahāvagga* defines Majjhimadesa as the region bounded by Kajaṅgala Nigama to the East, Salalavatī to the S.E., Setakaṇṇika Nigama to the South, Thuna to the West and Usīradhwaja to the North. See also pages 98-99.
3. *Ibid.* V. 13. 11, 12.
4. *R.S.*, *Vinaya.* p. 537. There is reference to a Bhikshshuṇī receiving Upasampadā by this method; nothing is said about a Bhikshu. But if this exception was applied to a Bhikshuṇī, same may have been the case with a Bhikshu under similar circumstances.

The Upajjhāya and the Saddhivihārika

After being ordained in the Pabbajjā initiation, the novice had to choose a spiritual teacher,[1] under whose guidance he endeavoured to attain the stage of full-fledged Bhikshuhood. The teacher was known as the Upajjhāya. Upajjhāya is the Pāli rendering of the Sanskrit Upādhyāya meaning 'one who is gone close up to.'[2] The term denotes a spiritual teacher in the Buddhist Order. He occupies the same status as the Āchārya in the Brahmanical system. According to Manu Upādhyāya means a professional teacher,[3] and the Āchārya occupies a higher position than him. In the Buddhist monastery the Upajjhāya occupied the place of a spiritual teacher, i.e. Āchārya ; and Āchariyo, that of an instructor or teacher, and he was only the deputy or substitute of the Upajjhāya. That the Āchariya was a teacher is suggested by references to the Āchariya's fee by the terms *āchariya-dhana*[5] and *āchariya-bhāgaṁ*[6]. In the Buddhist monastery, according to Buddha-ghosha, the Upajjhāya used to be a Bhikshu of ten years' seniority, whereas the Āchariya only of six years' seniority.[7]

The novice was known as the Saddhivihārika. Vedic *sadhrin* means towards one aim, and the Pāli *saddhi* means together.[8] Vīharika would signify residing or living. Saddhivihārika is described as co-resident, fellow-Bhikshu, or pupil in the *Pāli Dictionary*.[9] The novice lived in the company of his Upajjhāya and exerted himself for the attainment of the full-fledged Bhikshuhood; hence the term may be explained as signifying living together for the attainment of a definite aim. The relation that existed between the two, the teacher and the pupil, was one of mutual co-operation for their spiritual welfare. The Suddhivihārika was just like the Brahmachārin of the Brahmanical system. Rules for the Saddhivihārika of the Buddhist Saṅgha and those for the Brahmachārin of

1. *S. B. E.* XIII. 154
2. Rhys Davids, *Pāli Dictionary.*
3. *Manu.* II. 141
4. Rhys Davids, *Pāli Dictionary.*
5. *S.N.* I 177 ; *A.N.* V, 347.
6. *Jā.* V. 457; VI. 178 ; *Dhp. Comy.* I. 253.
7. *Comy. on Mahāvastu*, V. 4.2.
8. Rhys Davids, *Pāli Dictionary.*
9. *Ibid.*

the Brahmanical system as prescribed by Manu show a close resemblance.[3] Both were instructed to abstain from destroying life, telling a lie, taking strong drinks, dancing, singing and music, using scents and garlands, indulging in sexual acts, and impurity. The *Vinaya* texts do not mention ointments for the body, shoes and umbrella, playing dice and looking at women among the rules of negative character, which are prohibited by Manu; on the other hand, we find that Manu does not mention eating at forbidden hours and accepting gold and silver among the prohibited practices for the Brahmachārin. The reason for this seems to be that the Vedic Brahmachārin later became a Gṛihastha, whereas the Buddhist novice became a Bhikshu. The *Vinaya* text does not forbid the use of ointments, shoes and umbrellas for the novices, because these things were allowed on certain occasions, though normally prohibited. A Bhikshu suffering from skin disease could use ointments, and shoes could be put on outside the monastery. As Bhikshuṇīs lived in the Saṅgha, looking at them could not be prohibited, though looking with lustful eyes was not tolerated. Omission of the prohibition of dice does not necessarily mean that they were usually allowed to play it. But excavations have yielded dices from monastic sites, which would suggest that Bhikshus could relax themselves by playing dice. Similarly Manu's omission of eating at forbidden hours and acceptance of gold and silver does not mean that these practices were allowed for a Brahmachārin. As a Brahmachārin lived with the family of his Guru, there was no need of prescribing rules for the time of eating, as was the case with the Saddhivihārika who lived in the Bhikshu Saṅgha. Manu does not prescribe that gold and silver should not be accepted, but he stresses avoiding greed. The ideal before a Brahmachārin was to lead a life of strict discipline.

Though a few differences are found between the Buddhist

1. *S. B. E.* XIII; p. 211. The Saddhivihārika had to abstain from destroying life, stealing, impurity, lying, taking strong drinks, eating at forbidden hours, dancing, singing, music, seeing spectacles, using garlands, high and broad beds, accepting gold and silver. *Manu.* (II. 176-79) prescribes similar rules for the Brahmachārin.

and the Brahmanical systems in regard to the rules of the Saddhivihārika of the former and the Brahmachārin of the latter, the aims and the ideals of both were the same. The similarity is so close that the difference can be overlooked, and it can be very safely concluded that the Saddhivihārika of the Buddhist Saṅgha was the Naishṭhika Brahmachārin of the Brahmanical system, and that both had the same ideals before them.

Practically speaking, the relation of the Saddhivihārika and the Upajjhāya was that of a Guru and the Brahmachārin pupil, and the stage corresponded to the Brahmacharya and Vānaprastha combined in one. The duties of the Saddhivihārika in relation to his Upajjhāya was of doing proper service to him as did a Brahmachārin. The importance of the spiritual teacher was realised, and it was through doing proper service to him that knowledge could be attained. It is the long-lived Indian tradition and custom to honour and revere a teacher and to do proper service to him in order to acquire knowledge from him. The *Vaikhānasa Dharmapraśna*[1] lays down that a Brahmachārin should daily bow down before his Guru (teacher), should sit down, when the teacher sits down; when he leaves the seat, he should stand up earlier and walk after him ; he should occupy the lower seat and the bed; he should not do anything without his order, but he ought to carry on his studies and the usual daily routine, even without the teacher's order.

The Saddhivihārika had to render a number of services to the Upajjhāya. He gave the Upajjhāya the teeth-cleanser and water, prepared seat for him, served rice-milk, helped him when changing clothes, and cleansed the pots and the place, if dirty[2]. Such services were not rendered to a teacher by a pupil in the Brahmanical Order. The reason was that the teacher lived a family life, and his wife and children were there to serve him water, rice-milk, etc. He was instructed to be very cautious, when doing something. If he removed a chair, he was not to make any noise by knocking it against

1. *Vai. Dh. P.* I. 2.
2. *S*.B.E. XIII, pp. 154-55.

the door or the ground.[1] In addition to personal service to the Upajjhāya, he was also doing several works like sweeping the Vihāra, putting things in order, cleansing the privy if dirty, and so on.[2] From the *Jātaka* evidence we are told that the junior Bhikshus served the elders as their pages.[3] It is again said that Ānanda got the service of a young brother who served him with food and drink, tooth brush and water, looked after his privies, living and sleeping rooms and did all that was needed for hand, foot, and back.[4] The *Milindapañho* tells us that he accompanied his teacher, while going through the daily round for alms. Nāgasena on the very next day of his admission to the full order accompanied his teacher to the village.[5] This shows that if he accompanied his teacher for alms even after his Upasampadā, i. e. Full Brotherhood, he must have been doing the same, while he was still a novice and rendered a number of services to him. In later times when the Bhikshus began to use flower-garlands, the junior Bhikshus brought garlands for their elders.[6] These show that all types of services were taken from the junior Bhikshus for the comfort of the elders. It is also interesting that both shaved the hair of each others.[7]

The duty of the Saddhivihārika did not refer only to the physical needs and life of the Upajjhāya. More important was the moral responsibility. If the Elder, the Upajjhāya, took a false doctrine, it was the duty of the Saddhivihārika to discuss or cause others to discuss and see that he did not

1. *S.B.E.* XIII, p. 159.
2. *Ibid*, pp. 159-60.
3. *Jā.* II. 95-96 (No. 183).
4. *Jā.* II. 25 (No. 157).
5. *Milindapañho*, I. 29.

   उपसम्पन्नो च पना' यस्मा नागसेनो तस्सा रत्तिया अच्चयेन पुब्बण्ह-समयं निवासेत्वा पत्तचीवरमादाय उपज्झायेन सद्धिं गामं पिण्डाय पविसन्तो ।

6. *Jā.* II. 95-96 (No. 183). Generally this was done by the *Upāsakas* and this story represents them as living like junior Bhikshus and serving the elder ones. It is quite likely that the juniors who did several services for the elders used to bring garlands at a later stage, as observed above.
7. *S.B.E.* XIII, p. 162.

follow the wrong doctrine.[1] In case he was guilty of a grave offence and the Saddhivihārika was convinced of the guilt, he was to move the Saṅgha to take proper action against him and sentence to the Parivāsa, Mānatta, or any other discipline.[2] However, this thing did not exist in the Brahmanical Order. The Brahmachārin was not to take action against his teacher. How this practice appeared in Buddhism ? Here, it may be noted that in the Brahmanical system, when the education period came to an end, the pupil entered the household life. But in the Order of the Buddha he lived in the same community all his life. The relation of the tutor and the pupil was only of five years, and during this short period he was not barred from his right to find fault with his Guru. After this period he was also to become a full-fledged Bhikshu. If the Saṅgha wished to proceed against the Upajjhāya and he was not guilty in the eyes of the Saddhivihārika, it was his duty to make the Saṅgha change its attitude[3]. And, if a proceeding against him was instituted, he tried his best to help the Upajjhāya to aspire to get clear of the charge and make the Saṅgha revoke its sentence.

The Saddhivihārikas were to observe their duties properly. Those of them who did not observe proper conduct towards their Upajjhāyas could be turned away.[4] But the Upajjhāyas were not to misuse this power, and, it was prescribed that they had no right to turn away a guiltless Saddhivihārika.[5] They were not given any absolute right of turning away the Saddhivihārikas. If a saddivihāraka who was properly turned away begged pardon, he was forgiven.[6]

Seniority and Etiquette

The observance of respect and devotion towards the senior members was very much emphasised in the Buddhist Order. In the *Chullavagga* an interesting analogy is put forth to explain the importance of respect shown to the senior members. It

1. *S.B.E.* XIII, p. 161.
2. *Ibid.*
3. *Ibid.*, p. 162.
4. *S.B.E.* XIII, pp. 165-68.
5. *Ibid.*, pp. 167-68.
6. *Ibid.*, pp. 166-167.

is said that three friends—a partridge, a monkey, and an elephant, in course of a mutual discourse, found that the partridge was the oldest among them. From that day the elephant and the monkey honoured and revered him. They lived in mutual reverence, confidence, and courtesy.[1] The Bhikshus were instructed to be respectful, affectionate and hospitable to the teachers and superiors, or to those who ranked as teachers or superiors[2], and the laity was advised to honour parents, elder brother, and the teacher[3]. The *Dhammapada* says, "He who always greets and constantly reveres the aged, four things will accrue to him, viz., life, beauty, happiness, and power,"[4] In the *Manu-Smṛiti* we find a similar passage, which reads :

'Abhivādanaśīlasya nītyaṁ vṛidhopasevinah
Chatvāri tasya parivardhante Āyurvidyā Yaśo balam.'[5]

But age was not always counted. Both Brahmanical[6] as well as Buddhist writers[7] agree that virtue and wisdom should be regarded as the best determining factors of one's seniority, and one possessed of these qualities should be respected by all, though he may be young in age. The *Vinaya-Piṭaka* tells us that if a junior Bhikshu was speaking on Vinaya, the senior members receiving instructions were to occupy an equal or lower seat out of reverence for the Law.[8] It was not always the seniority in respect of age, but the wisdom possessed by the person was also to be respected properly. So far as the seniority of age is concerned, the difference of three years did not count, and members having this difference in age occupied equal seats.[9] It is also said that when teachers and superiors were walking without shoes, juniors were not to walk with shoes.[10]

1. *C.V.* VI. 6.3.
2. *M.V.* V. 4.2.
3. *K.S.* I. 226,
4. *Dhp.* 109.
5. *Manu.* II. 121.
6. *Manu.* II. 150.
7. *A.N.* II. 22-24.
8. *C.V.* VI. 13.1.
9. *C.V.* VI. 13.2.
10. *M.V.* V. 4. 2.

The *Jātaka* evidence indicates that the elder members of the Order got several privileges over the juniors. It is clearly stated that in the religion of the Buddha it was seniority which claimed respect of word and deed, salutation and service; it is the seniors who should enjoy the best lodgings, the best water, and the best rice[1]. Rice served in the Order was of two varieties[2]. Seniority was counted, when serving the rice-meal. While the senior members got rice of better quality, the juniors were served inferior variety of it[3]. Tickets were issued for both. The *Taṇḍulanāli Jātaka* (No. 5) states that once Dabba, the Mallian, had been assigned the task of allotting tickets for rice-meal. Udāyi complained that Dabba was not the only man who could give out the tickets. Udāyi complained, because he had received tickets for inferior variety of rice. Due to this complaint the Saṅgha appointed Udāyi himself as the distributor of tickets for rice-meal. He, instead of distributing tickets, divided the dining hall by making marks on the ground or on the walls, so that those who wanted to eat better rice would take their seats on one side ; and those who were for the inferior variety of it would sit on the other side. Now, most of the members wanted to take better variety of rice, and they sat on the seats assigned for it. Then the Brethren explained to Udāyi that the quality of rice served depended on the seniority of the Bhikshus, and the angry monks enraged at Udāyi's ignorance pushed him away from the place of ticket distribution[4].

It has been well indicated in the story of the three friends cited above that there was no one-sided duty. The inner idea was of mutual reverence, confidence, and courtesy. It was through mutual confidence that proper harmony in the Saṅgha could be maintained. For the respect the senior member received from the junior one, he had to guide him by his counsels and help in his difficulties.

But the Bhikshuṇīs were not saluted by the Bhikshus. The

1. *Jā*. I. 218 (No. 37).
2. *Jā*. Nos. 5, 37.
3. *Jā*. I. 123 (No. 5).
4. *Jā* I. 124.

वरभत्तं पन असुकवस्सग्गे ठितं लामकभत्तं असुकवस्सग्गे आहकंसु।

Chullavagga says, "You are not, O Bhikshus, to bow down before women, to rise up in their presence, to stretch out your joined hands towards them, nor to perform towards them those duties that are proper."[1] This clarifies the position that a Bhikshuṇī did not deserve the observance of etiquette from the junior Bhikshu, in spite of her seniority, before whom she was always to bow down. A woman in fact is the centre of the family life, and for one who renounces the world, she symbolises the worldly life. Probably a Bhikshu who symbolised the life of renunciation, did not bow down before the symbol of family or worldy life. Elsewhere we have referred to other factors responsible for assigning the Buddhist nuns a position inferior to that of the monks. The Bhikshuṇīs not only did not receive reverence from the Bhikshus, but they were also not to eat, while the Bhikshus were eating ; they had to stand aside.[2] They were entitled to receive reverence only from their own sex, and the senior and the junior Bhikshuṇīs occupied seats according to the rules of seniority.[3]

Thus we find that the elder members of the Saṅgha were to be shown proper respect, the exception being that of the Bhikshuṇīs, who were not saluted by the Bhikshus. Similar was the case with eunuchs and Bhikshus under probation[4]. Obviously, the Bhikshuṇī and the novice occupied an inferior position in the Saṅgha, and hence, none of them was saluted. A Bhikshu who was admitted to a higher degree was not to be saluted by one who got his admission into the Saṅgha before him[5]. In this case seniority in age seems to have determined the observance of respect. But in case a senior Bhikshu belonged to another community and spoke against the Dharma, he was not to be saluted.[6] How a Bhikshu who had taken refuge in the Dharma could respect one who spoke

1. *C.V.* X. 3.1.
2. *S.B.E.* XIII. 56.
3. *C.V.* X. 18.
4. *C.V.* VI. 6.5. The eunuchs were not admitted in the Order, and hence, the reference which tells us that the Bhikshu was not to salute them, speaks of an earlier stage.
5. *Ibid.*
6. *Ibid.*

against it. To speak or to act against the Dharma was an offence, and the offender was not to be shown proper respect. The Bhikshu who was guilty of an offence, or was liable to undergo a penance, or was undergoing one, was looked upon as unfit for receiving salutation.[1] In both these cases the Bhikshu fell down from his elevated position on account of his offence. Probably, in such cases, cessation of showing respect was prescribed as a measure to discourage future offences and also as a punishment to correct the offenders.

The ideal was that the elder Bhikshus should treat the juniors as their own sons, and the juniors should respect the elders properly. But gradually a tendency arose in some elders to ill-treat the juniors, and in some cases also the latter ceased to show devotion to the former. The *Jātaka* evidence shows that the younger Bhikshus were not even provided with quarters and slept in the "Service Hall" (Upaṭṭhānasālā)[2]. It is also said that Rāhula had to spend his nights at the privy, as he was denied a proper sleeping place. The elders from time to time tested him. They threw a little dust or hand-broom on the floor, and complained that Rāhula had thrown it. He used to remove the dust. The Buddha seeing Rāhula sleeping at the privy thought, "If they treat Rāhula like this, what will they not do to other youths, whom they admit to the Order."[3] This statement indicates that the junior ones were not receiving proper affection and regard from the elders. Another story tells us that a village lad, being abused and struck by an old Bhikshu, after being ordained, left the Order three times.[4] Such a treatment of the juniors by the senior Bhikshus may have been responsible, to a great extent, for the lack of courtesy and submission on the part of the former. Some of the junior Bhikshus gradually developed unruly habits. It is said in a *Jātaka* that the juniors in course of a journey occupied all available lodgings, and the elders had to sleep outside in the open place.[5] Sāriputta had to spend the whole

1. *C.V.* VI. 6.5.
2. *Jā.* I. 160.
3. *Jā.* I. 162,

राहुलं एवं परिच्चजन्ता अञ्ञे कुलदारके पब्बाजेत्वा किं करिस्सथ ।

4. *Jā.* III. 197-98 (No. 365).
5. *Jā.* No. 37.

night at the foot of a tree.[1] This incident is stated also in the *Chullavagga* (VI. 11. 1.), which attributes the discourteous behavour of the junior to the Chhabbaggiya Bhikshus. The incident indicates lack of courtesy among some Bhikshus as regards lodging places, but from this one can infer their attitude in other matters. It appears that in the Buddhist Order there were some Bhikshus who could not maintain the high ideal of showing respect to the elders. What was their percentage is difficult to say.

Mutual Relations

In the Buddhist Monastic Order, the feeling of mutual assistance and brotherhood was the main thing to be realised. The Buddha knew that no organisation could flourish without the intense feeling of brotherhood. The Buddhist Order was a missionary institution, and it had to practise this ideal itself, and also to teach the world the same. At the end of the Vassa residence, when all the Bhikshus assembled together, the Buddha enquired about their well-being, and asked them whether they had lived in unity, in concord, and without quarrel.[2] How the Bhikshus lived together in mutual concord and earnestness can be well understood through the way in which Anuruddha, Kambila, and Nandiya lived in a place.[3] The three Bhikshus lived together in one residence. One who came first from the village, after begging alms, prepared seats, got water for washing feet, got a foot-stool and towel in order, cleansed the slop-basin, put there water to drink and kept food ready. He who came back last ate, if there was any food left, and he also desired to eat, otherwise threw it away. He also put things in order.[4]

But in a good number of cases the Bhikshus lacked this ideal of selfless service to each other. They helped one who was of service, and neglected him who was of no service to them. A Bhikshu was ill, but no brother attended him, as he was of no service to the Bhikshus.[5] Thereupon the Buddha

1. *Jā.* No. 37.
2. *S.B.E.* XIII, p. 327.
3. *M.V.* X. 4. 2-5; *M.N.* III. 155-57.
4. *Ibid.*
5. *M.V.* VIII. 26.

said before the meeting of the Bhikshu-Saṅgha. "Ye, O Bhikshus, have no mothers and no fathers, who might wait upon you. If ye, O Bhikshus, wait not one upon the other, who is there indeed who will wait upon you? Whosoever, O Bhikshus, would wait upon me, he should wait upon the sick."[1]

Every encouragement was given to the inculcation of the feeling of mutual service and help during the period of sickness. To wait upon a sick Bhikshu was not always a thankless task. A Bhikshu who waited upon the sick was entitled to receive the robes and bowls belonging to him, after his death.[2]

In a huge organisation like the Buddhist Order, mutual relations could not be always ideal; because when people live at one place in large numbers and come into contact with one another, it is human nature to indulge in disputes and quarrels. Only a super-man can be expected to have no disputes with anybody. We gather that the Bhikshus disputed and quarrelled. Not only they quarrelled, but also the Bhikshuṇīs did the same with the Bhikshus.[3] In a dispute with the Bhikshus and the Bhikshuṇīs, the Bhikshu Chhanna forced his way into the apartments of the Bhikshuṇīs, took their side and disputed with the Bhikshus.[4] The ill-feelings which were generated in the heart resulted in intrigues to malign the opponents. The *Chullavagga*[5] tells us that some of the Bhikshus, who were against the Mallian Dabba, induced Mettiyā, the Bhikshuṇī to approach the Buddha and tell him that she was defiled one night by Dabba. Thus, bringing a false charge, they wanted to get rid of him. Sometimes the Bhikshus resorted to force. Once the Chhabbaggiyas forcibly seized the throats of the Sattaravaggiya Bhikshus, cast them out and occupied a newly built Vihāra.[6] At times relations became strained, leading to the use of abusive words, if a Bhikshu charged the other with the violation of monastic discipline, and the latter did not accept his fault. The *Aṅguttara-Nikāya* points out that if both the offending and the reproving monks did not practice strict

1. *M.V.* VIII. 26.
2. *M.V.* VIII. 27. 5.
3. *C.V.* IV. 14. 1.
4. *Ibid.*
5. *C.V.* IV. 4. 8.
6. *C.V.* VI. 11.1.

self-examination, there was the likelihood of mutual relations becoming protracted and bitter.[1]

Common ownership

The Bhikshus lived a community life. They took shelter in the Saṅgha and owned their allegiance to it. Their life was regulated by the Saṅgha, which fulfilled the requirements of individual Bhikshus. Property belonged to the Saṅgha, and no Bhikshu practised individual ownership, till the monasteries became degenerate and lost the old ideal. Even then the principle that the Saṅgha was the owner of the property dedicated to it did not die. No Bhikshu was to divert to the use of any individual property dedicated to the Saṅgha, knowing it to be so.[2]

Lodgings were the property of the Saṅgha. There was an apportioner of lodgings, and whosoever was in need of a lodging place was provided with such.[3] Lodgings were not kept exclusively for all times, except the three months of the rainy season.[4]

When Vihāras came into use, they were assigned to the groups of the Bhikshus. Once a new Vihāra was built by the Sattaravaggiya Bhikshus. The Chhabbaggiyas said to them, "Depart, Sirs, the Vihāra has fallen to us",[5] and driving them away, occupied the Vihāra as already referred to. They did so on the ground that the Vihāra was a common property belonging to the Saṅgha. No Bhikshu had the exclusive possession of a lodging place.

Robes were the common property of the Saṅgha, and no Bhikshu had a separate personal ownership over his robe.[6] If any Bhikshu received extra robes at the time of distribution, he had to return it within a period of ten days.[7] The Bhikshus were given the ownership of the robes by the Saṅgha, and after the expiry of individual ownership it again passed to the

1. *A.N.* I. 46-48.
2. *S.B.E.* XIII, p. 52.
3. *C.V.* VI. 11. 2.
4. *C.V.* VI. 11. 3.
5. *Ibid.* VI. 11. 1.
6. *S.B.E.* XIII. 18.
7. *Ibid.*

Saṅgha. If after the rainy season a Bhikshu became disqualified for the Saṅgha, or died, then the robe that would fall in his share became the property of the Saṅgha.[1] When a Bhikshu died, his set of robes and the bowl belonging to him were assigned by the Saṅgha to those who waited upon him.[2] The robes and the bowls belonged to the Saṅgha which could assign them to others. When a Bhikshus died, the Saṅgha became the owner of the property left by him.[3]

The following five things belonged to the Saṅgha and were not transferable, nor could be disposed off either by the Saṅgha or by a company of two or three Bhikshus, or by an individual.[4]

1. A Park (Ārāma).
2. A Vihāra or the site for a Vihāra.
3. A bed, a chair, a bolster, a pillow.
4. A brass vessel, a brass jar, a brass pot, a brass razor, an axe, hatchet, a spade.
5. Creepers, bamboos, grass like *muñja*, *babbaja*, etc., and things made of wood or crockery.

This shows that the material possessions of the Saṅgha ultimately belonged to it. They could be assigned to the individuals, but the ownership could not be transferred.

Dress, Ornaments and Decoration of the Person

Shaving the head or keeping matted hair is the usual practice of ascetics. The Buddha is represented in the sculptures with curly hair. But it is the sculptural convention to represent him with hair. The Buddhist texts reveal that he was shaven-headed. It was obligatory for the Bhikshus to shave at the intervals of two months, or when the hair had grown up to the length of two inches.[5]

The Buddha had specially prohibited the use of turban, but the rule was relaxed, in case one was sick.[6] The prohibition of tying the turban shows that it was not regarded as a fashion in the religious life. The Sānchī and Bhārhut

1. *M.V.* VIII. 30.
2. *Ibid.*
3. *M. V.* VIII. 27.5.
4. *C.V.* VI. 15.2.
5. *C.V.* V. 2.2.
6. *S.B.E.* XIII. 66.

reliefs show that it was used by men of substance, like the Seṭṭhis and the noblemen. The Vedic literature makes the earliest mention of Ushṇīsha in connection with the Vrātyas and describes it as white and bright, having cross windings and tied with a tilt[1]. The description closely fits some of the turbans of Sānchī and Bhārhut sculptures. The Vedic people other than the Vrātyas do not seem to have habitually tied the turban. It was on the occasion of the performance of great sacrifices, like the Rājasūya, when one proclaimed his sovereignty that it was compulsory to be tied. Probably it was non-Aryan in origin, but later was adopted by the Aryans, and used as a mark of royal dignity and authority. By the time of the Buddha it had become the householders' dress. In Ceylon it is the custom that when a novice is admitted to the Order, he is clad in the full dress of a householder which includes also the turban.[2] It was discarded by the monks, because it was the dress of the laity.

In the beginning no foot-covering was allowed to be used by the Bhikshus. But many noblemen from the highest rank of society had joined the Order. The sudden change from the most comfortable life to that of austerity caused them great difficulty and inconvenience. The incident of the Seṭṭhi Soṇa's feet being badly hurt made the Buddha to prescribe that foot-coverings (shoes) could be used, provided they were only of one lining[3] and with linings, if cast off by others;[4] because in the latter case they would not look attractive. But shoes with heal-coverings and coloured slippers were not permitted.[5] Simplicity and non-injury to living beings were the two principles that determined the type of shoes used. Wooden shoes, though common among the Hindu Sanyāsins, were not used by the Buddhist monks, so that insects might not to trodden and killed.[6]

Shoes were not to be used always. They were put on only for the sake of protecting the feet from being hurt. No one

1. *Vedic Index*, I. 104
2. Copleston, R.S., *Buddhism*, p. 268.
3. *M.V.* V. 1. 29.
4. *M.V.* V. 3.
5. *M.V.*V. 2. 1-3.
6. *M.V.* V. 6.4.

was allowed to use them inside the village, except when sick.[1] There can be three possible reasons for this rule. Firstly, other sects of mendicants did not use shoes. Secondly, it seems that while begging cooked food, they were probably looked upon as undesirable. Thirdly, it seems quite probable that roads outside the villages were rough, while inside them they were smooth and good. In the open Ārāma at night shoes could be put on to protect the feet from thorns and stakes, for which lamps and walking sticks were also used.[2] In order that beds may not be soiled, one used shoes before getting upon couches and beds.[3] Some disease or wound also necessitated the use of foot-coverings.[4] Social etiquette also played its part, and when elders were without shoes, juniors also walked barefooted as a mark of respect for the seniors,[5] as observed earlier.

But as time passed on there grew a number of monastic establishments, which began to evolve a mode of life in consonance with their surroundings and conception of Dharma. Shoes for the sake of ornamentation, adorned with various kinds of skins and feathers of birds and having coloured edges, were used by the Chhabbaggiyas and the Bhikshus of Bhaddiya.[6] Though such anti-monastic practices are attributed to the Bhikshus who were disliked by the orthodox Buddhist monks, it appears that a small section of them did not adhere to the strict rules regarding foot-coverings.

Buddhism aimed at simplicity, as other sects of mendicants did, though it avoided the extremes and instructed the Bhikshus to put on robes made of rags taken from a dust-heap.[7] At one place the Buddha is described as possessing rags from the dust-heap for making himself a robe.[8] This practice of putting on Paṅsukūla robes continued for 20 years after the Enlightenment of the Buddha, as is known from the

1. *M.V.* V. 12.
2. *M.V.* V. 6. 2.
3. *M.V.* V. 6.1.
4. *M.V.* V. 5.
5. *M.V.* V. 4. 2.
6. *M.V.* V. 2.3; V. 8.
7. *S.B.E.* XIII. 173.
8. *S.B.E.* XIII. 125.

Aṭṭhakathā.[1] But gradually it changed, and new robes supplied by the laity began to be used.[2] Option was given either to use robes supplied by the laity or the Paṅsukūla ones. Silken and woolen clothes were prohibited out of the motive of non-injury to living beings.[3] But the zeal of the lay disciples was so much pressing that robes of various fabrics were allowed, and the Bhikshus used robes made of silk, cotton, hemp, linen, wool, and coarse cloth.[4] Probably it was felt that the sentiments of the lay disciples should not be hurt.

All the robes were dyed. In the beginning they were dyed with cowdung and yellow clay.[5] They were also rendered ugly looking by being soiled with mud or black and dark blue spots.[6] Later six kinds of dyes were selected for colouring robes.[7] The white robe was the mark of the householder,[8] and hence it was not adopted by the Buddha. In the Brahmanical system also the Vānaprasthin and the Sanyāsin put on Kāshāya robe.[9] Antelope-hide was used by the ascetics of the Brahmanical system, but the Buddha, probably inspired by the idea of non-injury to living creatures, prohibited it for the monks.

In the beginning there was no rule as regards the number of robes, and hence, the Bhikshus kept many robes.[10] This was not in accordance with the ideals of the religious life, and therefore, the number was fixed to be three.[11] Every Bhikshu possessed a set of three robes—a double waist cloth (Saṅghāṭi) a single upper robe (Uttarāsaṅga) and a single undergarment

1. *R.S.*, *Vinaya*, p. 273, footnote.
2. *Ibid.*, p. 274.
3. *Ibid.*
4. *M.V.* VIII. 3. 1.
5. *M.V.* VIII. 10.1
6. *S.B.E.* XIII. 45.
7. *M.V.* VIII. 10.1
8. *M.N.* II. 244; III. 224; *A.N.* 65, 69; *K.S.* I.106; Schism Pillar Edicts of Aśoka also show that white robe was the eternal mark of the householder.
9. *Vai. Dh. S.* II. 6.2. III. 6.6, 9.
10. *R.S.*, *Vinaya*, p. 279-80.
11. *M.V.* VIII. 13.4—5.

(Antaravāsaka).[1] The question arises how the Bhikshus were managing to bathe with such a limited number of robes. But they were not bathing very often. It was only once in a fortnight that they bathed except in summer, in sickness, in a journey, or at times of rains.[2] For the rainy season they were provided with a special garment known as the Vārshikaśāṭikā, which was like a Lungī.[3] Sisters were also provided with extra garment known as the Udakaśāṭi, used for bathing or during the menses.[4] So that beds may not be spoiled due to skin diseases, a Pratichchhādana which was like a kopina, was used.[5] A bed covering, a piece of cloth to wipe the faces with, a water strainer, and a bag were to be possessed by every Bhikshu. The water strainer was kept with a view to killing no insects that could be drunk with water. The practice of straining water before drinking was common also among the Brāhmaṇa Sanyāsins.[6] In this respect the Jaina monks had gone a step further, because they have been covering their nostrils.

Robes were generally provided by the laity. The Saṅgha worked as an intermediary ; it received the robes and distributed them among the Bhikshus. The Bhikshus were entitled to receive their sets of robes from the Saṅgha of that very district where they had spent the rainy season.[7] If a Bhikshu spent the Vassa in two places, he got his robe from that district where he spent the major part of it; but if he lived for equal durations of period in both the places, he was entitled to receive half portion of robes from each[8]. The moment robes were received they became the property of the Saṅgha[9], which properly distributed them among the Bhikshus by appointing officers[10]. These officers were required to

1. *M.V.* VIII. 13.4-5.
2. *S.B.E* XIII. 44-45.
3. *M.V.* VIII. 15. 15; VIII. 20.2.
4. *R.S.*, *Vinaya.*, p. 283, footnote.
5. *Ibid.*, p. 285.
6. *Vai. Dh. P.* III. 7.9.
7. *M.V.* VIII. 25. 4.
8. *Ibid.*
9. *S.B.E.* XIII. 18; *M.V.* VII. 1.4.
10. *M.V.* VIII 5.2, VIII. 6.1; VIII. 8; VIII. 9.1.

possess the qualities of not going in the evil courses of lust, hatred, delusion, fear, and were aware of what had been received and what not.[1] The idea was that persons appointed for such function should be of high character, capable of maintaining impartiality. Before distribution, robes were assorted, estimated, and shared according to higher and lower groups[2]. Probably the quality of robes was counted when distributing; and while the elders got robes of superior quality, the juniors received inferior ones, as was the case with fooding and lodging.[3]

Ornaments were no doubt prohibited, but some Bhikshus (e.g., the Chhabbaggiyas) were using earrings, eardrops, strings of beads for the throat, girdles of beads, bangles, necklaces, bracelets, and rings.[4]

Anointment for the face was not allowed ordinarily, but a Bhikshu suffering from skin disease could anoint his face.[5] The practice of anointing the eye was quite common. Ointments used were black collirium, Sota, Rasa, Geruka, and Kapalla[6]. They were perfumed by Tagara, sandalwood, black Anusāri, Kālīya, and Bhadramuktāki[7]. Every Bhikshu kept ointment boxes and sticks made of bone, ivory, horn, Nala reed, bamboo, wood, lac, shells of fruits, bronze, centre of shank-shell.[8] Gold and silver ones were prohibited.[9] All these were kept in a bag carried on shoulder-straps or tied by a thread[10].

The *Jataka* evidence also informs us that a few Bhikshus decorated their persons. The *Chulla Nārada Jātaka* tells us that

1. *Ibid.*
2. *M.V.* VIII. 9.2.
3. *Jā.* I. 218. According to Buddhaghosha (*S.B.E.* XVII. 203) Bhikshus shared equal portions of the robes. But this does not seem to have been the case.
4. *C.V.* V. 2.1
5. *C.V.* V. 2.5.
6. *M.V.* VI· 11.2.
7. *Ibid.*
8. *M.V.* VI. 12.
9. *Ibid.*
10. *M.V.* VI. 12. 4.

a Bhikshu who had lost all desires for learning lived devoted to the adornment of his person. He anointed the upper corner of his eyes, kept long hair, put on costly robes and used coloured and precious bowl. Such cases may have been exceptions in the beginning.

Food

Certain articles of food were prohibited, but the rule was not rigid. Even meat, which was prohibited, was eaten under special circumstances. During famine meats of various animals recieved in alms were eaten.[1] Liquor was also prohibited, but a sick Bhikshu could take oil decoction mixed with strong drink.[2]

The Bhikshus used some liquid food. Salt-sour gruel mixed with water was taken[3]. Rice-milk taken as a delicious drink was highly praised by the Buddha as a source of life, joy, and strength, etc.[4] Honey was taken mixed with rice-milk.[5] The Bhikshus took rice-milk and honey as a morning breakfast.[6] But this practice was not permitted on those days when they were invited by the laity; because it was found that Bhikshus ate very little due to it at the houses of the lay disciples, which made them annoyed[7]. All the rules were flexible, and concessions were allowed for the sick ones, such as taking fat of bear, fish, alligator, swine, and ass mixed with oil and so on.[8]

Food was distributed among the Bhikshus by issuing tickets. There used to be a distributor of tickets[9]. Dabba was such an officer.[10] Udāyi also was appointed to this post for sometimes.[11] The tickets had marks to ascertain the

1. *M.V.* VI. 23. 10-15.
2. *M.V.* VI. 14. 1.
3. *M.V.* VI. 16. 3; *Jā.* I. 55.
4. *M.V.* VI. 24.
5. *Ibid.*
6. *M.V.* VI. 25. 1.
7. *M.V.* VI. 25.
8. *M.V.* VI. 2.
9. *C.V.* IV. 4.3.
10. *Ibid.*, *Jā.* No. 5.
11. *Jā.* No. 5.

quality of the food, which depended on the merit of the Bhikshus; the senior got better food and the junior ones got inferior one[1], as discussed elsewhere.

The Bhikshuṇīs

The Buddha was definitely against the entry of women in his Order, and even after he consented for their admission, he was not happy. He said to Ānanda, "If, Ānanda, women had not received permission to go out from the household life and enter the homeless state, under the doctrine and discipline proclaimed by the Tathāgata, then would the pure religion, Ānanda, have lasted long, the good Law would have stood fast for a thousand years. But since, Ānanda, women have now received that permission, the pure religion, Ānanda, will not now last so long, the good Law will now stand fast only for five hundred years."[2]

Why were women considered to be undesirable by the Buddha for religious life?

Ascetic Orders all over the world were hostile to women. The presence of women in the monastic order was likely to cause the fall of monks from the high ideals of moral and spiritual character. Man attributed his weakness and fall to the wickedness of woman. The Buddhist Order being a monastic organisation took an unfavourable attitude towards the entry of women in the Saṅgha. Again, though in the Vānaprasthāśrama women accompanied their husbands, they did so in their advanced age when their passions had subsided. In the Buddhist Order novices were admitted at the age of fifteen, and the presence of women was very likely to stir the suppressed desires for union, and lead to the defilement of the homeless state. As shown elsewhere, the presence of women led to a number of such cases which brought the Order into contempt. The patriarchal notion was also an important factor. Society looked upon women as a part of the family property. According to the Dharmaśāstras a woman given in marriage was also given to the family (*Kulāya hi diyate nārī*). She was also looked upon as unfit for enjoying complete

1. *C.V.* IV. 4.5; *Jā.* No. 5.
2. *C.V.* X. 1.6; *A.N.* IV. 278.

freedom (*nasvātantryamarhati nārī*). When her husband left the world, she went under the protection of her son. The wives of Yājñavalkya did not renounce the world, though they were very eager to follow the path of their husband. This shows that a woman was not to leave the family. Again, if a woman lived at the forest alone, without the protection of anybody, there was always some danger from antisocial elements. The *Vinaya* informs us that if women lived at the woods, they were raped by wicked persons.[1] Even if they bathed in a solitary place, they were attacked and defiled.[2] There was every chance of their being abducted by robbers. The wife of a Vānaprasthin accompained him, because in that case she enjoyed his protection. The Buddha had to face a delicate situtation. If he allowed women to enter the Saṅgha and to go to the forest for practising meditation, the latter could be a victim of antisocial elements; if they were allowed to live in the company of the Bhikshus, there was the possibility of mutual attraction, leading to defilement. It was due to these that after women were allowed to enter the Order, they were not permitted to go out of an *āvāsa* (residence) alone, or to go to a river alone, or to live at night alone, or to go out of the community alone.[3]

Why were women so eager to join the Order ? As there was a wave of asceticism, it was quite natural that women who are by nature more religious-minded than men, should be tempted to enter the homeless order of life. Those who were advanced in age would have liked to lead a life of religious austerities for the rest of their life and to gain the merit of the good work (Dharma). There were widows, who on account of the grief at the death of their husbands, lost all desire for the worldly life and entered the Order. Loss of near relations induced many to renounce the world. Paṭāchārā became mad at the tragic ends of a number of her near relatives—sons, husband, parents, and brother.[4] Similar was the case with Kisā-Gotamī[5]

1. R. S., *Vinaya.*, p. 537.
2. R. S., *Vinaya.*, 540.
3. *Bhikkhuṇī Pātimokkha-Saṅghādisesadhamma.*
4. *Psalms of Sisters*, pp. 70-71.
5. *Ibid.*, pp. 106-7; *Therīgāthā*, 218-19.

and Sundarī.[1] When a number of young men renounced the world and joined the Order, it was quite natural that their wives out of affection for them and also on account of disappointment followed the foot-prints of their husbands. It is said that 500 Śākya ladies whose husbands had renounced the world went to Vaiśālī and through Ānanda, the Thera asked the Buddha's permission for Ordination.[2] Similarly, Chāpā whose husband had entered the Order followed him, delivering her child to his grandfather.[3] When most of the family members joined the Order, some of the ladies renounced the world.[4] Failure of married life and lack of harmony in the family life was also responsible for women becoming Bhikshuṇīs. Isidāsī renounced the world, because she was abandoned by her three husbands successively.[5] Soṇā entered the Order, because she was not shown any respect by her sons and daughters-in-law.[6] Lastly, we find that despair in love also caused many to become Bhikshuṇīs. Bhaddā, daughter of a treasurer at Rājagṛiha, fell in love with a robber and saved his life. But the robber in return planned to kill her and acquire the costly jewels that she possessed. Knowing the plan of the robber, she killed him and became a Bhikshuṇī.[7] Thus we find that a number of factors were responsible for women becoming members of the homeless life.

Women got entrance in the Order of the Buddha as Bhikshuṇīs, but they were given a secondary position. As it has been already shown, they had always to bow down before the Bhikshus;[8] from the monks they were not entitled to receive proper respect suitable according to their seniority.[9] They were also not permitted to perform official works against the Bhikshus.[10]

1. *Therīgāthā*, 328.
2. *Psalms of Sisters*, p. 88.
3. *Ibid.*, pp., 130-31.
4. *Ibid.*, p. 55.
5. *Therīgāthā*, 406-33.
6. *Psalms of Sisters*, p. 62.
7. *Ibid.*, pp. 64-65.
8. *C.V.* X. 1. 4.
9. *C.V.* X. 3.
10. *C.V.* X. 20.

The existence of women in the Order created a new problem. Certain wives renounced the world with the permission of their husbands. In some such cases, those who did not know at the time of their admission, that they had already conceived, gave birth to children. The *Chullavaga*[1] says that a certain woman, who did not know that she had conceived, joined the Order among the Bhikshuṇīs. Afterwards her womb moved within her. Then she thought: "How shall I now conduct myself towards this child? " The Saṅgha allowed her to bring up the child till it attained to years of discretion. In order to facilitate the bringing up of the child, a companion was allowed to the mother Bhikshuṅī. A similar story is narrated in the *Nigrodhamiga Jātaka* (No. 12). It is said that the daughter of a wealthy merchant of Rājagṛiha decided to renounce the world with the hope of winning Arhatship. She conveyed this desire to her parents, who replied, "What my dear ? Ours is a very wealthy family and you are our only daughter. You cannot take the vow." She thought, "Be it so then, when I am married into another family, I will gain my husband's consent to take the vows." She was married and proved to be a devoted wife. In course of time she conceived, but did not know it. She got her husband's consent to join the Order. As time passed, the symptoms of pregnancy made their appearance. Other sisters noticing this brought the matter before Devadatta, who thought, "It will be a damaging report to get abroad that one of my sisters is with child and that I condone the offence. My course is clear :—I must expel her from the Order." Then without starting forward any inquiry, as if to thrust aside a mass of stone, he said, 'Away and expel this woman.' Later the matter was investigated by a Bhikshuṇī appointed by the Saṅgha and found that she had conceived before entering the nunnery; her expulsion was cancelled. This shows that in case of pregnancy normally the Bhikshuṇī was expelled. But if one entered the nunnery after conception which she did not know, she was not expelled. The *Nigrodhamiga Jātaka* tells us in continuation of the above story that the sister gave birth to a child. At that time king Presenajit was passing by the nunnery, and he thinking the

1. *C.V.* X. 25. 1.

care of a child to be a burden on the religious life of the sister took charge of it. The child was brought up in the king's family. It appears that in most of the cases the laity took charge of children born in the nunnery; while in a few, when no lay disciple came forward to accept such a child, it was brought up in the nunnery, till the years of discretion.

From the above account we gather that if a sister conceived before joining the Order, she was not expelled. But the possibility of conceiving in the nunnery cannot be ruled out; because, if both the Bhikshus and Bhikshnṇīs were in their youthful age, there was every possibility of such cases. And, to avoid such situations, it was laid down that if a novice practised sexual intercourse with a Bhikshuṇī, he would be expelled from the fraternity.[1] But as time passed on, the relation between a Bhikshu and a Bhikshuṇī in some cases ceased to be ideal, as already referred to.

Backsliding, Reverting to Worldly Life and Degeneration in the Monasteries

Probably it was mainly the suppression of desires at the unripe age, which was responsible for leading Bhikshus to the wrong path of backsliding and also reverting to the world. The *Jātakas* have preserved many such stories where Bhikshus are represented as backsliding. Most stories are no doubt narrated in order to warn the Bhikshus against the danger of falling a prey to the worldly desires, but they would not have been current without some basis. All the stories of this nature reveal that feminine charm was responsible for deflecting the Bhikshus from their ideals. The Buddha had predicted that the presence of sisters in the Saṅgha would bring disruption in the monastic life in about a period of five hundred years.[2] Novices easily could be a prey to backsliding, as was the case of Kaṇṭaka, who had defiled a Bhikshuṇī.[3] There were also such incidents in which Bhikshus were led astray by coming into contact with maidens in their prime of youth,

1. *M.V.* I. 60.
2. *C.V.* X. 1.6.; *A.N.* IV. 278.
3. R.S., *Vinaya*. p. 125.

belonging to the worldly life.[1] Young Bhikshus visiting the houses of lay disciples very often came into contact with youthful ladies, lost all desired for the life of renunciation and reverted to the world.[2]

Not always was the feminine charm responsible for bringing back Bhikshus to the world, but it was also the ill-treatment of the elders towards their juniors, as was the case with a village lad who, being abused and struck by an old man after he was ordained, left the Order.[3]

In a few cases the parents took active part in restoring their sons to the family life, as was done by the father of of Raṭṭhapāla[4] and a Rājagṛiha Seṭṭhi.[5] Sometimes the former wife or wives of the Bhikshu entreated him for reverting to the world.[6]

In some cases Bhskshus and Bhikshuṇīs probably changed their faith. Such Bhikshus could be readmitted in the Order, but this was not so with the Bhikshuṇīs.[7] This shows that Bhikshus could leave the Order and be readmitted. The Parivāsa rules state that if a Bhikshu left the Order, before the completion of the period of Parivāsa penalty imposed upon him, he had to go through it (Parivāsa) after his readmission.[8] The *Mahāvagga* tells us that some Upajjhāyas and Āchariyas used to go away from the Order, or they returned to the world.[9] This shows that reverting to the world was not limited to the new-comers, but some who had attained the position of Upajjhāyas left the Order.

1. *Jā.* II.33 (No. 159).
2. *Jā.* No. 477.
3. *Jā.* No. 365.
4. *M.N.* II 63-64.

   एहि त्वं, तात रट्ठपाल, सिक्खं पच्चक्खाय हीनाय' आवत्तित्वा भोगे भुञ्जसु पुञ्ञानि च करोहीति ।
5. *Jā.* No. 14.
6. *M. N.* II. 64,

   अथ खो आयस्मतो रट्ठपालस्स पुराणदुतियिको पच्चेकपादेसु गहेत्वा आयस्मन्तं रट्ठपालं एतदवोचुं: कीदिसा नाम ता, अय्यपुत्तक अच्छरायो, यासं त्वं हेतु ब्रह्मचरियं चरसीति ?
7. *R. S.*, *Vinaya.*, pp. 384, 539.
8. *Ibid.*, pp. 384, 386, 388.
9. *S.B.E.* XIII. pp. 178, 181, 182.

The Buddha preached the 'Majjhima-Patipadā', i.e. the middle path. He did not favour the method of severe austerities, preferred by his contemporary religious teachers, like Makkhali Gosāla, Mahāvīra, and others, or that practised by some of the Brāhmaṇa ascetics. His aim was that one should strive for spiritual realisation at the minimum torture to the body and the mind. The rules laid down for monastic discipline were not of severe asceticism. He allowed several concessions, so that the Bhikshus might not be put to a number of inconveniences. Among those who entered the monastery many found the monastic rules quite suitable for spiritual striving; but there were some who lacked intense urge for spiritual insight. The rules laid down by the Buddha seemed to them difficult to be followed. They were in favour of more concessions and liberalisation of the monastic discipline. It was this section of the Bhikshus that agitated at the Vaiśālī Council for the inclusion of the ten prohibited practices.[1] It is said that some Bhikshus openly began to practice them, which disturbed the conscience of the orthodox section. The study of the early Buddhist texts reveals that some of the Bhikshus did not live up to the high ideals preached by the Buddha. This was partly due to the lack of personal integrity on the part of the Bhikshus, and partly due to the overzealous devotion of the laity, who supplied elements of comforts for the monks.

The social instinct of a Bhikshu, which was suppressed during the early years of his life, must have been exerting for its full expression. The Bhikshu's life was cut off from the social life of a normal human being, and the society with all its varied activities appealing to the human heart was attracting the monks. Some of them who lacked personal intigrity responded to it. But this they could not do in a normal way.

The personal life of some of the Bhikshus was marked by greed and lust for sexsual pleasures. Acceptance of gold and silver was against monastic discipline, but, as informed by the *Chullavagga*[2] and the popular stories, some of the greedy

1. *Dīp.* IV. 47-49; V. 16.-18.
2. *C.V.* XII. 1.1.

Bhikshus began to accumulate money. The *Machchh-Udāna Jātaka* states how a junior Bhikshu deceived the elder of his one thousand Kārshāpaṇas.[1] The story shows that the elders received money which went into their pockets. It is further said that some Bhikshus became so greedy and dissatisfied with the mendicant's garb that they began to go out in search of good meals and invitations.[2] During the early stage of the Order, all invitations were looked upon as extra allowances. According to the rules and ideals of the monastic discipline, Bhikshus were to possess only limited requisites of their life and not to use luxury goods. But the lay disciples began to offer them such requisites of the Bhikshu life as bowls, robes, needle-cases, girdles, filters, etc. in plenty which they accepted to please them. Later it appears that the laity offered also luxury goods, which began to be utilised by some of the Bhikshus. It is gathered from the *Mahāvagga*[3] and the *Chullavagga*[4] that various luxury goods, such as sofas, cushions, divans, coverlets dyed with animal-figures, carpets inlaid with gold or silver, chairs of several types and so on were used by the Chhabbaggiya Bhikshus. What percentage of the Bhikshus used such luxury goods is difficult to say.

The coming into existence of large monasteries in different regions led to the development of degenerate Bhikshu-life in a number of such places. The *Chullavagga*[5] tells us that a Bhikshu travelling from Kāśī to Śrāvastī came across the Kīṭā-giri, where he saw the Bhikshus indulging in all sorts of worldly pleasures. He saw them making wreaths of flowers of various types, such as Mañjarikā, Vidhutikā, Vataṅsaka (or Vataṅsako), Āvela, Urachchhada, and sending them as presents to the wives, daughters, young women, sisters-in-law and female slaves of respectable families. They used to eat at the wrong time and drink strong drinks. They danced, sang, played music and wanton sports. They amused them-

1. *Jā.* II. 423.
2. *Jā.* IV. 70
3. *M.V.* V. 10.
4. *C.V.* VI. 2. 3-5.
5. *C.V.* I. 13.

selves at games of various types, both indoor and outdoor. They played dice, took part in chariot races and archery matches, and practised elephant and horse-riding, carriage-driving, swords-manship, wrestling and boxing. They invited dancing girls, saying, "Here you may dance sisters", and greeted them with applause. The *Mahākaṇha Jātaka* also describes the degenerate condition of a monastery and says that sons and daughters were born there. The *Jātaka* account may be taken as describing the conditions of a later period of the monastic life; but the *Chullavagga* being fairly early should be taken as referring to the life lived in some of the monasteries in our period.

The above account appears to be exaggerated, because all practices referred to do not seem practicable in a monastery. But one thing is clear that a number of indecent practices had crept into some of the monastic establishments. Some of the Bhikshus are described as going so far as to establish unfair relations with the female members of the laity's house and also as inviting dancing girls.

It was probably the development of a few monasteries, as described above, which led to the cessation of the ideal relations between the Bhikshus and the Bhikshuṇīs in a good number of cases. It is said that in some cases it became one of wives and husbands. The *Chullavagga*[1] says that the Chhabbaggiya Bhikshus uncovered their bodies, or their thighs, or their private parts and showed them to the Bhikshuṇīs ; they addressed them with wicked words or associated with them. People gave food to the Bhikshus and the latter gave it to the Bhikshuṇīs.[2] The *Pānīya Jātaka* says that many householders who had entered the monastery, found it difficult to get rid of the sinful thoughts of worldly desires, and they indulged in them. The mental lapse was the beginning of the physical lapse, which was to follow in the future. The statement that sons and daughters were born in the monasteries[3] is perhaps an exaggeration. But it indicates the relations between the Bhikshus and the Bhikshuṇīs in a few cases.

1. *C.V.* X. 9. 1.
2. *C.V.* X. 15. 1.
3. *Mahākaṇha Jā.* (No. 469).

It has already been shown that during the early stage of the Buddhist Order, the Bhikshus were having individual residences like those of Bhikshu Kassapagotta[1] and others, and the wandering Bhikshus used to visit such residences and live there for sometimes. But, when monasteries came into use, even then some Bhikshus, though in rare cases, built their own residences; and in place of the ideal religious life, lived the life of all comforts. The *Jātaka* evidence tells us that there were wealthy people who joined the monastic life, but found it difficult to break down all ties with their family estates and neglect their household affairs. A squire of Śrāvastī joined the Brotherhood. While joining, he caused to be built for himself a chamber to live in, a room for fire, and a store room; and not till he had stocked his store room with ghee, rice and other requirements did he join finally.[2] Even after he had become a brother, he used to send for his servants to cook for him, what he liked to eat; had an entire change of clothing for day and another for night, and he dwelt aloof on the outskirts of the monastery.[3] This description leads to the conclusion that while one entered the monastery, he could also manage his family affairs from a distance. He could live a comfortable life as he wished. His individual dwelling could be built at the outskirts of the monastery, his food could be dainty, and clothes plentiful. It is also said that such a life was discouraged by the orthodox monks, who did not commend the life of comforts. Such a dwelling was not confined to an individual, but in some cases a number of such Bhikshus who could not attain the ideal of the religious life, lived at the outskirts of the monastery. One story tells us that a number of aged friends who were wealthy squires of Śrāvastī joined the Brotherhood; but they failed to master the truth on account of their advanced age, and so did not follow sincerely the life of the Bhikshu.[4] All of them lived as a

1. *M.V*, IX. 1.1.
2. *Jā.* I. 126 (No. 6).
3. *Ibid.*
4. *Ibid.*, I. 497.

पब्बज्जानुरूपं समणधम्मं न करिंसु महल्लकभावेन धम्मं पि न परियापुणिसु ।

family together building a cluster of neighbouring huts on the skirts of the monastery.[1] When they went out for alms, they generally made for their wives and children's houses and ate there.[2]

Officers of the Saṅgha

The administration of the Saṅgha was well organised. There were a number of officers who managed its different departments. The system of appointing officers for the different types of works had very much facilitated the smooth and systematic working of the Saṅgha. The officers looked after the requirements of the Bhikshus and satisfied their needs. The condition of the Saṅgha was not allowed to be chaotic. It was very much orderly. When the government of a state is well organised and the administrative officers are conscious of their duty of looking after the welfare of the state, the subjects are happy. Such was the case with the Buddhist Monastic Order also. But the duties and functions of the two are quite different. A monastic order is concerned with the spiritual welfare of its members, although this does not mean that the members of a religious order have no material needs. It is true that the Buddha established a religious order of the homeless state, but he had not prescribed the path of extreme asceticism. A few material possessions were permitted to the monks, and these had to be procured and distributed properly.

The Buddhist Order was a huge organisation of the Bhikshu community living together. It is natural that when people live together in large numbers, many problems arise out of their mutual relations. In the Buddhist Order there was the possibility of Bhikshus entering into disputes and quarrels. They might form rival groups. Such situations were to be avoided, and ways for maintaining cordial relations were to be found out. The problem of moral discipline was very important. It was on the days of the Uposatha

1. *Jā*. I. 497.
पब्बजितकाले पि विहारपरियन्ते पण्णसाला करेत्वा एकको वसिसु।

2. *Ibid.*,
अत्तनो पुत्तदारस्स एव गेहं गन्त्वा भुञ्जिसु।

that by reciting the Pātimokkha (rules of monastic discipline) the Bhikshus were reminded of their discipline.[1] It was this procedure which fulfilled their spiritual needs. However, in their daily life, the Bhikshus learnt spiritual knowledge from their teachers—the Upajjhāyas and the Āchariyas. There was the problem of admission in the Saṅgha, for which the Pabbajjā and the Upasampadā Ordinations were conferred, according to the regulations laid down.

Now, coming to the material needs of a Bhikshu, we find that he did not suffer due to the mismanagement of the authorities of the Saṅgha. The Saṅgha appointed a number of officers to take charge of the different departments. The appointment was made through proper procedure which was the consent of the candidate, the motion before the Saṅgha, the resolution moved and the approval of the Saṅgha.[2] All appointments were made by the Saṅgha. Care was taken to appoint only such persons who on account of their good conduct enjoyed the confidence and respect of all the Bhikshus. There was a moral standard laid down, which determined the eligibility of a Bhikshu to be appointed as an officer. Only that Bhikshu could be made an officer who possessed the qualities of impartiality, fearlessness, and was free from delusions and did not indulge in the evil course of lust.[3] In addition to these moral qualifications, he was expected to be in full knowledge of the work, to which he was assigned. If he was to distribute lodgings, he was required to know the numbers of lodgings and those of the needy Bhikshus. If he distributed robes, he was expected to know the number of robes, the number of Bhikshus who had received robes and those who had not received and so on.

There was the problem of the management of lodgings. In the beginning this problem was not so important on account of the non-existence of monasteries and the existence of individual huts. But later on the management of the Ārāmas (parks) and the Vihāras became very important. Lodgings were the property of the Saṅgha, and it had to

1. *E. G., M.N.* III. 10.
2. *M.V.* VIII. 5. 1; *C.V.* IV. 9.
3. *C.V.* VI. 11.2.

allot residences to the individual Bhikshus. There was an officer known as the 'Śayanāsanaprajñāpaka' (distributor of lodgings)[1], whose duty was to find out those who were in need of a lodging place and to provide them with it. The Bhikshus were not to worry for lodgings, but simply to approach the officer-in-charge who allotted them rooms. The Ārāmas were kept in order, and there were a number of junior officers known as the Ārāmikas (those who kept the Ārāma in order).[2] They were under a superintendent (Ārāmikapreshaka)[3] who looked after their work. The laity were donating Vihāras for the Order. The new buildings in course of erection were to be in charge of a Bhikshu who superintended the work.[4] He was like an overseer of buildings. A Bhikshu was made the overseer of a Vihāra, because he was expected to know what type of building was most suitable as a residence of the Bhikshus.

Next came the management of robes. Robes were donated by the laity. In order to receive the robes properly, an Officer was appointed, known as the 'Chīvarapratigrāhaka' (receiver of robes).[5] The idea must have been that no disciple should be disappointed due to inadequate arrangements for receiving what the laity offered. It was not possible for a Bhikshu who received robes to look after them, so another officer, the Chīvaranidahaka[6] (incharge of robes) was appointed to take charge of the robes received and also to look after them, so that they might not be spoiled. His duty was simply to take charge of the robes, but he could not keep them in good condition due to the lack of proper place for storing them. Therefore, robes were kept in a store-room, under the charge of the Bhāṇḍāgārika (overseer of stores).[7] As the robes were, properly speaking, the property of the Saṅgha, and the Bhikshus received their share of robes from the Saṅgha, an officer to distribute them (robes) was appointed. He was the

1. *C.V.* VI. 21.2.
2. C.*V.* VI. 21·3.
3. *Ibid.*
4. *C.V.* VI. 5. 2.
5. *M.V.* VIII. 5.
6. *M.V.* VIII. 6.
7. *M.V.* VIII. 8.

Chīvarabhājaka (distributor of robes).[1] There was one more officer who received under-garments and probably distributed them also. He was called the Śāṭikāgrāhāpaka[2].

For the management of food also there were officers. The Bhikshus got their usual meals through tickets distributed by an officer of the Saṅgha called the Khādyabhājaka (apportioner of food).[3] Tickets were issued also for sending selected Bhikshus to the laity's houses. This was done during the period of scarcity. This officer who was called the Bhakta-Uddesaka[4] was a functionary appointed only during scarcity period. According to the types of food there were two more officers, namely, the Yavāgū-Bhājaka[5] who distributed rice gruel, and the Phalabhājaka[6] who distributed fruits.

There was an officer known as the Alpamātrabhājaka for disposing off trifles, like needles, scissors, strainers, etc.[7] Needles were needed for stitching robes, and each Bhikshu kept a needle. Scissors may have been utilised for cutting hair and nails. It may have been also used for cutting clothes. Strainer was necessary for each Bhikshu, because water was to be strained before drinking.

There was an officer of the novices known as the Śrāmaṇerapreshaka.[8] His functions are not known. Most probably his duty was to see that the novices performed their duties properly. He may have been keeping an account of the new-comers and of those who passed to the stage of Bhikshuhood. Many novices used to leave the Order, and this officer may have been keeping an account of such cases.

1. *M.V.* VIII. 9.1; *C.V.* VI. 21. 2.
2. *C.V.* VI. 21. 3.
3. *C.V.* VI. 4.3.
4. R.S., *Vinaya.*, p. 474.
5. *Ibid.* p. 475.
6. *Ibid.*
7. *C.V.* VI. 21. 3.
8. *Ibid.*

CHAPTER X

RURAL ECONOMY

Villages and Their Types

The available evidence points to the absence of urban life in Eastern India before the end of the second millenium B.C.. The majority of the population consisted of agricultural-pastoral peoples living in villages. The Vedic village under the Grāmaṇī was the main centre of the economic and social life of the people. Agriculture and cattle-rearing were the main occupations of the village people. The village seems to have consisted of a group of houses, surrounded by an enclosure as protection against wild beasts and enemies. It was surrounded by a belt of pasture land for the cattle beyond the arable fields.[1] Beyond the pasture land was the *aranya* or the uncultivated land which provided wood for the village. It was probably a no-man's-land.

By the 7th Century B.C. also we find smiliar arrangement of a village. During this period villages had houses together in a group, probably separated only by narrow lands.[2] Close to the dwellings was the sacred grove of trees of the primeval forest, left standing at the time of the forest clearing, for making dwelling houses and arable fields.[3] Beyond this lay the cultivable fields. Next to it existed an extensive stretch of pasture land for the cattle, and then the jungle which provided waste and wood for the village. This Buddhist account is similar to that presented by Pāṇini.[4]

1. *Ṛig.* I. 25. 16; III. 62. 16; V. 66.3.
   N.C. Bandopadhyay, *Economic life and Progress in A.I.*, Vol. I, p.108.
2. Rhys Davids, *B.I.*, p. 33.
3. *Jā.* II. 358, सब्बं बनं छिन्दित्वा खेत्तानि करित्वा कसिकम्मं करिंसु; IV. 359.
4. *India as known to Pāṇini*, pp. 141-2.

In the Pāli literature mention is made of Gāma[1], Gāmaka[2], Dvāragāma[3] and Pachchantagāma[4] as different types of villages. The Gāma and the Gāmaka were probably the ordinary village and the hamlet respectively, the difference being only of the size. The Nigama was probably a busy market village, differentiated from the quiet agricultural one. The Dvāragāmas were situated at the gates of cities, and probably they were suburbs, most of them being industrial villages. The Pachchantagāma was located at the border of the kingdom. Its situation was peculiar which had made its nature unstable. Due to border invasions, very often, they were deserted, and we come across villages in a ruined state (Purāṇagāmṭṭhāna[6]). Secondly, these villages were haunted by robbers, who used to make life insecure[7]. If was in these villages that one found it difficult to differenciate between a thief and an official of the state [8]. Such circumstances speak of the unstable economic condition of the Pachchantagāmas. These villages were not well looked after, and their economic condition was unstable; because much importance was attached to frontier towns, which were heavily guarded from all sides[9] on account of their being military bases that kept vigil on the frontiers.

During our period village life was marked by the rise of numerous industrial villages, which were exclusively inhabited by men of the same craft. Thus, we find villages

1. E.G., *D.N.* I. 193; *M.N.* I. 189, II.40; *A.N.* IV. 365; *Su. Ni.* I.4.
2. *Jā.* I. 283, 378; II.68.
3. *Jā.* III. 33.
4. *Jā.* I. 478; II. 76; IV. 326, 31.
5. *D.N.* I. 193; *M.N.* I. 166, 189, 271, 473; *S.N.* IV. 327, v. 2; *Peta.* II 13.18. *Jā.* I. 345,

   राजगहनगरस्स किर अविदूरे सक्खरं नाम निगमो ।
6. *M. V.* III. 10; *Jā.* I. 478; II. 102.
7. *Jā*, I. 296-97.
8. *Jā.* III. 9.
9. *A.N.* IV. 106-8; *Dhp.* 315,

   नगरं यथा पच्चन्तं गुत्तं सन्तरबाहिरं ।

like those of carpenters,[1] smiths[2], weavers[3], and so on. Another feature of the villages was that some of them were exclusively peopled by men of the same caste. We find villages of Brāhmaṇas (Brāhmaṇagāma)[4], Kshatriyas (Kshatriyagrāma[5], Vaiśyas (Baniyagrāma)[6], Chaṇḍāla (Chaṇḍālagāma)[7], Nesādas (Nesādagāma)[8], and so on. There were also villages of park-keepers (Ārāmika-gāma)[9] and robbers Choragāmaka)[10]. Villages, whether peopled by craftsmen, or by men of the same caste and profession, were the creation of the same principle. It appears that the economic factor of specialisation of labour was responsible for the localisation of various industries at separate villages and for the grouping of people of the same profession and caste.

Though there came into existence such villages which were peopled by men of the same caste, yet their number would not have been large. Society had not segregated castes and professions, and in an ordinary agricultural village or in a town the population would have been a mixed one, men of different castes, occupations and trade, following their own professions.

All the villages can be classified into two distinct types, i.e., the agricultural viilages and those inhabited by craftsmen or industrial ones. In the beginning all the villages were of the former type. Later, owing to the progress of

1. *Jā.* II. 18, 405; IV. 159, 207.
2. *Jā.* III. 281.
3. *Psalms of sisters,* p. 88.
4. The Buddhist evidence tells us of several Brāhmaṇa Villages in Magadha of our period such as Khānumata (*D.N.* I. 127), Ambasaṇḍā (*D.N.* II. 263-64), Ekanāla (*K.S.* I. 216), Pañchasālā (*K.S.* I. 143), Sālindiya (*Jā.* II. 293, IV. 276) and so on. We get references to Brāhmaṇa villages in *M.N.* I. 285, 400; *G.S.* I. 162; *A.N.* IV. 340-41.
5. *Vaiśālī-Abhinandana-Grantha,* pp. 85-86.
6. *Ibid.*
7. *Jā.* IV. 200, 376, 390; *The Mahāvaṁsa* (V. 41) speaks of a Chaṇdāla village to the east of Pāṭaliputra.
8. *Jā.* II. 36; IV. 413; VI. 71.
9. *M.V.* VI. 15. 4.
10. *Jā.* IV. 430.

पब्बतस्स उपरिवाते चोरगामको अहोसि ।

industries and the growth of their population, the craftsmen probably found it more convenient to migrate to their own settlements, where they lived in large numbers and pursued their crafts. The Buddhist[1] and the Jaina[2] sources refer to industrial villages outside the cities. It appears that the industrial villages formed the Dvāragāmas which supplied the needs of the cities, and expressions like Dvāragāmavāsī Vaḍḍhaki,[3] Dvāragāmavāsī Kumbhakāra[4], etc. probably refer to the inhabitants of such villages.

The Muchalagāma, described as a small village in Magadha, consisted of thirty families only..[5] We do not get reference to any village smaller than this. This shows that the smallest village or the hamlet was inhabited by at least thirty families. There is also no mention of any village consisting of more than a thousand families. This shows that there was no village larger than this size. Big villages are described as consisting of either five hundred[6] or a thousand families.[7] These were mostly villages inhabited by the craftsmen.

Agriculture

Vedic Aryans had made sufficient strides in the field of agriculture. Agriculture and cattle-farming both were practised; the latter being a means of the former as well as a source of food by supplying milk, curd, butter and also meat. It was due to the need of rains for cultivating the land that Indra, the rain god was so much invoked.[8] Vedic people's knowledge of cultivation is revealed well from these hymns: "Harness the ploughs, fit the yokes now that the womb is ready, sow the seeds therein, and through our praise,

1. E. G., *Jā.* IV. 207 speaks of a village of carpenters outside the city.
2. *Uvāsagadasāo*, VII. 184, tells us of a village of 500 potters outside the city of *Palāsapura*.
3. *Jā.* IV. 344.
4. *Jā.* III. 376.
5. *Jā.* I. 199,
   तस्मिं च गामे तिंस' एव कुलानि होन्ति ।
6. *Jā.* II. 18.
7. E.G., *Jā.* I. 234.
   कुलसहस्सवासे केवट्टगामे ।
8. *Ṛig.* VII. 101.3; X 105.1; X. 50.3.

may there be abundant food, may (the grain) fall ripen, towards the sickle."[1] "Set up the cattle trough, bind the straps to it, let us pour out the water of the well which is full of water, fit to be poured and not easily exhausted."[2] The importance of agriculture can be assessed from the story of king Janaka's ploughing the field[3]. Knowledge of cultivation seems to have made considerable progress. We are told of heavy ploughs, with sharp point and a smoothed handle, harnessed by 24 oxen.[4] The *Saṁhitās* and the *Brāhmaṇas* speak of the different seasons for the cultivatiom of different grains and also of the double crop[5] and inform us about the operations of ploughing, sowing, reaping, and threshing.[6] Later Vedic sources further speak of manure and irrigation and also of the enemies of the farmer. They tell us that moles destroyed the seed, birds and other creatures injured the young shoots, draughts and excessive rains were to be feared.[7] The *Atharvaveda* prescribes several spells and charms to avoid calamities and secure a good harvest.

In the *Ṛigveda*, Yava and Dhānya are mentioned as the cereal and grain crops cultivated.[8] *Ṛigveda* refers to Saptasindhu where rice was not in abundance. Later we find the *Bṛihadāraṇyaka Upanishad* mentioning ten kinds of grains; they are rice and barley (Vrīhi-yavāh), sesasum and beans (Tila-māsāh), Panicum Milicum and Italicum (Aṇupriyaṅgavah), maize (Godhūmah), lentils (Masūrah), pulses, and Vetches or Delichos-Uniflorus (Khala-kulah).[9]

The Buddhist as well as the Brahmanical sources reveal that the contemporary agricultural society had attained further progress than the earlier one. The process of cultivation had become more perfect, and some new crops were added to the list referred to above. New devices of agricultural methods, as in the field of irrigation, were also introduced.

1. *Ṛig*. X. 101. 3.
2. *Ṛig*, X. 101.5
3. *Rāmāyaṇa*, II, 181, 28.
4. *CHI*, vol. I, p. 135.
5. *Tai. Saṁ*. IV. 2; VII. 2.10; *Kau. Br.* XIX. 3.
6. *Śat. Br.* I. 6.1.3.
7. *CHI*, Vol. I., p. 136.
8. *Vedic Index*, I. 398; II. 187.
9. *Bṛi. Up.* VI. 3.13; *S. B. E.* XV. 214.

The Buddhist sources give a more detailed account of the various processes of agriculture than the Brahmanical ones. They make references to the ploughing of the fields, watering them, sowing of seeds, fencing of fields, getting the weeds pulled up, reaping the crops, arranging them in bundles, getting it trodden, picking of straw, removing the chaff, winnowing and garnering of the harvest, as the various successive stages of the agricultural process.[1] Out of these processes Pāṇini makes mention of ploughing (Karsha, Halayati)[2], sowing (Vāpa)[3], weeding (Mūlābarhaṇa)[4], reaping or harvesting (Lavana)[5], threshing (Khala)[6], and winnowing (Nishpāva)[7]. The account of the process of cultivation presented before us by the contemporary literature is practically the same as is practised by the farmers of to-day. We are further informed that for the purpose of ploughing, big ploughs were also used.[8]

Crops

Both the Buddhist and the Brahmanical sources refer to rice (Vrīhi), wheat (Godhūma) and barley (Yava) as the main crops. Rice of many varieties seem to have been cultivated. Sāli, Vīhi, and Taṇḍula are the terms used for rice in the Pāli *Nikāyas*[9] and the *Jātakas*[10], which probably denote its different varieties. The *Gṛihyasūtras* refer only to Vrīhi[11].

1. *C.V.* VII. 1.2; *C.S.* I. 209, 221; *A.N.* IV. 237-8; *Jā.* No. 36.
2. *Pāṇini*, III. 1.21; III. 1.117; III. 2.183; IV.4.81; IV. 4.97, V. 4.121.
3. *Pāṇini*, III. 1.126; IV. 3.44; V.4.58.
4. *Pāṇini*, IV. 4.88.
5. *Pāṇini*, VI. 1.140.
6. *Pāṇini*, IV. 2. 50, 51. The threshing floor where reaped crop was stocked was known as Khala; the plot set apart for threshing was called Khalya (V. 1. 7); the adjoining threshing floors were named Khalya or Khalini (IV. 2. 50-51), the same as *Khalihāna* of today. For a full account of the agricultural process represented by Pāṇini, see V.S. Agrawala, *India as known to Pāṇini*, pp. 194-202.
7. *Pāṇini*, III. 3.28.
8. *S.N.* III. 155, कसको महानङ्गलेन कसन्तो ।
9. *M.N.* I. 57; III. 90.
10. *Jā.* I. 429. 484; II. 110, 135, 378; IV. 276; VI. 367.
11. *Āśva. G.S.* I. 17.2; *Sāṅ. G.S.* I. 24.3; I. 28.6.

Pāṇinī refers to Vrīhi, Śāli[1], and Mahāvrīhi[2]. This shows that even Vrīhi was of two varieties, i.e. ordirary and the best one. Sāli of Magadha is highly praised by Patañjali (I. 19). Later we find Suśruta mentioning Mahāśāli[3]. Yuan Chwang probably refers to this variety grown in Magadha, which he describes as of an unusual sort, large and scented, having shining colour and used by the richer classes[4]. According to Hwui Li Mahāśāli rice was grown only in Magadha, and Yuan Chwang while staying at Nālandā was entertained with this rice[5]. Pāṇini makes mention of some more varieties of rice such as Hāyana (III. 1.48), Shashṭikā (V. 1.90), and Nīvāra (III. 3.48). obviously, these varieties were cultivated in eastern India, which has been predominantly a rice producing region in the country. Other cereals harvested were barley (Yava)[6] and millet (Kaṅgu)[7]. The former is referred to also in the *Gṛihyasūtras*[8] and by Pāṇini[9]. The latter refers also to Godhūma (wheat) and Gavedhukā (Coix Barbata)[10]. Among pulses cultivated were grams (Kalāye)[11], beans (Mugga)[12], pear (Māsa)[13] and Kolatthi[14], among which the *Gṛihyasūtraṣ* mention only Mudga[15], while Pāṇini refers to Mudga[16], Māsha[17], Kulattha[18] and Masūra.[19] Among oil seeds the Buddhist

1. *Pāṇini*, V. 2.2.
2. *Pāṇini*, VI. 2.38.
3. *S ūtra-Sthāna*, 46.7.
4. Beal, Life of Hiuen-Tsiang, p. 109.
5. *India as known to Pāṇini*, p. 103.
6. *A.N.* IV. 108; *Jā.* II. 110.
7. *Jā.* VI. 580.
8. *Āśva. G.S.* I. 9.6; I. 17.2.; *Sāṅ G. S.* I. 24.3; 1.28.6; III. 1.3; IV.4.9.
9. *Pāṇini*, V. 1.7; V. 2.5.
10. *Pāṇini*, IV. 3. 136.
11. *Su. Ni.* III. 10; *Jā.* II. 74.
12. *M.N.* I. 57, 80; III 90; *A.N.* IV. 108; *Su. Ni.* III. 10; *Jā.* 1.429.
13. *M.N.* I. 57; III. 90; *A.N.* IV. 108.
14. *K.S.* I. 189.
15. *Sāṅ. G.S.* I. 22.5; *Pā. G.S.* I. 15.4.
16. *Pāṇini*, IV. 4. 25.
17. *Pāṇini*, V. 1. 7, V. 2.4.
18. *Pāṇini*, IV. 4.4.
19. *Pāṇini*, IV. 3. 136.

literature mentions sesame (Tila),[1] castor oil seed (Eraṇḍa)[2], and mustard oil seed.[3] The *Gṛihyasūtras*[4] and Pāṇini[5] refer to Tila; the former mentions also mustard oil seed (Sāṅ. G. S. III. 1.3.).

Among the fibre crops we get mention of cotton (Kappāsa)[6], silk (Kosseya)[7], linen (Khoma)[8], and silkcotton (Simbali, Sālmali or Simula).[9] Cotton and hemp get mention in the *Gṛihyasūtras*.[10] Pāṇini knows cotton by the terms Karpāsa[11] and Tūla[12], linseed by Umā[13], and hemp by Bhaṇgā.[14] The *Jātakas* also speak of cotton-fields[15] and forests of silk-cotton (Simbalivana)[16].

Betel was also cultivated in abundance.[17] It has remained an important and paying cultivation in North Bihar and in the district of Gayā in South Bihar. The Magahī betel of the latter is well known all over the country.

Vegetable cultivation was not neglected. People cultivated gourds, pumpkins, pot-herbs, cucumbers, convolvulus[18], etc. Garlic (Nāḍi)[19] was also produced and was probably utilised for flavouring vegetables.

1. *M.N.* I. 57, 80, III 90; *A.N.* IV. 108; *Jā.* VI. 335.
2. *Jā.* I. 423; II. 440.
3. *Sutta Ni.* III. 10; *Jā.* I. 244, II. 363.
4. *Āśva. G.S.* I. 9.6; 11. 4.4; IV. 4. 13; *Sāṅ G.S.* I. 28. 6; III. 1.3; *Pā. G.S.* I. 15.4; II. 6.17.
5. *Pāṇini*, V. 2.4; V. 1.7.
6. *Jā.* III. 286; VI. 336.; VI. 47,
   कप्पासकोस्सेयं खोमकोटुम्बरानि च ।
7. *Jā.* VI. 47.
8. *Jā.* VI. 534.
9. *Jā.* I. 202, 203; III. 39; V. 269; IV. 277.
10. *Ā. Śrauta Sū.* V. 4. 17; *Sāṅ G.S.* I. 24. 11.
11. *Bilvādi-gaṇa.* IV. 3. 134.
12. *Pāṇini*, III. 1.25.
13. *Pāṇini*, V. 2.4.
14. *Ibid.*
15. *Jā.* VI. 336. It is said that a lady was keeping watch over the cotton-field.
16. Jā. IV. 277.
17. *Jā.* I. 266, 291; 11. 320; VI 367.
18. *Jā.* V. 37; I, 312,
    साकञ्च' एव-आलाबु-कुम्भण्डी-एलालुकादीनि च वपित्वा तानि पि विक्किणन्तो···।
19. *Jā.* VI. 536.

Measures were taken to protect the standing crops from being destroyed by animals from the nearby forests. The peasants, anxious to kill the haunting animals and birds, and to save the crops from destruction, dug pitfalls around the fields, fixed stakes, set stone-traps and planted snares.[1] They also guarded the fields by fences and placards.[2] Wealthy cultivators kept watchmen (Khettarakkhaka, Khettagopaka, Khettarakkhaṇaka) who guarded their fields day and night.[3]

Crops were also damaged by natural calamities like drought and flood.[4] There is reference to famine striken people moving to where they would get ample food.[5] There is also mention of villages being washed away by floods.[6] It appears that the problems of flood and draught were the same in ancient times as they are to-day for the country.

The importance of irrigation was realised and arrangements were made for irrigating the cultivated fields. The Buddhist sources reveal that there were engineers who constructed canals for watering the fields.[7] The *Kāma Jātaka* (No. 466) refers to making of little embanked squares for water. The Śākyas and the Koliyas had made a dam on the river Rohiṇī,[8] and similar may have been the case elsewhere too. The Brahmanical sources support the Buddhist account by making references to irrigation by rivers, wells, and canals.[9] The *Arthaśāstra* of Kauṭilya dealing with

1. *Jā.* I. 143.

   मगधरट्ठस्मिञ्च सस्समये किट्ठसम्बाधे अरञ्ञे मिगानं परिपन्थो होति । मनुस्सा सस्सखादकानं मारणत्थाय तत्थ तत्थ ओपातं खनन्ति सूलानि रोपेन्ति पाषाणयन्तानि सज्जेन्ति कूटपासादयो पासे ओड्डेन्ति । बहू मिगा विनासं आपज्जन्ति ।

2. *Jā.* I. 153; IV. 262-3.
3. Jā. II. 110; III. 52; IV. 277.
4. *A.N.* III. 104; *Jā.* II. 135, 149, 367; V. 401; VI. 487,
5. *A.N.* III. 104.
6. *Dhp.* 287.
7. *Dhp.* 80; *Theragāthā*, 19, 877.

   उदकं हि नयन्ति नेत्तिका ।

8. *Kunāla Jā.* (No. 536).
9. *Bhāshya*, I. 1.24, 1. 82,

   शाल्यर्थं कुल्याः प्रणियन्ते ।

   (*India as known* to *Pāṇini*, p. 204).

irrigation tells us that the Mauryan state received from the cultivators a portion of their produce as the irrigation tax (Udakabhāgam), which varied from one third to one-fifth, and that fields were irrigated with water from rivers, lakes, tanks, and wells (Nadīsarastaṭākakūpoddhāṭam).[1] It is further told that for lifting water some sort of machine was also used.[2]

Society had realised the importance of agriculture, and the state took interest in the workings of the cultivators. No cultivator was to sit idle and waste labour. Land could be confiscated and given to others from those who did not cultivate them.[3]

The state took proper steps to see that the village community was not disturbed by undesirable elements, which would come in the way of the agricultural activities. Production of food stuff was the main occupation of the agricultural community, and it was in the interest of the country that food production was not to be lowered down. Keeping in view this factor, it is said in the *Arthaśāstra* that no ascetic other than a Vānaprasthin, no company other than one of local origin and no guild of any kind other than the local co-operative fields, shall find their way into the villages of the kingdom. There should be no place intended for plays and amusements in the villages.[4]

"In order that there may be an assurance of plentifulness of money, free labour, commodities, grains, oils and other liquids, actors, dancers, singers, drummers, buffons, and bards shall not be allowed to disturb the work of the villagers."[5]

1. *Kau.* II. 24.
2. *Ibid.*
3. *Kau.* II. 1.
4. *Kau.* II. 1.
   वाणप्रस्थादन्यः प्रवाजितभावः सजातादन्यः सङ्घस्सामुत्थायिकादन्यस्समयानुबन्धो वा नास्य जनपदमुपनिवेशेत् । न च तत्रारामविहारार्थाः शालास्स्युः ।
5. *Kau.* II. 1,
   नटनर्तनगायनवादकवाग्जीवनकुशीलवा वा न कर्मविघ्नं कुर्युः निराश्रयत्वात् ग्रामाणां क्षेत्राभिरतत्वाच्च पुरुषाणां कोश विशिष्टद्रव्यधान्यरसवृद्धिर्भवतीति ।

To encourage cultivation it was prescribed that waste land should be reclaimed.[1] He who cut down a portion of the forest usually became the owner of the land thus reclaimed.[2]

Land Holdings

It seems that there were many grades of land-holdings, down from the poor farmer possessing a few acres, upto the wealthy cultivator owning hundreds of acres. The Buddhist sources refer to considerable big plots possessed by some Magadhan cultivators. Thus, the *Sutta-Nipāta* tells us that in the Brāhmaṇa village Ekanāla in Magadha, the Brāhmaṇa, Kasibhāradvāja was the owner of a big plot of cultivable land which needed 500 ploughs for ploughing it;[3] other *Jātaka* refers to another wealthy cultivator possessing one thousand *Karisas* (probably 800 acres) of cultivable land in the village Sālindiya to the east of Magadha.[4] Probably such plots were only a few, and most of the land-holdings were small ones which could be managed single handed, or with the help of sons and other family members or hired labourers.[5] Hired labourers were employed, probably during the harvesting days, when more hands were needed as is the case even to-day. Ordinarily, the poor farmer is seen ploughing his field himself.[6] We get reference to agricultural persuit carried on with the aid of two oxen only.[7] There were poor farmers who could not possess a pair of oxen,

1. *Kau.* II.
2. *Manu.* IX. 44.
3. *Su. Ni.* I. 4,
   तेन खो पन समयेन कसिभारद्वाजस्स ब्राह्मणस्स पञ्चमत्तानि नङ्गलसतानि पयुत्तानि होन्ति वप्पकाले।
4. *Jā.* III, 293; IV. 276,
   तत्थ कोसियगोत्तो नाम सालिन्दियवासी ब्राह्मणो सहस्सकरीसमत्तं खेत्तं गेहत्वा सालिं वपापेसि।
5. *Jā.* I. 277; III. 162-63.
6. *Jā.* I. 277.
   बोधिसत्तो एकस्मिं गामके कस्सको अहोसि। सो एकदिवसं अरञ्ञन्तरस्मिं छड्ढितगामके खेत्ते कसिं कसति।
7. *Jā.* II. 165.

and hence they had to borrow from others.[1] The wealthy farmers mostly depended on their labourers for cultivating their fields.

It is not possible to determine the smallest unit of a land-holding. There is no difinite statement from which the minimum land-holding can be determined. But as there was no acute problem of the pressure of population on the land as we find it at present, there were not probably such small holdings on the produce of which a family could not be maintained.

The plots of land under different owners were separated by boundary stones (*thambhe*)[2]. In the *Mahāvagga*[3] the Buddha compares the rice fields of Magadha with the patchwork of robes. The rice fields are described as devided into short pieces (*achchibaddhan*), in rows (*palibaddhan*), by outside boundaries (*mariyādabaddhan*) and by cross boundaries (*singhāṭakabaddhan*). Pā.ini shows that arable lands were divided into separate holdings (*kshetra*) and were held under individual ownership.[4] Manu also speaks of the boundary disputes of fields and prescribes rules for their settlement.[5] The *Jatakas* tell us that the fields were surveyed by the king's officers and taxes were fixed accordingly.[6] According to Pāṇini this officer was called the Kshetrakara.[7] It is said in a *Jātaka* that the merchants of a village, finding the royal officers arrived at for making a survey of the fields, requested the king's brother for sending a letter to him and procure them remission of taxes.[8] About the method of surveying the fields, we are told that a cord was fixed to a stick and one end was given

1. *Jā*. II. 300.
   एकं सहायकं द्वे गोणे याचित्वा सब्बं दिवसं कसित्वा तिणं खादापेत्वा गोणे सामिकस्स निय्यादेतुं गेहं अगमासि।
2. *Jā*. IV. 281.
3. *M.V.* VIII. 12.1.
4. *India as known to Pāṇini*, p. 142.
5. *Manu*. VIII. 262-65.
6. *Jā*. IV. 169.
   अपरभागे राजकम्मिका खेत्तप्पमाणगहणत्थाय तं गामं आगमिसु।
7. *Pāṇini*, III. 2.21.
8. *Jā*. IV. 169.

to the owner of the field.[1] We are also informed of a Rajjugāhaka-Amachcha[2] who was probably a settlement minister. Megasthenes informs us that there were officers whose duty was to measure lands for purposes of assessment of revenue.[3] Thus, we find that land-survey was properly done, and it appears that the officer entrusted with this task was of the status of a minister.

Cattle Farming

Cattle-wealth was held in the highest esteem during the Vedic period. The early Aryans were probably pastoral people who gradually settled down as agriculturists. The Buddhist sources reveal that agriculture and cattle-farming were in a considerably good condition during our period. Cows are described as yielding milk, curd, butter, and ghee.[4] Though cattle-meat was eaten by some, cow was looked upon with respect. The *Sutta Nipāta* says, 'Like unto a mother, a father, a brother, and other relatives the cows are our best friends, in which medicines are produced.[5] There is reference to Gorakkhā as a livelihood.[6] The pasture grounds were known as *gochara* both in Pāli and Sanskṛit.[7] People reared cattle which were during the day time taken out for grazing by the cowherds (Gopālakas) and returned by the evening to the owners. But probably this practice did not apply to the wealthy people, who possessed them in large numbers. Their cattle were reared by the Gopālakas themselves from whom

1. *Jā*. II. 376,

   सोपि एकदिवसं जनपदे खेत्तं मिनन्तो रज्जुं दण्डके बन्धित्वा एकं कोटिं खेत्तसामिकेन गाहापेत्वा एकं अत्तना अग्गहेसि ।
2. *Ibid.*
3. *Frg*. 34. (M'crindle, *Ancient India*, p. 86).
4. *Bṛ. Up.*, I. 5.2; VI. 3. 13. *A.N.* II. 95.;
5. *Su. Ni.* II. 7.13.
6. *A.N.* IV. 281, 286.

   जीविकं कप्पेति यदि कसिया यदि वणिज्जाय यदि गोरक्खेन ।
7. *Dhp.* 135; *Jā*. IV. 327, VI. 335; *Pāṇini*. III. 3.119.

the owners received the dairy produces.[1] Probably the Gopālakas maintained dairies for the cattle, as is evident from the account of Kauṭilya.

It is from the *Arthaśāstra* of Kauṭilya, which confirms and supplements the above account, that we are enabled to have a clear idea of the cattle-farming activities. The dairies were maintained by the Gopālakas who accepted herds, either for wages, or on a fixed amount, or on share of the dairy producc.[2] Cattle which were lost, abandoned, or useless were also maintained.[3] The dairies were run under the supervision of the Superintendent of the Cows (Go-Adhyaksha).[4] This was probably a new innovation of the Maurya administration, and was instituted with a view to giving further incentive to cattle-farming and ensuring smooth running of the dairies.

Not only cows, oxen, bulls, and buffaloes; but also sheep (Ajādinam), mules (Ajāvīnam), horses (Aśvādinam), asses (Khara), camels (Ushṭra) and hogs (Varāha) were maintained in dairies.[5] The *Arthaśāstra* informs us that in addision to milk, butter, ghee, cheese, and butter-milk obtained from cows, wool was procured from the sheep, and meat from eatable animals, and skin (Charma) from various animals.[6]

The state took every step to encourage and safeguard cattle-wealth. We have already seen that it had instituted the office of the Superintendent of Cows. It had further

1. *Ja.* I. 388,

   बोधिसत्तो महाविभवो सेट्ठि अहोसि···तस्स' एको गोपालको किट्ठसम्बाधसमये गावो गहेत्वा अरञ्ञं पविसित्वा तत्थ गोपल्लिकं कत्वा रक्खन्तो वसति, सेट्ठिनो च कालेन कालं गोरसं आहरति ।

   The *Saṁyutta-Nikāya* (IV. 181) says that when a Gopālaka wished to enter the monastery, he was told by the Buddha to returṅ the herds to his master (*tena hi tvaṁ Nanda Sāmikānaṁ gāvo niyyādehīti*). This suggests that the Gopālaka was maintaining the cows of his master.

2. *Kau.* II. 29,

   गोऽध्यक्षो वेतनोपग्राहिकं करप्रतिकरं भग्नोत्सृष्टकं भागानुप्रविष्टं व्रजपर्यग्रं नष्टं विनष्टं क्षीरघृतसञ्जातं चोपलभेत ।

3. *Ibid.*
4. *Ibid.*
5. *Ibid.*
6. *Ibid.*

legislated that causing injury or to steel a cow was a great crime, for which one would be punished by death penalty[1]. It was a great merit to rescue or to recover a cow, either local or foreign from the thieves, for which the rescuer would receive proper reward[2]. To ensure safety to the herds, the pasture grounds were kept clear from thieves and beasts such as tigers by hunters with the aid of hounds[3]. Thus we find that all possible measures were taken to enrich the cattle-wealth of the land.

1. *Ibid.*
2. *Ibid.*
3. *Ibid.*

CHAPTER XI

ARTS, CRAFTS PROFESSIONS, AND INDUSTRIES

By the Vedic period the society had crossed the primitive stage of economic life, and various arts and crafts had come into existence. Rural industries were in the process of further development, and crafts had a tendency of being multiplied and subdivided. Carpentry had become specialised, and in addition to the ordinary carpenter (Takshā)[1], there was the Rathakāra, who specialised in chariot making. Weaving was practised[2], and the weaver was known as the Vāya[3]. Woolen[4] (Urṇa) and linen[5] (Tārpya) gaıments were probably used first, and cotton came in use later on. Pottery[6], tanning[7], and wine-distilling[8] were also important professions. Various metals had come into use, and one finds the mention of gold[9] (Hiraṇya), silver[10] (Rajata), copper[11] (Loha), iron[12] (Ayasa), lead[13] (Sīsa), tin[14] (Trapu), and probably bronze (Ayasa or Lohāyas). The *Vājasaneyī-Saṁhitā* enumerates Hiraṇya, Ayas, Śyāma, Loha, Sīsa, and Trapu[15]. Thus we find that the crafts were in the process of gradual evolution.

From the ninth century B.C. onwards the imperialist element in the country was being more and more asserted, and

1. *Ṛig.* IX, 112, 1.
2. *Ṛig.* II. 3.6; VI. 9.2.; *A. V.* X. 7.42.
3. *Ṛig.* X. 26.6.
4. *Ṛig.* I. 126.6; X. 75.8, *Vāj. saṁ* XIX ; *Mait. Saṁ.* III. 11.9. *Kā. Saṁ.* XXXVIII. 3.
5. *A. V.* XVIII. 4.31; *Tai. Saṁ.* II. 4.11.6, *Śat. Br.* V. 3.5.20.
6. *Vāj. Saṁ.* XVI. 27; *Māi. Saṁ.* 1.8.3; *Vāj. Saṁ.* XXX. 7.
7. *Ṛig.* VI. 48.
8. *Tai. Saṁ.* XI. 6.
9. *Ṛig.* V. 62.8; *Tai. Saṁ.* V. 7.13.
10. *Śat. Br.* XII, 8.3.11; *Tai Saṁ.* II. 2.9.7; III. 9.6.5.
11. *A.V.* XI. 3.17; *Vāj. Saṁ.* XIII. 13; *Śot. Br.* V. 4.12; XXII. 2.2.8.
12. *Ṛig.* IX. 1.2, IX. 80.2; 30.15; V. 62.8.
13. *A. V.* XII; 2.1.
14. *A.V.* XI. 3.17.
15. *Vāj. Saṁ.* XVII. 2.1.

her army was being rapidly expanded. Crafts connected with military needs may have been fairly advanced. Herodotus refers to the iron-tipped arrows used by Indian soldiers of the army of the Persian ruler XerXes, and Ktesian, his contemporary pays tribute to the excellence of the two swords of Indian steel presented to Arta Xer Xes Mnemon.[1] Again, due to the development of Urban life also several crafts may have made progress. It was due to the progress of certain crafts and industries that finished goods loaded on hundreds of waggons were despatched to the distant parts of the country and to the foreign lands, over roads and water-ways. It would appear both from the Buddhist and the Brahmanical sources that arts and crafts made considerable advancement during this period. It is very likely that carpentry, pottery, metallurgy, smithy, etc. may have been in a flourishing condition.

Textile Industry and Luxury Goods

The Budhist as well as the Brahmanical sources refer to various textile fabrics such as linen (Khomaṁ), cotton (Kappāsikaṁ), silk (Kosseyaṁ), wool (Kambalaṁ), and hemp (Sāṇaṁ) out of which threads were spun and woven into cloth of various varieties and qualities.[2] The *Dīgha-Nikāya* mentions unfinished goods like cotton, hemp, etc., threads spun out of them, and woven clothes, showing thereby that spinning and weaving[3] were well known. There are references which describe the Kāśī clothes as very fine,[4] but it does not mean that the industry was not advanced in other cities of this period, because it is a convention of the Buddhist storytellers to make Kāśī the scene of incidents referred to by them. It is very likely that the flourishing cities such as Śrāvastī, Kauśāmbī, Rājagṛiha, Pāṭaliputra, Champā, Vaiśālī, Kusinārā, and Mithilā would have been manufacturing plenty of textile goods of high quality both for domestic as well as foreign market.

1. Sharma, R. S., *Light on Early Indian Society and Economy*, pp. 60-61.
2. *M.V.* VIII. 3.1; *Peta.* II. 1. 17; *India as known to Pāṇini*, pp. 125-26.
3. *D N.* II. 350-51. The *Pātimokkha* refers to yarn, weaving and the weaver (*S.B.E.* XIII. 28).
4. *G.S.* I. 128; 225-26; *A.N.* III. 50; *Jā.* III. 11; VI. 49, 50, 144.

From very early times spinning and weaving have been among the domestic industries. There are references in the *Vinaya* texts to Bhikshus spinning yarn and weaving them into clothes. References to the weaver (Pesakāra),[1] the loom (Tanta),[2] weaving appliances (Tantabhaṇḍa),[3] the place of weaving (Tantavitaṭṭhānaṁ)[4] and so on would suggest that weaving was fairly common in the society.

Textile goods manufactured were of numerous varieties. The Buddha prohibited for the Bhikshus the use of various luxury goods which he said were used by some Śramaṇas and Brāhmaṇas, and it is very likely that they were of indigenous manufacture. We get mention of hair coverlets with very long fleece (Goṇaka), patchwork counterpanes of many colours (Chittaka), white blankets (Paṭika), woolen coverlets embroidered with flowers (Paṭalika), quilts stuffed with cotton and wool (Tūlika), coverlets embroidered with figures of lions and tigers, etc. (Vikatika), rugs with fur on both sides (Uddalomī), rugs with fur on one side (Ekantalomi), coverlets embroidered with gems (Kaṭṭhissaṁ), silk-coverlets (Kosseyyaṁ), big carpets, probably of woolen for the dance of sixteen nautch girls (Kuttakaṁ), elephant housings or rugs (Hatthattharaṁ), horse-rugs (Assattharaṁ), chariot-rugs (Rathattharaṁ), carpets with awings over them or with red pillows for the head and the feet (Sauttarachchhadaṁ-Ubhato Lohitakūpadhānaṁ) and so on.[5] Blankets may have been made from materials like horse's tail (Vālakambala) and feathers of owl (Ulumpakkhaṁ), which are said to have been put on by ascetics.[6] The *Jātakas*

1. *S.B.E.* XIII. 28; *D.N.* I. 51; *Ja.* IV. 475, for the weaver, two terms are used, viz., the *tantavāya* and *pesakāra*.
2. *Jā.* I. 356.
3. *Vinaya.*, II. 135.
4. *Jā.* I. 356.
5. *M.V.* V. 10.3; *D.N.* I. 15 (*Dia.* I. 12),
आसन्दि पल्लङ्कं गोनकं चित्तकं पटिकं पटलिकं तूलिकं विकतिकं उद्दलोमिं एकन्तलोमिं कट्ठिस्सं कोसेय्यं कुत्तकं हत्थत्थरं अस्सथरं रथत्थरं अजिनप्पवेणिं कदलिमिग पवरपच्चत्थरणं स-उत्तरच्छदं उभतो-लोहितकूपधानं इति वा । *M.N.* I. 76; *G.S.* I. 120; 164.
6. *D.N.* I. 167; III. 41; *M.N.* I. 78; *A.N.* II. 206.

tell us that embroidered clothes were also manufactured. Kings put on turbans worked with gold (Kañchanapaṭṭaṁ);[1] state elephants were decorated with golden clothes (Hemakappanavāsasa).[2] Costly and dainty fabrics of silk and fur are said to have been worked out into rugs, blankets, cushions, coverlets, and carpets.[3] The Buddhist account which describes the textile industry as well advanced gets support from the Brahmanical sources. Pāṇini refers to the weaver (Tantuvāya), the place of weaving, the loom, the process of weaving and the manufactured textile goods.[4] The mention of blanket-maker (Kambalakāraka)[5] and several kinds of blankets shows that it was a specialised industry. The *Arthaśāstra* of Kauṭilya tells us that threads (Sūtra), coats (Varma), cloth (Vastra), and ropes were manufactured by skilled artisans.[6] Various kinds of garments, blankets, and curtains were among the finished goods.[7]

It appears from the Buddhist literature that a number of luxury goods were manufactured for the use of the wealthy persons. The Buddha prohibited the use of luxries for the monks. Divans seem to have been manufactured on a large scale, and the rich people are described as using divans with animal figures carved on the supports.[8] Couches of ivory, wood, gold, silver, etc. were also made.[9]

1. *Jā*. V. 322.
2. *Jā*. IV. 404; V. 258.
3. *Jā*. I. 149 (*rattakambala*); II. 274; III. 184; VI 280 (*Varapotthakattharaṇaṁ*).
4. Agrawala. *India as known to Pāṇini*, pp. 231-32.
5. *Ibid*.
6. *Kau*. II. 23,

   सूत्रवर्मवस्त्ररज्जूव्यवहारं तज्जातपुरुषैः कारयेत् ।
7. *Ibid*.

   वस्त्रास्तरणप्रावरणविकल्पानुत्थापयेत् ।
8. *M.V.* V. 10.3; *D.N.* I. 7.
9. *S.N.* III. 144-5,

   दंतमयानि सारमयानि सोवण्णमयानि रुपियमयानि गोणकत्थतानि पटिकत्थतानि पटलिकत्थतानि कदलिमिगपवरपच्चत्थरणानि ।

Ointments, garlands, cosmetics, bracelets, necklaces, walking sticks, turbans, and diadems seem to have been produced in plenty. Chairs and bed-steads, thrones and carriages, were probably inlaid with gold.[1] Popular stories refer to mirrors of gold (Kañchanādāsa).[2] Excavations have yielded mirrors of copper. Shoes of various designs were manufactured too.[3] All these are referred to under different industries.

Carpentry

References in the Buddhist literature to the Dārukammika as the wealthy carpenter or the timber merchant,[4] the Yānakāra as constructing chariot-wheels,[5] the Tachchaka as carving wood,[6] and carpenters constructing wooden buildings[7] suggest that carpentry during this period had attained a considerably advanced stage; it was a specialised profession and that the carpenter's art had attained perfection to a great extent. It appears from references to wooden constructions[8] that the most appreciable work that the carpenters were doing was building houses and palaces. Prior to the development of stone-architecture, it was the woodens architecture which was common in the country, and the renowned wooden palace of Chandragupta Maurya is well known. We get references in the *Nikāyas* to ordinary houses of wood[9] and

1. *Jā* I. 486, III. 375, *Suvaṇṇakhachitaṁ*; IV. 422, V. 204; VI. 231, *Suvaṇṇavikate pīṭhe*; VI. 580.
2. *Jā* II. 297; IV. 270,
   सुमज्जिते आदासे मुखं ओलोकेन्तस्स ।
3. *M.V.* V. 2.3; *C.V.* VI. 2. 3-5.
4. *A.N.* III. 391.
5. *M.N.* I. 31,
   समीति यानकार पुत्तो रथस्स नेमिं तच्छति ।
6. *Dhp.* 80,
   दारुं नमयन्ति तच्चका ।
7. *Jā.* II. 18; IV. 153, 159.
8. *MV.* III 8; *Jā.* IV. 153, 159.
9. *M.N.* I. 190,
   सेय्यथापि आवुसो कट्ठञ्च पटिच्च वल्लिञ्च पटिच्च तिणञ्च पटिच्च मत्तिकञ्च पटिच्च आकासो परिवारतो अगारन्त' एव...।

peaked houses having roof-beams.[1] The *Jātakas* often refer to wooden palaces. The *Mahā-Ummaga Jātaka* speaks of the building of the city rampart of Mithilā, restoration of old buildings and so on, for which the carpenters were sent to the forest for bringing the required timber on 300 boats.[2] The *Alīnachitta Jātaka* (No. 156) gives a picturesque description of the work of carpenters engaged in the building industry. As heavy logs were needed for the purpose of house-building, they thought it the best course to go inside the forests, acquire the necessary materials, and transport them through rivers to their workshops. Accordingly, they went inside the forest in vessels, and according to the needs of the type of the building under construction, shaped beams and planks, put together the framework, numbering all the pieces and then transported them through the river. They would then build the houses and deliver them to the customers and get their wages.[3]

Next to the house-building industry, carpentrs had specialised themselves for constructing boats and ships,[4] carts and chariots[5] of all sorts, and machines (Yantāni).[6]

They also made furniture of various types which were utilised by people of different sections in the society of our period. In the *Jātakas* they are represented as constructing

1. *G. S.* I. 240.
2. *Mahā-Ummaga Jā.* English, Vol. VI, p. 197.
3. *Jā.* II. 18,
   ते नावाय उपरिसोतं गन्त्वा अरञ्ञे गेहसम्भारदारूनि कोट्टेत्वा तत्थ' एव एकभूमिकद्विभूमिकादिभेदे गेहे सज्जेत्वा थम्भतो पट्ठाय सब्बदारुसु सञ्ञं कत्वा नदीतीरं नेत्वा नावं आरोपेत्वा अनुसोतेन नगरं आगन्त्वा ये यादिसानि गेहानि आकंखन्ति तेसं तादिसानि कत्वा कहापणे गहेत्वा पुन तत्थ' एव गन्त्वा गेहसम्भारे आहरन्ति ।
4. *Jā.* IV. 159; V 427,
   वड्ढकिसतानि आदाय उद्धगङ्गं गन्त्वा सारदारूनि गाहापेत्वा तिसमत्ता नावा मापेत्वा···।
5. *Jā.* IV. 207,
   दारूनि आहरित्वा रथं कत्वा जीविकं कप्पेसि ।
6. *Jā.* V. 242,
   तस्मा यन्तानि कारेन्ति राजा भरति वड्ढकिं ।

Pīṭha and Mañchaka[1]. They must have been making Āsana,[2] Apassayapīṭhaka,[3] Kochchha[4] Sirisayana,[5] Chatussadaṁ,[6] Pallaṅkaṁ,[7] Samugga,[8] Nisseṇi[9], etc., which get mention in the popular stories.

They worked with instruments such as the hatchet, the chisel, and the mallet,[10] etc. The *Gṛihya-Sūtras* support the Buddhist account of the advanced stage of carpentry; but they refer mostly to those articles made by carpenters which were needed for sacrificial purposes, such as the ladle (Sruch, Sruva, Dhruvā),[11] Pātrī,[12] Agnihotrahavanī,[13] Spoon (Darvi, Upabhṛita),[14] and sword (Sphya),[15] etc., all made of wood. Building chariots[16] is often referred to. Pāṇini also refers to the carpenter by the term Takshā and shows that he played an important part in the rural economy.[17]

House Building

Urban life in the Gangetic Valley had developed by the time of the *Śatapatha Brāhmaṇa.*[18] Rise of towns and cities involves progress in the art of building, which seems to have been

1. *Jā.* I. 350; IV. 159,
   मंचं करिस्साम, पीठं करिस्साम।
2. *Jā.* VI. 413.
3. *Jā.* III. 235.
4. *Jā.* V. 407.
5. *Jā.* I. 398; III. 264; VI. 10.
6. *Jā.* IV. 422.
7. *Jā.* III. 257; IV. 422; VI. 40.
8. *Jā.* I. 373.
9. *Jā.* III. 477. The *Āchārāṅga-Sūtra* (*S.B.E.* XXII, p. 154) speaks of benches, stools, trays, seats, beds, etc. as furniture of wood.
10. *Jā.* II. 405,
    वासिफरसुनिखादनमुग्गरे;
    IV. 344; VI. 427.
11. *Āśva. G.S.* IV. 3. 5-6; *Śāṅ. G.S.* I. 9. 14; *Pā. G.S.* I. 1.3.
12. *Āśva. G.S.* IV. 3. 4-10.
13. *Ibid.*
14. *Ibid.* IV. 3. 3; *Pā. G.S.* II. 14. 13, 20, 24.
15. *Āśva. G.S.* IV. 3. 4.
16. *Āśva. G.S.* I. 8. 1. III. 12. 2; *Pā. G.S.* I. 8. 18; I. 10. 1-3.
17. *Pāṇini*, V. 4. 95; III. 1. 76; III. 3. 80.
18. *The Excavations at Kauśāmbī*, 1957-59, pp. 12-13.

carried on with the co-operation of the carpenter, the worker in bricks, the clod-hopper, and the architect. The art of constructing citadels had already developed, and the remains of the defences at Kauśāmbī, Rājagṛiha and other cities assigned to this age make it fairly clear that the capital cities were protected with massive defences of similar nature. Mithilā is described in the *Jātakas* as a prosperous city with defences, watch-towers, and gates.

We have already seen that the wooden buildings were constructed by the carpenter. The master carpenter (Mahāvaḍḍhaki) appears as levelling the ground, cutting posts, and measuring the site with thread.[1] Apart from the wooden structures, houses were built of bricks and mud (Iṭṭhakā cha mattikā cha).[2] Probably such houses were of durable nature. Most probably houses of bricks and mud were having wooden ceilings and roofs.

In the *Jātakas* the stone-cutter (Pāshāṇakoṭṭaka)[3] also figures as taking part in house-building. He is represented as cutting stones out of the ruined material of a former village (Gāma).[4] But there is no direct evidence of stone-architecture prior to the Mauryan age; and the *Jātakas* in this respect may be taken as referring to the Mauryan and post-Mauryan periods. Stone may have been used for the foundations of the buildings in the pre-Mauryn age, but whether it was cut into specific sizes is doubtful.[5]

It is said that Mahāgovinda planned the city of Rājagṛiha and several other capitals of Northern India, and designed palaces.[6] It appears from the *Jātakas* that the architect (Vatthuvijjāchariyo) was a personality whose co-operation was also indispensable for building mansions.[7]

1. *Jā*. 332,

   भूमि समं कारापेत्वा खाणुके कोट्टेत्वा सुत्तं पसारेसि ।
2. *Jā*. VI. 429.
3. *Jā*, I. 478.
4. *Ibid*,

   पुराणगामट्ठाने पासाणे उप्पाटेत्वा कोट्टेति ।
5. Stone was used for the Cyclopean wall at Rājagṛiha, but it was not cut into specific sizes.
6. *Vimānavatthu comy.*, p. 82.
7. *Jā*. II. 297; IV. 323.

In building palaces as many as eighteen manual arts were employed,[1] and the architect was the foremost and indispensable for the purpose. He was skilled in divining good sites.[2] Detailed information about him is not available. That he was an important figure is known from the *Mahābhārata* also, which tells us that he was well grounded in the science of building and was a Sūta by caste.[3]

Buddha's prohibition to have imaginative paintings on the walls of the monasteries[4] and the *Jātaka* description of the construction and decoration of a play hall[5] suggest that the practice of decorating the walls of buildings with various paintings was in vogue. The painter (Chittakāra) seems to have been giving the finishing touch to the work of the architect, the carpenter, and the stone-cutter. He probably painted frescoes on the clay and wooden walls after being plastered.

Lastly, the contributions of the workers in bricks (Iṭṭhakavaḍḍhaki)[6] and the clod-hoppers (Gahapatisippakāra)[7] cannot be neglected, who were indispensable for the construction of buildings.

Mining and Metallurgy

The contemporary Buddhist as well as the Brahmanical sources mention seven kinds of metals. They are Iron (Aya) copper (Lohaṁ), tin (Tipu), lead (Sīsaṁ), silver (Rajata or

1. *Jā.* VI. 427.
2. *Jā.* II. 297-98,

   वत्थुविज्जाचरियो पगुणविज्जो अन्तोभूमियं सत्तरतनट्ठाने दोसं पस्सति ।

   IV. 324.
3. *Mbh. Ādiparva*, 51. 15,

   स्थपतिबुद्धिसम्पन्नो वास्तुविद्याविशारदः ।
   इत्यब्रवीत् सूत्रधारः सूतः पौराणिकस्तदा ॥
4. *C.V.* VI. 3.2.
5. *Jā.* VI. 332-33.
6. *Jā.* VI. 333.
7. *Jā.* VI. 438.

Sajjha), gold (Suvaṇṇa, Jātarupaṁ)[1], and bronze (Kaṅsa).[2] Later we find Kauṭilya adding to the above list mercury (Vaikṛintaka) and brass (Ārakūṭa).[3] Megasthenes tells us that numerous metals lay underneath the ground—gold, silver, copper, iron, tin and others, employed in making articles of use and ornaments as well as instruments of war.[4] The Buddhist literature does not enable us to know in detail about the science of mining. But a few references suggest that mines were dug for obtaining the metals.[5] During the Mauryan period mining was an industry under state-monopoly.[6] The Superintendent of Mines was in charge of the Department of Mining.[7] Rules of mining operations are described in detail, and the methods of identifying metals by means of colour, appearance, smell, hardness, and softness are suggested.[8] Mining may have been carried on even during the ealier period on the lines suggested by Kauṭilya.

Smithy

The economy of this period was marked by the widespread use of iron. The Kammāra (blacksmith), i.e. Karmāra of Pāṇiṇi,[9] occupied an important position among the artisans.

1. *D.N.* II. 351 (XXIII. 29),
   अयं वा लोहं वा तिपुं वा सीसं वा सज्झं वा इदं पहूतं सुवण्णं छड्डितं । *A.N.* III. 16.
   Jā. II. 296,
   जरूदपानं खणमाना वाणिजा उदकत्थिका ।
   अज्झगंसु अयो लोहं तिपु सीसञ्च वाणिजा ।
   रजतं जातरूपञ्च मुक्ता बेलुरिया बहू ।
   Agrawala, *India as known to Pāṇini*, p. 231.
2. *M.V.* VI. 14. 2; *M.N.* I. 25-31.
3. *Kau.* II. 12.
4. M' Crindle, *M.* & *A.*, p. 30.
5. *Bhūridatta Jā.* (VI. 212).
   And the brick mound, search as you may, contains
   No veins of iron for the miner's pains.
6. *Kau.* II. 12.
7. *Ibid.*
8. *Ibid.*
9. Agrawala, *India as known to Pāṇini*, p. 234.

In the Buddhist literature, we come across descriptions of the smith's furnace (Ukkā)[1] and get references to his anvil (Adhikaraṇī)[2] and pincers (Saṇḍāsa)[3]. The existence of the villages of blacksmiths consisting of a thousand families suggests that this craft was in a flourishing condition.[4] The smiths made mainly agricultural and household implements like razors, axes, ploughshares, goads, spades, hangers, hammers, instruments for cutting bamboos, grass-cutters, pegs, three-fronged iron forks, vessels, needles, etc.[5] The Brahmanical sources refer to a few among these.[6] Manufacture of weapons for war such as spear, sword, arrow, axe, and coats of mail seems to have been another important job of the smith. Keeping in view the military strength of states in North-Eastern India during this period, it can be said that production of war material must have been a considerably large scale industry and absorbed a good number of the blacksmiths. The *Gṛihya-Sūtras* mention sword, spear, armour, Paraśu and arrow among the weapons.[7] Iron was also introduced for improving the means of transport. According to a *Jātaka* a sheath of iron, two inches wide, was put round the outer edge of the wheel to make it strong.[8]

The Blacksmith's craft had attained specialisation to a great extent. The Usukāra is mentioned as engaged in making only the arrow. In the *Dhammapada*[9] and the

1. *Jā*. VI. 189, 437,

   कम्मारानं यथा उक्का अन्तो झायति नो बहिं ।

2. *Jā*. III. 285.
3. *Jā* I. 223; II. 342; III. 138.
4. *Jā*. III. 281.
5. *Jā*. I. 247, 312; 464; II. 59, 241, 405; III, 224, 281 285. V. 45,

   वासिफरसुकुद्दालनिखादनमुट्ठिकवेलुगुम्बदच्छेदनसत्थितिणलायन
   असिलोहदण्डखानुक-अयस्मिं घाटकेहि अत्थो ।

6. Agrawala, *India as known to Pāṇini*, p. 234.
7. *Sāṅ. G.S.* I. 13.1; *Pā G.S.* II. 6.16; III. 15.21; *Āśva. G.S.* I.15.3; III. 12.10.
8. *Jā*. IV. 210.
9. *Dhp*. 80, 33.

   फन्दनं चपलं चित्तं दुरक्खं दुन्निवारयं
   उजुं करोति मेधावी उसुकारो व तेजनं ।

10. *Theragāthā*, 19, 877.

Theragāthā[1] he is referred to as straightening or bending it. In one place he is described as heating an arrow in a pan of coal, wetting it with sour rice-gruel, and closing one eye and looking with the other, making the arrow straight.[2] This shows that arrow-making was a separate art from the general smithy.

The *Jātakas* refer to the highly skilled workmanship of the blacksmith. In one place he is described as making a delicate and strong needle which pierced a dice and floated on water.[7] He is also described as making a sheath for it which pierced the dice along with it. One cannot believe the floating of a needle on water, and such exaggerated accounts of skill attributed to the Bodhisattva are to be taken with a grain of salt. But the manufacture of fine needles cannot be doubted, because they were in common use. Thus we find that the Buddhist literature gives a more detailed account of the work of the blacksmith than what we get from the Brahmanical sources.

Industry of Precious Metals

The Suvaṇṇakāras and the Maṇikāras are mentioned as workers in precious metals and gems.[3] The goldsmith (Suvaṇṇakāra) or his apprentice (Antevāsī) is a number of times referred to as working at the furnace.[4] We get descriptions of how gold used to be worked out. It was put in the furnace and blown; at times water was sprinkled, and at times it was left to be cooled.[5] The *Aṅguttara-Nikāya* refers to

1. *Jā*. VI. 66,
उसुकारो अंगारकपल्ले उसुं तापेत्वा कञ्जिकेन तेमेत्वा एकं अक्खिं निमीलेत्वा एकेन ओलेकेन्तो उजुं करोति ।

2. *Jā*. III. 282,
उत्तमजातिकं अयं गहेत्वा एकं सुखुमं घनं सूचिं कत्वा पासे विज्झित्वा ओदके ओपिलापेत्वा अपरमपि तथारूपमेव तस्सा कोसकं कत्वा पासे विज्झि ।

3. *Jā*. V. 438-9; VI. 276.

4. *M.N.* III. 243; *G.S.* I. 231, 236.

5. *M.N.* III. 243,
सेय्यथापि, भिक्खु, दक्खो सुवण्णकारो वा सुवण्णकारन्तेवासी वा

the refininig of gold in these words : 'Then the goldsmith or his man heaps that sterling gold into a crucible and blows it (till it melts), melts it together but does not run it out of the crucible. That sterling gold is then blown till it melts: it is molten but not flawless, it is not done with yet, its impurities are not yet strained off. It is not pliable or workable nor glistening...But a time comes, Bhikshus, when the goldsmith or his man blows that gold till it melts, melts it down and runs it out of the crucible. Then that gold is melted, molten, flawless, done with, its impurities strained off.'[1] After this process ornaments or other articles were made.[2] Pāṇini also refers to the work of the goldsmith, though he does not go into such detail as the Buddhist literature. But he informs us that the goldsmith had to perform the threefold task of making ornaments from new gold and silver, melting old ornaments to make new ones and the work of polishing.[3] The goldsmith sometimes used to collect gold from river beds and refine it.[4] He is once referred to as finishing an exquisite gold image for a king, according to his order.[5] Such descriptions suggest that the industry was divided in finding ore metal, refining it and making finished articles.

That the work of the goldsmith was in a flourishing condition is suggested by the mention of a number of precious metals and various ornaments. During the period

उक्कं बंधेय्य उक्कं बंधित्वा उक्कामुखं आलिंपेय्य उक्कामुखं आलिंपेत्वा संडासेन जातरूपं गहेत्वा उक्कामुखे पक्खिपेय्य, तं एनं कालेन कालं अभिधमेय्य कालेन कालं उदकेन परिप्फोसेय्य कालेन कालं अज्झुपेक्खेय्य· · · ·।

1. G.S. I. 231.
2. *M.N.* III 243; G.S. I. 231, 236.
3. Agrawala, *India as known to Pānini*, pp. 234-35.
4. *M.N.* III. 102,
नेक्खं जम्बोनदं दक्ख-कम्मारपुत्त-उक्कामुखे सुकुसलसम्पहट्ठं पण्डुकम्बले निक्खितं भासति च तपति च विरोचति च ।
A.N. II. 29.
5. *Jā*. V. 282,
सो कम्मारजेट्ठकं पक्कोसापेत्वा बहुं सुवण्णं दत्वा, 'एकं इत्थिरुपकं करोहीति'· · ·सुवणं गहेत्वा सयं इत्थिरुपकं अकासि ।

under review both men as well as women were fond of wearing ornaments. The *Vinaya-Piṭaka* describes the Chhabbaggiya Bhikshus as putting on various ornaments.[1] From the Buddhist, the Jaina, and the Brahmanical sources it is disclosed that several types of ornaments for the different parts of the body were made out of the various metals like gold and silvier. We get mention of Paṭṭikā, Muddikā (ring), Vallikā or Kuṇḍala (ear-ring), Kāyūra or Graiveyaka (necklace), Suvarṇamāla or Kañchanamāla (golden chain), Pāmaṅga (ear-drop), Ovattikā (bangles), Hattharana (bracelet), Mekhalā (waist-band), etc.[2]

One does not find only men and women decorating their presons with ornaments, but as the *Saṁyutta-Nikāya*[3] and the *Jātakas*[4] inform us, elephants, horses, and chariots, etc. were decorated with golden ornaments (Sovaṇṇālaṅkāra), golden banners (Sovaṇṇadhaja), golden network (Hemajālapatichchhādana) and the like.

In addition to ornaments, golden dishes (Suvaṇṇathāla),[5] bowls and cups (Suvaṇṇapāti, Suvaṇṇabhiṅkara, Suvaṇṇasaraka)[6] for eating and drinking, vessels (Suvaṇṇakalasa)[7] and silver dishes (Rajatathāla)[8] and similar objects seem to have been produced. Mirrors (Ādāsa) were made by giving fine polish to the surface of the metal.[9] Popular stories state that

1. *C.V.* V. 2. 1.
2. *C.V.* V. 2.1; *M.N.* III. 243,
यदि पवट्टिकाय यदि कुण्डलाय यदि गीवेय्यकाय यदि सुवण्णमालाय ।
G.S. I. 232, 236; A.*N.* III. 16;
Jā. I. 134, II. 122, 373, III. 153, 377; IV. 60, 493; V. 202 215, 259, 297, 400, 438; VI. 144-45, 217, etc.
Āchāraṅga Sūtra, II. 2, 1, 11 (*S.B.E.* XXII, pp. 123-24); *India as known to Pāṇini*, p. 234.
3. *Jā.* III. 145.
सोवण्णालङ्कारानि सोवण्णधजानि हेमजाल पटिच्छन्नानि ।
4. *Jā.* II. 48, 143, IV 404; V. 258-59; VI. 39; 487-8, 510.
5. *Jā.* III. 224.
6. *Jā.* II. 90, 371; III. 10. 277; IV. 384; VI. 39, 510.
7. *Jā.* IV. 384.
8. *Jā.* III. 224; IV. 107.
9. *Jā.* II. 297; IV. 270.

orders of the kings were engraved on golden plates[1] which may have been true in some cases. Chairs, bed-steads, thrones and royal cars appear to have been inlaid with gold[2]. Probably relief-work was also practised, which is suggested by the description of a celestial car in a *Jātaka* story.[3]

Trade in ornaments seems to have been extensive. The handicraft was probably specialised for making particular kinds of ornaments. Gold-ornaments were set with gems, and the art of cutting and polishing the latter was known.[4] This also seems to have been a specialised art. Similar was probably the case with the art of inlaying.

Pearls, Gems, and Precious stones

The Buddhist literature refers to Muktā (Pearls), Maṇi (crystal), Beluriya (beryl), Bhaddaka (luck-stone), Saṅkha, Silā, Pawāla (coral), Lohitaṅka (ruby), and Masāragalla which were exploited from the ocean.[5] Lohitaṅka and Sasyaka (emerald) are common to the *Sūtras* of Pāṇini[6] and Kauṭilya's *Arthaśāstra*[7]. Most of the gems and precious stones mentioned above may have been used for making ornaments[8] and inlay work. The art of skilfully cutting precious stones and giving

1. *Jā*. IV. 7, 335; V. 59, 125,
राजा· · ·सुवण्ण पट्टे लिखापेत्वा अरञ्ञं पाविसि ।
2. *Jā*. I. 470; *Jā*. II. 48; IV. 404; V. 259; VI. 487-8.
3. *Jā*. V. 408-9,
अलङ्कतं कञ्जनचित्तसन्तिकं;
4. *M.N.* II, 17; III. 121; *K.S.* I. 272; *Jā*. IV. 233, 256, *Sumajjitamaṁgulikā*, *Sumajjita Kañchanapaṭṭa*.
5. *A.N.* IV. 255, 258, 262,
मुक्ता-मणि बेलुरियञ्च भद्दकं ।
A.N. IV. 199, 203; *Udāna*, V. 5,
महासमुद्दो बहुरतनो अनेकरतनो, तत्रिमानि रतनानि सेय्यथीदं मुक्ता, मणि, वेलुरियो, सङ्खो, सिला, पवालं, रजतं, जातरूपं, लोहितङ्को, मसारगल्लो ।
Jā. I. 351; II. 6; IV. 60, 85; VI. 116-20, 175, 276, 403, 493.
6. *Pāṇini*, V. 4. 30; V. 2. 68.
7. *Kau*. II. 11.
8. E.G., we come across Maṇikuṇḍala (*Jā*. III. 153; IV. 422; VI. 238), Maṇivalaya (*Jā*. III. 377), Maṇipatimā (*Jā*. IV. 7).

them various shapes was known. We often get references to Beluriya (Vaiḍūrya) cut into eight facets, well polished, and made perfect from all aspects.[1] Similar may have been the case with others. Probably gold ornaments (such as rings) were set with gems.[2] It appears that cutting gems and precious stones into various shapes and polishing them was a specialised art by itself and that setting them on ornaments was the work of the goldsmith. In addition to setting them on golden ornaments, they may have been made into necklaces.

Ivory Work

Nepal Terai was the home of elephants, and so the wealthy cities of Eastern Uttar Pradesh and Northern Bihar must have been the most flourishing centres of ivory industry. The cities where ivory-work was localised were having the quarters of the ivory-workers.[3] They were good experts in their handicraft and could carve out any shape out of ivory.[4] They made bangles, trinkets and articles of diverse forms.[5] Costly carvings, ornaments, handles for mirrors and inlayings of royal chariots were prepared by them[6]. As to their instruments for shaping the ivory pieces, only a kind of saw (Kakacha or Kharakakacha) is known.[7] Ivory was obtained from the forests, either from the dead elephants, or after killing them,[8] or from the living ones.[9] Tusks of the living ones were very valuable. This industry most probably had given rise to a class of people whose profession was to collect elephant tusks from the forests. This work was probably done by the hunters.

1. *M.N.* II, 17; III· 121; *K.S.* I. 89.
2. *Jā.* IV. 233, 256, V. 453.
3. *Jā.* I. 320, II. 197.
4. *D.N.* I. 78; *M.N.* II. 18.
5. *Jā.* II. 197,
   दन्तकारवीथियं दन्तकारवलयादीनि करोन्ते दिस्वा···।
6. *Jā.* V. 302, VI. 223.
7. *Jā.* I. 321, VI. 261.
8. *Jā.* VI. 61.
9. *Jā.* I. 320-21. II. 197, V. 45, 49.

Garland Making and Perfumery

People of our period were fond of flowers and perfumery. In addition to the daily consumption, they were lavishly and profusely consumed on festive occasions. There were a number of flower-gardens (Pupphārāmas) from where flowers were taken to the garland-makers (Mālākāras), who made beautiful garlands and bouquets with them.[1] Garland-making seems to have been a specialised art, and one could be seen apprenticing himself to the skilled garland-maker.

The perfumer (Gandhaka) was a respectable man, popular among the fashionable people,[2] who were fond of scenting their person. Thc *Jātakas* refer to perfumery shops.[3] Several kinds of perfumes were manufactured from various materials.[4] The *Mahāvagga* refers to sandalwood, Tagara, black Anusāri, Kāliya, and Bhadramuktaka which were used for perfuming ointments.[5] The *Nikāyas* refer to scents produced from roots (Mūlagandha), Sāra, flowers (Pupphagandha), Phegu, Tacha, Papaṭi, fruits (Phalagandha), leaves (Pattagandha), and juice (Rasagandha)[6]. Best fragrances are said to be those produced from sandalwood, Kālānusāri, and Vassikā.[7] Sandalwood was the most favourable one,[8] from which scented powder (Chandanasāra) and probably oil were made.[9] We get references to crimson (Harichandana) and

1. *M.N.* I. 386-87,
सेय्यथापि भन्ते नानापुप्फानं महापुप्फरासि, तमेनं दक्खो मालाकारो वा मालाकारन्तेवासी वा विचित्रं मालं गन्थेय्य, एवमेव खो भन्ते सो भगवा अनेकवण्णो अनेक सतवण्णो ।
D.N. I. 51; *Jā.* I. 120; II. 321, III. 405; IV 82; V. 292; *Dhp.* 53.
2. *Jā.* I. 129, 238; IV. 82; VI. 336.
3. *Jā.* I. 290; IV. 81.
4. *M.N.* III. 6-7; *S.N.* III. 156, 251-2; *G.S.* I. 205-6; *Ja.* II. 373; VI. 290, 336.
5. *M.V.* VI. 11. 2.
6. *M.N.* III. 6-7; *S.N.* III. 156, 251-2; *G.S.* I. 205-6.
7. *M.N.* III. 6-7; *S.N.* III. 156.
8. *Jā.* III. 160, 512; V. 156, 302; VI. 144.
9. *G.S.* I. 128; *Jā.* II. 373; *Jā.* VI. 480 speaks of sandalwood powder being prepared for perfuming the body.

red sandalwood[1] (Lohitachandana). An expression like Kāsika-Chandana[2] suggests that Kāśī was the centre for manufacturing sandalwood fragrances. But the possibility of the existence of this industry in cities like Pāṭaliputra, Vaiśālī, Śrāvastī and others cannot be ruled out.

Among flowers from which perfumes were produced were Vassikā, Mallikā, lotus, and Piyaṅgu.[3] Perfume prepared from the last was prominent,[4] and the Sabbasaṁhāraka, a compound of several scents or different chemicals was regarded as a rich one.[5] Agara, Tagara and other flowers also described as fragrant may have been used for perfuming.[6]

Pottery

In the *Nikāyas* we often get mention of the expert potter and his apprentice.[7] The former is called the Kumbhakāra.[8] Pāṇini knows him by the terms Kulāla or Kumbhakāra.[9] From the literary as well as the archaeological evidence it is quite clear that the potter's art was in an appreciably flourishing condition during the pre-Mauryan and Mauryan periods. The *Jātakas* tell us that there existed potters' villages where various types of bowls, jars, and vessels of all types were made.[10] Vessels were moulded by skilful hands on the wheel,[11] the practice which has remained constant till the present day. There is also mention of the potter's oven[12] which was used for burning moulded or hand-made articles. Artistically decorated pieces of pottery were not unknown. Vessels were

1. *M.N.* III. 6; *A. N.* III. 237; *Therīgāthā*, 298.
2. *S. N.* V. 407; *A.N.* III. 391, IV. 281; G.*S.* I. 128.
3. *M.N.* III. 6; *S.N.* III. 156; *Dhp.* 54; *Jā.* VI. 336.
4. *Jā.* VI. 336.
5. *Ibid.*
6. *Jā.* VI. 530, 535, 537.
7. *M.N.* II. 18,

   दक्खो कुम्भकारो वा कुम्भकारन्तेवासी वा ।
8. *D.N.* I. 51; *M.N.* II. 46; III. 118; *K.S.* I. 49-50.
9. *Pāṇini*, IV. 3. 118; *India as Known* to *Pāṇini*, p. 230.
10. *Jā.* III. 368, 376, 385. 508; V. 291.
11. *Jā.* IV. 6; V. 291; *Uvāsagadasāo* p. 106,
12. *K.S.* II. 58.

also engraved with various designs.[1] In addition to the household articles, various types of toys were also produced.[2] This is supported from the large finds of terracotta figurines of various objects from the pre-Mauryan and Mauryan strata at several sites in North-East India.

Dyeing

Dyeing appears to have been an important occupation. Both the Buddhist and the Brahmanical sources are acquainted with dyed clothes. The washerman or the dyer (Rajaka)[3] dyed clothes after properly washing them. New as well as washed clothes were dyed.[4] There would have been no need of dyeing clothes after washing, unless new clothes were already dyed. The *Vinaya-Piṭaka* informs us that dyed clothes of the colours of blue, light yellow, crimson, brown, black, brownish yellow, and dark yellow were prohibited for the monks.[5] This suggests that clothes of these colours were used by the laity. We are told that after washing properly, the washerman dyed the clothes with blue, yellow, red, or saffron colours.[6] The *Jātakas* mention garments, rugs and curtains as dyed scarlet, orange, yellow and red,[7] and umbrellas as red (Jambonadaṁ Chhattaṁ).[8] They also mention various colours such as white (Seta), dark-blue (Nīla), brown (Piṅgala) yellow (Halidda), golden (Sovaṇṇa), silvery (Rajatāmayā),

1. *Jā.* V 291,
सो नाना वण्णानि खुद्दकमहन्तानि भाजनानि कत्वा पभावतिया अत्थाय भाजनं करोन्तो नानारूपानि समुट्ठापेसि।
2. *Jā.* VI. 6, 12,
3. *D.N.* I. 51.
4. *M.N.* I. 36, 384-85.
5. *M.V.* VIII. 29.1.
6. *M.N.* I. 36;
सेय्यथापि भिक्खवे वत्थं संकिलिट्ठं मलग्गहितं तं एनं रजको यस्मिं रंगजाते उपसंहरेय्य, यदि नीलकाय यदि पीतकाय यदि लोहितकाय यदि मञ्जेट्ठकाय, दूरत्थवण्णमेव' अस्स।
S.N. V. 121.
7. *Jā.* IV. 258; V. 211.
8. *Jā.* VI. 218.

red (Ratta, Indagopa), black (Kāli), madder like (Mañjeṭṭha),[1] etc. It can be presumed that these colours were utilised for dyeing clothes.

More light is thrown on the washerman or the dyer by Kauṭilya. He says that clothes which were to be washed only, were to be returned within one to four nights; those which required light colouring, in five nights; which were to be made blue, in six nights, and those that were to be made as red-flower, lac, or saffron, or required much skill, in seven nights.[2] Kauṭilya also prescribed punishment, if the Rajaka sold, mortgaged, or let out on hire other's clothes; he was to be fined 12 Paṇas.[3] Later he is mentioned by Manu.[4] The *Milinda-Pañho* also refers to the dyer's street.

Dyes, Gums, Drugs, and Chemicals—We have seen that the washerman dyed clothes in various colours. The practice of dyeingclothes presupposes the existence of the industry of dye-making. In the *Vinaya-Piṭaka* we find the Bhikshus dyeing their robes with dyes prepared from roots, trunks and barks of tress, leaves, flowers, and fruits.[5] The *Jātakas* also suggest that leaves like Haritāla and Hiṅgulaka were used as the raw material for this industry.[6] Dyes were boiled[7], decidedly to give a fast colour to clothes. Apart from dyeing clothes, dyes were needed for ladies, decorating their hands and feet. They usually adorned themselves with Lākshārasa[8], which would have been an important produce of the dye-manufacturing industry. The Buddhist literature refers to various

1. *Jā*. VI. 279.
2. *Kau*. IV. 1,
पञ्चरात्रिकं तनुरागं षड्रात्रिकं नीलं पुष्पलाक्षामञ्जिष्ठारक्तं गुरुपरिकर्मयत्नोपचार्यं जात्यं वासः सप्तरात्रिकं ततः परं वेतनहानिं प्राप्नुयुः ।
3. *Ibid*.
परवस्त्रविक्रयाधानेषु च द्वादशपणो दण्डः ।
4. *Manu*. IV. 81.
5. *M. V*. VIII. 10. 1.
6. *Jā*. V. 416.
7. *M.V*. VIII. 10.2.
8. *Jā*. III. 183; VI. 218.

dyes such as red, yellow, blue, saffron, black, Pāṇḍu and so on.[1]

Gums, drugs, and acids also seem to have been produced on a large scale. Science of medicine was not in a primitive stage. The *Mahāvagga* and the *Dīgha-Nikāya* show that it had progressed to such an extent as to necessitate the use of gums, drugs, and chemicals. The *Mahāvagga* mentions seven kinds of gums—Hiṅgu, Hiṅgu-laka, Sipātikā, Taka, Takapatti, Taka-paṇṇī, and Sajjulasa.[2] In the *Dīgha-Nikāya* we get reference to drugs administered into the nose, and to the use of emetics, purgatives and other medicines[3]. The *Mahāvagga* mentions a number of roots,[4] leaves[5] and fruits[6] used as medicines. Probably drugs and chemicals were made of the various roots and leaves. The advancement of the medical science in the *Jātaka* also suggests this. In one of the *Jātakas* we find a dead body being preserved safely with the aid of oil.[7] For the purpose of the mineral industry, acids were also produced. This is suggested by the expression like 'verdigris removed by acid'.[8] Acids were probably used to refine the metals.

Fishing and Meat Production

Mention in the Buddhist literature[9] that people sought livelihood as mutton-butchers, pork-butchers, fowlers, hunters fishermen, and the like suggests that fish and meat (machchha-maṁsaṁ) were freely eaten and had given rise to the industries of fishing and slaughtering or hunting animals. The fishermen are mentioned by the term Machchhaghātakas and Kevaṭas[10].

1. *M.N.* I. 127. II. 17. III. 121; *S.N.* III. 87; V. 121. *A.N.* I. 35; III. 230; IV. 263-4. V. 47. *Vimāna* II. 5.1,
नीला पीता च काला च मञ्जेट्ठा अथ लोहिता ।
2. *M.V.* VI. 7.
3. *D.N.* I. 69.
4. *M.V.* VI. 3.1.
5. *M. V.* VI 5.1.
6. *M.V.* VI. 6.1.
7. *Jā.* II. 155.
8. *Jā.* III. 344; V. 95.
9. *K.S.* II. 171; *A.N.* II. 207, III. 301-3, 383.
11. *A.N.* II. 207. 383. *Jā.* I. 234.

Fishermen often lived in colonies in large numbers at one place and caught fishes in the rivers and pools.[1] They used nets (Jāla)[2] and basket-traps etc. (Kuminādīni)[3] for fishing. Traps were set in pits and holes of rivers.[4] Gangā is described as yielding plenty of fishes.[5] Fishermen are described as selling fish as fish-mongers.[6]

We get descriptions of meat being carried to market places in poles[7] or on carts.[8] We come across villages of hunters[9] and their settlements at the forests.[10] There is reference also to slaughterhouses.

The occupation of hunting was practised by the hunters, who killed animals, either by shooting with bows and arrows[11] or by entrapping.[12] The hunter first gathered the information of the animal from the footprints at the water-place which he traced and then set the snares and killed the victim with sword and spear (Asiñchasatiñcha).[13]

For hunters (Luddakas) we get expressions like

1. *Jā.* I. 234,
   कुलसहस्सवासे केवट्टगामे·····। जालहत्थं नदियञ्च तलाकादिसु च मच्छे परिसेयन्तं·····।;
   II. 36, IV. 413; V. 337. *Therigāthā*, 291. f.
2. *Jā.* I. 427, 482.
3. *A.N.* I. 29; *Udāna*, VII. 4,
   पमत्त बन्धुना बन्धा मच्छा व कुमिनामुखे ।
   Jā. I. 427.
4. *Jā.* II. 238,
   तदा मनुस्सा नदीकन्दरादिसु तत्थ तत्थ मच्छगहनत्थाय कुमिनानि ओड्डेंसु ।
5. *Jā.* II. 424.
6. *A.N.* III. 301-2.
   मच्छिकं मच्छिबन्धं मच्छे बधित्वा बधित्वा विक्किणमानं ।
7. *Jā.* VI. 170.
8. *Jā.* III. 49.
9. *Jā.* VI. 71 f.
10. *Jā.* IV. 430.
11. *Jā.* II. 200.
12. *Jā.* III. 184-85; IV. 170.
13. *Ibid.*

Vaṭṭakaluddaka[1] (quail-trapper), Godhaluddaka[2] (iguana-trapper), Sākunika or Tittiraluddaka[3] (Partridge-catcher), and Migaluddaka[4] (deer-hunter) which suggest that hunting had become specialised; and that hunters were differentiated according to the animals or birds they used to catch and kill.

Birds were caught with snares and nets.[5] The fowler is described as catching quails by flunging the net over birds when they had drawn together, and whipping the sides of the net, so as to get them all hudded up in a heap and then cramming them into basket.[6] Then he sold them in the market.[7]

As regards hunting, we are told by Manu that the occupation was followed by the mixed castes such as the Medas, Āndhras, Chuñchus, Mudgas, Kshattras, and Uggas.[8] But we have seen that even high caste people like the Brāhmaṇas sometimes took up this profession for the sake of livelihood.[9] The *Jātakas* inform us that mainly the Nesādas were engaged in hunting, and those who took to this occupation were styled as Luddakas, which was a general term to denote hunters.

Liquor Distilling

The Buddhist evidence refers to Meraya, Surā, Vāraṇa, Majjha and Āsava as the various varieties of liquor distilled.[10] Among these Pāṇini makes mention of Madya[11] (intoxicating

1. *Jā*. III. 64.
2. *Jā*. II. 153; III. 170. 184-85.
3. *Jā*. Nos. 33, 533.
4. *Jā*. I. 208
5. *Ibid.*
6. *Manu*. X. 48-49.
7. *Jā*. I. 208, 434.
8. *Jā*. I. 488
9. *Jā*. II. 200; VI. 170.
10. *A.N.* II. 53, IV 5,246; *Itivuttaka*, 74; *Jā*. I. 349; 362, IV. 217. 222, 367 : V, 467.
11. *Pāṇini*, III. 1.100.

liquor), Surā[1] (wine in general), and Maireya[2] (special wine) which may be taken as largely distilled during this period. The *Arthaśāstra* of Kauṭilya refers to six varieties of liquor, viz., Medaka, Prasannā, Āsava, Arishṭa, Maireya, and Madhu.[3]

Our sources further tell us how liquor was distilled. Pāṇini speaks of the process of distilling.[4] The Buddhist texts inform us that rice and fruit-mixture,[5] and sugarcane[6] were utilized for extracting liquor. Pāṇini further speaks of the distillery (Āsuti) and the distiller.[7]

The Food-Vendor

In the cities there were quarters (Odaniyaghara) where lived the curry-maker and the food-vender (Odanika), who prepared and sold food.[8] The Odanika is described as making a luscicous display of his stuff.[9] He is referred to as the Bhojanadātṛi[10] by Kauṭilya and later as the Ālarika in the *Milindapañho*.[11]

Sugar Making

Bihar and Uttar Pradash seem to have been the prominent sugar producing areas during our period as they are to-day. In the *Vinaya-Piṭaka* we get description of carts loaded with sugar. The sick Bhikshus were allowed to eat sugar, and the healthy ones were permitted to drink it.[12] It is evident that sugar was made from sugarcane juice. It is said in a *Jātaka*

1. *Pāṇini*, II. 4.25.
2. *Pāṇini*, VI. 2.70.
3. *Kau.* II. 25.
4. Agrawala, *India as known to Pāṇini*, p. 119.
5. *Jā.* V. 12.
6. *Jā.* IV. 161.
7. *Pāṇini*, V. 2. 112.
8. *Jā.* III. 287; VI. 276. He is also called Ālārika (*Ja.* V. 296; VI. 580).
9. *Jā.* I. 397,
नानाग्गरसानं दिब्बभोजनानं भाजनानि पूरेत्व ओदनिकापनं पसारेत्वा निसीदिंसु ।
10. *Kau.* IV. 8; II. 4.
11. *Milindapañho*, 331.
12. *M.V.* VI. 27.

story that a wicked king crushed his subjects, like sugarcane in a machine.[1] This shows that sugarcane crushing machine was used. We get mention of lump as well as powdered sugar.[2] Probably jaggery and Bhurā were produced. Pāṇini refers to sugarcane in *Sūtra* VIII. 4.5; and the manufacture of Guḍa (jaggery) is implied in rule IV. 4.103, on which the illustration Gauḍika, meaning excellent for making Guḍa presumes sugarcane. He does not seem differentiating between the lump and the powder sugar, as in the case of the Buddhist literature.

Cane and Leaf Work

The workers in cane, bamboo, and leaf were known as the Nalakāras, Veṇukāras, and Velukāras. They went to the forest to work, because they got the available raw material there.[3] They made lutes, baskets, ropes, and mats.[4] They made palmleaf fans (Tālavantaṁ, Vālavījanaṁ) and leaf-sun-shades (Paṇṇachchhattakaña) also in large numbers.[5] Their handicraft appears to have been considerably skilled, and probably they not only g ive various shapes to the finished articles, but also decorated artistically by drawing figures on them.[6] Ornaments of palm-leaf (Tālipata)[7] for the ears also seem to have been largely made. Such ornaments are even today used by the aboriginal tribes.

Leather Work

Leather industry also seems to have been in a fairly advanced stage. The Chammakāra (cobbler) manufactured various types of leather goods. Shoemaking was the most

1. *Jā.* II, 240.
2. *Jā.* I. 238; IV. 379; V. 384.
3. *Jā.* II. 302, IV. 251.
4. *Jā.* IV. 251, 318; VI. 341, 370.
5. *Jā.* III. 79, 283; V. 291-92; VI. 218.
6. *Jā.* V. 292.
तालवन्तं कत्वा तत्थ 'एव सेतच्छत्तं अपानभूमिञ्च वत्थं गहेत्वा ठितं पभावतिं' चाति नानारुपानि दस्सेति ।
7. *Jā.* No. 159.

important aspect of his handicraft. In the *Vinaya-Piṭaka*[1] shoes and slippers of various designs are mentioned, which reveal the skill and workmanship of the leather-worker. Shoes were probably adorned with skins of lion, tiger, panther, atelope, otter, cat, squirrel, and owl.[2] Boots were made of various hues like the wings of partridges.[3] They were painted with rams' and goats' horns and ornamented with scorpion's tails.[4] Shoes and slippers were having the colours of blue, yellow, red, brown, black, orange, and yellowish.[5] The *Jātakas* also show that shoes of various types were manufactured, and sometimes they were set with gold[6] and wrought with various threads.[7] Pāṇini informs us that shoes were also manufactured to the order of the purchaser as per measurement of his foot.[8]

The worker in leather did not cofine himself to shoe-making only. He made leather sacks (Chammabhastaṁ)[9], shields of hundred layers[10] and leather parachutes[11] (Chammo-chhatta). He also seems to have been making ropes, sword-case, and traps.[12] Pāṇini refers to various leather goods finished by the leather-worker such as straps (Nadhrī, III. 2.182), leather thong (Vardhra, IV. 3.149)[13] and rope

1. *M.V.* v. 2.
2. *M.V.* v. 2.4.
3. *M.V.* V. 2. 3,
   तित्तिरपत्तिका'ति तित्तिरपत्तसदिसविचित्र वद्धा ।
4. *Ibid.*,
   मेण्डविसाणवद्धिका'ति कण्णिकाट्ठाने मेण्डकसिगसंठाने वद्धे योजेत्वा कता । अजविसाण-वद्धि'कादिसु'पि एस' एव नयो । विच्छिकालिका'ति तत्थ' एव विच्छिकानं-गुत्थ संठानेवद्धे योजेत्वा कता ।
5. *M.V.* V. 2. 1—2.
6. *Jā.* IV. 379; VI. 370.
7. *Jā.* VI. 218,
8. The expression for per measurement of the foot is *anupadaṁ baddhā*, and such a pair was called *anupadīnā* (V. 2.9).
9. *Jā.* V. 45.
10. *Jā.* VI. 454.
11. *Jā.* V. 45.
12. *Jā.* I. 175, II. 153, III, 116; IV. 172, V. 47, 106, 375; VI. 51.
13. Agrawala, *India as Known to Pāṇini*, p. 234.

(Varatrā).[1] He further makes a distinction between skinning (tvachayati)[2] and objects made entirely of leather.[3] It appears that the leather-workers' craft was not of a mean order.

Leather-workers had organised themselves under a guild and are mentioned among the eighteen guilds.[4]

1. *Kāśikā* on V. 1. 15.
2. *Pāṇini*, III. 1. 25.
3. *Pāṇini*, V. 2.5.
4. *Jā*, VI. 427.

CHAPTER XII

TRADE AND TRADE ROUTES

Our sources by making references to long distant land and sea trades, river transport, shipwrecks, caravans, scenes of market-places, of sale and purchase, hawking on donkeys and bullock carts, visits of merchants to various cities for transacting trade and so on reveal that during the period under review India's trade was in an appreciably flourishing condition. It is also revealed from our sources that there was not only a network of trade routes within the country, connecting its important towns and cities through roads and water-ways, but some of them led to foreign lands also.

References to the caravans and Seṭṭhis from Śrāvastī[1] and merchants from Orissa visiting Rājagṛiha[2], Rājagriha Seṭṭhis visiting Vaiśālī[3] and the like would suggest the existence of trade transactions between the important towns of Eastern India such as Rājagṛiha, Vaiśālī, Śrāvastī, Vārāṇasī, Champā, and others. Most of the routes connecting these places are known from the wanderings of the Buddha. That the above cities had trade transactions through land routes with distant lands like Gāndhāra, Kamboja and Sind, etc. is shown by references to the visits of merchants from Gāndhāra and Kashmir to Videha,[4] visits of horse-dealers from Punjab and Sind to the eastern region,[5] caravans from the east marching to the west[6], etc. References to trade between the east and the west confirm the existence of brisk land-trade

1. *Jā.* I. 92,
2. *M.V.* 1. 4. 2.
3. *M.V.* VIII. 1.2.
4. *Jā.* III. 365. The king of Videha is described as enquiring from the tradesmen about the health of his friends, the kings of Gāndhāra and Kashmir.
5. *Jā.* No. 160—tells us that Sindhu horses were used in Videha.
6. *D.N.* II. 342; *Jā.* Nos. 1, 85,

बोधिसत्तो सत्थवाहो हुत्वा पञ्चहि सकटसतेहि पुब्बन्ता अपरन्तं गच्छन्तो · · ·।

between the Eastern and Western regions of India. We are in a position to show that there were short distant as well as long distant trade routes, which connected towns of Eastern India with each other and with other centres of trade in the country.

From our sources it appears that there were four minor, but important trade routes which connected the trade, centres of Eastern India; a fifth road led to Kaliṅga's capital.

Rājagṛiha-Kapilavastu Route—The details of this route are known from the journeys of the Buddha. It started from Rājagṛiha and passed through Nālandā, Pāṭaligāma, Vaiśālī, Bhoganagara, Pāvā and Kuśīnagara.[1]

Rājagṛiha-Śrāvastī Route—The Buddhist literature discloses that this route had two courses. According to one, starting from Rājagṛiha it went via Pāṭaligāma,[2] Vaiśālī,[3] Bhaddiya,[4] Aṅguttarāpa,[5] Āpaṇṇa,[6] Kusinārā[7] and Ātumā.[8] According to the other course, from Vaiśālī it passed through Vārāṇasī.[9]

Rājagṛiha-Mithilā Route—The details are not available, but it passed through Vaiśālī.[10]

Rājagṛiha-Champā Route—Halting places between these two places are not given. Buddha had travelled along this route.[11] We are also told of people resting on the borders of Aṅga and Magadha.[12] This speaks of the period when Aṅga was not merged in Magadha. It appears almost certain that there was

1. *D.N.* II. 72-137.
2. *M.V.* VI. 28. 1.
3. *M.V.* VI. 29-30.
4. *M.V.* VI. 34.17
5. *M.V.* VI. 34-17.
6. *M.V.* VI. 35. 1.
7. *M.V.* VI. 36. 1.
8. *M.V.* VI. 37.1.
9. *M.V.* VIII. 14-15.
10. Bhīma & Kṛishṇa had travelled from Mithilā to Rājagṛiha which is known from the *Mahābhārata* (*Sabhāparva*, XX).
11. *M.N.* I. 339.
12. *Gūthapāṇa Jā.* (No. 227).

a regular route between Rājagṛiha and Champā. The latter was also connected with Mithilā, as we get description of carts moving on the road connecting these cities.[1]

Rājagṛiha-Kaliṅga Route—The *Mahāvagga* speaks of a road which passed through Bodha-Gayā to Orissa.[2] Evidently it was the Rājagṛiha-Kaliṅga road. As the above source speaks of merchants from Utkala, the existence of trade relations between Magadha and Utkala or Kaliṅga cannot be doubted. This road may have been repaired and put in proper condition during the days of the Nandas, who had occupied Kaliṅga and carried out constructional activities at the capital, according to the Hāthīgumphā inscription of King Khāravela.

In addition to the above trade routes, there were three long distant routes, which started from Rājagṛiha to far off trade-centres. They were the following :

Rājagṛiha-Pushkalāvatī Route or the Uttarāpatha

This route connected Rājagṛiha with Takshaśilā and Pushkalāvatī, which were busy centres of trade in the North-West extremity of India. Takshaśilā was just like an international trade-centre and established commercial relations between India and the West. This route was the same which is referred to as Uttarāpatha by Pāṇini (V.1.77.) and was known to the Greeks as the 'Northern Route'. It was utilised during the Mauryan Period; Shershah repaired it, and to-day it is known as the Grand Trunk Road within India. It seems to have passed through Pāṭaliputra, Vārāṇasī, Kauśāmbī, Mathurā, Indraprastha, and Sākala. From Pushkalāvatī it probably branched off to Kashmir to the North-East and to Bactria to the North-West. It was through the Rājaṛiha-Pushkalāvatī route that Kṛishṇa and Bhīma had travelled from Indraprastha to Rājagṛiha.[3] According to the writer of the *Mahābhārata* they went

1. *Jā.* VI. 31-32.
2. *M.V.* I. 4. 2. The name of two merchants travelling on this road is given as Tapussa and Bhallika.
3. *Mbh, Sabhāparva,* XX.

first to Mithilā and thence to Rājagṛiha. They appear to have travelled through Ayodhyā, taking a nothern course. During the Moghul period, the Northern route was via Jaunpur, and the same seems to have been in the knowledge of the author of the *Mahābhārata.* There seems to have been a direct route from Rājagṛiha to Kauśāmbī, which was resorted to by the Buddha, but unfortunately details of it are not referred to.[1] There seem to have been two courses upto Mathurā; one which passed through Śrāvastī and extended to the North-East as far as Mithilā, through which traders from Gāndhāra and Kashmir visited the Videhan capital[2]; the other, the Southern course of the route may have passed through Pāṭaliputra, Vārāṇasī, and Kauśāmbī and extended to the east as far as Champā.

It was by one of these routes that students from various parts of Eastern India such as Mithilā,[3] Vaiśālī, Rājagṛiha[4], etc. used to go to Takshaśilā, the renowned seat of learning, for their education. The famous Magadhan physician Jīvaka had gone there from Rājagṛiha, for being trained in the science of medicine and surgery.[5] That Jīvaka had been there during the days of Bimbisāra, Pāṇini hailing from the North-West came to Pāṭaliputra during the days of Nandas, and that Chandragupta Maurya had studied at that seat of learning show how Takshaśilā had been connected with the cities of North-East India through the famous Uttarāpatha route.

Rājagṛiha-Pratishṭhāna Route

From the Buddhist and the Brahmanical works we are told of a route leading to Patiṭṭhāna from Rājagṛiha. According to Pāṇini this route was known as the Kāntārapatha[6] because of its passing through the forest region. It was the same as the above route (Rājagṛiha-Pushkalāvatī) upto

1. *C.V.* VII. 2.5 speaks of Buddha's direct journey from Kauśāmbī to Rājagṛiha.
2. *Jā.* III. 365.
3. *Suruchi Jātaka* (No. 489) refers to a prince of Mithilā going to Takshaśilā; *Vinīlaka Jātaka* (No. 160) speaks of a Videhan prince going there.
4. *Darimukha Jā.* (No. 378); *Nigrodha Jā.* (No. 445).
5. *M.V.* VIII. 1.6. The *Darimukha Jā* (No. 378) speaks of a Magadhan prince going to Takshaśilā.
6. Agrawala, *India as Known to Pāṇini*, p. 242.

Kausāmbī, from where it passed through Vansahvaya, Vedisa, Gonaddha, Ujjeni, Mahissati and then to Patiṭṭhāna.[1] Caravans going to Bharukachchha from Rājagṛiha, Pāṭaliputra, Vaiśālī and other trade centres would have been going through this route upto Mahishmatī from where it seems to have been branched off to Bharukachchha. From Kausāmbī there was another course leading to Śrāvastī[2] through which traders from East Uttar Pradesh and North Bihar may have been going to the trade centres of South-West India.

Rājagṛiha-Sindhu Region Route

There is also evidence of trade relations between North-Eastern India and the Sindhu region. The *Jātakas* speak to busy trade transactions going on between the east and the west. The *Apaṇṇaka* (No. 1) and the *Vaṇṇuṭatha* (*No.* 2) *Jātakas* speak of caravans starting from Vārāṇasī and passing through a desert. The desert through which marched the caravans was very likely the sandy desert of Rajasthan, and the route led to the Sindhu region. We are often told of horses and donkeys brought from Uttarāpatha and Sindhu to the eastern region[3] which is generally Vārāṇasī. Horses from the Sindhu region are very often described as of good breed[4]. In view of the big army maintained by Magadhan kings, it is but natural to conclude that Sindhu-horses would have got a favourable market in the capilal of the Magadhan empire.

Up to Mathurā this western route was the same as the Rajagṛiha-Pushkalāvatī route, but there it branched off to the direction of the Sindhu region. This route was connected

1. *Su. Ni.* V. 1. 36,
   अलकस्स पतिट्ठानं पुरिमं माहिस्सतिं तदा ।
   उज्जेनिं चापि गोनद्धं वेदिसं वनसह्वयं ॥
   कोसंबिं चापि साकेतं सावत्थिं पुरुत्तमं ।
   Jīvaka had travelled through this route upto Ujjainī, via Kauśāmbī, when he had been sent by the Magadhan ruler Bimbisāra to treat the haughty king of Avantī, Pradyota (*M.V.* VIII. 1. 23-27).
2. *M.V.* VI. 13. 6-8; *Su. Ni.* V. 1. 36.
3. *Jā.* I. 124, 178, 181, II. 31. 287; V. 259-60.
4. E.g., *Jā.* I. 178, VI. 14, 265, 404.

with Śrāvastī and Kapilavastu to the North-East and also with Vaisālī, as described in the *Sutta Nipāta*. It is very likely that traders from North Bihar would have preferred to travel through Śrāvastī than via Pāṭaliputra, as in the case of the Pratishṭhāna route.

River Transport

In ancient times river-routes were more convenient and less costly and sometimes safer and quicker than roads, and rivers such as Gangā, Yamunā, Sarayū, Soṇa, Gaṇḍakī, Kosi and others seem to have been fully utilised for navigation. There must have been brisk trade transactions among river ports like Champā, Pāṭaliputra, Vārāṇasī and Kauśāmbī being connected through the waterway. Pāṭaliputra was also the centre which connected North and South Bihar. That boats were sailed as far as Sahajāti to the North-West in the Gangā is known from the *Chullavagga*[1]. The same source speaks of the disembarkment of Ānanda at Kausāmbī on a boat with 500 Bhikshus from Magadha.[2] As Kauśāmbī was a capital city, it must have been a great trade-centre having close commercial contacts with other river-ports and trade-centres like Vārāṇasī and Pāṭaliputra.

Heavy transport was carried on mainly through the rivers. Recent excavations at Kumrahar have revealed that Chunar sandstone or heavy pillars were brought to Pāṭaliputra through the Gangā for constructing the Mauryan Pillared Hall[3]. During this period ships were utilised in the rivers as far as practicable, then big boats were used and still further small boats served the purpose. Streams which passed through forests were utilised by the carpenters for transporting logs, for building and other purposes. The river-ports were connected with trade-centres on the land, and hence, the rivers established a co-ordinated means of transport for facilitating easy and swift trade.

1. *C.V.* XII· 2. 1.
2. *C.V.* XI. 1. 12.
3. Excavations have revealed that a canal was constructed right upto the hall for transporting the huge sandstone pieces. Mauryan Pillars in different parts of the country were also transported through rivers.

Oversea Trade

There are ample references in the Buddhist literature to show that people of North-East India were keenly interested in maritime activities and that they sailed to foreign lands for transacting business. Illustrations cited by the Buddha before the Magadhan and other Bhikshus of boats sailing on the ocean for six months[1], merchants going to the ocean with direction showing birds (tīradassī-sakuna),[2] merchants crossing the ocean[3], and so on would suggest that Majjhimadesa of the Buddhist literature was acquainted with seafaring in the Buddha's time. When the *Theragāthā* speaks of merchants sailing on the sea with the hope of earning wealth,[4] and when the popular stories tell us of several shipwrecks[5], spacious ships[6], ship-building activities[7] and of seafarers from Videha and Champā sailing to Suvaṇṇabhūmi,[8] they furnish us with the evidence that people of Noth-East India, during the period under study, were carrying on brisk oversea trade. The description in the Ceylonese chronicles of prince Vijaya's voyage to Ceylon from Bengal with his 700 followers[9] presupposes a regular sea-trade and intercourse. The *Baudhāyana-Dharmasūtra*[10] shows that

1. *S.N.* III. 155; V. 51; *A.N.* IV. 127,
सेप्पथापि भिक्खवे समुद्दिकाय नावाय वेत्तवन्धनवद्धाय छम्मासानि, उदके परियादाय हेमन्ति केन थले उक्खित्ताय वातातपपेरतानि बन्धनानि तानि पावुस्सकेन मेघेन अभिप्पवुट्ठानि (or वट्टानि) अप्पकरिसेन एवं पाटिस्सम्भन्ति ।
2. *D. N.* I. 222.
3. *D. N.* II. 89.
4. *Theragāthā*, 530,
आसाय वाणिजा यन्ति समुद्दं धनहारका ।
5. *E.G, Jā.* II. 111, 127-29; V. 75; *Jā.* No. 196 speaks of a shipwreck at Tambapaṇṇidīpa.
6. *E.G, Jā.* Nos. 466, 539.
7. *Jā.* IV. 159; VI. 427,
आनन्द त्वं तीणि वड्ढकिसतानि आदाय उद्धगङ्गं गत्वा सारदारुनि गाहापेत्वा तिसमत्ता नावा मापेत्वा····।
This passage speaks of ship construction at Mithilā.
8. Mahājanaka *Jā.*
9. *Dīpavaṁsa* IX. 10-28; *Mahāvaṃsa*, VI,
10. *Bau. Dh. S.* I. 1. 20.

navigation was peculiar to Brāhmaṇas of the North. Manu[1] and Baudhāyana[2] by placing the profession of seafaring among prohibited practices for the Brāhmaṇas reveal that it was taken up mainly by the Vaiśya Community. But one should not overlook the fact that the Dharmaśāstra permits the pursuit of trade for the Brāhmaṇas in time of distress. It was probably the uncertainty of life and low estimation of the career from the orthodox point of view that some of the Dharmaśāstra writers prohibited the Brāhmaṇa community from resorting to seafaring, but till the days of Baudhāyana, Brāhmaṇas of the North did not give up this life. When we refer to the *Sūtras* of Pāṇini, the mention of various terms connected with navigation leaves no doubt as regards the practice of seafaring during this period.[3] He refers to Samudra (Ocean)[4] and two kinds of islands, viz., near the seacoast (Anusamudra) and in the main ocean. Goods imported from the former type of islands are called Dvaipya; whereas those from the latter, Dvaipa or Dvaipaka.[5] Boat-ferry is called Nāvya.[6] Merchants are valued in terms of the number of ship-loads of merchandise possessed by them such as Dvināva-Dhana (one having two cargo-boats), or Panchanāvapriya (one sailing with five ship-loads).[7]

They are also referred to as either owning the whole cargo-boat or sharing a part of its merchandise.[8] He further makes mention of various types of boats, e.g., Utsaṅga,[9] Uḍupa (ḍoṅgī—it is described as shaped like the half-moon), Utpata (probably a longish fishing boat) and Piṭaka (a basket

1. *Manu.* III. 158.
2. *Bau. Dh. S.* II. 1. 41.
3. Agrawala, *India as known to Pāṇini*, pp. 155-56.
4. *Pāṇini*, IV. 4. 118.
5. *Pāṇini*, IV. 3.10.
6. *Pāṇini*, IV. 4. 9.
7. Agrawala, *India as known to Pāṇini*, p. 155.
8. Agrawala, *India as known to Pāṇini*, p. 156.
9. *Pāṇini*, IV. 4. 15 It was originally made out of the hollow of a tree. It is known as *Chang* in Sind and was similar to Roman *Cumba* (*India as known to Pāṇini*, p. 156). The boatmen of Chotanagpur construct their *ḍoṅgīs* by digging the hollow of a tree; they are unfamiliar with the practice of making boat as in the Up country. It appears that Pāṇini refers to this boat, which must have been used in the hilly regions for crossing small rivers, as is the case in Chotanagpur today.

like coracle).[1] The *Arthaśāstra* of Kauṭilya makes it quite clear that during the days of Chandragupta Maurya Indian navigation was in a highly advanced stage. The state had instituted an officer known as the 'Nāvadhyaksha' as the Superintendent of ships.[2] We need not enter into details of the Mauryan shipping, but we can safely assume that Pāṭaliputra would have been the main centre of navigation in Magadha during the pre-Mauryan and Mauryan periods.

Our sources reveal that seafaring was not in its infancy. It was well developed and proper training was given in the science of navigation, which was known as the Niyāmakasippa.[3] We do not know exactly the nature of training imparted to the young seafarers. They were probably trained in the knowledge of various trade routes, directions of winds, how to train and utilise the Disākākas, how to escape shipwrecks and the like. There was no compass to tell them the directions, nor had man by that period invented the wireless system, through which the outside world could be contacted for help in moments of emergency. While sailing on the waters birds were of great help for the navigators. In every ship the mariners kept a direction guiding crow (Disākāka) or other bird (tīradassī sakuna)[4] which would fly to the direction of land, if there was any visible, otherwise it would come back to the ship. Thus they were enabled to know whether they were sailing near a land or were still in a region where there was no trace of it. It seems that accomplished mariners had to possess a thorough knowledge of training and utilising birds for the purpose of knowing directions. Shipwrecks were quite common and probably instructions were given how to escape such occasions. Sea-trade was always precarious and life was never secure. Parents dissuaded their sons from taking up this career. But the attractions of the adventures and thrills of navigation impelled many to choose this profession.

1. *Ibid*; *India as known to Pāṇini*, p. 156, There is also reference of Bhastra (raft of inflated skins), and Bharata (float of wood). The former is used in Punjab, N.W.F.P. and Afghanistan.
2. *Kau.* II. 28.
3. *Jā.* IV. 137.
   सोलस्सवस्सकाले येव नियामकसिप्पे निप्फत्तिं पत्वा····।
4. *D.N.* (XI. 85) I. 222; *Jā.* III, 126. 267.

The mariners (Niyāmakas) had organised themselves into guilds, the head of which was known as the Niyāmakajeṭṭhaka. It has been already seen that the term Jeṭṭhaka was used to denote the head or the Alderman of a guild, and that almost all the crafts of this period had formed their guilds under their respective Jeṭṭhakas. The Niyāmakajeṭṭhaka was probably the captain, the owner of the ship and the leader of the traders travelling with him. Decidedly, his responsibilities were heavy, as the lives of his fellow travellers would have been endangered, if due to his negligence the ship lost its route.

The *Jātakas* tell us that traders from ports on the Gangā sailed to the eastern lands. The *Saṅkha Jātaka* describes the journey of the Brāhmaṇa Saṅkha from Vārāṇasī to Suvaṇṇabhūmi[1] (Burma and portions of Indo-Chinese Peninsula). The *Sīlānisaṁsa Jātaka* refers to a seafaring nymph as bringing shipwrecked people to Vārāṇasī from the far off sea.[2] References are made to voyages from Champā to Suvaṇṇabhūmi. Prince Mahājanaka is said to have travelled in a ship with probably 350 men (or 700 caravans) and reached there.[3] Traders from Vaiśālī also seem to have been going to Suvaṇṇabhūmi and other places for trade. In later times we find contact between Vaiśālī and the Arakan.[4] The *Valāhassa Jātaka* speaks of trade between Vārāṇasī and Tambapaṇṇidīpa.[5] All these suggest that vessels from the ports on the Gaṅgā were sailed to lands beyond the bay of Bengal. The vessels starting from Vārāṇasī

1. *Jā.* IV. 15-17,
2. *Jā.* II. 112.
3. *Mahājanaka Jā.* (No 539.) He is said to have travelled with probably 350 men; as the expression Sattajaṅghasatāni=700 legs may be taken as denoting the suggested number (*Jā.* VI. 34).
4. Vaiśālī was the name of a famous city in Arakan, and according to local chronicles it was built in 789 A.D. by a king of the Chandra dynasty. For two centuries the city retained its position as a strong-hold of Indian culture, specially, Buddhism. At present it is a small village of eighty houses. Its relation with Vaiśālī is difficult to ascertain, but Burmese traditions are acquainted with Indian Vaiśālī and show that Burmese people had great respect for Vaiśālī (Majumdar, R. C., in *Vaiśālī Abhinandana Grantha*, pp. 43-44.)
5. *Jā.* II. 127-29.

must have been anchoring at Pāṭaliputra and Champā, both being important river-ports. At these ports traders must have probably bartered their goods, loaded their vessels with local produces and then proceeded further to the foreign market. It is not unlikely that traders from Pāṭaliputra and Champā sailed for the eastern lands with their ships carrying locally manufactured goods. These cities must have been busy centres of trade and commerce. It was this sea-trade which was largely shared by the people of the kingdoms of Magadha and Vaiśālī. Though only Suvaṇṇabhūmi and Tambapaṇṇidīpa are mentioned, it can be assumed that trade was carried on with many other islands of the East Indies. The *Mahāniddesa* tells us that India's trade to the east existed with Kālamukha, Suvaṇṇabhūmi, Vesuṅga, Verāpatha, Takkola, Tamali, Tambapaṇṇi, and Jāvā. First two of these places can be identified with Arakan coast and lower Burma. Next two correspond to Ptolemy's Besyngeitai, Berbai, and Takkala[2]. Tamali has been identified by Sylvain Levi with Tāmraliṅga in the Malaya Peninsula.[3] The *Apadāna* states that traders from Malaya and China visited India.[4]

Thus we find that traders from the sea-ports on the Gangā went to the eastern lands across the sea. During the earlier part of the period under review, Vārāṇasī and Champā were important ports; but when Pāṭaliputra rose to imperial status, it became the biggest and the most busy centre of trade in North-East India.

The *Baveru Jātaka* speaks of trade with Baveruraṭṭha,[5] a birdless country which appears to be Babylon and there is evidence, both foreign and indigenous to establish India's trade relation with Babylon and the countries on the Mediterranean during the 6th century B.C.[6] Mr. Kennedy who worked on this subject concluded that maritime commerce between

1. Majumdar, R.C., *Suvarṇadvīpa*. p. 57; S. Levi, *Etuder Asiatiques*, Vol. II, Chap. II.
2. Majumdar, R.C., *Suvarṇadvīpa*, p. 57.
3. *Ibid.*,
4. *Apadāna*, I. p. 2.
5. *Jā*. III. 126; Buhler, *Origin of Indian Alphabet*, p. 84.
6. Mukherjee, R. K., *Indian Shipping*, Chap. I.

India and Babylon flourished in 7th and the 6th, but more specially in the 6th century B.C.[1] Jackson writing on India's ancient trade has observed that the Buddhist *Jātakas* and some of the Sanskrit law-books tell us that ships from Bhroach and Sopara traded with Babylon from the 8th to the 6th century B.C.[2] The *Suppāraka Jātaka* says that a band of travellers sailed from the port of Bharukachchha and passed through six seas, under the leadership of a skilled mariner.[3] The seas, thus mentioned, are Khuramāla, Aggimāla, Dadhimāla, Nīlakusamāla, Nalamāla, and Balabhāmukha[4]. These seas have been identified with the Persian gulf, the Arabian coast, Nubia on the North-East corner of Africa, the canal joining the Red sea and the Mediterranean, the Mediterranean and some portion of the Mediterranean.[5] If this identification is correct, it can be established that Indians possessed the knowledge of a sea-route from the Western coast to the Mediterranean. During the 5th cen. B.C. certain Indian commodities, e.g., rice, sandalwood and peacocks were known by Indian names to the Greeks and others.[6] It cannot be denied at the present knowledge of the subject that during our period Indians traded with the countries on the Mediterranean, and this trade seems to have been carried on mainly from the Bharukachchha and Suppāraka, the two famous centres of trade in Western India, to which were caravans from the trade-centres of the north-eastern region of the country regularly visiting, as shown by the Buddhist sources.

1. *J.R.A.S.* 1898.
2. Jackson, A.M.T., quoted by Mukherjee, *Indian Shipping*, p. 90.
3. *Jā.* IV. 138-43.
4. *Ibid.*
5. *J. B. O. R. S.* VI, 195 (Jayaswal's Article); Mukherjee, *Indian Shipping*, Chap. I; R. L. Mehta, *Pre-Buddhist India*, P. 228.
6. Mukherjee, R.K., *Indian Shipping*, p. 88.

CHAPTER XIII

ORGANISATION OF INDUSTRY AND TRADE

Guilds

Our sources reveal that during the period under review the organisational genius of people played an important role in the progress of trade and industry. There are frequent references to guilds in the Buddhist and the Brahmanical sources, and the existence of cities such as Śrāvastī, Kauśāmbī, Vārāṇasī, Rājagṛiha, Vaiśāli and others, where trade was brisk and a number of industries like smithy, carpentry, ivory-work, making luxury goods, etc. were considerably advanced, suggest that the agencies to organise and control them must have been in existence. Both the Brahmanical and the Buddhist sources make references to guilds; but whereas the former refers to the guilds of cultivators, traders, herdsmen, and artisans,[1] the latter makes mention of eighteen guilds.[2] It is obvious that the Buddhist evidence refers to the guilds of the eighteen Śilpas, but there is no authoritative enumeration of these crafts. The Tahskaśilā University made a claim to specialise in them. Among the subjects taught there which may be called Śilpas figure archery, mililary art, medicine, magic, snake-charming and the art of finding treasures.[3] Besides the above six, the Buddhist literature includes among the Śilpas conveyancing and law, mathematics, accountancy, agriculture, cattle-breeding, commerce and administrative training[4]. There is specific mention of carpenters, smiths, leather-workers, and painters as having been organised into guilds.[5] When music and engineering are added to the above

1. *Gau. Dh. S.* XI.
2. *Ja.* VI. 22, 427. Generally we get the expression *sabbaseṇiyo* (*Jā.* I. 267, 314; IV. 43, 411), which is used for 18 guilds, the total conventional number.
3. *M.V.* VIII. 1.6. *Jā.* Nos. 80, 185; Altekar, A.S., *Ancient Indian Education, Appendix*, IV.
4. *M.N.* 1. 85; *A.N.* IV. 281.
5. *Jā.* VI. 427,
वड्ढकिकम्मार-चम्मकाराचित्तकारादिना-सिप्पकुसल अट्ठारससेणियो ।

list of Śilpas, their number reaches nineteen. The number eighteen is a traditional one, and it can be said that there were various Śilpas, all organised into guilds.

The Buddhist as well as the Brahmanical sources reveal that the guilds were autonomous bodies, having their own laws. The latter source informs us that the corporate existence of the guild was recognised by the state.[1] Guilds exercised considerable control over the members[2]. Probably the settlement of disputes among its members and the solution of the problems of trade and business fell under the jurisdiction of the guild. It could also settle the disputes between wives and husbands.[3] That guild organisations were well disciplined and maintained solidarity is suggested by a *Jātaka* story which describes the shifting of 1000 families of carpenters overnight.[4]

The exact nature of the relation of the guild to the state is not known. The guild laws were recognised by the state; they were also consulted by the king very often. Probably there was a permanent representative of the guilds at the royal court or in the ministry. The *Uraga Jātaka* tells us that two of the guild leaders were included among the Kośala Mahāmātras. The same may have been the case in other kingdoms. A blacksmith is called Rājaballabha in one of the *Jātakas*,[5] which suggests his close association with the royal court. In some of the stories kings are described as calling all the guilds (Sabbaseṇiyo) on certain occasions.[2] Probably

3. *Gau. Dh. S.* XI. 22-23,
देशजातिकुलधर्मश्चाम्नायैरविरुद्धाः प्रमाणम् ॥
कर्षकवणिक्पशुपालकुसीदिकारवः स्वे स्वे वर्गे ॥
4. *M.N.* I. 286,
इध गहपतयो एकच्चो मुसावादी होति, सभागतो वा परिसगतो वा ञातिमच्झगतो वा पूगमज्झगतो वा राजकुलमज्झगतो वा अभिनीतो सक्खिपुट्ठोः ।
5. *Vinaya*, IV. 226.
6. *Jā.* IV. 159.
1. *Jā.* III. 281,
तत्थ कम्मारसहस्स जेट्ठकम्मारो राजवल्लभो अट्ठो महद्धनो ।
2. *Jā.* I. 267; IV. 411. In one place we are told that the king called all the guilds for witnessing his almsgiving (Bose, A. N., *Social and Rural Economy of Northern India*, Vol. II, p. 242).

the Seṭṭhi visited the royal court as a representative of the business community and the same may have been the case with the heads of the guilds. When Manu says that the king was to decide the case after examining laws of the Śreṇīs,[1] he suggests that guilds were represented at the royal court.[2]

On occasions like disputes among the guilds, it was probably the state-interference which settled them. We are told in a *Jātaka* of a king inaugurating the office of the Bhāṇḍāgārika, who carried with it also the judgeship over all guilds [3] There may have been a permanent arrangement for the settlement of guild disputes. According to Rhys Davids the Mahāseṭṭhi or the Lord High Treasurer acted as a sort of the Chief Alderman over the guilds.[4] Probably there was no hard and fast rule as to the office of the judge for guild disputes, and it was at the discretion of the king to make appointment to that post. Naturally, such a man would be one conversant with the affairs of trade and business and workings of the guilds. It would appear from the Seṭṭhi's close association with the king's court that generally he filled the post of judgeship over guilds.

Our sources reveal that people had realised the importance of saving money as a security for times of distress. Manu and Vātsyāyana stress the need of saving a portion of the income, which should be done by the wife who would control expenditure.[5] The earliest method of saving money was by burying bullion and jewellery inside ground, which is so frequently referred to in the popular stories.[6] Usually

1. *Mauu.* VIII. 41,
जातिजानपदान्धर्मान्श्रेणिधर्मांश्च धर्मवित् ।
समीक्ष्य कुलधर्मांश्च स्व धर्मं प्रतिपादयेत् ॥
2. For guild disputes see Bose, A.N., *Rural and Social Economy of Northern India*, Vol. II. p. 242; *JRAS*. 1901; *I.H.Q*. 1944, p. 175.
3. *Jā*. IV. 43.
4. *B. I.* p. 60.
5. *Manu*. IX. 11.
6. *Jā*. Nos. 39. 40, 73, 482, etc.

floors of houses, forests, or river-banks were preferred for this purpose. But there was no safety, for house-floors could be dug out ; flood washed the treasure away, if buried at the river-banks; and if deposited at the forest, somebody would trace and remove the hoard. King Dhananada's immence wealth was washed away by flood, and the same happened to Anāthapiṇḍika's hoard of coins.[1] But at a time when there was always fear of being robbed by armed robbers, there was no other safe way, but to hide the money underneath the earth. Muslim travellers have referred to this practice, and several finds of hoarded treasures of ancient coins testify to the prevalence of this method of saving money. Till recently Indian villagers regarded it to be a safe way of keeping money. But on account of paper currency and the extension of banking facilities to the rural areas it has now gone out of vogue.

Money-saving would not have been only by means of hoarding underground, but also through lending to banking corporations, if in existence. The Seṭṭhis were private bankers who used to lend money on interest, as did Anāthapiṇḍika.[2] In the capitals like Rājagṛiha, Vaśiālī and others there may have been such Seṭṭhis who would be accepting money from others on interest and investing it in trade, and also lending on interest for the same to smaller tradesmen.

In addition to the Seṭṭhis as private bankers, probably guilds also carried on banking business. Some scholars think that they never existed as such, but such an extreme view is untenable. When Kauṭilya speaks of Upanidhi (deposits) of the guilds,[3] or when he says, "King's spies disguised as

1. *Jā.* I 227,
अट्ठारसकोटियो नदीतीरे निदहित्वा ठपिता वतोदकेन नदीकूले भिन्ने महासमुद्दं पविट्ठा ।

2. *Ibid.*
बहू वोहारोपजीविनोपि'स्स हत्थतो पण्णे ओरोपेत्वा अट्ठारसकोटियसंखं धनं इणं गण्हिंसु ।

3. *Kau.* IV. 1, 'Those who can be expected to relieve misery, who can give instructions to artisans, who can be trusted with deposits, who can plan artistic work after their own design, and who can be relied upon by guilds of artisans, may receive the deposits of the guilds. The guilds (Śrenī) shall receive their deposits back in time of distress.'

merchants may borrow from corporations bar gold and coin gold for various kinds of merchandise to be procured from abroad"[1], he shows that guilds functioned as banks. That Takshaśilā merchant guilds minted coins is almost certain in the light of the Negama coins. In cities like Rājagṛiha, Śrāvastī, Vaisālī and others, where brisk trade and business were being carried, the guilds of Śreshṭhins may have been functioning as banking institutions.[2] At a stage when commercial life was considerably advanced, it is not improbable that banking may have been taken up by guilds.

Localisation of Industries and Partnership

Localisation is an important factor for the progress of industries. It gives impetus to specialisation and efficiency of labour. During the period under discussion industries made remarkable progress, and the main feature of the economic life was the development of various cottage industries, which were localised. It is evident from the fact that villages inhabited almost exclusively by one type of craftsmen had come into existence—there are references to villages of Smiths, potters, carpenters, saltmakers, etc.[3] which were generally in the vicinity of towns, probably forming their suburbs, as already referred to elsewhere.

When the *Mahā-Ummaga Jātaka* describes Mithilā as composed in part of four suburbs extending beyond each of its gates called Nigamas[4], the workshops in the streets of which were open to view, and when Kauṭilya laying down rules for the planning of a town allots separate quarters for different types of traders, artisans, and craftsmen[5], there

1. *Kau.* V. 2.
2. The Vaiśālī excavations have yielded seals of the Gupta period, which in the opinion of Block belonged to the corporations or guilds of bankers, traders, and merchants (*A.S.R.* 1902-3). Spooner thought that banking was as prominent in Vaiśālī as we should have expected it to be (*A.S.R.* 1913). Situation may have been similar during the earlier period; but there is no positive evidence to prove this.
3. *Suprā,* chap. X.
4. *Jā.* VI. 330.
5. *Kau.* II. 4.

remains no doubt that during the period under consideration, there were some industries which were localised in separate streets of towns and cities. The stories tell us of the separate streets of weavers[1], caterers[2], washermen[3], ivory-workers,[4] etc.

The practice of having partners in trade, either permanent[5] or for specified purposes,[6] seems to have been fairly common. This would have been much helpful for the smaller traders to transact large scale trade. It was specially of much use for the Satthavāhas and the seafares, whose life was generally unsafe. The *Jarupadāna Jātaka* refers to land traders (Satthavāhas) transacting trade under a Jeṭṭhaka.[7] Two traders of Sāvatthi became partners and went to the west with a large caravan.[8] Similar may have been the case with traders of Rājagṛiha, Vaiśāli, Pāṭaliputra and other centres of trade.

The existence of the phenomenon of partnership in trade and commerce indicates that co-operative undertakings were fairly common. Kauṭilya mentions thereon in connection with the agricultural and commercial activities undertakings, which probably applied to cultivators as well as merchants. The partners were to divide their earnings, either equally or in proportion to their investments, or as agreed upon among themselves.[9] The practice of co-operative

1. *Jā.* I 356; IV. 484, *tantavitaṭṭhānavīthi.*
2. *Jā.* III. 49, *odonikagharavīthi.*
3. *Jā.* IV. 81, *rajakavīthi.*
4. *Jā.* I. 320, *dantakāravīthi,*
5. *Jā* I. 404, II. 181; IV. 350.
6. *D.N.* II. 342; *Jā* I. 111.
7. *Jā.* II. 294.
8. *Jā.* II. 181,

   सावत्थिवासिनो हि कूटवाणिजो च पण्डितवाणिजो च द्वे जना पत्तिका हुत्वा पञ्चसकटसतानि भण्डस्स पूरेत्वा पुब्बन्तरो अपरन्तं विचरमाना बोहारं कत्वा बहुलाभं लभित्वा सावत्थिं पच्चागमिंसु ।
9. *Kau.* III. 14,

   सङ्घभृतास्सम्भूयसमुत्थातारो वा यथा सम्भाषितं वेतनं समं वो विभजेरन् ।

undertakings continued to be an important aspect in the field of trade in the later period, and it is referred to by Nārada, who lays down rules for the qualifications of the partners and the principle for sharing loss, expenses, and profits.[1]

1. *Nārada*. III. 1. 3-4, 'People should carry on business jointly with persons of noble parentage, who are active, clever, intelligent, familiar with coins, skilled in revenue and expenditure, honest and enterprising. The loss, expenses and profits of each partner are proportionate to the amount contributed by him.'

CHAPTER XIV

CURRENCY, PRICES, FEES, SALARIES, AND WAGES

Gold, Silver and Copper Coins

The Buddhist and the Brahmanical literary sources as well as the archaeological evidence throw considerable light on the coinage of this period. The literary sources reveal that coins of various denominations were struck in gold, silver, and copper; sometimes they were minted in lead (Sīsa) also.

So far as the gold currency is concerned, as yet no specimens belonging to our age have been found and we have to rely only on the literary sources. They refer to Nishka,[1] Suvarṇa[2] and Śatamāna[3] as the main denominations of the gold currency. References to transactions in the gold currency suggest that it was beconming more and more common during this period. The *Vinya-Piṭaka* refers to the incident of Jetavana being covered with gold coins,[4] of which we find also sculptural representation. This description may be taken as legendary. But Pāṇini tells us that objects bought for one, two or three Nishkas were to be known as Naishkikam, Dvinaishkikam and Trinaishkikam respectively.[5] Persons owning wealth worth a hundred or a thousand Nishkas were to be known as Naishkaśatika and Naishkasāhasrika respectively (*Sūtra*, V.2). Nishka, weighing 320 *rattis* was too big a gold coin for daily use and its submultiples, quarter Nishkas and Māshakas or 1/16 Nishkas, were also issued. In the *Udaya Jātaka* there is mention of the gold Māshakas.[6] Bhandarkar thinks that these

1. *Jā.* I. 3757-6; IV. 460; *Pāṇini*, V. 1. 30, V. 2.119.
2. *Jā.* VI. 69, 186, 462, 463.
3. *Pāṇini*, V. 1. 27.
4. *C.V.* 4. 7.
5. *Pāṇini*, V. 1. 30. *dvitrip ūrvānnishkāt*.
6. *Jā.* IV. 106-8.

सुवण्णमासक पुरां एकां सुवण्णपाति ।

were small medallic pieces of gold.[1] The *Sūtras* of Pāṇini (VI. 2.55) make it clear that the term Suvarṇa was applied to gold coins. In one of the *Sūtras* Pāṇini refers to pieces of gold equal to the standard weight.[2] We also come across the expression Hiraññā-Suvaṇṇa.[3] Hiraññā seems to have been applied to uncoined bullion in gold. The term Śatamāna is referred to only by Pāṇini and Kātyāyana. Pāṇini shows that it was used as a medium of exchange, as he tells us that Śātamāna denoted an object bought for a Śatamāna.[4] Kātayāyana speaks of the *dakshiṇā* of golden Śatamāna.[5] As suggested by the name, the Śatamāna corresponded to the weight standard of 100 *rattis*=175 grains.

The silver coins of the age were the Śatamānas and the Kārshāpaṇas (of 16 Māshas=58.56 grains, which was 2/5th of the weight of Suvarṇa, i.e. the gold coin). Śatamāna as the silver currency has been referred to by Kātyāyana, which shows that by the time of the *Śrauta-Sūtras* (*c.* 600 B.C.) silver Śatamāna had come into use. The bent bar coins are regarded as the specimens of this standard. The Paila hoard coins, which adhere to the weight standard of 24 *rattis*, seem to have been Pāda-Śatamānas. Our sources reveal that the standard currency of this period was the Kārshāpaṇa. It is accepted by almost all the scholars that coins known as Kārshāpaṇas were current during the lifetime and before the birth of the Buddha, and that they were closely associated with the economic life of the masses. But there is a good deal of disagreement among scholars in accepting Kārshāpaṇa as a silver currency of the period under review.

1. Bhandarkar, *C.L.* 1921.
2. *Pā.* IV. 3, 153.
   जातरूपेभ्यः परिमाणे ।
3. *Jā.* VI. 69, 462, 493.
4. *Pāṇini,* V, 1. 27.
   शतमानेन क्रीतं शातमानम् ।
5. *Kātyāyana-Śrauta-Sūtra,* XVI.
   शतमानं दक्षिणा सौवर्णम् ।

The view that Kārshāpaṇa was not a silver coin does not seem to be tenable. Kārshāpaṇa was so called because theoretically in weight it corresponded to one Karsha,[1] and this name was not restricted to coins of any metal; that there were Kārshāpaṇas of gold, silver, and copper is revealed by the Buddhist and the Brahmanical sources. The *Jātaka-Nidānakathā* speaks also of the lead Kahāpaṇa (Kārshāpaṇa).[2] Amarasiṁha, the lexicographer also makes mention of silver Kārshāpaṇa, which according to the commentator Kshīras-vāmin was of the weight standard of one Karsha=80 *rattis*.[3] Prices referred to in the Buddhist literature suggest that Kārshā paṇa was a silver currency. That the price of a pair of oxen was 24 Kāhāpaṇas and a horse cost 1000 Kāhāpaṇas seem to suggest that the Karshāpaṇa in which the prices are stated was a silver coin. Prices were very cheap in our age, yet we can hardly imagine that the bull could have cost only 12 copper pieces. Bhandarkar has therefore observed that prices mentioned in the *Jātakas* must have been silver coins, as copper or gold would be too low or too high price for animals.[4] The charge of Ambapālī as 50 Kahāpaṇas per night would appear to be correct in the case of the silver currency; copper would be too low for a courtesan of her status. *Arthaśāstra* of Kauṭilya speaks of the minting of the silver coins called Paṇa, Arddha-Paṇa, Pāda-Paṇa, and Ashṭabhāga-Paṇa, and of copper coins called Māsha, Arddha-Māsha, Pāda-Māsha (Kākaṇi) and Ashṭabhāga-Māsha (Ardha-Kākaṇi).[5] Kane's view that Paṇa of Kauṭilya was a copper currency does not appear to be convincing[6]. His main arguments are that (1) Manu, Yājñavalkya, and Śukra refer to copper pieces as coins bearing stamps; (2) Manu states that a labourer was to be paid a Paṇa for a day; (3) Kauṭilya's *Arthaśāstra* mentions high figures as the salary of officials, which would not have been possible, had the currency been other than the copper one (4) Nārada

1. Bhandarkar, *C.L.* 1921, pp. 83, 86.
2. *Ibid.*, p. 142.
3. *J.N.S.I. VXIV*, p. 131.
4. Bhandarkar, *C.L.* 1921, p, 78.
5. *Kau.* II. 12.
6. Kane, P.V., *History of Dharmaśāstra*, Vol. III, pp. 120 f.

states that silver Kārshāpaṇa was current in the South. As regards the first and the second arguments it may be pointed out that silver and copper currencies were independent of each other and existed side by side, and it has already been seen that Kārshāpaṇa was applied to coins of all the metals in ancient India. Kane gives much stress on the statement of Nārada that silver Kārshāpaṇas were current in the South. But Nārada may be referring to his own time, and one doubts whether his statement is true even of the 5th or 6th century A.D. Silver coins were not then current in South India. Kane maintains that fees and salaries referred to in the *Arthaśāstra* are too high, if Paṇa is accepted as a silver coin, e.g., a Mantrin was paid 48,000 pieces of coins (Paṇas) per annum. But Kauṭilya also states that agricultural labourer was to be paid only $1\frac{1}{4}$ Paṇas per month supplemented by food.[1] Here Kauṭilya apparently speaks of the silver Paṇa (Kārshāpaṇa). The *Jātakas* speak of one or one and a half Māsakas as the earning of a menial labourer,[2] which is very near to the above account of the *Arthaśāstra*, according to which 2/3 Māshaka was the daily wage of a labourer. When the *Arthaśāstra* states that 48,000 Paṇas constituted the salary of a Mantrin, it seems to suggest a copper currency; but when it tells us that the labourer got $1\frac{1}{4}$ Paṇas as monthly wage, it speaks of the silver coin. And it is difficult to come to a conclusion. Probably both silver and copper Kārshāpaṇas were current.

Large finds of silver punch-marked coins of the pre-Mauryan and the Mauryan periods would support the literary evidence that silver currency was in vogue during our period. It should be accepted that the Kahāpaṇas of the Buddhist sources, Kārshāpaṇas of the Brahmanical evidence, Paṇas of Pāṇini and *Arthaśāstra* are the silver punch-marked coins, which conform to the 32 *rattis* standard.

Silver punch-marked coins have been found in large numbers throughout India and Afghanistan. Several

1. *Kau.* II. 24.
2. *Jā.* III. 325-6.

hoards of these coins such as the Golakhpur,[1] Patraha,[2] Machhuatoli,[3] Ramna,[4] Gorhoghat,[5] Paila[6], Bhirmound[7] and others have been studied and published by different scholars. The study of the various hoards shows that the punch-marked coins fall into two distinct categories of the pre-Mauryan and Mauryan, and that the circulation of these silver pieces during our period cannot be doubted. The Golakhpur hoard of 108 coins and the Ramna hoard of 48 coins have been assigned to the pre-Mauryan age by Walsh on convincing grounds. 709 out of 2873 coins of the Patraha hoard[7] and one third of the Machhuatoli hoard fall under the category of the pre-Mauryan currency.[8]

The classification of pre-Mauryan and Mauryan coins is largely on the basis of fabric and the grouping of symbols. It is generally accepted that the thin, broad and large-sized coins belong to the pre-Mauryan period; whereas the small, thick, and finely executed ones belong to the Mauryan age. There is thus a marked difference in the manufacture of pre-Mauryan and Mauryan coins.

The later class of coins are more numerous and found all over India, which suggests their being issued by the imperial Mauryas. The crescented hill is regarded as the Rājāṅka of Chandragupta Maurya, and its association with the Mauryan monuments has been well established.[9] Moreover, hoards show that a good number of the coins regarded as pre-Mauryan are restamped with the Mauryan monagram (crescented hill) on the reverse, which is an additional proof of the existence of a pre-Mauryn currency. Silver punch-

1. *J.B.O.R.S.* 1919. pp. 16-72.
2. *Memoir* No. 62 of the *A.S.I.* 1940.
3. *J.B.O.R.S.* 1939, pp. 91-117.
4. *Ibid.*
5. *Ibid* 1919, pp. 463-94.
6. *J.N.S.I.* II; *N. S.* No. XLVII of *J.A.S.B.*
7. Walsh, *Memoir No.* 59 *of the A.S.I.*
8. The above No. is according to Walsh's classification. *J.N.S.I.*, IV, pp. 81-132. According to P. L. Gupta there are only 341 coins of the pre-Mauryan type in the Patraha hoard. *J.N.S.I.*, XII, p. 147.
9. *J.A.S.B.* 1337, *N.S.* No. XLVII,

marked coins had a long circulation, and that is why they were known also as Purāṇas. Restamping during the Mauryan age testifies to their long circulation. Under these circumstances the pre-Mauryan and Mauryan classification of the silver punch-marked coins should not be doubted.

By the 7th century B.C. the kingdoms of Magadha, Kośala and others had started minting coins.[1] Bhandarkar comes to the conclusion that the large finds of punch-marked coins represent coinages of three different regions of India with their headquarters at Takshaśilā, Pāṭaliputra, and Vidiśā.[2] The coins of the Paila hoard are regarded as the indigenous coins of Kośala before its inclusion in the Magadhan empire.[3] These coins follow a different weight standard, viz. of 24 *rattis* .

It is suggested both from the literary as well as the archaeological evidence that Magadha had her own coinage during this period. It is difficult to say as to who was the first Magadhan ruler who started minting coins. According to the *Mahābbārata* the kings of the Bṛihadratha dynasty were having bull as the standard.[4] Bull is one of the pre-Mauryan symbols, and the coins having this symbol may have been issued by the later rulers of the Bṛihadratha dynasty in c. the 8th century B.C. This would show that coinage in Magadha had a hoary antiquity. The coinage of Magadha during the time of Buddha and Bimbisāra was of the standard of 20 Māshakas, according to the *Sāmantapāsādikā* of Buddhaghosha on *Vinaya-Piṭaka*,[5] and according to a *Jātaka* story the four Māsaka piece was of lower value than a Pāda.[6] This gets support from Pāṇini and

1. Durga Prasad, *J. A. S. B.* 1937, *N.S.* No. XLVII.
2. Bhandarkar, *C.L.* 1921, p. 99.
3. Mr. Walsh and Durga Prasad, who studied the Paila hoard, agreed in maintaining that the coins were indigenous issue of Kośala before her absorption in Magadha (Ref. *J.N.S.I.* II, p. 29; *N.S.* XLII of *J.A.S.B*)
4. *J. B.O.R.S.* 1919, p. 36.
5. Bhandarkar, *A.I.N.*, p. 111; Agrawala, *India as known to Pāṇini*, p. 269,

तदा राजगहे बीसतिमासको कहापणो होति, तस्मा पञ्चमासको पादो ।

6. *Jā.* III. 448; *A.I.N.*, p. 112.

Kātyāyana, who speak of the silver coin of 20 Māshakas; the former calls it Viṅśatika.[1] Fortunately there are actual specimens of the silver Viṅśatika which were found at Rājagṛiha and are at present in the Lucknow Museum.[2] We may accept the view of V.S. Agrawala that the Viṅśatika was related to the weight standard of 40 *rattis* in silver.[3]

Pāṇini (V.1. 24) refers to another silver coin named Triṅśatka, which is not referred to by other authorities. Specimens of silver punch-marked coins of the weight of 58 *rattis* were found from Bihar by Durga Prasad.[4] This should be identified with Triṅśatka. The loss of two *rattis* may be explained as being lost due to circulation.

Indigenous coinage of Magadha must have undergone considerable change after her attaining an imperial status. Under the prosperous reigns of the Haryaṅkas and the Nandas coins must have been issued on a large scale. It is not unlikely that they may have introduced a uniform system of coinage throughout their domain. We may accept the suggestion of V.S. Agrawala that the Nandas standardised Magadhan coinage according to the traditional standard of 16 Māshakas.[5] The Sanskṛit grammar has retained the illustration Nandopakramaṇi mānāni, i.e. the task of standardising weights was first accomplished by a Nanda king. In view of the extensive territories of the Nandas and their possession of immense wealth, and considering the weight standard of the coins which were in circulation immediately before the Mauryas, the view that the Nandas introduced a uniform currency would appear to be quite correct. A new standard was introduced by the Nandas and it was of the 32 *rattis*.[6] It appears that during the days of the Nandas the old coin Viṅśatika as well as the new Kārshāpaṇa of 32 *rattis* were in circulation.

1. *Pāṇini*, V. 1.24; V. 1. 32; V. 1.27.
   शतमान-विंशतिक-सहस्र-बसनाद् अण ।
2. Agarwala, *India as known to Pāṇini*, p. 270.
3. *Ibid.* p. 271.
4. *J.U.P.H.S.*, July, 1939, p. 33.
5. Agrawala, *India as known to Pāṇini*, p. 271.
6. Presidential address to the Numismatic society of India, 1950, *J.N.S.I.*, XII, p. 197.

The Buddhist as well as the Brahmanical sources refer to several divisions of the silver Kārshāpṇas, and we are enabled to know of the Kārshāpaṇa, Arddha-Kārshāpaṇa, Pāda-Kārshāpaṇa (four Māshakas), Tri-Māshaka, Dvi-Māshaka, Māshaka, Arddha-Māshaka, Kākaṇi and Arddha-Kākaṇi.[1] In the light of the specimens of silver punch-marked coins found so far, all these subdivisions seem to have been minted, except the Kākaṇi, which seems to have been a copper token coin. Till a few years ago, it was doubted if the half Māshaka, a tiny silver piece of one *rattis* (1.8 grains) only, could have been minted. Agrawala expressed his opinion that the Addha-Māshaka of silver would be too minute to be handled, and hence it did not exist.[2] But later he had the opportunity of examining some of the half Māshaka pieces.[3] In the catalogue of Allan four specimens of the silver Māshakas are described.[4] Walsh has made mention of 79 minute coins, weighing 2.3 to 2.86 grains. These are decidedly silver Māshakas. The theoretical weight of the Māshaka is two *rattis*=3 to 3.5 grains.[5] V.S. Agrawala found a hoard of 100 pieces containing Māshakas and half Māshakas.[6] These tiny coins bear symbols only on the obverse.

The punch-marked coins bear punched symbols on them. Pāṇini speaks of Rūpa which is significant of the punching of coins.[7] This is made clear by Kauṭilya, who makes

1. *Vinaya*, 294, II. 15-16; *C.V.* XII. 1.1. III. 49; *A.N.* V. 83; *Jā.* I; 340 III. 448; *Pāṇini*, V. 1. 34; *Kau.* II. 12; *Bhāshya*. I. 3. 72. I. 239; *Manu.* VIII. 404.
2. *India as known to Pāṇini*, p. 268.
3. *Ibid.* & Presidential address to the Numismatic Society of India, 1950, *J.N.S.I.* XII, p. 196.
4. Allan, *Catalogue of Indian Coins*, Ancient India, pp. 286-87.
5. *A.I.N.* p. 52.
6. Presidential address to the Numismatic Society of India, 1950, *J.N.S.I.* XII, p. 196.
7. *Pāṇini*, V. 2. 120.

mention of the royal officer Rūpadarśaka,[1] whose duty was to supervise the minting and punching of coins, and to see if the punches were made properly. Patañjali refers to the officer Rūpatarka,[2] whose duty seems to be the same.

The varieties of symbols on the punch-marked coins and the arrangement in which they appear, have been dwealt upon at length by several scholars.[3] They have made efforts to trace the origin of the symbols in the remains of the Harappā culture, in the Buddhist antiquities, in ancient literature and so on.

The study of the pre-Mauryan punch-marked coins reveals that generally they bear five distinct symbols on the obverse. Out of these five symbols a variety of the Shaḍarachakra, the six-armed symbol and the sun are universal. The 3rd, 4th, and the 5th symbols, however, change, thus giving rise to different groups of five symbols in a series. Generally groups of four symbols are formed and only the 5th is changed. Sometimes we get only four symbols instead of five. At times the number of the obverse symbols is 6 to 7. The total number of symbols is high, and more than 200 of them have been identified by several scholars. We get several varieties of the same symbol; thus in the Takshaśilā hoard alone 40 varieties of the Shaḍarachakra have been identified.[4] On account of the varieties of symbols several classes and types of the coins are formed; for instance, the Golakhpur hoard forms 34 groups of five symbols.[5]

Some of the coins are of blank reverse, whereas others bear small symbols which vary from one to nine. Reverse symbols are smaller than the obverse ones. They are usually regarded as the marks of the checking authority,

1. *Kau.* II. 12.
2. *Vārttika* to Pāṇini's Sūtra, I. 4. 52.
3. On symbols references may be made to *J.R.A.S.* 1924, Cunnigham, *Coins of A. I*; *A. S. R.* 1905-6 (Spooner's article), Thomas, *Numismatica Orientalia*, pt. 1; Bhandarkar, *A. I. N.*; Walsh, Memoirs of *A.S.R.* No. 59; Durga Prasad, *J.A.S.B.* 1937, *N.S.* 30; Allan's *Catalogue of coins*, *A.I.*, Kosambi, D.D., *J. B.O.R.S.* 1934 and so on.
4. *J. N. S. I.* XI, p. 114.
5. Durga Prasad, *J.A.S.B.*, 1934, Vol. XXX, *N.S.* No. XLV. The BhirMound hoard forms 120 varieties (*J. N. S. I.* XII, p. 136).

be it the bankers or the state. It was believed formerly that the earlier coins were those which had few reverse marks. But it is rightly suggested by Durga Prasad that the numbers of the reverse marks of the punch-marked coins are the determining factor of their circulation period—more reverse marks means longer circulation. This is shown by the fact that the coins of the thinner and broader fabric, having several reverse marks, are in worn out condition.

Certain classes of the punch-marked coins of the early fabric are found practically in the same percentage in Patraha, Rairh and Takshaśilā hoards.[1] This would show that findspots, even widely apart, contain punch-marked coins of the same class among the pre-Mauryan type of coinage. These coins seem to be a common issue by a central authority and probably were minted by the Nandas. 'M' class of the Takshiśilā hoard is found practically in the same percentage at Takshaśilā and Patraha, but in a higher percentage at Rairh. The percentage at Takshaśilā and Patraha is 4.1% and 3.8% respectively, but 26% at Rairh. Most probably coins minted in Magadha under the Nandas migrated to Takshaśilā and Rairh due to army movements in early Mauryan period. Some of the coins seem to have been taken to these places by Chandragupta and Kauṭilya, who may have taken a large collection of these coins to pay the army fighting with the Greeks.

Very few specimens of copper punch-marked coins are available, and it appears that they were not issued on a large scale as was the case with silver currency. A hoard of copper punch-marked coins was found at Madhepur in the Bhagalpur district ;[2] out of which 54 speciments were acquired by the

1. Walsh, *J. N. S. I.*, IV.; *J.B.O.R.S.* 1939; P. L. Gupta, *J.N.S.I.* XII, pp. 147-48.
P. L. Gupta has given the following table of the percentage of these classes of coins :

	Class M.	*Class A.*	*Class C.*	*Class D.*
Takshaśilā hoard	54%4·1	482 45·6%	102 9.8%	147 10.4%
Patraha hoard	13 3·8%	113 33·13%	32 9·4%	33 9·7%
Rairh hoard	63 26.0%	82 35·66%	19 8.3%	21 9·1%

2. *A.S.R.* 1625-26, p. 154; Allan, *Catalogue of coins, Ancient, India*, pp. LXXVIII-LXXIX.

Indian Museum, Calcutta. Their weight varies from 163.9 to 286.7 grains. There are some specimens in the British Museum also, which are regarded by Allan as belonging to Magadha of the Mauryan period. The symbols on the copper pieces are similar to those on the silver punch-marked issues ; the fitst, second and third symbols are Sun, Shaḍarachakra and hill. The copper Kārshāpaṇa weighed 144 grains according to the calculation of Cunnigham. According to the *Amarakosha* (*Vaiśyavarga*, 85-86) 5 *guñjas*=1 *ādyamāsha* and 16 *ādyamāshas*= 1 *Karsha*, which would be equal to one *tolā*.

So far as the problem of the copper cast coins is concerned, they are found commonly in excavations, and their association with the pre-Mauryan stratum has been established by the excavations at Kauśāmbī.[1] As they are found over wide areas, it is not unlikely that a few types may have been issued by the Nandas and copied by the Mauryas. Excavations at Kumrahar and Bulandibagh show that the copper cast coins were current from the Mauryan to the Kushāṇa period, and it appears that they were the currency of the common man ; stray silver pieces are found, showing thereby that they were preserved carefully. Symbols found on the cast coins such as the hollow cross, taurine, tree in railing and its branch are common to Mauryan punch-marked coins ; but it is not unlikely that these types may have been inherited from the earlier ruling dynasties.

Copper cast coins are available in square, rectangular and round shapes. The common types of the square and rectangular ones bear groups of four symbols on each sides. On one side, generally occur the elephant, swastika, banner, taurine, and hollow cross. On most of the coins elephant and banner are constant ; the third and the fourth symbols are changing. On some coins elephant, banner and taurine are constant, and the fourth symbol changes. On the other side we get four groups of symbols such as the crescented hill, taurine, hollow cross, tree in railing and banner.

The round shaped coins show elephant on one side and the crescented hill on the other.

1. Sharma, G.R., *The Excavations at Kauśāmbī*, 1957-59, p. 81.

Prices

The *Jātakas* very often refer to the prices of various things. As the stories refer to the day-to-day happenings of people, it is quite reasonable to expect from them correct information as regards prices of articles that were available in the market of our period. But as stories generally exaggerate things and obscure the truth, we find that in most of the cases prices given are fantastic and fabulous.[1] In some of the cases it is with a view to glorifying the Bodhisattva that highly exaggerated figures are mentioned. And, there are only a few references which may be taken as mentioning the actual market-prices of certain objects. Thus, it appears that articles of food were probably cheap. According to the *Vinaya* texts a small quantity of ghee or oil could be bought for a Kahāpaṇa only.[2] Meat for a chameleon could be bought for a Kākaṇi or an Addha-Māsaka,[3] and a fish cost only seven Māsakas.[4] A jar of liquor was available for one Māsaka.[5] It is further said that a Māsaka was sufficient for an ordinary wage-earner to buy a garlaṇd, perfume and some strong drink.[6] Animals of inferior quality

1. The *Jātakas* tell us that a golden dish (*Jā.* II. 319), a dinner-dish of a royal horse (*Jā.* I· 178), a robe made out of Kāśī muslin (*Jā* III. 11; VI. 403, 450), and an ornament for a lady (*Jā.* III. 435; golden necklace—*Jā.* VI. 480) cost each 1,00,000 Kahāpaṇas; a golden necklace (*Jā.* II. 373), a robe for a court-lady (*Jā.* II. 24) and a Śivi robe (*Jā.* IV. 401) each ost 1,000 Kahāpaṇas; a pair of shoes were worth 100 to 1,000 Kahāpaṇas (*Jā.* IV. 15); the price of a thorough-bred horse was 6,000 Kahāpaṇas (*Jā.* II. 289) and that a team of chariot horses (*Jā* VI. 404) was 90,000 Kahāpaṇas, the cost of a jewelled housing of an elephant was 22,00,000 Kahāpaṇas (*Ja.* VI. 488); ornaments were worth 1,000 to 1,00,000 Kahāpanas (*Jā.* II 373; III. 435; VI 480); sandalwood perfume cost 1,00,000 Kahāpaṇas (*Jā.* I. 340; II. 373) and so on do not reflect the actual market prices. They are fanciful and unbelievable.
2. *Vinaya*. IV. 248-50
3. *Jā.* VI. 346.
4. *Jā.* II. 424,
   सो तेसं सत्तमासके दत्वा मच्छं भरियाय पेसेसि ।
5. *Jā.* I. 350,
   मासकमत्तं दत्वा अन्तरापणतो सुरादारकं आहारापेत्वा....।
6. *Jā.* III. 446,
   तवाड्ढमासको ममाड्ढमासको ति मासको होति, ततो एकेन कोट्ठासेन मालं एकेन कोट्ठासेन गन्धं एकेन सुरं गहेत्वा कीलिस्साम ।

are described as cheap ; while those of superior quality are mentioned to be dear. A thoroughbred horse probably cost 1,000 Kahāpaṇas.[1] A donkey cost only eight Kahāpaṇas.[2] A pair of oxen could be bought for 24 Kahapāṇas.[3] A nice plump dog could be had for one Kahapāṇa and a cloak.[4] A dead mouse was worth only one Kākaṇi.[5] We do not get detailed information as regards the price of land. According to a reference in the *Majjhima-Nikāya* a monastic cell (Vihāra) would be worth 500 Kahāpaṇas.[6] In a *Jātaka* story a play-hall for 600 boys worked by voluntary labour is estimated to have been worth 1,000 Kahāpaṇas.[7]

There are references to show that prices were determined by haggling.[8] Mrs. Rhys Davids has rightly observed that the act of exchange between producer or dealer and consumer was both before and during the Jātaka age a free bargain, a transaction unregulated by any system of statute-fixed prices.[9] This state of affair was unwelcome to some merchants. They wished that commodities should be sold in the market on fixed prices. A caravan-leader observed that haggling over prices was killing time, and he preferred to sell his wares at the prices already fixed.[10]

There was the absence of such stable agency which would fix prices and enforce the traders to sell at that rate. In the Buddhist literature we come across an official of the state known as the court-valuer (Agghakāraka, Agghāpanaka, Agghāpanika)[11], whose duty was to fix prices of the articles bought

1. *Jā.* II. 306.
2. *Jā.* VI. 343.
3. *Jā.* II, 305.
4. *Jā.* II, 247.
5. *Jā*, I. 120.
6. *M.N.* (No. 52) I. 353.
7. *Jā.* VI. 332.
8. *Jā.* I. 111-13, 195; II, 289, 424-25; III, 126-27; VI. 113.
9. *J.R.A.S.* 1901, p. 874.
10. *Jā.* I. 99,
अग्घट्ठपनं नाम मनुस्सानं जीविता बोरोपन सदिसं, अहं पच्छतो गन्त्वा एतेहि ठपितग्घेन' एव भण्डं विक्किणिस्सामीति ।
11. *Jā.* I. 124,

for the royal household, but not for the whole society. He is also mentioned as the Atthadhammānusāsaka-Amachcha.[1] It was only the king who could alter the prices already fixed by this official.[2] But there was every possibility of the wrong estimation of prices by him ; because he could be bribed by the producers, who would like to sell their goods at a high price. At the same time he would have liked to fix a low price to please the king. But on such possibilities it would not be justified to conclude that the court-valuer did not always fix reasonable prices of commodities. In ancient days religious sentiments and conceptions of morality controlled human activities to a great extent, and the court-valuer would have been directed by them, while fixing prices. It would have been a great achievement of the state, had it been able to institute the system of the valuation of prices for the whole community. It was the Mauryan state which appears to have made remarkable achievement in fixing market-prices. During the Mauryan period the Price-Expert was responsible for the regulation of market-prices.[3] According to Śtrabo, prices were regulated by municipal bodies.[4] Manu prescribes that the king himself should settle prices every 5th or 14th day in consultation with the merchants, keeping in view the expenses of production.[5] The *Arthaśāstra* tells us that the dealers were allowed to derive a profit of five per cent above the fixed prices of local produce and of 10 percent on foreign goods.[6] It was a crime to raise the prices or to realise more profit. Raising of prices or realising profit, even to the extent

तदा अम्हाकं बोधिसत्तो तस्स अग्घकारको अहोसि, हत्थिअस्सादीनि च' एव मणिसुवण्णादीनि च अग्घापेति, अग्घापेत्वा भण्डसामिकानं भण्डानुरुपम् एव मूलं दापेसि।

Comy. on Theragāthā, 20, 393; *Jā*. 125; V. 270.

1. *Jā*. II. 30-31.
2. *Ibid.*
3. *Kau*, IV. 2.
4. *Str*. XV. 1.50.
5. *Manu*. VIII. 401-2
6. *Kau*. IV. 2,

अनुज्ञातक्रयादुपरि चैषां स्वदेशीयानां पण्यानां पञ्चकं शतमाजीवं स्थापयत् परदेशीयानां दशकम्।

of ½ Paṇa above the permitted one, was liable to a fine of five Paṇas in the former case, and of 100 to 200 Paṇas in the latter[1].

These rules were there, but how far did the state actually control the market ? We have also seen that during our period there was no agency of price-control, and that it was during the Mauryan age and later that such an agency came into existence. We have also seen that there were punishments prescribed for the law-breakers who raised prices. But Kauṭilya himself admits that the trading community was able to raise, or to lower the market-prices, and that they could derive cosiderable profit, even to the extent of hundred percent.[2] The Mauryan state, conscious of the evil of such tactics of the business community, had prescribed punishment for the unscrupulous merchants. Merchants conspiring, either for preventing the sale of goods, or for selling or purchasing merchandise at higher prices, were liable to a fine of 100 Paṇas[3]. Even later lawgivers like Yājñavalkya and Nārada prescribe punishments for such antisocial activities of creating disorder in the market[4].

But probably sanctions of the law-books did never succeed in controlling market-prices. It has been shown above that even during the Mauryan age prices could be lowered or raised high by the business community. The state itself owned a number of big industries, and in course of time fell in line with the merchants in pursuing business methods and tactics. The *Arthaśāstra* prescribes that when certain commodities become very widely circulated in the market, the state should increase

1. *Ibid*,
ततः परमर्धं वर्धयतां क्रये विक्रये वा भावयतां पणशतं पञ्चपणाद्विशतो दण्डः ।
2. *Kau.* III. 4,
वैदेहकास्तु संभूय पण्यानां उत्कर्षोपकर्षं कुर्वाणः पणे पणशतं कुम्भे कुम्भशतं इत्याजीवन्ति ।
3. *Kau.* IV. 2,
वैदेहकानां वा सम्भूय पण्यं अवरुद्धता अनर्घेण विक्रिणता क्रीणतां वा सहस्रं दण्डः
4. *Yājña.* II. 249; *Nārada*, V. 125.

the prices by taking suitable steps.[1] But to what extent did the state adopt such methods is not known.

Fees and Salaries

As regards fees and salaries also we find generally exaggerated statements,[2] as in the case of prices. However, a few references appear to be very near the reality. Thus the *Mahāvagga* tells us that a courtesan's fee for one night was 50 to 100 Kahāpaṇas.[3] According to the *Jātakas* she received 1,000 Kahāpaṇas every night.[4] The *Arthaśāstra* tells us that the salary of the chief courtesan was one thousand Kārshāpaṇas.[5] Though the popular stories give high figures as the fee of the courtesans, they should not be regarded as totally false ; because their charges may have varied according to the beauty possessed by them. Moreover, stories speak of those courtesans who could be approached only by the nobles and the Seṭṭhis. We do not know of the fees of the ordinary ones.

A teacher's honorarium for the whole course was probably 1,000 silver Kahāpaṇas.[6] In one of the *Jātakas* it is said to have been only seven gold Nishkas[7], which seems to be quite insufficient. But it is well known that a teacher in ancient India was not guided by monetary gains, nor could he demand a fee from his pupil. Looked from this point of view the above

1. *Kau.* IV. 2,
यच्च पण्यं प्रचुरं स्यात्तदेकीकृत्याधर्मारोपयेत् । प्राप्तेऽर्घे वाऽर्घान्तरं कारयेत् ।
2. E.G., a highly accomplished archer received 1,000 Kahāpaṇas daily (*Jā.* V. 128) ; the tracker of foot-steps was paid 1,000 Kahāpaṇas (*Jā.* III. 505) ; a forest convoy was paid 1000 Kahāpaṇas for safely leading a caravan through a forest region (*Jā.* II. 335; V. 22, 471); The *Vinaya* account (*M. V.* VIII. 1) representing Jīvaka as receiving 16,000 to 1,00,000 Kahāpaṇas for curing a disease is also fabulous and is stated by the story-teller only to glorify the most renowned physician of his time.
3. *M.V.* VIII. 1. 1-3.
4. *Jā.* III. 435, 475; IV. 248.
5. *Kau.* II. 27.
सहस्रेन गणिकां कारयेत् ।
6. *Jā.* II. 47, 278; IV. 38; V. 128.
7. *Jā.* IV. 224.

amount as an honorarium would not appear as an improbability. Honorariums amounting to a thousand current coins could be paid by well-to-do families. According to the *Majjhima-Nikāya* the Brāhmaṇas were given an allowance of 500 Kahāpaṇas (probably per annum).[1] The *Arthaśāstra* informs us about the salaries of royal officers of various grades which ranged from 60 to 48,000 Paṇas per annum.[2] The spies according to their qualities were paid salaries between 250 to 1,000 Paṇas. The messenger got 10 Paṇas per Yojana; but for each Yojana beyond 10 and below 100, he received 20 Paṇas. Probably similar may have been the earnings of various officers during the pre-Mauryan period also.

Wages

Our sources disclose that labourers fell into two distinct catagories of the day-labourers, working on the basis of daily wages, and of those who worked on the basis of monthly wages or were employed as servants. Both the Buddhist and the Brahmanical sources use the term Kammakāra or Karmakara in the sense of a labourer or wage-earner[3]; but the former sometimes uses the term Bhataka most probably for a wage-earner on monthly basis.[4] Probably Pāṇini uses the term Vaitanika in the same sense.[5] He makes a difference between the unskilled manual labourer (Karmakara)[6] and the artisans (Śilpins) also.[7]

A labourer earned only 1½ Māsaka daily according to a *Jātaka* story.[8] In the *Bhāshya* of Patañjali a day's wage is said to have been four Māshakas only.[9] According to Kauṭilya the

1. *M.N.* (94), II. 163.
2. *Kau.* V. 3.
3. *A.N.* III. 37-8; *Pāṇini*, III. 2. 22.
4. *Jā.* IV. 277. In the edicts of Aśoka also we get the term Bhataka in this sense.
5. *Pāṇini*, IV. 4. 12.
6. *Pāṇini*, III. 2. 22.
7. *Bhāshya*, III. 1.26. 14; II. 36.
8. *Jā.* III. 326,

अहं भतिया मासकमड्ढमासकं संवरित्वा किच्छेन मातरं पोसेमि।

9. *Bhāshya*, I. 3. 72; I. 293.

agricultural labourer was to be paid only $\frac{2}{3}$ Māshaka daily supplemented by food.[1] This is very near to the *Jātaka* account referred to above. Thus authorities seem referring to different sections of the society. Pāṇini and Patañjali probably refer to the wages prevalent in the cities where they lived. As gathered from the *Jātakas* and the *Arthaśāstra* of Kauṭilya an ordinory labourer seems to have been earning from 15 to 45 Māsakas, i.e. from about one to three Kahāpaṇas per month. If supplemented by food, the daily wage was $\frac{2}{3}$ Māsaka per day ; and probably in the absense of food supply, it would have been $1\frac{1}{2}$ Māsaka or so, i.e. about the double of the amount supplemented by food. Hence it appears that one earned two men's food by a day's labour and that a man's food cost about $\frac{2}{3}$ Māsaka. There are references to show that the earning of the labourer was not sufficient enough for ensuring him a happy life, and that he lived a wretched life.[2]

1. *Kau.* II. 24. The labourer was to be paid 1 Paṇa and a quarter per month supplemented by food.
2. E. G., *Jā* I. 475 tells us that three Brāhmaṇa girls working as hired labourers passed their days in difficulty. In another place we find a labourer supporting his mother with difficulty (*Jā.* III. 326). In one story we find that a wage-earning couple was able to spend only one Māsaka on a festival day (*Jā.* III. 446).

CHAPTER XV

THE CARAVANS

Cities such as Rājagṛiha, Pāṭaliputra, Vaiśālī, Champā, Śrāvastī, Vārāṇasī, Kauśāmbī, etc., which were centres of trade, must have been scenes of the visits of caravans and of local traders going with their caravans to distant places. Visits of caravans to Rājagṛiha from Śrāvastī has been already referred to. The *Vinaya* texts refer to caravan from Rājagṛiha starting to the west.[1] The Buddhist sources show that caravan life was an important aspect of the trading community of the period. The caravan-leaders were known as the Satthavāhas, who undertook all the long distant land trades. It was really creditable for them to traverse hundreds of miles, when neither the means of communication were good nor life was safe. There were no metalled roads, and the rough ones levelled by the wheels of the moving carts passed through dense forests, inhabited by wild beasts and haunted by highway robbers, who had made life quite insecure. The Satthavāhas had also to pass through deserts, where it was not easy to trace the route, and very often they were led away to the unknown wilderness. Journeys were long. Not to speak of days, but weeks and months passed, yet the caravans did not reach their destination.

The *Jātakas* infrom us that there were five major dangers that awaited the travellers. They were of robbers, wild beasts, draught, demons, and famine.[2] In ancient days the problem of the robbers was among the most acute ones which the caravan-leaders and travellers had to confront with. The robbers lived in bands of considerably large numbers; they were well armed and attacked the caravans and looted them.[3] It is said in one place that robbers armed with bows, clubs and other weapons attacked a caravan, when

1. *Sutta-Vibhaṅga, S. B. B.* XIII. 15.
2. *Jā.* I. 99.
2. *Jā.* I. 332-33.

all the members of it were in slumber.[1] Vigilence for the whole night was required to face such situations. At the forests, there were guards who guided and led caravans safely, for which they were generally paid substantial amount, which according to the popular stories was one thousand Kahāpaṇas.[2] In the forests there were poisonous leaves, flowers, and fruits, etc. and there was every possibility of traders losing their lives by eating them. The *Phala Jātaka* (No. 54) informs us that a party of traders perished completely due to eating unfamiliar poisonous fruits. In such cases the oxen, carts, and wares would be distributed among the people of the nearby villages, who reached there earliest.[3]

Passing through deserts was more dangerous. Water scarcity was the most acute problem. As the caravans carried jars filled with water in carts, there was every chance of dying when water exhausted. The *Jātakas* mention also demons, who troubled caravans passing through deserts. The *Apaṇṇaka-Jātaka* (No. 1) tealls us that demons made a Satthavāha to throw away his water jars, and finding his men exhausted on account of thirst, attacked at night and killed them all.[4] It is just possible that the method of bringing about the destruction of the caravan parties by destroying their water reservoirs was employed by robbers, who knew that it was easy to attack and loot a caravan, when its members had become weak due to thirst on account of the unavailability of water, and hence could not give any effective resistence to the attackers.

Due to the existence of such problems on the path, the Satthavāhas had to make ample and proper equipments for a safe journey. They equipped the party with sufficient provision to survive before starting. In the hot burning deserts there could be no hope of life without water. Days could be passed without food, but lack of water could ultimately result in the ruin of the whole party. The caravan people used to dig

1. *Ibid.*
2. *Jā.* 335, V. 22, 471.
3. *Jā.* I. 271.
4. *Jā.* I. 101.

wells even for bathing,[1] but it was a difficult task to find out the spot where water could be available easily by digging. Therefore, the caravan-leaders thought it to be the safest, wisest and the most sensible step to carry drinking water. Big jars filled with sweet drinking water were loaded on the carts.[2] They had also to carry with them firewood, oil, and rice, etc.[3] They also got themselves armed with weapons to face the robbers.[4]

At the time of starting for the destination, the Satthavāha had to see that he was not accompanied by other caravan-leader. It was unwise for the Satthavāhas to travel together. Caravans usually consisted of several waggons, sometimes numbering upto five hundred, and if even two Satthavāhas started together, it would have been a hard matter to get food, water, and other requirements for all men, nor would there be available ample grass for the oxen.[5] Therefore, some preferred to go earlier, while others liked to start after the first parity had gone, allowing a gap of about six weeks[6]. In both cases there were abvantages. The leader of the party which started earlier thought that by going before those who would follow him, he would derive the advantage of having a road not yet cut up; his oxen would have the pick of fresh grass; his men would get fresh herbs for curry; the water would be undisturbed; and he would fix his own price for

1. Water was procured by digging in the forest regions also (*Jā*. II, 294.295.
2. *Jā*. I. 101,
सो तत्थ उदकचाटियो पूरेत्वा बहुं उदकं आदय···।
3. *Jā*. I. 107,
दारुदकतेलतण्डुलादीनि सकटेहि आदाय·····।
4. *S.B.E.* XIII, p. 37; *Jā*. I. 103.
5. *Jā*. I. 98,
एकतो मग्गे गच्छन्ते मग्गे पि नप्पहेस्सति मनुस्सानं दारुदकादीनि पि बलिवद्दानं तिणानि पि दुल्लभानि भविस्सन्ति।
6. *Jā*. I. 101,
बोधिसत्तो पि खो बालसत्थवाहपुत्तस्स निक्खन्तदिवसतो मासद्धमासं वीतिनामेत्वा पञ्चहि सकटसतेहि नगरा निक्खम्म अनुपुब्बेन कन्तारमुखं पापुणि।

the barter of goods.[1] The caravan-leader who preferred to go after a gap of six weeks saw other advantages for his party. He thought that the first party would level the road where it was rough, and the grass grazed by the oxen of the caravan would have again grown afresh, sweet and young ; his men would also find the fresh growth of herbs for curry, where the old ones would have been picked ; where there was no water, the first party would dig wells and thus solve the water problem for the following party, which would easily get drinking water without any trouble. The party ahead would also fix the prices of the wares and the party following would sell at the fixed rate, without haggling over prices.[2]

These considerations were necessary for an easy journey and a favourable market. The clever merchant always gained by fixing a suitable time for his start, while the foolish one with his own cost facilitated the journey of the other.

After proper equipments were made the caravan started on the fixed day. It proceeded in a well organised and disciplined manner. The leader (Satthavāha) of the party rode in the front, in his carriage, with the attendants arround him, in order to escape the dust whenever the wind blew against it ; but when the wind blew from bebind, he rode in like fashion in the rear of the column.[3]

When the caravan reached at the entrance of a forest or a desert, the Satthavāha, by beating of drums assembled his men and gave them necessary instructions to be followed, so that no calamity might befall on them on account of the mis-

1. *Jā*. I. 98,
मयि पुरतो गच्छन्ते बहू आनिसंसा, मग्गेन अभिन्नेन एव गमिस्सामि, गोणा अवामट्ठतिणं खादिस्सन्ति मनुस्सानं अनामट्ठं सूपेय्यपण्णं भविस्सति पसन्नं उदकं यथारुचि अग्घं ठपेत्वा भण्डं विक्कणिस्सामीति ।

2. *Jā*. I. 99.
3. *Jā*. I. 100,
सत्थवाहा च नाम यदा धुरवातो वायति तदा यानके निसीदित्वा उपट्ठाकपरिवुता रजं परिहरन्ता पुरतो गच्छन्ति, यदा पच्छतो वायति तेन' एव नयेन पच्छतो गच्छन्ति ।

take of the members. A Satthavāha is seen addressing his men thus—"Let not even a palmful of water be used without my sanction. There are poisonous trees in this wilderness ; so let no one among you eat any fruit, flower or leaf which he had not eaten before, without asking me."[1] Wearied and long journeyed travellers would have found tender fruits very tempting, which might have caused misery and suffering to many caravans.

when the caravan passed through forests, usually nights were given to rest with complete vigilence against the robbers. The carts were unyoked and ranged in a circle so as to form a strong laager. Supper was taken early, and oxen were made to lie down in the middle with men around them. The Satthavāha with the leading men of the band stood in guard, with sword in hand throughout the whole night, waiting for the day to dawn. As the morning light gave the signal of day-break, the oxen were fed, everything needful was done, and the band proceeded further.[2]

Journey through the desert was hard as well as interesting. It was not possible to travel during the day time, as it became hot like a burning bed of charcoal-embers.[3] The sun was also scorching. There was heat both from above and below. But nights were quite soothing, pleasant, and comfortable. Therefore, during the day time the caravan took rest. It formed a circle, spreading an awning over head, and after an early meal all men sat down for rest for the whole day. With the disappearance of the daylight, they took their evening meals, and

1. *Jā.* I. 10-12. It is said in a *Jātaka* story that a complete party of traders perished due to eating poisonous fruits (*Jā.* I. 271.).
2. *Jā.* I. 103,

सकटानि मोचापेत्वा सकटपरिवत्तकेन खन्धावारं बन्धापेत्वा कालस्स' एव मनुस्से च गोणे सायमासमत्तं भोजापेत्वा मनुस्सानं मज्झे गोणे निपज्जापेत्वा सयं बलनायके गहेत्वा खग्गहत्थो तियामरत्तिं आरक्खं गहेत्वा ठितको व अरूणं उट्ठापेसि । पुनदिवसे पातो च सब्बकिच्चानि निट्ठापेत्वा गोणे भोजेत्वा····।

3. *Jā.* I. 107,

as the earth became cool, yoked the carts and proceeded further.[1] The description of proceeding through the desert is really interesting and enchanting, which is compared to the sailing of ship through the waters of ocean.[2] The guide who led the caravan through the desert was known as the Thalaniyāmaka[3] (desert-pilot). It was through his knowledge of the stars that the party of the caravan was made to move in the right direction. He sat in the front cart upon a couch, looking up to the stars in the heavens, and directing the course thereby.[4] If the Thalaniyāmaka, who was the only man to show the right path fell asleep, there was every chance of being misguided and taken away to unknown regions. The *Vaṇṇupatha Jātaka* mentions a desert-pilot who had been without sleep for many nights and fell asleep with the result that the oxen retracted their steps, and when his eyes opened he found the caravan at the same place from where it had started.[5] There was another danger of throwing away the water-jars with the wrong assumption that the path had deen traversed. Because the carts carrying water-jars moved heavily, therefore if such a region was reached where water was available in abuncance, or the journey was nearing its end, the jars were usually broken and thrown.[6] If water was exhausted it was through

1. *Jā*. I. 107,
रत्तिं एव गन्त्वा अरुणग्गमने सकटानि परिवत्तं कत्वा मत्थके मण्डपं कारेत्वा कालस्स'एव आहारकिच्चं निट्ठापेवा छायाय निसिन्ना दिवसं खेपेत्वा अत्थं गते सुरिये सायमासं भुञ्जित्वा भूमिया सीतलाय जाताय सकटानि योजेत्वा गच्छन्ति ।
2. *Jā*. I. 107,
समुद्दगमनसदिसम् एव गमनं होति ।
3. *Ibid.*
4. *Jā*. I. 108,
नियामको पुरिमस कटे आसन्दिं सन्थरापेत्वा आकासे तारका ओलोकेन्तो इतो पाजेथा'ति बदमानों निपज्जि ।
5. *Jā*. I. 108,
सो दीघं अद्धानं अनिद्दायनभावेन किलन्तो निद्दं ओक्कमि, गोणे निवत्तित्व आगतमग्गम् एव गण्हन्ते अञ्ञासि ।
6. *Jā*. I. 101,
चाटियो भिन्दापेत्वा पसतमत्तम'पि उदकं अनवसेसेत्वा सब्बं छड्ढेत्वा सकटानि पाजापेसि ।

digging the earth that life could be saved. It was the growth of certain plants and grasses, specially the Kuśā, which indicated the presence of water underneath.[1] But it was not an easy task, as one had to dig considerable depth to get water. There was possibility of finding rocks instead of water. If water was available after digging, flags were hoisted[2], so that other bands passing through the same route might avail the water-reservoir.

At last, after encountering a number of difficulties and disappointments, the caravan could reach the destination. Then, the Sathavāha went to the city, bartered the merchandise, and in exchange received other goods of the same value,[3] or earned considerable profit amounting to double or four times of the wares sold.[4]

1. *Jā*. I. 108,
एकं दब्बतिणगच्छं दिस्वा इमानि तिणानि हेट्ठा उदक सिनेहेन उट्ठितानि भविस्सन्तीति चिन्तेत्वा कुद्दालं गाहापेत्वा तं पदेसं खणापेसि ।
2. *Jā*. I. 109,
उदकवाटसमीपे धजं बन्धित्वा इच्छितट्ठानं अगमिंसु ।
3. *Jā*. No. 90 (I. 377-78).
4. *Jā*. I. 109,
ते तत्थ भण्डं विक्किणित्वा द्विगुणं चतुग्गुणं भोगं लभित्वा अत्तनो वसनटठानम् एव अगमिंसु ।

CONCLUSION

The above survey of life in Northern India in the pre-Mauryan times shows certain special features of social and religious aspects of life. We have no account of any assault on the caste system before the advent of Buddhism and Jainism. But we find that during this period the Buddha and Mahāvīra and their followers raised their voice against the notion of caste superiority. The Buddha was theoretically in favour of abolishing caste distinction, but conditions were not in his favour, and eventually he became a protagonist of the Kshatriya superiority. The passage in the *Mahābhārata*, which points out to the necessity of caste equality, may have been inspired by the movement in Magadha during this age. The Buddha's contribution for the infusion of the feeling of equality was undoubtedly notable, at least in the spiritual world, though ineffective in the temporal life. It was the Buddhist Order where even a barber like Upāli could rise to the position of the head of the Saṅgha.

North-East India was the centre of an important religious movement. New sects such as Buddhism, Jainism, and Ājīvikism rose to prominence in addition to some minor ones. But popular Brahmanism prevailed. The Vedic gods did not go out of the scene due to the advent of new schools of religion and philosophy, but they were worshipped by the masses. Though the Buddha opposed the authority of the *Vedas* and the Brāhmaṇas, he is not found preaching against the worship of Prajāpati or Indra; for he did not go against the popular religious beliefs and practices, except those which caused slaughter of life.

The process of assimilation and amalgamation of the religious practices of the non-Aryans into the fold of Brahmanism had become almost complete by this period, and we find that Yakshas, Nāgas and so on which were originally non-Aryan deities were worshipped in Eastern India by the masses.

The most remarkable feature of the age in the sphere of religious movement was the development of the monastic life.

Though the homeless stage of life existed in India long before our period, but it was not so popular as during this age. The advent of the well organised Buddhist Monastic Order was an event of great significance in the religious history of the country. We find that the Bhikshu-life was modelled after the Brahmacharya, Vānaprastha and Sanyāsa stages of life in the Brahmanical system. The period of Pabbajjā which marked the necessary preliminary for the Bhikshuhood, combined in itself, the Brahmacharya and the Vānaprastha Aśramas; whereas the Bhikshuhood corresponded to the Sanyāsa Aśrams. The rlues made by the Buddha in connection with the organisation of his Order are, indeed, very interesting and throw considerable light on the contemporary conditions.

Prior to the advent of the Buddha's Order occasionally a few women renounced the world, and even the ascetic organisations contemporary to that of the Buddha, generally did not encourage the entrance of females in the monastic fold. But under Buddhism the practice of women embracing the monastic life became very wide.

The picture of the social life of the age as presented before us reveals that on the whole people were happy, leading a life studded with joyful occasions. Organisation of festivals, where took place unrestricted eating, drinking and merry-making by various ways, was a special feature of the social life. The cities and towns of the age were centres of important festive celebrations. Life in the urban areas was luxurious to a certain extent, and they were also famous for the presence of courtesans, who were regarded as essential for adding to the gaity of the city life.

It was in Magadha of this age where developed the earliest Prākṛit literature of the country. Buddha preferred to preach in the dialect of the masses, and his teachings were compiled after his Nirvāṅa in the Pāli language. Later inspired by the Buddha's teachings, king Aśoka made remarkable contribution for the spread and development of Pāli which also cannot be overlooked. Thus we find that this age cccupies a significant position in the history of the country.

BIBLIOGRAPHY

Original Sources

BUDDHIST CANONICAL WORKS

Aṅguttara-Nikāya — Ed. R. Morris and E. Hardy, 5 Vols., P.T.S. London, 1883-1900.
Tr. F.L. Woodward and E.M. Hare, *The Book of the Gradual Sayings*, 5 Vols. P.T.S. London, 1932-36; I & II. Vols, 1951-52.

Dhammapada — Text, Ed. Rahula Sankrityayana, Rangoon, 1937.
Translation, *S.B.E.* X, Oxford, 1950.

Dīgha-Nikāya — Ed. T.W. Rhys Davids and J. Erstlin Carpenter, 3 Vols., R.T.S. London, 1890-1911.
Tr. T.W. and C.A.F. Rhys Davids. *Dialogues of the Buddha, S.B.B.*, 3 Vols., P.T.S. London.
Tr. Rahula Sankrityana in Hindi *Dīgha-Nikāya,* Mahābodhi Sabhā, Sārnāth, 1936.

Itivuttaka — Ed. Ernst Windisch, Oxford, 1948, Tr. *S.B.E.* In Nāgarī Script—Rangoon, 1937 and Mahābodhi Sabhā, Sārnāth, 1951.

Jātaka — Text, ed. Fausböll, 6 Vols., Trubner & Co. Ltd., London, 1877-1896.
English Translation, edited by Cowell, Cambridge University, 1895-1907.

Khuddaka-Pāṭha — Ed. Helmer Smith, P. T. S. London, 1915.

Majjhima-Nikāya — Ed. V. Trenckner and R. Chalmers, 3 Vols, P.T.S. London, 1948-51;

Tr. Rahula Sankrityayana in Hindi, Mahābodhi Sabhā, Sārnāth, 1933.

Nidāna-Kathā Ed. N.K. Bhagavat, Bombay, 1935.

Petavatthu Ed. Rahula Sankrityayana, Rangoon, 1937.

Saṁyutta-Nikāya Ed. M. Leon Feer, and Mrs. Rhys Davids 5 Vols. P.T.S. London, 1884-1904.
Tr. Mrs. Rhys Davids. Luzac & Co., Vols. I-II, 1950-52.

Sutta-Nipāta Ed. Anderson & Smith, P. T. S., S.B.E., 1948; in Nāgarī Script, Ed. Rahula Sankrityayana, Rangoon, 1937.

Theragāthā Ed. Oldenberg, P.T.S. London, 1883; Ed. N.K. Bhagavat, Bombay, 1939.

Therīgāthā Ed. N.K. Bhagavat Bombay University, 1937. Tr. Mrs. Rhys Davids, *Psalms of Sisters*, P. T. S. London, 1909.

Udāna Ed. Rahula Sankrityayana, Rangoon, 1937.

Vinaya-Piṭaka Tr. T. W. Rhys Davids and H. Oldenberg, S.B.E., Vols. XIII, XVII, XX, Oxford, 1881-85.
Tr. Rahula Sankrityayana in Hindi, Mahābodhi Sabhā, Sārnāth, 1935.
Pātimokkha, Bh. O. R. I., Poona, 1937.

Vimānavatthu Ed. Rahula Sankrityayana, Rangoon, 1937.

BUDDHIST NON-CANONICAL WORKS

Dīpavaṁsa Ed. & Tr. Oldenberg, Williams and Norgate, London & Edinbergh, 1879.

Mahāvaṁsa Ed. & Tr. Geiger, P. T. S. London, 1912.

Mahāvastu Ed. E. Senart, 3 Vols., Paris, 1882-97.

Milinda-Pañho Ed. R.D. Vadekar, Bombay University, 1940.

Puggala-Paññati Ed. G. Landsberg & Mrs. Rhys Davids, P.T.S. London, 1914.

JAINA SOURCES

Āchārāṅga-Sūtra	Tr. H. Jacobi, *S.B.E.*, Vol. XXII, Oxford, 1884.
Bhagavatī-Sūtra	With Comy. of Abhayadeva, 3 Vols., Bombay, 1918-21.
Kalpa-Sūtra	Tr. H. Jacobi, *Jaina Sūtras, S.B.E.* Vol., XXII, Oxford, 1884.

BRAHMANICAL SOURCES

VEDIC

Atharvaveda	Ed. Śrīpāda Śarmā, Aundha Nagara, Bombay, 1938.
Aitareya Brāhmaṇa	Ed. Martin Haug, Govt. Central Book Depot, Bombay, 1863.
Aitareya Āraṇyaka	Ed. Keith, Oxford, 1909.
Bṛihadāraṇyaka Upanishad	Ed. U. T. Viraraghavacharya, Venkateśvara Oriental Institute, Tirupati, Chittoor (S. I.) 1954. Translation, S.B.E., Vol. XV.
Chhāndogya Upanishad	Ed. U. T. Viraraghavacharya, Venkatesvara Oriental Institute, Tirupati, Chittoor (S.I.) 1952. Translation, S.B.E. Vol. I.
Kaṭhopanishad	B.D. Basu, Allahabad, 1911.
Maitrāyaṇī Saṁhitā	Ed. Dr. Leopold Von Schroeder, Leipzig, 1923.
Muṇḍakopanishad	B. D. Basu, Allahabad, 1911; *S. B. E.*Vol. XV.
Pañchaviṁśa Brāhmaṇa	Tr. W. Galand, A. S. B., Calcutta, 1931.
Śatapatha Brāhmaṇa	Ed. Weber, Leipzig, 1924.
Taittirīya Saṁhitā	Ed. Śrīpāda Śarmā, Svādhyāya Maṇḍala, Aundha Nagara, Bombay, 1945. Ed.
Taittirīya Brāhmaṇa	Shamasastry, Govt. O. L. S., Mysore, 1921.
Taittirīya Āraṇyaka	Ānandāśrama Sanskṛit Series, 1926. Ed.
Ṛigveda	Śrīpāda Śarmā, Aundha Nagara, Bombay, 1940

GṚIHYA-SŪTRAS

Āpastamba Gṛihya-Sūtra S. B. E., Vol. XXX.

Āśvalāyana Gṛihya-Sūtra S. B. E., Vol. XXIX.

Baudhāyana Gṛihya-Sūtra Ed. R. Shamasatry, Oriental Library, Mysore, 1920.

Gobhila Gṛihya-Sūtra Ed. C. K. Tārkālaṅkāra, Calcutta, 1908.

Hiraṇyakeśin Gṛihya-Sūtra Ed. J. Kirtse, Imp. Academy of Science of Vienna, 1889.

Pāraskara Gṛihya-Sūtra Ed. M. G. Bākre, Bombay, 1917.

Sāṅkhyāyana Gṛihya-Sūtra *S. B. E.*, Vol. XXIX.

DHARMA-SŪTRAS

Āpastamba Dharma-Sūtra Ed. G. Bühler, Bombay Saṅskrit Series, 1932. Translation, *S. B. E.*, vol. II.

Baudhāyana ,, Ed. L. Srinivasacharya, Govt. O. L. S. Mysore, 1907.

Gautama ,, Ed. L. Srinivasacharya, Govt. O. L. S., Mysore, 1917.

Vaśishṭha ,, *S. B. E.*, Vol. XIV.

Vishṇu ,, *S. B. E.*, Vol. VII.

SMṚITIS, EPICS, GRAMMAR AND OTHER WORKS

Ashṭādhyāyī- of Pāṇini Tr. S. C. Vasu, Indian Press, Allahabad and Pāṇini Office Vārāṇasī, 1891-1898.

Kauṭilya's Arthaśāstra Ed. and tr. R. Shamasastry, Mysore, first edition, 1915 and second edition, 1923.

Mahābhāshya of Patañjali Ed. Kielhorn, Bombay, 1892-1909.

Manu-Smṛiti Ed. G. D. Paṭhaka, Vārāṇasī, 1948.

Mahābhārata Chitraśālā Press, Poona, 1929-33.

Nārada-Smṛiti *S. B. E.*, Vol., XXXIII.

Rāmāyāṇa Pandit Pustakālaya, Vārāṇasī 1951.

Vaikhānasa-Dharma-Praśna Ed. Ganapati Sastry, Trivendrum Sanskrit Series, 1923.

DICTIONARIES AND INDEXES

Dictionary of Pali Proper Names Malalasekera, John Murray, London 1937-38.

Pāli Dictionary Ed. Rhys Davids, P. T. S., London, 1921.

Vedic Index Macdonell and Keith, London, 1912.

GENERAL WORKS

Agrawala, V. S. *India as known to Pāṇini*, University of Lucknow, 1953.

Altekar, A. S. *The Position of Women in Hindu Civilisation*, The cultural Publication House, Banaras Hindu University, 1938.

Ibid. *Education in Ancient India*, Nand Kishore Bros. Banaras, 1944.

Ibid *The Kumrahar Excavation Report*, 1951-54, K. P. J. R. Institute, Patna, 1956.

Allan, J. *Catalogue of Coins, Ancient India*, London, 1936.

Bandopadhyaya, N. C. *Economic Life and Progress in Ancient India*. University of Calcutta, 1945.

Barth, A. *The Religions of India*. Tr. Rev. T. Wood, London 1921.

Barua, B. M. *Gayā and Bodha-Gayā*, Calcutta, 1934.

Barua, B. M. *Inscriptions of Aśoka*, University of Calcutta, 1943.

Basham A. L. *History & Doctrine of The Ājīvikas*, Luzac & Co. Ltd., London, 1951.

Beal *Life of Hiuen-Tsang. London*, 1911.

Bhandarkar, D. R. *Carmichael Lecturers* 1921, *Ancient Indian Numismatics*, University of Calcutta, 1921.

Upadhayaya, Bharat Singh—*Pāli Sāhitya Kā Itihāsa*, Hindi Sāhitya Sammelan, Prayāg, 2008 Vikramī.

Chanan, D. R. *Slavery in Ancient India*, PPH, Bombay, 1960.

Bose, A. N. *Social and Rural Economy of Northern India* (B. C. 600—A.D. 200) Vol. II, University of Calcutta, 1945.

Copleston, R. S. *Buddhism*, printed by W. B. & Co. Plymouth, 1908.

Das, S. K. *Economic History of Ancient India.* Calcutta 1944.

Dutta, N. N. *Early Monastic Buddhism.* 2 Vols. Calcutta 1941.

Dutta, S. K. *Early Buddhist Monachism*, London & New York, 1924.

Fick, Richard *Social Organisation in North-East India in Buddha's Time*, Tr. S. K. Maitra, University of Calcutta, 1920.

Hopkins, E. W. *Religions of India*, Boston, 1895.

Horner, I. B. *Women Under Primitive Buddhism*, George Routledge & Sons, London, 1930.

Jain, J. C. *Life in Ancient India as Depicted in the Jain Canons*, New Book Co. Ltd., Bombay, 1947.

Jaini, J. R. *Outlines of Jainism*, Cambridge University Press, London, 1940.

Kane, P. V. *History of Dharmaśāstra*, three vols., Bh. O. R. I., Poona, 1941.

Law, B. C. *India as Described in Early Texts of Buddhism and Jainism*, Luzac & Co. Ltd., London, 1941.

Law, B. C. *History of Pāli Literature*, 2 Vols. Kegan Paul, London, 1933.

Law, B. C. *Mahāvīra, His Life and Teachings*, Luzac & Co. Ltd., London, 1937.

M, Crindle, *Ancient India as described by Megasthenes and Arrian*, Calcutta, 1926.

Mehta, R. L. *Pre-Buddhist India*, Bombay, 1939.

Motichandra, *Sārthavāha*, Bihar Rāshtrabhāshā Parishad, Patna, 1953.

Mukherjee, R. K. *A History of Indian Shipping*, Longmans, London, 1912.

Mukherjee, R. K. *Ancient Indian Education*, MacMillan, London, 1951.

Oldenberg, H. *The Buddha*, Williams & Norgate, London and Edinburgh, 1882.

Rapson, E. J. *Cambridge History of India*, Vol. I, Cambridge, 1935.

Rhys Davids, Mrs. *Outlines of Buddhism*, Metheren & Co. London, 1934.

Rhys Davids, T. W. *Buddhist India*, Calcutta, 1950.

Sharma, G. R. *The Excavations at Kauśāmbī*, Allahabad, 1960.

Sharma, R. S. *The Śūdras in Ancieut India.* Motilal Banarsidass, Delhi 1959.

Ibid. *Light on Early Indian Society and Economy*, Manaktala, Bombay. 1966.

Thomas, E. J. *Early Buddhist Scriptures*, Kagan Paul, London, 1935.

Thomas, E. J. *History of Buddhist Thought*, Kegan Paul, London, 1953.

Weber, A. *A History of Indian Literature*, Kegan, Paul, London, 1914.

Winternitz, M. *A History of Indian Litcrature* Vol. II Tr. Mrs. S. Ketkar & Miss H. Kohn, University of Calcutta, 1933.

JOURNALS, REPORTS AND MEMOIRS

Annals of the Bhandarkar Oriental Research Institute, Poona.

Indian Antiquary, Bombay.

Indian Historical Quarterly, Calcutta.

Journal of the Bihar & Orissa Research Society, Patna.

Journal of the Bihar Research Society, Patna.

Journals & Proceedings of the Asiatic Society of Bengal, Calcutta.

Journal of the Royal Asiatic Society, London.

Journal of the Department of Letters, Calcutta.

Journal of the Numismatic Society of India, Bombay.

Journal of the Uttar Pradesh Historical Society, Lucknow.

Archaeolagical Survey Reports and Memoirs of the Deptt. of Archaeology, Govt. of India.

INDEX

Abhijñāna Śakuntalam, 41
Aboriginal, 85, 232
Āchariya (Āchārya), 6, 160, 184,190,
—bhāgam, dhana, 160
Āchāraṅga-Sūtra, V, X, 99,214(Fn.)
Achelakas, 126, 131, 138, 139
Achela Kassapa, 157
Acids, 228
Actor, 202
Abhaya, prince, 65, (Fn.)
Ādāsa, 221
Adharma, 41
Addhariyas (Aitareyas), 112
Adhikaraṇi (anvil), 218
Afghanistan, 243 (Fn.), 257
Africa, 246
Aggasāvaka, 93
Agghakāraka, Agghāpanaka,
Agghāpanika, 266
Aggimāla, sea, 246
Agivachchhagotta, Parivrājaka, 134
Agni, IX, 70, 112, worship of 114
Agnihotra,, 141, 114
Agnihotrahavanī, 214
Agrawala, V. S., 260, 261
Agriculture, 79, 193, 196, 197
process of 198, 202, 205, 247
Ahi, Nāga, 118
Ahiguṇḍika, 15, 82, see snake-charmer
Ahiṅsā, 101, 103, 143
Ahipāraka, *senāpati*, 43 (Fn.)
Aitareya Brāhmaṇa, 22, 37, 120, 123
Ajakalāpaka, Yaksha, 117,
Chetiya, 117
Ajanta fresco, 142
Ajātaśatru, king of Magadha, i, 2, 41, 45, 54, 96, 101
Ajita, Parivrājaka, 133
Ajita-Kesakambalī, 131, 107
Ājīvikas, V, X, 104, sects of 107, 125. 100, 130, 131, 139, 140-42, 149
Ājīvikaseyya 141, Ājīvikasabhā, 142
Ājīvikism, i, ix, 104, 105, 107, 108, 279
Ālārika, 231
Ālāra Kālāma, 6
Alderman, 244, 249
Allakappa, 96
Allan, J. 261, 264
Alms, 189
Almsbowl, 186
Alapamātra-bhājaka, 192
Amātyamaṇḍala, 13
Amarā, 54
Amarakosha, 264
Ambapālī, courtesan, 64, 65, 66(Fn.) 67, 92, 256
Ambapālī grove, 65, 92
Ambasaṇḍā, village, 194(Fn.)
Ambaṭṭha, Brāhmaṇa, 8, 9, 116
America, 28
Amittatāpanā, girl, 50
Ānanda, XI, 93, 97, 163, 179, 181, 240
Anāthapiṇḍika, Seṭṭhi, 13, 14, 88, 151, 250
Andamanese, 120
Āndhras, 230
Aṅga, 95, 111, 128, 140, 141, 236
Aṅgati, king of Videha, 106
Aṅgulimāla, 44, 152
Aṅguttarāpa, 8(Fn.) 236
Aṅguttara Nikāya 24, 28, 38, 39, 56 134, 139, 170, 219
Annabhāra, Parivrājaka, 133, 134
Annaprāśana, 74
Aññatitthiya, Parivrājakas, 132, 157
Anopama, 41
Antaravāsaka, 176
Anugāra, Parivrājaka, 134
Anuloma, marriage, 43
Anuruddha, Bhikshu, 97, 169
Anusāri, 177, 224
Aparigraha, 103, 143, 144
Āpastamba, 4, 18, 52, 63, 71, 72 74, 77, 136
————*Dharma-Sūtra*, 23, 39
————*Gṛhya-Sūtra*, 39, 52, 83
Apadāna, 245
Āpaṇṇa, 236
Apassayapīṭhaka, 214
Apportioner of food, 192
————lodgings, 151, 171
Apprentice, 76, 225
Apsaras, 120
Arabia, 246
Ārāma, 150, 151, 172, 174, 190,191
Ārāmika, 191
————gāma, 195
————Preshaka, 191
Araṇya, 193

Aranyānī, 119
Āraṇyakas, 110
Arakan, 244, 245
Ārakūṭa, 146, 217
Archer, Archery, 81, 94, 247, 269 (Fn.)
Architect, 215, 216
Arhatattva, 107, Arhatship, 182
Arindama, king, 10
Arjuna, 118
Armour, 218
Army, 208, 209, 239, 263
Arishṭa, 231
Ārsha, marriage, viii, 52
Arta Xerxes Mnemon, 209
Arthaśāstra, v, vii, 25, 30, 33, 201, 202, 206, 211, 222, 231, 242, 256, 257, 267, 270; see Kauṭilya
Artisan, 217, 247, 251, 270, see Śilpin
———, skilled 211
———, higher 3
Ārya, 1, 24, 173
Ārya-Ashtāṅgika-Mārga, 102
Aryans, Vedic, 118, 119, 120, 196, 205
Aryan gods, 118
Āsā, deity, 115
Āsana, 214
Āsava, 230, 231
Ascetics, Asceticism, 31, 34, 58, 66, 106, 112, 123, 1262-7, eating meat, 75, drinking liquor, 86
———, Ājīvika, 105
———, Jaṭila, 90
———, Brāhmaṇa, 91
Orders of 57, 123, 124, 125, 131, 149, 179
See monks and Order
Āshāḍha, month, 83, 122
Ashṭādhyāyī of Pāṇini, v, see Paṇini
Ashṭakā, 140
Asia, S. E., 120
Aśoka, iii, 72, 80, 96, 98, 105, 130, 131, 270 (Fn.), 280
Āśrama, 134, 137, of Guṇa Kassapa 105, of Jaṭilas 90, 128, of Ṛishis 125, of Sundarika Bhāradvāja 114, four Āśramas 123, 156
Asteya, Jaina, 103, 143, 144
Āsura, marriage, viii, 52
Āsuti, 231
Āśvalāyana, 52
———*Gṛhya-Sūtra*, 42, 52
Āśvin, month, 85 (Fn.)
Aśvapati, king, 130
Aśvattha, 120
Āṭānāṭiya-Sutta, 92
Ātman, 124
Aṭṭhaka, Ṛishi, III
Aṭṭhakathā, 175
Atharvaveda, 55, 75, 109, 116, 120, 197
Atthadhammānusāsaka-Amachcha, 267
Atri, 19
Ātumā, 236
Audience Hall, 13
Aupapātika-Sūtra, 101, 132
Aurasa, 56
Avadānaśataka, 87
Avadhūta 129
Āvāsa, 180
Avantī, 98, 239 (Fn.)
Āvela, 186
Avestā, 44
Aviruddhakas, 131
Aya, 216, Ayasa, Lohāyasa, 208
Ayodhyā, 125, 238

Babylon, 245, 246
Bactria, 237
Bahuputta Chetiya, 137 (Fn.)
Balabhāmukha, sea, 246
Bali, 88
Bangles, 221
Baniyagrāma, 195
Bankers, 250
Banners, 221
Barabar, hill, 105
Bards, 202
Barua, B. M., 141
Basket-maker, 11, 20
———trap, 229
Basham, A. L., 101 (Fn.), 107 (Fn.), 142
Baveruraṭṭha, 245
Bauddha-Saṅgīti, 94
Baudhāyana, 48, 242
———*Dharma-Sūtra*, 52, 135, 241
Beluriya (Vaiḍūrya), 222, 223
Bengal, 74, 244
Berbai, 245
Besyngeitai, 245
Betel, Magahī, 200
Beṭṭhadīpa, 96
Bhaddā, Bhikshuṇī, 181
Bhadda Assājāniya, Brāhmaṇa, 3 (Fn.)
Bhaddaka, stone, 222
Bhaddiya, monastery, 174, 236
Bhadramuatāki, 177, 224
Bhagalpur, district, 263
Bhagavagotta, Parivrājaka, 133
Bhagavatī-Sūtra, v, 100, 103-4
Bhakta, Bhatta (Bhāta) 68, 69

Bhakta-Uddeśaka, 192
Bhakti, cult, 112
Bhallika, merchant, 237 (Fn.)
Bhāṇḍāgārika, 191, 249
Bhandarkar, D. R., 254, 256, 259
Bhaṅgā, 200
Bharata, float of wood, 243 (Fn.)
Bhārhut, iv, 115, 117, 137, 149, 172-73
Bharukachchha, 239, 246
Bhastra, raft, 243 (Fn.)
Bhataka, 14, 270
Bherīvādaka, 15, 82, see drummer
Bherīvādaka-kula, 15, 82
Bhikshu-Āśrama, 156
Bhikshus, Buddhist, x-xii, 2, 5, 13, 24, 35 (Fn.), 61, 69, 77, 90, 91, 96, 132, 135, 136, 138, 139, 145, 146, 149, 150, 152, 154-61, 163-69, 171, 172, 175-78, 180, 185-92, 210, 220, 221, 227, 231, 240, 241
Bhikshuṇīs, 46, 159, 161, 166, 167, 170, 181, 182, 183, 184, 187
Bhikshu Saṅgha, 65, 150, 154, 158, 161, 162, 170
Bhīma, 236 (Fn.), 237
Bhirmound, 258, 262 (Fn.)
Bhoganagara, 236
Bhoja, 129
Bhojanadātrī, 231
Bhṛigu, ṛishi,...111
Bhroach, port,...246
Bhurā, 232
Bhūtas, 121
Bihar, i-iii, v, viii, 57, 64, 74, 90, 91, 92, 93, 94, 104, 118, 125
Bimbādevī, 69
Bimbīsāra, king of Magadha, 7 (Fn.), 8 (Fn.), 41, 45, 64, 92, 96, 101, 104, 239 (Fn.), 259
Bindusāra, Maurya king, 142, 238
Blacksmith, 218, 219, 248
Blankets 210, 211
Blanket-maker, 211
Blessed one (Buddha), 94, 95 (F.n.)
Bloch, Th., 251 (Fn.)
Boat, 213, 240, 241, 242
———ferry, 242
Bodhisattva, 28, 219, 265
Border Countries, 159
Bowls, 221, 225
Bows, 229
Bracelets, 212, 221
Brahmā, god, 90, 112, 113
———Prjāpati, Sahampati, 90, 113, Sanan-Kumāra, 113
Brahmacharya, 135, 136, 143, 144, 156, 162, 280
Brahmachārin, xi, 78, 79, 135, 140, 156, 160, 161. 162, 164
Brāhma, marriage, viii, 52, 53
Brahman, 123, doctrine of 124,
Brahmadeyya, 6, 7 (Fn.)
Brahmajāla-Sutta, 8, 9
Brahma-Sūtra, 103 (Fn.)
Brahmavidyā, 22
Brāhmaṇas, i, vi, ix-x, 1, 9, 11, 18, 19, 29, 31, 39, 42, 49, 50, 71, 72, 74, 76-79, 83, 88, 95, 96, 105, 107, 109, 110, 111, 112, 114, 124, 125, 129, 130, 131, 145, 203, 210, 230, 242, 270, 271 (Fn.), authority of 101, 108
Brāhmaṇa-gāma, 92, 195, 203, see village
———Gṛihapati 12, 39
———Guest, 72
———Nigama, 99
———Snātaka, 4
———Vāchanikāni, 7
———Mahāsālas, 8, 110, 126
Brāhmaṇas (texts), iv, 1, 22, 38, 89, 116
Brahmanism, ix, 108, 109, 110, 120, 126, 279
Brass, 217
Bride, 25, 41-43, 46, 47, 50-55
———groom 25, 41, 43, 50-55
———price 53, 54
Bṛihadāraṇyaka-Upanishad, 22, 124
Bṛihadratha, Dynasty, 259
British Museum, 264
Bronze, 208, 217
Buddha, i, iii, iv, vi-ix, x-xii, 1, 9, 24, 37, 65, 69, 75, 88, 90-96, 104, 108-9, 117-18, 124, 125, 128, 131, 133-37, 139, 141, 146, 149-54, 157, 158, 164, 166, 168-70, 172-75, 178-81, 185, 189, 204, 206 (Fn.), 210, 211, 216, 235, 236, 238, 241, 255, 259, 279, 280, Gotama, Gautama, 89, 96, 129
Buddhism, Buddhists, ix, x, 108, 126, 157, 159, 164, 279, 280, spread of Buddhism 90-93, 95, 96, 99, Schisms 94, 97, 98, against the authority of Vedas & Brāhmaṇas 109, 110, 112, hostile to Ājīvikas 105, teachings of Buddha 101-4.
Buddhist Brethren, 166
———, Brother hood, 154, 155
———, Council, iii, 96, 97 (Fn.)
———, Laymen, see Laity
———, theology, 97
Buddhaghosha, 160, 177 (Fn.), 259
Bühler, G., iv
Buildings of wood, 212, 215
Bulandibagh, 264

Bulis, of Allakappa, 96
Bull, standard, 259
Bull worship, 121
Bullion, 249, 255
Butter, 70, 205, Butter-milk, 206
Burma, 244, 245

Calcutta, Indian Museum, 264
Camels, 206
Canals, 201
Canon, Buddhist, i, 97 (Fn.)
Car, celestial and royal, 222
Caravans, xiii, 14, 235, 239, 244, 252, ...269 (Fn.), 272-77
Caravan-leader, 266, 274, see Satthavāha
Carriage, 212
Carpenters, 195, 196 (Fn.), 208, 212-16, 240, 247-48
Carpets, 210
Carts, 213, 229, 231, 235, 237, 272, 273, 277
Caste, 2, Vedic period, 1, higher and dispised, 3, 16, 39; characteristics of 12, unorganised, 15, professional, 15
Caterer, 252
Cattle, breeding, farming & rearing of; 12, 193, 196, 197, 205, 206, 207, 247, meat of 70, slaughter of 73
——butcher, 71, 73
Cereals, 197, 199, 208, 209
Ceylon, 173, 241
Ceylonese Chronicles, 241
Chaidya Kāsu, king, 22
Chair, 212, 212
Chammakāra, 232
Chammabhastaṁ, 233
Chammochhatta, 233
Champā, 6 (Fn.), 7 (Fn.), 14 (Fn.), 64 (Fn.), 92, 99, 101, 104, 209, 235-238, 240, 241, 244, 245, 272
Chaṇḍālas, 3, 16, 17, 18, 19, 82, 130
Chaṇḍāla-gāma, 195, see village
——————work, 117
Chaṇḍālī, viii, 16
Chandanasāra, 224
Chandra, dynasty, 244 (Fn.)
Chandragupta, Maurya, 81, 212, 238, 243, 258, 263
Chang, 242 (Fn.)
Chanki, celebrated Brāhmaṇa, 2
Chāpā, Bhikshuṇī, 181
Chāpāla Chetiya, 137 (Fn.)
Chaplain, 31, 86
Chariot, 84, 208, 212,-14, 221, 223
——————races, 80, 81, 187
Chārvākas, 102, 108
Chātaka, 74
Chāturmāsyas, 83, 84
Chaturthīkarma, 48
Chāturyāma-Saṁvatsara, 103
Chatussadaṁ, 214
Chavadāhaka, 18
Chemicals, 228
Cheta, fish, 74
Chhabbagiyas, Bhikshus, xi, 94, 97, 169-71, 174, 177, 186, 187, 221
Chhandāvas, 112
Chhāndogya-Upanishad, 123
Chhandokas (Chhāndogyas), 112
Chhanna, Bhikshu, 170
China, 245
Chiñchamanavikā, a lady, 95 (Fn.)
Chintāmaṇivijjā, 9
Chisel, 214
Chitralatā, garden of Indra, 114
Chittakāra, 216
Chīvarabhājaka, Chīvaranidahaka, Chīvarapratīgrāhāpaka, 191, 192
Chorapapāta, 137 (Fn.)
Chotānāgpur, i, 55, 85, 242 (Fn.)
Christian era, 105
Chulasachchaka, sutta, 92
Chullavagga, iii (Fn.), 61, 95 (Fn.), 97 (Fn.), 164, 167, 169-70, 182, 185, 240
Chuñchus, 230
Chunar, 240
Citadel, 215
Cities, 12, 13, 16, 19, 64 (Fn.), 71, 92, 196, 209,214 courtesans of 64, 67, scenes of festivals, 82, 83, defences of 213, 215, industries and trade of 223, 225, 235, 237, 245, 247, 252, 271, 272, of Yakshas, 116
Clansmen, 42
Clod-hopper, 215, 216
Cobbler, 232
Coins, 53, 250, 251, 254-56, 260
———,Cast, 264
———,punch-marked, 257,-65 259, 261, 262, 263, 264, hoards of 250, 258, 262, 263
Cook, 11
Copper, 208, 212, 216, 217, coins of 254, 256, 257, 264
Cosmetics, 212
Couches, 211
Council, of Buddhists, 96, 97, 98
Council Hall, of Śākyas, 10
Court-Valuer, 266, 267
Courtesans, VIII, of Vaiśālī and

Rājagṛiha 64, 92. income of 65, 256, 269, character of 66
Co-wives, 39, 40 (Fn.), 41
Crafts, 16, 79, 244
Craftsmen, handicraftsmen, 14, 195, 196, 251
Creator, 3, 101
Crucible, 220
Cultivators, 13, 202, 203, 247
Cumba, 242 (Fn.)
Cunningham, A., 264
Cup, 221
Curd, 70, 205
Curtain, 10, 226
Curry-maker, 231
Cyclopean wall, of Rājagṛiha, 215 (Fn.)

Dabba, Mallian, 166, 170, 178
Dadhimāla, sea, 246
Dairy, 206
Daiva, marriage, VIII, 52
Dakshiṇā, 255
Dancer, VII, 202, dancing girl, 187
Dantakāra, 15 see ivory-worker
Dāru-kammika, 212
Darvi, sacrificial spoon, 214
Dāsa, Varṇa, 1
Dāsas, Dasis, vii, 22, 33, 36, see slaves
Daśaratha, king of Ayodhyā, 130
Dasuttara-Sutta, 92, 93
Dabtor, 26, 152
Deccan, i, xiii
Deer-hunter, 71, 72
Dalicos-uniflorus, 197
Deliverance, 108
Desert, 116, 239, 272, desert-pilot, 277
Desire, 108
Devadaha, 87
Devadatta, 4 (Fn.), 94, 96, 182
Devadhammikas, 112
Devanandā, 10
Devaputta, 116
Devatā, 116
Devavatikas, 112
Dhamma, wheel of 90, recitation of 94, compilation of the rules of iii, 97, taking refuge in 158
Dhammadinnā, Bhikshuṇi, 46, 150
Dhammapada, 46, 165, 218
Dhanananda, king, 250
Dhaniya, Brāhmaṇa herdsman, 38, 62
Dhānya, 197
Dharma, 167, 168, 174, 180, Dharma-kārya, 153
Dharmaśāstra, viii, 18, 23, 40, 42, 48, 53, 54, 56, 57, 58, 62, 63, 71, 73, 74, 77, 131, 135, 136, 138, 179, 242
Dharma-Sūtras, i, v, 23, 39, 48, 110
Dhataraṭṭha Mahārājā, 115
Dhruvā, 214
Diadems, 212
Dice, 219
Dīghamāṅgalikā, 17
Dīghanakha, Parivrājaka, 133, 134
Dīgha-Nikāya, 8, 24, 34, 81, 84, 103, 126, 131, 209, 228
Dīghatālā, 54 (Fn)
Dīpāvalī, 122
Dīpavaṃsa, iii (Fn.), 97
Diśākāka, 243
Distiller, 231
Diwans, 211
Dongī, boat, 242
Donkeys, 235, 239, prices of 266
Dramatic representations, 81
Draupadī, 38
Drought, 201, 272
Drummer, 202
Drugs, 228
Durga Prasad, 259 (Fn.), 260, 263
Dutta, N., x
Dutta, S. K., x
Dvādasāh, sacrifice, 72
Dvaidhishavya, 55
Dvāragāma, 194, 196
Dvijas, 110
Dvinaishkikam, 254
Dvināvadhana, 242
Dyer, 227

East Indies, 245
Egypt, 44
Eight-fold Path, 102
Eknāla, Brahmaṇa village, 92, 195, 203
Ekantalomi, 210
Ekasāṭikas, order of 131
Elephant Festival, 85
Elephant-housings, 210, decoration of elephants, 211, 221, parade of 81, 86
Endogamy, 4
Enlightenment of Buddha, 174
Eraṇḍa, 200

Fairies, 120
Famine, 35 (Fn)., 178, 201, 272
Fans, 232
Farmer, 203, 204
Festivals, 77, 78
Fick, R., ii, iv, 12

Filter, 186
Fire-worshippers, 132, 140, 157
Fishermen, 228, 229, Fish-monger 229
Flood, 201
Florist, 11
Flower-garden, 224
Food-Vendor, 231
Foot-coverings, for Bhikshus, 173, 174
Fowler, 71, 228, 230
Furnace, 218, 219
Furnitures, 213

Gaggarāpokkharaṇī, 92, 94, 136
Gahapatis, caste, vii, 3, 11, 12
Gahapatisippakāra, 216
Gairikas, 131
Gāma, Gāmaka, 194, 215
Games, 80, 187
Gaṇasatthā 135
Gaṇḍakī, river, 240
Gandhabba, 15, see musician
————kula, 15
Gandhaka, 224, see perfumer
Gāndhāra, 235, 238
Gangā, river, 229, 240, 244-45
Gangetic valley, i
Gāndharva, marriage, viii, 52, 54
Gaṇikāghara, 67
Garbhādhāna, 48, 49
Garden-house, 145
Gārgya, *gotra*, 44
Gārhasthya, 6, 79
Garland, 82, 212, 265, garland-maker, 224
Garments, 221, 226
Gates, 215
Gāthās, of *Jātakas*, 126
Gautama, 7, 48, 78, 125, 129
Gavampati, 90
Gavedhuka, 199
Gayā, 69, 104, 117, 141, 200, Gayā-sīsa, 91, 94
Gaya Kassapa, Jaṭila, 90, 140
Gems, 210, 219, 222, 223
Geruka, 177
Ghee, 69, 119, 188, 205, 206, 265
Gijjhakūṭa, 92, 94, 136
Girdles, 186
Gītā, 10, 103 (Fn.)
Goads, 218
Go-Adhyaksha, 206
Goat-butcher, 71
Gobhila, 47
Gochara, 205
God, 3
Gods, 75, 78, 112, 120
Godha-luddaka, 230
Godhūma, 197, 198, 199
Gogerly, 107
Goghātaka, Goghataka-sūnaṁ, 73
Golakāla, 54 (Fn.)
Golakhpur, 258, 262
Gold, 86, 208, 211, 217, 219, 221, 222, 233, 251, 254-256
Goldsmith, 219, 220, 223
Goṇaddha, 239
Goṇaka, 210
Gopālaka, 15, 205, 206, see cowherds and herdsmen
Gorakkhā, 205
Gosāla, Makkhali, Ājīvika Leader, v, 89, 95, 131 associations with Mahāvīra, 99, 104, 129 rival of Mahāvīra, 100, death of 101, teachings of 105, 106, 107, 142, 185, at Polāspura, 141
Gotama, Buddha, 89, 96
Gotamanigrodha, 137 (Fn.)
Gotra, 43, 44, Sagotra 44,
Grain, 197, 202, grannery, 33
Grāmaṇī, 193
Graiveyaka, 221
Grand Trunk Road, 237
Greece, 20
Greeks, 237, 246, 263, Greek writers, 72
Gṛihastha, 79
Gṛihyasaṅgraha, 47
Gṛihya-Sūtras, i, v, 78, 110, 112, 119, 198, 199, 200, 214, 218
Guḍa, 69, 232
Guest, 83
Guild, xii-xiii, 234, 244, 247,-51
Gums, 228
Guṇa Kassapa, Ājīvika ascetic, 105, 106
Gupta, dynasty, 34
Gupta, P. L., 263 (Fn.)
Guru, xi, 7, 161, 162, 164
Guṇaratna, Tamil writer, his works 107 (Fn.)

Hamlet, 194, 196
Hammer, 218
Hangers, 218
Harappā, 262, Harappan Civilisation and people, 120, 121
Harichandana, 224
Haridwār, 99
Haritāla, 227
Haryaṅkas, 260
Hatchet, 214
Hāthīgumphā inscription, 237

Hatthi-Maṅgala, ix, 85, *Hatthi-Sutta*, 85
Hattharaṇa, 221
Hāyana, 68, 199
Hazaribagh, district, 98
Herdsmen, 39, 247
Heretics, 95, 96
Hermits, 124, 125, 126
Herodotus, 209
Hindu fold, 118, Hindu Order, 142, Hindu Sanyasins, 137, 139, 173, Hindu Society, vii, 7, 53, 109, Hindus, 60 103 (Fn.), 119
Hiraṇya, 208
Hiraṇya Gṛihya-Sūtra, 47
Hiraññа-Suvaṇṇa, 255
Hiṅgu, 228, Hingulaka, 227, 228
Hiri, deity, 115
Hoernle, 142
Holy Order, 1
Holy Triad, 158
Homeless Order, 130, 135, 180, see Order
Honorarium, of teachers, 14, 269, 270
Horses, thoroughbred, 84, from Sind, 206, 221, 239, price of 266, Horse-race 81, Horse-rugs 210
Huen Tsang, 68 (Fn.)
Hunters, 19, 20, 72, 223, 228, 229, 230
Hutton, 120
Hwui-Li, 68

India, i, viii, ix, xi-xiii, 22, 27, 29' 40, 45, 57, 65, 124, 237, 246, 257, 258, 259, 269, 280, people of 109, Eastern, i, 19, 87, 89, 193, 199, 235, 236, 238, Western, 236, 237, 246, Northern, i, 47, 64, 69 83, 84, 121, 215, 279. N. E., IX, 68, 89, 218, 226, 235, 241, 245, 279, Central, 99, people of 109
Indian, art, 87, commodities, 246, population, 120, society, 38, 125, soldiers, 209, tradition, 162
Indian Archipelago, 120
Indian Museum, Calcutta, 264
Indo Chinese Peninsula, 244
Illīsa, Seṭṭhi, 76
Indra,, xi, 70, 88, 112, Sahassanetta, Sahassākkha, Samantachakkhu, 113
Indrakūṭa, Yakkha, 117, hill, 117
Indraprastha, 237
Industries, xii, 208, 247
——————,cane and leaf-work, 232
——————,carpentry, 208
——————, cottage, 251
——————, domestic, 210
——————, dye-making, 226, 227
——————, drugs, gums, chemicals, 228
——————,fishing & meat production, 228, 229
——————, garland-making & perfumery, 224, 225
——————, house-building, 212-215
——————, ivory-work, 211, 223, 247
——————, jewellery, 249
——————, leather-work, 232, 233
——————, liquor-distilling, 230, 231
——————, mining & metallurgy, 208, 209, 212, 216-222
——————, pearls, gems, precious metals, 222, 223
——————, pottery, 208, 209, 225, 226
——————, smithy, 209, 217, 219, 247
——————, rural, 208
——————, tanning, 208
——————, textile, 209, 210, 211
Inlay work, 222
Iranians, 44
Irrigation, 201, tax of 202
Isāna, deity, 112
Isidāsī, Bhikshuṇī, 39, 46, 181
Isigili, hill, 137 (Fn.)
Isigili-sutta, 125
Isipattana (Sārnāth), 90
Island, 116, 242, 245
Italicum, 197
Italy, 28
Iṭṭhakavaḍḍhaki, 216
Ivory-worker, 223, 252

Jābālopanishad, 123
Jackson, A.M.T., 246
Jacobi, H., 143 (Fn.)
Jainas, Jainism, i, v, ix-x, 102, 104, 109, 110, 126, hostility to Ājīvikas, 100, 105, opposition to Brāhmaṇas & Vedas 108, Canons, 10, 99, 103, commentator, 131, philosophy, 103, pilgrims, 100, temple 101, Tīrthaṅkara, 99, 103, Digambara, 142, monks, 77, 100, 101, 131, 139, 143-46, 176, Order of 143, 145-47, 149
Jāla, 229
Jāli, prince, 35
Jamadagni, ṛishi, 111
Jambuka, Ājīvika, 142
Jambukhādaka, Parivrājaka, 133, 134

Janaka, king of Mithilā, 22, 130, 197
Janamejaya, king, 118
Jānussoṇi, wealthy Brāhmaṇa, 8
Jarāsandha, king, 118

Jātaka, *Alinachitta* 213
——, *Apaṇṇaka* 239, 273
——, *Baveru* 245
——, *Chitta-Sambhūta*, 16, 17
——, *Chulla-Nārada* 177
——, *Chulla-Seṭṭhi* 31
——, *Chulla-Sutasoma* 40, 58 (Fn.)
——, *Dasa-Brāhmaṇa* 8
——, *Darimukha* 238 (Fn.)
——, *Dummedha* 83
——, *Illīsa* 69
——, *Jarupadāna* 252
——, *Kachchhapa* 44
——, *Kāma* 88, 201
——, *Kaṇavera* 67
——, *Kaṭṭhahāri* 54
——, *Kuṇāla* 15
——, *Machchh-Udāna* 186
——, *Mahājanaka* 13, 244 (Fn.)
——, *Mahākaṇha* 187
——, *Mahā-Ummaga* 54, 213, 215
——, *Mātaṅga* 17
——, *Nanda* 30, 50, 56
——, *Nidānakathā* 10, 87, 256
——, *Nigrodhamiga* 181
——, *Pañchuposatha*, 121 (Fn.)
——, *Pānīya* 187
——, *Phala* 273
——, *Ruhaka* 61
——, *Sañjīva* 84
——, *Saṅkha* 244
——, *Saṅkichcha* 84
——, *Santhava* 114
——, *Sigāla* 16, 86
——, *Silānisaṅsa* 244
——, *Sona-nanda*, 35
——, *Sulasā* 66
——, *Suppāraka* 246
——, *Susīma* 56, 85
——, *Takkala* 61
——, *Takkāriya* 16, 66
——, *Taṇḍulanāli* 166
——, *Uchchhaṅga* 56
——, *Udaya* 254
——, *Uddālaka* 31
——, *Ummadantī* 62
——, *Uraga* 248
——, *Valāhassa* 244
——, *Vaṇṇupatha* 239, 277
——, *Vātamiga* 30
——, *Vessantara* 28, 35, 50, 58 (Fn.)
——, *Vidhurapaṇḍita* 25, 26
——, *Vinīlaka* 238 (Fn.)

Jātakas, iv, x, 1, 13, 18, 20, 23, 49, 52, 53, 55, 58-62, 65-68, 73, 75-78, 81, 82, 84, 86, 95, 105, 106, 115, 126, 127, 129, 132, 135, 138, 139, 163, 166, 168, 177, 183, 187-88, 198, 200, 204, 210, 213, 215, 218-19, 221-22, 225-28, 230, 233, 239, 246, 248, 256, 259, 269, 271-73
Jātarupa, 217
Jāti, 42
Jaṭilas, 90, 91, 114, 128, 140, 141, 157, see Fire-worshippers
Jaunpur, 238
Jāvā, 245
Javelin-dancer, 82
Jāyā, 37
Jetavana, 88, 137, 254
Jeṭṭhaka, xii, 15, 244, 252
Jina, 104, image of 101
Jiṇṇapaṭi-Saṁhāraka, 18
Jīvaka, physician, 65, 92, 94, 238, 239 (Fn.), 269 (Fn.)
Jivaka's Āmravana, 137
Jīvaka-Sutta, 92
Jñātis, 58
Juggler, 18, 82
Jujaka, Brāhmaṇa, 50
Jyeshṭhā, 45

Kahāpaṇa, coin, 24, 65, 256, 257, 265, 266, 269, 270, 273
Kajaṅgala Nigama, 98
Kakacha, Kharakakacha, 223
Kākaṇi, 256, 261, 265, 266
Kālamukha, country, 245
Kāla-Silā 137 (Fn.)
Kālāśoka, Śaiśunāga, 97
Kalāye, 199
Kālī, courtesan, 65, 66
Kaliṅga, 80, 101, 236, 237
Kalpa-Sūtra, v, 10, 99
Kāliya, 177, 224
Kaliyuga, 60
Kambala, 209
Kambila, 169
Kamboja, 235
Kammakāra (Karmakara), 270
Kammāra, 15, 17, see smith
Kammāra-Jeṭṭhaka, 15
Kammāsadamma Nigama, 134 (Fn.)
Kāmpilya, town, 64 (Fn.)
Kāma-Sūtra, 50
Kañchanamāla, 221
Kandaraka, *sutta*, 92, Parivrājaka, 133
Kaṅgu, 199
Kaṅkajola, 98
Kānā, 61

Kane, P. V., 256, 257
Kanhā, princess, 38
Kaṅsa, 217
Kaṇṭaka, Bhikshu, 183
Kāntārapatha, 238
Kapalla, 177
Kapilavastu, 87, 92, 93, 96, 136,236, 240
Kappāsa, 200, 209
Kāraṇḍava, sutta, 92
Karisa, 8 (Fn.), 203
Kārttika, month, 83, 84, 85
Karma, 105, Karman, 108
Karsha, 256
Kārshāpaṇa, coin, 186, 255-57, 260, 261, 264
Kāshāya robe, 139, 146, 175
Kashmir, 235, 237, 238
Kassapa, Mahā Kassapa, 93, 97 (Fn.)
Kassapa brothers, Jaṭilas, 90, 111, 140
Kassapagotta, Bhikshu, 188
Kassapasīhanāda-Sutta, 92, 137, 139
Kāśī, i, 45, 186, 209, 225
Kasibhāradvāja, wealthy Brāhmaṇa, 8, 95, 157, 203
Kasibhāradvāja-Sutta, 92
Kāśika-Chandana, 225
Kaṭāhaka, slave, 29, 32
Kāṭhaka-Saṃhitā, 75
Kathāvāchanas, 7
Kaṭṭhahāraka, 15
Kattikā (Kaumudī-Mahotsava), ix, 84, 85 (Fn).
Katriyana, Parivrājaka, 134
Kātyāyana, v, 255, 260
Kauśāmbī, 14 (Fn.), 64, 98, 209, 215, 237, 238, 239, 240, 247, 264
Kauṭilya, 24, 26, 27, 35, 40,49, 57 -59, 80, 119, 121, 201, 206, 211, 217, 222, 227, 231, 242, 251, 252, 256, 261, 263, 268, 270, 271
Kāyūra, 221
Keniya Jaṭila, 8
Kennedy, 245
Kevaṭa, 228
Khādya-bhājaka, 192
Khaggavishāṇa-Sutta, 125
Khalakulah, 197
Khalya, Khalini, Khalihāna 198 (Fn.)
Khāṇḍava-vana, 118
Khānumata, village, 7 (Fn.) 195 (Fn.)
Khara, Yakkha, 117
Khāravela, king of Kalinga, 80, 237
Kh ettagopaka, Khettarakkhaka, Khettarakkhaṇaka, 201
Khoma (Kshauma) 200, 209
Khuddaka-Nikāya, iv
Khuramāla, sea, 246
King, 13, 18, 22, 25, 41, harems ol 23, 40; crganiser of festivals, 80, 81, 82; of Magadha, 84, 91,239, relationship with guilds, 248-251, controller of prices, 267
Kiriyavāda, 104
Kisā-Gotamī, Bhikshuṇī, 180
Kisa Sankichcha, 104 (Fn.)
Kītāgiri, 94 (Fb.), 186
Kochchha, 214
Kokālika, Bhikshu, 4 (Fn.), 150
Kokanuda, Parivrājaka, 133
Kolatthi (Kulattha), 199
Kolitagāma, 93
Koliyas, 201
Koṇḍadamaka, 15
Kopina, 176
Kośala, i, 4, 31, 45, 94 (Fn.), 104, 110, 259
Kosī, river, 240
Kosseya, 200, 209
Koṭigāma, 65
Kṛichchhra, penance, 63, 78 (Fn.)
Kṛishṇa, 236 (Fn.), 237
Kshatra, 230
Kshatriyas, vi-vii, l, feeling of superiority, 9, 10, above all, 9, 10, 109, 279, prince, 11, traders and cultivators, 11, 12, marriage of 39, 43, initiation of 49, as ascetics, 130, qualities of a true Kshatriya, 130. permitted to drink, 76, 78, 79
Kshatriyagrāma, 195
Kshetra, 204
Kshetrakara, officer, 204
Kshīrasvamin, commentator, 256
Ktesian, 209
Kubera, 116
Kula, 42
Kulāla, 225
Kummāsa (Kulmāsha), 69
Kumbhakāra, 15, 196, 225, Rāja-kumbhakāra, 20
Kumini, 229
Kumrahar, 240, 264
Kund Kundāchārya, Jaina philosopher, 103 (Fn.)
Kuṇḍala, 221
Kuṇḍala-Kesā, Bhikshuṇī, 46
Kuṇḍaliya, Parivrājaka, 133
Kuru, 98
Kusa, prince, 59
Kusāvatī, 59
Kushāṇa, 121, 264
Kusinārā, 96, 209, 236; Kuśīnagara, 236

Kūṭadanta, celebrated Brāhmana, 2, 6, 7(Fn.), 95, 110, 111
Kūtāgārasālā, 97
Kuṭumbika, caste, vii, 12

Labourer, landless, 3, day-labourer, 14, 270, free, 202, hired, 203, voluntary, 266, earnings of 257, 270-71
Laduyāyi, Parivrājaka, 134,
Laity, Buddhist, 165, 173, 175, 176, 178, 182, 185-187, 191, 192
Lakshamaṇa, 125
Lākshārasa, 227
Lakshmī, goddess, 115, 122
Land-holdings, 203, 204, Land-survey, 204, 205
Laṅghanasippa, 82
Laṅghanaṭaka, 15
Law, 248, 249, Good Law, 179
Law-books, 14, 42, 109, 246, 268, see Dharmaśāstra
——givers, 11, 19, 44, 54, 60, 63, 268
Law, B. C., ii
Lead, 208, 216
Leather-worker, 233, 234, 247
Lentils, 197
Levi, Sylvain, 245
Lichchhavis, 4, 43(Fn.), 96, 100
Linen, 209
Liquor, 75-79, 178, 230, 231, 265
Loha, 208, 216
Lohichcha, Brāhmaṇa, 6(Fn.)
Lohita-Chandana, 225
Lohitaṅka, 222
Lokapālas, 115
Lokāyata, 6
Loom, 210, 211
Lord (Buddha), 10, 93, 94
Lord High Treasurer, 249
Lucknow Museum, 260
Lotus, 225
Luddaka, 20, 229, 230
Lumbinī-vana, 87
Luxury goods, 186, 209, 210, 247

Machchhaghātaka, 20, 228
Machhuatoli, 258
Machines, 213, 232
Maddakuchi, 137
Madhepur, 263
Madhu, 22
Madhuparka, 72, 73
Madhyadeśa, 57; Majjhimadesa, i, iii, 98, 99, 241, defined, 98-99, 159(Fn.)
Madhyama-Pratipadā, 102- Majjhima-Patipadā, 143, 185
Madra, 47(Fn.), 59
Magadha, i, xiii, 7 (Fn.) 29, 57, 64, 68, 70, 83, 84, 87, 91, 92, 94-96, 101, 103-105, 110, 111, 117-21, 128, 134, 140-41, 196, 199, 203, 204, 236-37, 240, 243, 245, 259, 260, 263, 264, 279, 280
Magadhan, Ājīvika, 104, coinage, 260, dialect, 104, Bhikshus, 241, empire, 239, 259, king, 239, 259, noblemen, 31.
Maghavā, 113
Magandikas, order of 131
Māgandiya, Parivrājaka, 133
Magic, 247
Mahābhārata, 24, 38, 40, 47, 50, 118, 119, 216, 237, 238, 259, 279
Mahābhāshya, v, see Patañjali
Mahāgovinda, architect, 215
Mahājanaka, prince, 244
Mahākappas, 16
Mahākassapa, iii (Fn.), 93, 96, 97, 104
Mahāmātra, 248
Mahānāma-Khattiya, Śākya, 4, 31
Mahāniddesa, 245
Mahāparinibbāna-Suttanta, 70, 97 (Fn.), 131
Mahārāshṭra, 122
Mahāsachchaka, sutta, 92
Mahāsakuludāyi, sutta, 92
Mahāsāla, 8
Mahāseṭṭhi, 249
Mahāsīhanāda, sutta, 92, 139
Mahātittha, village, 94
Mahāvagga, 12, 70, 90, 91, 98, 99, 131, 184, 186, 204, 224, 228, 237, 269
Mahāvaṁsa, iii(Fn.), 96
Mahavana, 92, 137, 149 (Fn.) i, v,
Mahāvīra, i, v, vi 10, 45, 89, 95, 129, 142, 146, teachings of 103-4, clash with Gosāla 100-101
Mahiddhi, god, 112
Mahinda, iii (Fn.)
Mahissati, Mahishmatī, 239
Mahosadha, prince, 54
Maitrāyaṇī, *gotra*, 44
Majjha (Madya), 230
Majjhima Nikāya, 15, 44, 59, 99, 126, 153, 266, 270
Makara, 74
Mālākāra, 224, Mālākāra-Jeṭṭhaka, 15, Rāja Mālākāra, 20
Malaya, 120, 245
Mallas, 96, Mallian, 166,170
Mallet, 214
Mallikārāma, 137

Mañchaka, 214
Mānatta, 164
Mānava-Gṛihya-Sūtra, 47
Manes, 74, 76
Maṇi, 222, Maṇikāra, 219
Maṇimāla, Yakkha, Chetiya, 117
Maṇimekhalā, deity, 115
Maṇi Nāga, temple, 119
Mañjarikā, 186
Mangalas (of Jainas), 109
Maṅgala-sutta, 109
Mantras, 9
Mantrin, 257
Manu, *Manu-Smṛiti*, v, 7, 18, 24, 26, 27, 40, 42, 49, 54, 57, 58, 63, 72, 74, 78, 79, 136, 160, 161, 165, 204, 227, 230, 242, 249, 256, 267
Mārgasīrsha, month, 145
Market, 72, 121, 230, 239, 268; —place, 229, 235,—village, 194,—town, 144,—price, 265, 267, 268, foreign, 209, 245
Marriage, Vedic period, 37, caste of parties, 41, 42, 43, gotra, viii, 44, age, 46-50, selection of 51, marriage of brother-sister, 44, 45, of cousins viii, 45, of widows 56, 60, polygamy vii, 38-40, polyandry, vii, 39, marriage day, 53
Mariners, 243, 244, 246
Māsa, 197, 199
Masaka (Māshaka), 254, 257, 259, 260, 261, 265, 270, 271
Māsha, 256
Masūra, 197, 199
Mātali, charioteer, 114
Mātaṅga, ascetic, 19, 130
Mathematics, 247
Mathurā, 64, 98, 117, 237, 238, 239
Mauryas, i, iv, v, 30, 59, 206, 238, emperor, 101, architecture of 215, coinage of 257, 258, 259, 263, 264, control of price, 267, 268; mining of 217, monuments of 258 pottery of 225, 226, trade routes 237, shipping, 243
Medas, caste, 230
Medaka, liquor, 231
Medicines, 228, 238, 246
Mediterranean, 245, 246
Megasthenes, v, 209, 205, 217
Mekhalā, 221
Mendicant, 106, 124, 129, 186, see ascetics
Meraya (Mairaya), 76, 230, 231
Merchant, 14, 17, 31, 32, 39, 64, 67, 235, 241, 242, 266, 267, 268, 275, see Seṭṭhis
Mercury, 217
Mettiyā, Bhikshuṇī, 170
Miga-luddaka, 72
Migasira, Parivrājaka, 134
Milinda-Pañho, 50, 163, 227, 231
Military art, 247
Mirror, 212, 221, 223
Missaka, garden in heaven, 114
Missakasāra, palace of Indra, 113
Mithilā, 40, 54, 64 (Fn.), 82 (Fn.), 99, 105, 106, 125, 209, 213, 215, 237, 238, 241 (Fn.), 251
Mlechchhas, 24
Moggaliputta Tissa, iii (Fn.)
Moggallāna, 91, 93-95, 150, Mahāmoggallāna, 128
Moghul, 238
Moliyasīvaka, Parīvājaka, 133, 134
Monasteries, x, 31, 61, 123, 183, 185-90, 216
monastic cell, 266
Monks, x, xi, 75, 93, 185, 188, 189, 211, 226
Moon, worship of 114
Moranivāpa, Parivrājakārāma, 134, 136
Mortar, 29
Mother Goddess, 88
Muchalagāma, 196
Mugga (Mudga), 199, 230
Muktā, 222
Mukunda, 88
Mulagandha, 224
Mules, 206
Muṇḍakasāvakas, order of 131,
Muṇḍaka-Upanishad, 123
Municipal bodies, 267
Muṇis, 123
Muslim travellers, 250
Mutton-butcher, 228

Nāḍi, 200
Nadhri, 233
Nāga, tribe, 118
Nāga-Devatā, 118, Nāgapañchamī, 119
Nāgas, worship of x, 88, 118, 119, 121, 279, fire of 128, image & temple, 118
Nāgasena, 163
Nagnikā, 47
Naishkikaṁ, Naishkaśatika, Naishkasāhsrika 254
Naishṭhika, 140, 162
Nakkhata, 81
Nāla, village, 104

Nālāgiri, elephant, 94, 95 (Fn.)
Nālakagāma, 134
Nalakāra, 232, Rājupaṭṭhāka- Nalakāra 20
Nalamāla, sea, 246
Nālandā 68 (Fn.), 93, 94, 104, 137, 236
Nanda, slave, 30
Nanda Gopālaka, 157, 206 (Fn.)
Nanda Vachchha, 104 (Fn.)
Nandana, garden of Indra, 114
Nandas, i, iv, v, xiii, 101, 237, 238, 260, 263, 264
Nandivardhana, prince, 45
Nandiya, Parivrājaka, 133, 169
Nāpita, 16, Nahāpita, 20
Nārada, v, 26, 36, 60, 253, 256, 257, 268
Nārada-Smṛti, 34, 35, 36
Naṭas, 15, 82
Naṭaka, 82 (Fn.), Naṭakakula, 15
Nāṭakāni, 81
Navigation, 242, 243
Nāvya, 242
Necklace, 212, 221, 223
Needle, 219, needle-case, 186
Negama coins, 251
Nagrito, 120
Nerañjarā, river, 90, 137, 140, 141
Nesādas (Nishādas), vii, 3, 8, 16, 19, 20, 230, Nisādagāma, 195
Net, 229, 230
Nidānas, 102
Nidāna Kathā, 10
Nigama, 194, 251
Nigaṇṭhas, Order of 99, doctrine of 103, lay disciples, 100
Nigṇaṭha Nātaputta, 99, 131
Nighaṇṭu, 6
Nigrodha, Paṛivrājaka, 133
Nikāyas, 23, 98 (Fn.), 132, 133, 198, 212, 224
Nīlakusamāla, sea, 246
Nimi, king, 130
Nirvāṇa, Buddha's, 97, Mahāvīra's, 103
Nishka, coin 254, 269
Nissaya, 94 (Fn.)
Nisseṇi, 214
Nīvāra, 68, 199
Niyāmaka, 244, Niyāmaka-Jeṭṭhaka, 244
Niyaṭi, doctrine of 105, 106; Niyativāda, 106
Niyoga, 55, 56, 57
Noble Truths, 102
No-mans-land, 193
Non-Action, theory of 107
Non-Aryans, 38, 173, 279, cult, religious practices of 119, 120, deity, 118, ruler, 118, land, 118, 120
Novice, 77, 173, 179, 183, 192
Nubia, 246
Nuns, 93, see Bhikshuṇī, Nunnery, 183
N.W.F.P., of Pakistan, 243 (Fn.)

Odana, 68
Odanika, 231
Ointments, 177, 211, 224
Oldenberg, H., 97 (Fn.)
Orabbhika, 20, see butcher
Orāons, 55
Order, of Ājīvikas, 104, 105, of Buddhists, i, vi, x-xii, 1, 2, 31, 34 (Fn.), 57, 90, 91, 94-96, 130, 151-55, 157-60, 164, 166, 168-70, 173, 179-84, 186, 188-89, 191, 192, 280; of Jainas, 131, 142-48, of Brahmanical ascetics, see ascetics, Vānaprasthins and Sanyāsins, others, 131
Ordination, 149, 181
Orissā, 235, 237
Ornaments, 18, 33, 66, 177, 217, 220-23, 232, 265 (Fn.)
Outcaste 3, 17, 18, see Chaṇḍālas
Oxen, 203, 256

Pabbajita, 156, 157
Pabbajjā, ordination, 153-58, 160, 190, 280
Pachchantagāma, 121 (Fn.), 194
Pāda, coin, 259, Pāda-Māsha, Pāda-Paṇa, 256
Paila hoard, 225, 258, 259 (Fn.)
Painter, 216, 247
Paiśācha, marriage, viii, 52
Paishṭi, liquor, 78
Pajjusana, Jaina, 144 (Fn.)
Pakudha Kachchāyana, 106, 107, 131
Palāyi, Parivrājaka, 134
Pāli, language & literature, 11, 132, 136, 160, 194, 205, 280
Pāli Dictionary, 160
Pallaṅkaṁ, 214
Pāmaṅga, 221
Paṇa, coin, 35, 227, 256, 257, 268, 270
Pañchanāvapriyah, 242
Pañchasālā, village, 195 (Fn.)
Pañchaśikha, musician, 114
Pāṇḍavas, 38
Paṇḍuputta, Ājīvika, 104, 142
Panicum Milicum, 197
Pāṇigrahaṇa, 53 (Fn.)
Pāṇini, 44, 48, 53, 68, 69, 80, 87, 120 193, 198-200, 204, 211, 214,

217, 220, 222, 225, 230-33, 237, 238, 242, 254, 255, 257, 259-61, 270-71
Pannachhatta, 232
Paṇṇasālā, 137
Paṅsukūla robe, xi, 138, 174-75
Pāpa-Chaṇḍālī, 17
Papaṭi, 224
Parāśara, 60
Pāraskara Gṛihya-Sūtra, 39, 48, 74
Paraśu, 218
Pariśishṭaparvan, 101
Parivāsa, 156, 157, 164, 184
Parivrājakas, 125, 131-32, 135-38
Parivrājakārāma, 134
Parjanya, Pajjuna, deity, 114
Pārśvanātha, 103
Pāshāṇakoṭṭaka, 215
Pasture 205, 207, —land, 193
Pasupālaka, 15
Pasura, Parivrājaka, 134
Paṭāchāra, Bhikshuṇī, 47 (Fn.), 180
Paṭalika, 210
Pāṭaliputra, iv, v, 14, 29, 64, 101, 195 (Fn.), 209, 225, 237-40, 243, 245, 252, 259, 272,
Pāṭaligāma, 236
Patañjali, 44, 120, 199, 262, 270, 271
Paṭhavijayamanta, 9
Paṭika, 210
Paṭikaputta, Parivrājaka, 133
Pātimokkha, 190, 209 (Fn.)
Patiṭṭhāna, Pratishṭhāna, 64 (Fn.), 238, 239, 240
Patna, 85 (Fn.)
Pattagandha, 224
Patraha hoard, 258, 263
Pātrī, 214
Patriarchial notion, 179
Paṭṭikā, 221
Pauper, 83
Pāvā, 96, 99, 100 (Fn.), 236
Pavārika's Āmravana, 137
Paviṭṭhakolita, Parivrajaka, 134
Pawāla, 222
Peacock, 246
Perfumer, perfumes, 82, 234
Pesakāra, 20, 210, see weaver
Pessa, Parivrājaka, 133
Pestle, 29
Phalabhājaka, 192
Phalagandha, 224
Phalgu, river, 137, 141
Phālguṇa, month, 83
Phārusaka, garden, 114
Phegu, perfume, 224
Phusati, princess, 47 (Fn.), 59
Pig-butcher, 71, 72
Pilotaka, Parivrājaka, 133
Pippala, worship of 120
Pisāchillikas, 131
Pishṭaka, Piṭhā, 70
Piṭaka (Buddhist) i, iii, 23, coracle, 242
Pīṭha, 214
Piṭhakhajjaka, Khājā, 69
Piyajātika-Sutta, 59
Piyaṅgu, 225
Play-hall, 216, 266
Plough, 196-98, 203, ploughshares, 218
Ploughing-Festival, ix, 88
Pokkharasāti, wealthy Brāhmaṇa, 8, 10
Polāsapura, town, 141, 196 (Fn.)
Popular religion, ix, 108
Pork-butcher, 228
Potaliputta, Parivrājaka, 133, 134
Potaliya, —, 133
Poṭṭhapāda, —, 9, 133
Potter, 11, 128, 196 (Fn.), 225, see Kumbhakāra
Pradyota, king, 239 (Fn.)
Prākṛit lit., 280
Prajāpati, god, ix, 279
Prājāpatya, marriage, viii, 52, 53, 112, 113
Prajñā, 103
Prasannā, 231
Prasenajit, king, 4, 7 (Fn.), 10, 31, 45
Pasenadi, 110
Pratichchhādana, 176
Pratiloma, marriage, 43
Pravahaṇa, 80
Pravrajyā, 123, see Pabbajjā
Pretas, 121
Prices, 265-68, price-control, 268, Price-Expert, 267
Priests, 75, 89, 109, 110
Ptolemy, 245
Public Halls, 132
Pukkusas, vii, 3, 16, 19, 20
Pukkusāti, 157
Punarbhu 55, 57
Puṇḍarika, Parivrājaka, 134
Panjab, 235, 243 (Fn.)
Puṇṇā, slave girl, 29
Puṇṇagi, 90
Pupphagandha, 224
Pupphārāma, 224
Purāṇas, coins, 258
Pūraṇa Kassapa, 106, 107, 131, 142
Purohita, 22, 29
Purukutsa, 22
Pushkalāvatī, 237
Puvā, 69

Rāhula, 153, 168

Rairh, 263
Rājaballabha, 248
Rājagṛiha, iii, iv, 4 (Fn.), 13, 23, 31, 32, 33 (Fn.), 64, 65, 80, 83-85, 91-94, 96, 99, 100, 104, 117, 134, 136, 137, 142, 181-82, 184, 209, 215, 235-39, 247, 250-52, 260, 272
Rajaka, 226, 227
Rājanya, 1
Rajasthan, 239
Rājasūya, sacrifice, 173
Rajata, 208, 216, Rajatathāla, 221
Rajjugāhaka-Amachcha, 205
Rākshasa, marriage, viii, 52, 55
Rāma, 40, 125
Rāmagāma, 96
Rāmāyaṇa, 80, 125
Ramnā hoard, 258
Rasa, 177, Rasagandha, 224
Ratan-Sutta, 92
Rathakāra, vii, 16, 20, 104, 142, 208
Raṭṭhapāla, 184
Raṭṭhapāla-Sutta, 34, 39, 153
Ratti, 254-56, 259-61
Rebirth, 108
Red Sea, 246
Revenue, 205
Rhys Davids, T. W., iv, 97 (Fn.), 132, 249, Mrs., 266
Rice, 29, 33, 68, rice-fields, 204, rice-gruel, 69, 219, rice-milk, 69
Ṛigveda, 1, 22, 37, 70, 75, 89, 123, 197
Ṛishis, iii, 112, 125
River-route, 240, river-port, 240, 245
Robbers, 45, 66, 152, 180, 181, 194, 250, 272-74, 276, robber-chief, 55
Robes, of Bhikshus 174-77, 186, 190-92, 277
Rohiṇī, *nakshatra*, 88, river, 201
Rohita, 74
Rohitassa, 129
Rome, 28
Roruka, town, 64 (Fn.)
Rudra, 88
Rugs, 210, 211, 226
Rujā, princess, 106
Rūpa, 261, Rūpadarśaka, Rūpatarka, 262

Sabbasaṁhāraka, 225
Sabhiya, Parivrājaka, 133, 134, 157
Sacrifices, ix, 6, 23, 24, 37, 71, 72, 75, see Yajña
Saddhā (Śraddhā), deity 115
Saddhivihārika, xi, 23, 160-64
Sāketa, city, 64 (Fn.)
Sahajāti, town, 240
Sajjha, 133
Sajjulasa, 228
Sākala, town, 237
Sakka, Śakra, god, 77, 113, 114, 129
Sakkapañha-sutta, 92
Sakula-Udāyi, Parivrājaka, 133, 134
Sakunika, 20, 230
Śakuntalā, 41
Śākyas, 4, 31, 45, 96, 201, Order of 131, 157, ladies joining Buddha's Order, 181
Sāla, trees, flowers, groves of, 87
Sālabhañjikā festival, 87, 88
Salalavatī, river, 98
Sālavatī, courtesan, 64, 65, 67
Sāli (Śāli), 68, 198-99, Mahāsāli, 68, 199
Sālindiya, village, 195 (Fn.), 203
Sāmā, courtesan, 65, 67
Samādhi, 103
Samāja, Samajja, Samajyā, 80, 81
Samaṇa, Buddha, 91, 128
Samaṇa Maṇḍikāputta, Parivrājaka, 133
Samaṇḍaka, Parivrajaka, 133
Samandakāni—, 133
Sāmaṇera, 156, Sāmaṇerapreshaka, 192
Samaññakāni, Parivrājaka, 134
Sāmaññaphala-sutta, 84, 107, 131
Sāmantapāsādikā, 259
Samāpatti, 128
Saṁbodhi, 90, 92
Sambulā 62
Saṁhitās, 22
Samudra, 242
Samugga, 214
Saṁyutta Nikāya, 117, 126, 206 (Fn.), 221
Sānchī, iv, 137, 149, 172, 173
Sandaka, Privrājaka, 134
Sandalwood, 224, 225, 246
Saṇḍāsa, 218
Saṅgha, xii, 13, 91, 94, 145-46, 149, 151-53, 157-59, 161-62, 164, 166-67, 171-72, 176, 180, 182, 183, 189-91, 279, schisms, 97
Saṅghāṭi, 175
Sangīti, 93, 94
Sañjaya, Parivrājaka, 91, 95, 133-35; prince 47 (Fn.)
Sañjaya Belaṭṭhiputta, 107, 131
Saṅkha, Brāhmaṇa, 244
Saṅkhadhamaka, 15, 82, Saṅkhavādaka, 15
Saṅkhyāyana G. S., 88
Sānaṁ, 209

Sanskrit, 160, —grammar, 260
Santhal Pargana, district, 98
Sanyāsa-Āśrama, Sanyāsins, x, 34, 57, 123, 125, 132, 133, 135, 138, 139, 143, 146, 156, 173, 175, 176, 280
Sappiniyā, river, 134, 136
Saptabhaṅgī Naya, 103
Sāpuga, 98 (Fn.)
Sāra, 224
Sarabha, Parivrājaka, 133, 134
Sarandada Chetiya, 137 (Fn.)
Sarayū, river, 240
Sārnāth, 90, 158
Sarpayajña, 118
Sāriputta, 68, 69, 91, 93-95, 116, 134, 150, 152, 168
Sasyaka, 222
Śatamāṇa, coin, 254, 255
Śatapatha Brāhmaṇa, 51, 70, 214
Śāṭikāgrāhāpaka, 192
Sattapaṇṇiguhā, 137, (Fn.)
Sattaravaggiya Bhikshus, 170-71
Satthā, 135
Satthavāha, 252, 272-76, 278
Sattu, 69
Satya, of Jainas, 103
Sautrāmaṇi, sacrifice, 76
Sāyanāsanaprajñāpaka, 191
Seafarer, seafaring, 115, 241-44, 252
Sea-trader, sea-route, 246,
Seals, Gupta 251 (Fn.)
Sela, learned Brāhmaṇa, 6
Seṇiya, Bhikshu, 157
Service Hall, 168
Setakaṇṇika, 98 (Fn.)
Seṭṭhis, vii, 3, 13, 31, 32, 42, 76, 79, 90, 173, 184, 235, 249, 250, 269, Śreshthin, 251
Settlement minister, 205
Shaḍarachakra, symbol, 262
Shashṭikā, 68, 199
Shershah, 237
Sheep-butcher, 7
Ship, 213, 240, 241, 243-45, 277; shipwreck, 115, 241, 243, 244
Sickle, 197
Sigālovāda-Sutta, 81
Sihanāda-Sutta, 92
Sīhanāda, of Sāriputta, 93
Silā, 222
Śilas, Jaina, 101, Buddhist, 103
Śilpas, Śilpins, 247, 248, 270, Sippa, 20
Silver, 208, 211, 216,17, 220-21, coins of 254-57, 259-60, 264
Sīmbalivana, 200
Sind, Sindhu, 235, 239, horses of 234 (Fn.), 239
Siri, Sirimā, deity, 115
Sirisavatthu, Yakkhanagara, 116
Sirisayana, 214
Sīsa (Sisaṁ), 208, 216, 254
Sister, Buddhist, 182, 183, see Bhikshuṇī
Śiśunāga, king, i
Sītā, earth, 88
Sītambavana, 137 (Fn.)
Sītavana, 137
Śiva, Śaivism, 121, 122
Śivi, 45, —robe 265 (Fn.)
Skanda, 88
Slaughter-house, 71, 229
Slaves, 4, 22f., 152, 186, slave-owners, 27
Smith, 195, 217, 218, blacksmith, 247
Smṛitikāras, 54, 60, see law-givers
Snake-charmer, vii, 82, 247
Snātaka, 24
Soma, 75, 112
Soṇa, Brāhmaṇa, 10, Seṭṭhi, 173, river, 240
Soṇā, Bhikshuṇī, 181
Soṇadaṇḍa, wealthy Brāhmaṇa, 2, 6, 7 (Fn.), 92, 95
Sonpur fair, 85 (Fn.)
Sopārā, port, 246
Sorrow, 108
Sota, 177
Sovaṇṇālaṅkāra, Sovaṇṇadhaja, 221
Sparta, 28
Spear, 218, 229
Sphya, 214
Spies, 251
Spooner, D. B., 251 (Fn.)
Squire, 30, 50, 73, 188
Śrāddha, 71, 72, 73, 76
Śramaṇas, 105, 210. see Samaṇas and Bhikshus.
Śrāvaṇa, month, 119
Śrāvastī 14 (Fn.), 64, 85, 88, 92, 99, 104, 136, 137, 186, 188, 209, 225, 235, 236, 238-40, 247, 251, 272, Sāvatthi, 110, 252
Śrauta-Sūtra, 255
Śreṇī, 249
Srucha, 214
Sruva, 214
Stone Architecture, 212, 215
——cutter, 215-16
Store-keeper, 27, 29, 32
Strabo, 267
Stūpa, iv, 96
Subāhu, Seṭṭhi, 90
Subhadda, Parivrājaka, 133, Bhikshu, 97 (Fn.)
Su-Brahmā, 128
Sūchiloma, Yakkha, 117

Suchimukhī, Parivrājikā, 133
Suddhavāsa, 128
Suddhodana, king, 153
Śūdras, vii, 20, 24, 31, 39, 43, 54, 130, 131
Sugar, sugarcane, 231, 232
Sujātā, 43, 62
Sūkara-maddava, 70
Śūkra, 256
Sulasā, courtesan;, 65, 66
Sulāgava sacrifice, 73
Sumedhā, princess, 40(Fn.)
Suṁsumāragiri, 98
Sun, deity, 114, symbol, 262
Sūnā, 71, see slaughter-house
Sunakkhata, sutta, 92
Sundarī, a lady, 95(Fn.), 181
Sunetta, learned Brāhmaṇa, 6
Sunṛita, Jaina, 143
Sūpa, 68, 69
Surā, 75, 76, 78, 230, 231
Surā-Nakkhata, festival, ix, 77, 78, 86
Surgery, 238
Suruchi, prince, 40
Susīma, Parivrājaka, 133
Suśruta, 199
Sūta, caste, 216
Sutavā, Parivrājaka, 133
Sūtra, thread, 211
Sūtra, lit., 47, 49, 51, 56
Suttas, Buddhist, iii,
Sutta Nipāta, 37, 50, 62, 117, 126,138 203, 205, 240
Sutta-Piṭaka, iii-iv
Suvaṇṇa, Suvaṇṇakāra, 217, 219; Suvaṇṇabhinkara, Suvaṇṇakalasa, Suvaṇṇamāla, Suvaṇṇapāti, Suvaṇṇasaraka, Suvaṇṇathāla, 221
Suvaṇṇabhūmi, 241, 244, 245
Svarga, 40
Svāvidha, 72
Sword, 209, 214, 218, 229, 233
Syādvāda, Jaina, 103
Śyāma, 209

Tacha, 224
Tagara, 177, 224, 225
Taittirīya Brāhmaṇa, 37, 83
——————*Saṁhitā*, 22, 55
Taka, Takapatti, Takapaṇṇi, 228
Takkala, Takkola, 245
Takshā, 208, 214, Tachchaka, 212
Takshaśīlā, iv, 18, 237, 238, 247, 251, 259, 262-63
Tālipata, 232
Tamali, Tāmraliṅga, 245
Tambapaṇṇidīpa, 117, 241(Fn.), 244, 245
Taṇḍula, 198
Tanta,—bhaṅda, —Vitaṭṭhānaṁ, 210
Tantuvāya 211, 210(Fn.)
Tapas, Tāpasas, x, 127, 131, 132, 134, 139, see ascetics
Tapodārāma, 196
Tapussa, merchant, 237(Fn.)
Tarasadasyu, king, 22
Tārpya, 208
Tārukkha, wealthy Brāhmaṇa, 8
Tathāgata, Buddha, 179
Tattvārtha-Sūtrā,—*Nigama*, 103
Tāvatiṅsa, heaven, 113
Taverns, 76
Tadaṇḍikas, order of 131
Temples, 145
Terracottas, 226
Tevijja, sutta, 92
Thalaniyāmaka, 227
Theras, iii, 97, 181
Theragāthā, 219, 241
Theravāda, 94(Fn.), 97
Therīgathā, 39, 41, 46, 126, 141
Thieves, 152, 194, 207
Thrones, 212, 222
Thullakoṭṭhita, 98
Thūṇa, Nigama, 98(Fn.), 99
Tila, 69, 197, 200, Tilakuṭa, 69
Timbaraka, Parivrājaka, 133
Tiṇṇahāraka, 15
Tīradassī Sakuna, 241, 243
Tīrthaṅkara, Jaina, 103
Tissa Kumāra, 30
Tittiraluddaka, 230
Tittiriyas, Taittiriyas, 112
Todeyya, wealthy Brāhmaṇa, 8
Towns, 214, 251-52, of frontier 194
Trade, Trader, 14, 79, 236, 242, 244-49, 250-52, 266, 273 276 (Fn.), partnership in trade, 252
Trade-centres, 237, 239, 240, 246
———routes, xii, 235, 236, 237, 243
———,oversea, 241-46
Trapu, Tipu, 208, 216-17
Treasurer, 42, 181
Trinaishkikam, 254
Tri-Ratna, 103
Triṅśatka, coin, 260
Tripiṭaka, iii, vii, 98
Tula, Tulika, 200, 210
Tumbler, 82
Tuṇḍila, 66
Turban, 117, 172-73, 211-12

Udakabhāgam, 202
Udakasāṭi, 176
Udamantha, Udakamantha, 69

Udāna, 117, 131, 140
Udayana, king, 41
Udāyi, king, 101, Bhikshu, 166, 178
Uddālaka, ascetic, 31
Uddalomī, 210
Udichcha Brāhmaṇa, 3, 4, 6 (Fn.)
Udena Chetiya, 137 (Fn.)
Udumbarā, princess, 54
Udumbarika-Sīhanāda-Suttanta, 92
137-38
Uḍupa, 242
Uggas, 230
Uggahamāṇa, Parivrājaka, 133-35
Uggatasarīra, wealthy Brāhmaṇa, 110
Ujjainī, 64 (Fn.), 99, 239 (Fn.), Ujjeni, 239
Ukkā, 218
Ukkāvela, 134
Umā, 200
Umāsvāti, 103
Umbrella 226
Ummadantī, 43 (Fn.)
Upabhṛita, 214
Upajjhāya, xi 94 (Fn.), 98 (Fn.), 160, 162-64, 184, 190, Upādhyāya 160
Upaka, Ājivika, 104
Upākarma, 71
Upāli, Thera, 2, 93, 97, 279; lay disciple of Mahāvīra, 100
Upanidhi, 250
Upanishads, iv, 22, 57, 89, 103 (Fn.), 110, 116, 120, philosophy of x, 141
Upāsakas, 163 (Fn.)
Upasampadā, 91, 149, 153-59, 163, 190
Upatissa, Parivrājaka, 134
Upaṭṭhānasālā, 168
Upayamana, 53 (Fn.), 5
Uposatha, 98 (Fn.), 189
Urachchhada, 186
Urṇa, 208
Uruvelā, 90, 91, 111, 114, 137
Ushṇīsha, 173
Usīradhvaja, 98 (Fn.), 99
Usukāra, 218
Utkala, 237
Utpata, 242
Utsaṅga, 242
Utsarga, 71
Utsava, 80
Uttarāpatha, 237-39
Uttar Pradesh, i, iii, xiii, 57, 64, 90, 99, 104, 125, 223, 231, 239
Uttarāsaṅga, 175
Uttiya, Parivrājaka, 133-34
Uvāsagadasāo, v, 141, 196 (Fn.)
Vachchhagotta, Parivrājaka, 92, 133, 134, 157
Vaḍḍhaki, 15, 196, Vaḍḍhaki-jeṭṭhaka, 15, Mahā-vaḍḍhaki, 215
Vaikhānasa-Dharma-Praśna, v, 162,
Vaikṛintaka, 217
Vaiśālī, viii, 14 (Fn.), 64, 92, 95, 96-97, 99, 101, 134, 136-37, 181, 209, 225, 235-36, 238-40, 244-45, 247, 250-52, 272
Vaiśya, 1, 7, 12, 39, 43, 49, 76, 78, 79, 242, Vessa, 8, 11
Vaitanika, 270
Vājasaneyī Saṃhitā, 208
Vajji, Vajjians, i, 97, 98, 134
Vājirā, 45
Vallikā, 221
Vāmaka, *ṛishi*, 111
Vāmadeva, *ṛishi*, 111
Vanakammika, 15
Vānaprastha, Vānaprasthin, x, 23, 131-32, 135-36, 138-40, 156, 162, 175, 179-80, 209, 280,
Vaikhānasa, 156
Vanasahvaya, town, 237
Varadhara, Parivrājaka, 133-34
Vāraṇa, 230
Vārāṇasī, 14 (Fn.), 55, 64, 84, 86, 90, 235-40, 244-45, 247, 272
Varatrā, 234
Vardhra, 233
Varma, 211
Varṇa, 1, 11
Varshāvāsa, 138 (Fn.), 144-45, Vassa, 92, 150, 169, 176
Vārshikaśāṭikā, 176
Varuṇa, god, 112
Varyā, 48
Vāsabhakhattiyā, 4, 31
Vāsava, 133
Vaśishṭha, 48, 49, 57-59, 78, 136
Vassikā 224, 225
Vastra, 211
Vasudevaka, 112
Vāsudeva-Kṛishṇa, 112
Vataṅsaka, 186
Vatsa, i
Vātsyāyana, 249
Vaṭṭagāmani, king, iii (Fn.)
Vaṭṭaluddaka, 230
Vatthuvijjāchariyo, 215
Vāya, 209
Vedas, vi, ix, 49, authority of 101, 108, gods, ix, mantras, 88, 112, people of 80, 173, 196, religion of ix, 89, 90, 109, 115, 131, 140, 279, teachers ṛishis, priests of 5, 71, 72, slaves in 22, 23, society of 37, 38, 55, 56
Vedabhamanta, 9

Vejayanta, chariot, 114, palace, 113
Vekhanasa, 133
Velukāra, Veṇukāra, 20, 232
Veluvana, 91, 96, 136, 149 (Fn.)
Veṇas, vii, 3, 16, 20
Veṇī, 16
Verāpatha, 245
Vessavana Mahārājā, 115
Vesuṅga, 245
Videha, 105, 106, 235, 241, capital of 238
Videhas, 22
Viddhutikā, 186
Vidiśā, 259, Vedisa, 239
Viḍuḍābha, king, 31
Vihāras, x, 151, 163, 170-72, 190-91, price of 266, see monastery
Vijaya, prince, 241
Vikatika, 210
Village, xii, 13, 70, 82, 215, types of 194, agricultural, 195, 202, 204, of castes & professionals, 15, 92, 94, 195, 203, 225, 229, 251, of craftsmen, 195, 196, 218, 251. slaves of 23, 32, Vedic 193
Vimala, 90
Vinaya (monastic discipline), xi, 2, 77, 165
————dhara, 159,
Vinaya, *Vinaya-Piṭaka*, iii, x,23, 25, 65, 80, 92, 94, 140, 141, 165, 180, 221, 226, 227, 231, 233 254, 259, 269 (Fn.), rules of 77
Vinśatika, coin, 260
Virulhaka Mahārājā, 115
Virupakkha————, 115
Vishṇu Dharma-Sūtra, 78
Viśvāmitra, ṛishi, 111, 125
Vrātya, 173
Vrīhi, Vīhi, 68, 197-99, Mahāvrīhi, 199
Vyākaraṇa, 6

Wages, 33, 213, 257, 270-71; Wage-earner, 265, 270, 271 (Fn.)
Walsh, 258, 261
War, 217, weapons of 218, war-captives, 25, 27, 34
Washerman, 226-27, 252
Watch-tower, 215
Water-strainer, 176, 192
Waterway, 209, 235, 240
Weaver, 20, 195, 208-11, 252
Wheel, potter's 225
Widow, 55, 56, 180
Wine-distilling, 208, 231
Winternitz, M., iii

Xer Xes, 209
Yajña, 108, 109, 114, Mahāyajñas, 8 (Fn.), 110, Pākayajña, Pañchamahāyajña, 109, Assamedha, Purisameddha, Sammāpāsa, Vajapeyya, 111
Yājñavalkya, v, 22, 70, 123, 180, 256, 268
Yakkha, Yaksha, worship of x, 88, 116, 117, 279
Yakkhabhavana, x, Yakkhanagara, 116
Yama, 44, 112
Yamī, 44
Yānakāra, 212
Yasa, Seṭṭhi, 12, 90, 158
Yati, 123
Yātrā, 80
Yava, 197-99
Yavāgū, 69, Yavāgū-bhājaka, 192
Yoga, 127, Yogī, 128
Yuan Chwang, 199
Yudhishṭhira, 24, 38
Yūpa, 111

Zamindars, 25.

Corrigenda

Page	Para or Fn.	Line	Read	For
3	Fn. 7	2	कण्हो	कण्ह
4	Fn. 1	1	जातिं	जांतिं
—	—	—	Jā. I. 373	Jā. I. 3731
—	—	3	Udichcha	chcha
6	Fn. 6	2	Lohichcha	Lohicha
8	1	2	Kasibhāradvāja	Kasibhārdvāja
—	2	1	*Brahmajāla-Sutta*	*Brahmajālā-Sutta*
9	1	5	Asilakkhaṇa	Asiakkhaṇa
14	Fn. 1	4	Vaiśālī	Vaśālī
24	Fn. 7	1	पञ्च	पच्च
29	Fn. 3	3	भण्डागारिककम्मं	भण्डागारिकम्मं
31	1	30	grand-father's	grand fathers'
34	Fn. 1	2	स्वामिनश्चाङ्गैरूपस्थान	स्वामिनश्चाङ्गे'रूपस्थान
35	Fn. 6	2	debtor	debter
36	1	8	Nārada	Nārda
37	Fn. 3	1	कृत्स्नतरमिवात्मानं	कृत्स्नतरमिनात्मानं
41	Fn. 5	2	मे	ये
43	Fn. 3	5	जातिसम्पन्ना	जातिसम्पन्वा
47	Fn. 3	5	दद्याद्गुणवते	दघाद्गुणवते
—	Fn. 5	2	तस्माद्वस्त्रविक्षेपणार्हा	तस्माद्वस्त्रविक्षेपणा हा
52	Fn. 2	1	न च	नं च
53	Fn. 5	2	*sva-karaṇa*	*sva-karṇa*
54	3	7	*kaṭṭhahāri*	*kaṭṭahāri*
—	Fn. 1	3	कम्मं	कुम्भं
55	2	9	aboriginals	aboroginals
56	Fn. 1	2	इयं	दयं
62	Fn. 1	5	view	viwe
64	Fn. 1	4	Rhys Davids	Rys Davids
71	2	5	sought	saught

72	3	2	Migaluddakas	Mig-luddakas
88	1	1	Jetavana	Jatavana
92	1	13	*Āṭānāṭiya*	*Āṭānāṭiva*
96	2	12	Lichchhavis	Lichahavis
97	Fn. 1 Para 2	12	Kassapa	Kasapa
101	3	7	differed	differred
104	1	1	non-violence	non-voilence
115	Fn. 3	1	धतरट्ठस्स	धतरट्वस्स
119	4	1	Araṇyānī	Arṇyānī
123	1	1	Gradual	Gradula
129	Fn. 1	3	सुत्तस्स	सुत्तस्य
—	Fn. 4	1	ब्राह्मणेसु	ब्राह्मणानं
133	1	14	Subhadda	Subhaddha
141	Fn. 1	3	हिमपातसमये	हिमपातासमये
143	2	2	Asteya	Aiteya
147	2	7	violence	viloence
148	1	4	monks	manks
157	2	3	Buddha	Budda
—	Fn. 2	1	अञ्ञातितित्थियपूब्बो	सचेभन्तेअञ्जतित्थय- पूब्बो
—	—	3, 4	आकंखति	आकंखंति
—	—	5	भिख्खू पब्बाजेन्ति	भिक्ख पब्बजेन्ति
182	1	last	Prasenajit	Presenajit
184	4	1	Bhikshus	Bhskshus
194	1	12	Purāṇagāmaṭṭhāna	Purānagamṭṭhāna
201	2	5	drought	draught
206	2	5-6	produce	producc
212	2	11	wooden	woodens
—	Fn. 9	3	परिवारितो	परिवारतो
251	Fn. 2	2	Bloch	Block
254	2	6	becoming	beconming
265	Fn. 1	6	cost	ost
272	2	3	drought	draught
274	2	11	advantages	abvantages
275	Fn. 1	1	विक्किणिस्सामीति	विक्कणिस्सामीति